Theatre History Studies

2014 VOLUME 33

Edited by
ELIZABETH REITZ MULLENIX

PUBLISHED BY THE MID-AMERICA THEATRE CONFERENCE
AND THE UNIVERSITY OF ALABAMA PRESS

Copyright © 2014
The University of Alabama Press
Tuscaloosa, Alabama 35487-0380
uapress.ua.edu
All rights reserved
Manufactured in the United States of America

Template Designed by Todd Lape / Lape Designs
Production by Illinois State University's English Department's Publications Unit
Production Director: Steve Halle
Production Intern: Taylor Hobson
Typeface: Minion
Articles appearing in this journal are abstracted and indexed in *Historical Abstracts* and *America: History and Life*.

∞

The paper on which this book is printed meets the minimum requirements of American National Standard for Information Sciences-Permanence of Paper for Printed Library Materials, ANSI Z39.48-1984.

MEMBER
CELJ
Council of Editors of Learned Journals

Cover: Cover of sheet music for "Apres la Guerre," 1917.
Cover Design: Todd Lape/Lape Designs

Editor
Elizabeth Reitz Mullenix, Miami University of Ohio

Book Review Editor
Robert B. Shimko, University of Houston

Editorial Assistant
Laura Ferdinand Feldmeyer

Book Review Editorial Assistant
Alicia Hernández Grande

Editorial Board
John Fletcher, President of MATC
Felicia Hardison Londré, University of Missouri–Kansas City
Ron Engle, University of North Dakota

Consulting Editors
Rosemarie K. Bank, Kent State University
Howard Blanning, Miami University of Ohio
Terry Brino-Dean, James Madison University
Peter A. Campbell, Ramapo College of New Jersey
Jonathan L. Chambers, Bowling Green State University
Dorothy Chansky, Texas Tech University
Stacey Connelly, Trinity University
Tracy C. Davis, Northwestern University
Lesley Ferris, Ohio State University
Anne Fletcher, Southern Illinois University
Sara Freeman, University of Puget Sound
Andrew Gibb, Texas Tech University
Leah Lowe, Vanderbilt University
Scott Magelssen, University of Washington
Mark Mallet, Richard Stockton College
John Poole, Illinois State University
Denis Salter, McGill University
Catherine Schuler, University of Maryland
Robert A. Schanke, Central College
Alan Sikes, Louisiana State University
Jeffrey Ullom, Case Western Reserve University

Past editors of *Theatre History Studies*
Ron Engle, 1981–1993
Robert A. Schanke, 1994–2005
Rhona Justice-Malloy, 2005–2012

Theater History Studies is an official journal of the Mid-America Theatre Conference, Inc. (MATC). The conference encompasses the states of Illinois, Indiana, Iowa, Kansas, Michigan, Minnesota, Missouri, Nebraska, North Dakota, South Dakota, and Wisconsin. Its purposes are to unite people and organizations within this region and elsewhere who have an interest in theatre and to promote the growth and development of all forms of theatre.

President
John Fletcher, Louisiana State University

President Elect
Peter A. Campbell, Ramapo College of New Jersey

Vice President, Conference Coordinator
Elizabeth A. Osborne, Florida State University

Associate Conference Coordinator
Christine Woodworth, Hobart and William Smith Colleges

Secretary
Kate Roark, Blackburn College

Treasurer
Tyler A. Smith, Ball State University

Webmaster
Mark Mallett, Richard Stockton College

Immediate Past President
Scott Magelssen, University of Washington

*Theatre History Studie*s is devoted to research in all areas of theatre history. Manuscripts should be prepared in conformity with the guidelines established in the *Chicago Manual of Style,* and emailed to mullener@muohio.edu, or submitted in duplicate, and sent to Elizabeth Reitz Mullenix, PhD, Dean of the College of Creative Arts, Miami University of Ohio, Oxford OH, 45056. Consulting editors review the manuscripts, a process that takes approximately four months. The journal does not normally accept studies of dramatic literature unless there is a focus on actual production and performance. Authors whose manuscripts are accepted must provide the editor with an electronic file, using Microsoft Word. Illustrations (preferably high-quality originals or black-and-white glossies) are welcomed. Manuscripts will be returned only if accompanied by a stamped, self-addressed envelope bearing sufficient postage.

This publication is issued annually by the Mid-America Theatre Conference and The University of Alabama Press.

Subscription rates for 2012 are $15 for individuals, $30 for institutions, and an additional $8 for foreign delivery. Back issues are $29.95 each. Subscription orders and changes of address should be directed to Allie Harper, The University of Alabama Press, Box 870380, Tuscaloosa, AL 35487 (205-348-1564 phone, 205-348-9201 fax).

Theatre History Studies is indexed in *Humanities Index, Humanities Abstracts, Book Review Index, MLA International Bibliography, International Bibliography of Theatre, Arts & Humanities Citation Index, IBZ International Bibliography of Periodical Literature,* and *IBR International Bibliography of Book Reviews,* the database of *International Index to the Performing Arts.* Full texts of essays appear in the databases of both *Humanities Abstracts Full Text* and *SIRS.* The journal has published its own index, *The Twenty Year Index, 1981–2000.* It is available for $10 for individuals and $15 for libraries from Elizabeth Reitz Mullenix, PhD, Dean of the College of Creative Arts, Miami University of Ohio, Oxford OH, 45056; (513) 529-3053.

CONTENTS

List of Illustrations   {ix}

Introduction   {1}
— ELIZABETH REITZ MULLENIX

Civil War Memories on the Nineteenth-Century Amateur Stage: Preserving the Union (and Its White Manly Parts)   {4}
— BETHANY D. HOLMSTROM

Corporeal *Disasters of War*: Legibilities of "Spain" and the Jewish Body in Helen Tamiris's *Adelante!*   {35}
— LISA JACKSON-SCHEBETTA

A Doughgirl with the Doughboys: Elsie Janis, "The Regular Girl," and the Performance of Gender in World War I Entertainment   {56}
— DEANNA TOTEN BEARD

Staging Hibernia: Female Allegories of Ireland in *Cathleen Ní Houlihan* and *Dawn*   {71}
— TANYA DEAN

Germanification, Cultural Mission, Holocaust: Theatre in Łódź during World War II   {83}
— ANSELM HEINRICH

Resistance to War: Carl Zuckmayer's *Des Teufels General*   {108}
— GENE A. PLUNKA

CONTENTS

"Imposing the Standards of Boston on Japan": *Kasutori* Performance, Censorship, and the Occupation   {130}
— DAVID JORTNER

Locating Fascism by Dislocating War: Stage For Action's *Skin Deep*   {151}
— CHRYSTYNA M. DAIL

Binding and Unbinding Insurrection in Madagascar: Jean Luc Raharimanana's *47*   {169}
— HADDY KREIE

Beyond Political Propaganda: Performing Anticommunist Nostalgia in 1950s' Taiwan   {193}
—LI-WEN (JOY) WANG

Marilyn Monroe: Soldier in Greasepaint   {209}
— KRISTI GOOD

Birnam Wood: Scotland, Nationalism, and Theatres of War   {226}
— ARIEL WATSON

BOOK REVIEWS

John W. Frick, *"Uncle Tom's Cabin" on the American Stage and Screen*
— REVIEWED BY ROSEMARIE K. BANK   {251}

Amy E. Hughes, *Spectacles of Reform: Theatre and Activism in Nineteenth-Century America*
— REVIEWED BY AMANDA BOYLE   {253}

Verna Foster, ed., *Dramatic Revisions of Myths, Fairy Tales and Legends: Essays on Recent Plays*
— REVIEWED BY PETER A. CAMPBELL   {256}

Bruce McConachie, *Theatre & Mind*
— REVIEWED BY SHAWNA MEFFERD CARROLL   {258}

Milly S. Barranger, *Audrey Wood and the Playwrights*
— REVIEWED BY MIRIAM M. CHIRICO   {260}

CONTENTS

Karl M. Kippola, *Acts of Manhood: The Performance of Masculinity on the American Stage, 1828–1865*
— REVIEWED BY FRANCISCO COSTA   {263}

Lynne Kendrick and David Roesner, eds., *Theatre Noise: The Sound of Performance*
— REVIEWED BY DANIEL C. DENNIS   {265}

Tom Rutter, *The Cambridge Introduction to Christopher Marlowe*
— REVIEWED BY RODNEY DONAHUE   {268}

Christin Essin, *Stage Designers in Early Twentieth-Century America: Artists, Activists, Cultural Critics*
— REVIEWED BY ANNE FLETCHER   {270}

Claire Warden, *British Avant-Garde Theatre*
— REVIEWED BY SARA FREEMAN   {272}

Wendy Arons and Theresa J. May, eds., *Readings in Performance and Ecology*
— REVIEWED BY JENNIFER GOODLANDER   {275}

Jim Linnell, *Walking on Fire: The Shaping Force of Emotion in Writing Drama*
— REVIEWED BY JEANMARIE HIGGINS   {278}

Soyica Diggs Colbert, *The African American Theatrical Body: Reception, Performance, and the Stage*
— REVIEWED BY KEITH BYRON KIRK   {280}

Andrew L. Erdman, *Queen of Vaudeville: The Story of Eva Tanguay*
— REVIEWED BY FRANKLIN J. LASIK   {282}

Robert W. Goldsby, *Molière on Stage: What's So Funny?*
— REVIEWED BY FELICIA HARDISON LONDRÉ   {285}

Simon Shepherd, *Direction*
— REVIEWED BY LEWIS MAGRUDER   {287}

CONTENTS

Carol Martin, ed., Dramaturgy of the Real on the World Stage
— REVIEWED BY WILLIAM PALMER   {289}

Eyad Houssami, ed., *Doomed by Hope: Essays on Arab Theatre*
— REVIEWED BY GEORGE POTTER   {291}

Jonathan Hart, *Shakespeare and His Contemporaries*
— REVIEWED BY JANE PURSE-WIEDENHOEFT   {294}

Michael Y. Bennett, *Words, Space, and the Audience: The Theatrical Tension between Empiricism and Rationalism*
— REVIEWED BY ADAM SHEAFFER   {296}

Sara Warner, *Acts of Gaiety: LGBT Performance and the Politics of Pleasure*
— REVIEWED BY ALAN SIKES   {299}

Books Received   {303}

Contributors   {307}

ILLUSTRATIONS

HOLMSTROM

Figure 1. Capt. Harry McMullen as Uncle Joe and W. D. Jobson as Frank Rutledge {5}
Figure 2. Cast of *The Drummer Boy* {6}
Figure 3. The drummer boy is shot by Frank Rutledge {7}
Figure 4. Robert Gordon, Union veteran, in civilian clothes {11}
Figure 5. Robert Gordon as Tom Elliot {12}
Figure 6. Robert Gordon as Tom Elliot in Union uniform {13}
Figure 7. Robert Gordon as Tom Elliot, wounded at Shiloh {14}
Figure 8. Robert Gordon as Tom Elliot in Andersonville Prison {15}
Figure 9. Robert Gordon as Tom Elliot, returned home on furlough {16}
Figure 10. Robert Gordon in a masquerade {16}

JACKSON-SCHEBETTA

Figure 1. Goya, "And there's nothing one can do about it" {38}
Figure 2. Production photo of *Adelante!* {51}

BEARD

Figure 1. Cover of sheet music for "Après la Guerre" {63}
Figure 2. A familiar image of Elsie Janis with a steel Brodie helmet {65}

JORTNER

Figure 1. Maeyuki Sachiko at the Naniwa Theatre for the show *Dorimuto Kokaiki* (The Log of the Cruise to the Dream Islands) {136}

ILLUSTRATIONS

GOOD

Figure 1. Marilyn Monroe, USO Show, Korea 1954   {210}
Figure 2. Marilyn Monroe poses, USO Show, Korea 1954   {211}
Figure 3. USO Camp Show   {218}

Introduction

—ELIZABETH REITZ MULLENIX

> I didn't realize quite how much of a theatrical business the army is.
> PLAYWRIGHT GREGORY BURKE, IN THE PREFACE TO *BLACK WATCH*

> If we really saw war, what war does to young minds and bodies, it would be impossible to embrace the myth of war. If we had to stand over the mangled corpses of schoolchildren killed in Afghanistan and listen to the wails of their parents, we would not be able to repeat clichés we use to justify war. This is why war is carefully sanitized. This is why we are given war's perverse and dark thrill but are spared from seeing war's consequences. The mythic visions of war keep it heroic and entertaining.
> CHRIS HEDGES, *DEATH OF THE LIBERAL CLASS*

American Civil War buffs are no doubt familiar with the oft-repeated words of the Confederate general Robert E. Lee, who declared at Fredericksburg in 1862 (a battle that saw 18,000 casualties in four days), "It is well that war is so terrible—lest we should grow too fond of it." As Lee's now-hackneyed words imply, war is a paradox. It is both horrifying and compelling, galvanizing and devastating, a phenomenon that separates and decimates while at the same time creating and strengthening national identity and community bonds. Indeed, the myth of war, according to the award-winning war correspondent and author Chris Hedges, is a force that gives us meaning. And, as theatre scholars well know, it is the stuff of great drama.

This special issue of *Theatre History Studies* contributes to an ongoing conversation about theatre and war, a popular topic amongst academics for obvious reasons. The American Society for Theatre Research (ASTR) will continue its working group on theatre and war this year, a dialogue that began in 2010. In April 2013 and 2014 theatre scholars Ilka Saal and Barbara Ozieblo organized a workshop entitled "Teatrum Belli: Theater of War, Theater as War, War as Theatre" in Thessaloniki; and I have spoken with two different scholars this summer who are working on anthologies on the subject. The essays in Volume 33 of THS explore plays about war, performance during times of war, and theatre done both to resist and foster war. In poignant ways, all the authors in this volume also write about nationhood and about how war—through propaganda and through protest—defines a people.

In her excellent essay in this volume that examines the nexus between theatre, Scottish nationalism, and war, Ariel Watson observes, "War plays are about the mobility of human populations and identities; they are about countries in flux and in conflict, strangers in a strange land reflecting on the Verfremdungseffekt of performing nation outside its boundaries. They are about occupiers and the occupied, and the ambivalences of identity in between." Because wartime ravages and glories play with the very essence of humanity, as Watson implies, the subject of national and international conflict is a staple theme upon the world stage.

Indeed, the authors in this volume investigate constructions of nationalism (Watson and Tanya Dean) as well as notions of occupied and occupier, nostalgia and utopia, and patriotism and revolution—themes that transcend particular conflicts and countries. The essays are arranged chronologically so as to survey a march of war, both civil and international, that spans three centuries. This arrangement allows for obvious comparisons between authors (think European fascism and its multiple applications), but also maps the scope of war's major themes as ideas prevalent in one historical moment seem to rift off the ideologies and propaganda of wars past and present. For example, while this volume begins with Bethany D. Holmstrom's piece on the construction of memory in post–American Civil War drama, her ideas about nostalgia resonate with Li-Wen (Joy) Wang's thoughts about the Chinese Civil War. Chrystyna Dail's essay about post–World War II antifascist theatre and Lisa Jackson-Schebetta's work about performance and the Spanish Civil War caused me to think about how war engenders feelings of utopia (a world without violence and conflict) as well as nostalgia. Utopia's impulses are the same as nostalgia's—a reaching forward rather than a looking back—as both spaces are constructed by the memory and experience of war. Theatre helps to point in those directions, and such pointing can be either progressive or oppressive (as demonstrated by Anselm Heinrich's history of Nazi propaganda in the Polish city of Łódź). Propaganda, of course, helps to establish and maintain both the good and the bad, but also works to construct identities within theatres of war, as made clear in DeAnna Toten Beard's and Kristi Good's essays about gender construction, celebrity, and

INTRODUCTION

national identity in both World War II-era Europe and the Korean War period, and during World War I. In his fascinating essay about erotic performance in Kasutori theatre, David Jortner examines the way that propagandistic impulses can also lead to confusion, as was the case in postwar occupied Japan when the Allies used censorship of erotic performance to promote—paradoxically— larger ideological notions of freedom and democracy. And finally, no volume about war would be complete without essays examining the power of protest and revolution, as do Gene Plunka's essay about a post–World War II play, Carl Zuckmayer's *Des Teufels General* and Haddy Kreie's fascinating study of revolution in twentieth-century Madagascar and the performative work of memory and forgetting in a postwar nation.

I hope you find this special edition as compelling as I do. Many thanks to all who made it possible.

Civil War Memories on the Nineteenth-Century Amateur Stage
Preserving the Union (and Its White Manly Parts)

—BETHANY D. HOLMSTROM

One summer night in 1868, nineteen-year-old Laura Cooke attended a production of *The Drummer Boy, or the Battle of Shiloh* in Sandusky, Ohio. Her father, Jay Cooke, referred to as "*the* financier of the Civil War," was behind a wartime bond program that greatly increased the Union's coffers and allowed him to build the family a summer home—Cooke Castle—on nearby Gibraltar Island in Lake Erie.[1] Samuel Muscroft, a veteran as well as the author of the evening's production, appeared in the lead role as the hero Mart Howard, while Sandusky residents and veterans took on the majority of the other roles. Laura Cooke noted her reactions in the margins of a program during the show.[2] After writing about her frustration that they only got a few minutes of music before the curtain (as well as jotting down when she took a nap during act 2), she also recorded her reaction to the violence depicted on the stage at Norman Hall that June evening.[3] In act 4, on the corpse-strewn battlefield of Shiloh, a Southern patriarch dies and renounces his loyalty to the Confederacy as his ex-slave Uncle Joe (played by a local white veteran in blackface) bemoans "Massa" Rutledge's fate: "He done turned rebel, but he was a good Massa to me" (fig. 1).[4] Closing the act is a tableau of the decoration of soldiers' graves, which would become a major rite of mourning in the United States. It is here that Cooke responded to the production in an intriguing (and problematic) way. She scribbled in the space available at the close of the act's program listing: "Too awfully sad + true to life—heart breaking," and then noted later that her theatre companions (including her brother Jay Jr.) began to cry upon the death of the drummer boy at the hands of the rabid Confederate villain in Andersonville Prison in act 5 (figs. 2 and 3). This reaction raises several questions. What did Laura Cooke, the daughter of a wealthy financier, a mere twelve years old at the war's outbreak, know of the "truth" behind war? What battlefield scenes had she witnessed first-hand to attest to the authenticity of this tragedy? And, assuming that she had not actually witnessed the overwhelming carnage of the war—the bodies piled at Shiloh, the conditions in the squalid prison camps—what had she seen and heard that led her to believe that this dramatic representation of battle was indeed "true to life"?

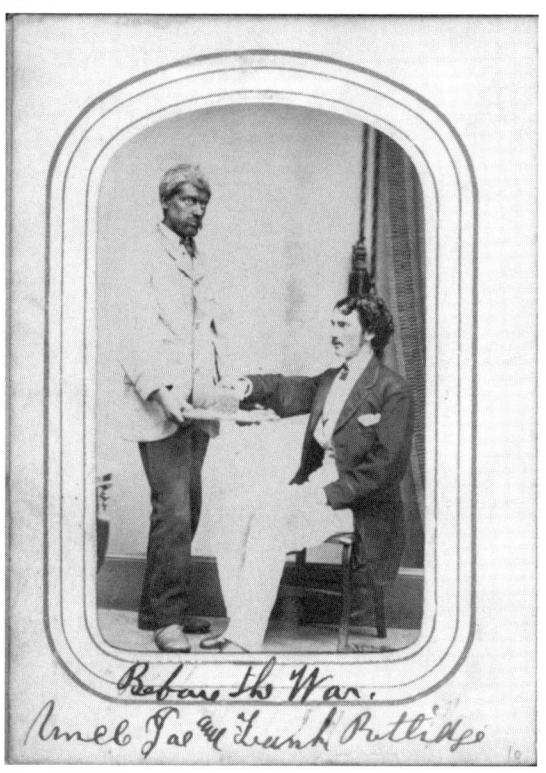

Figure 1. (Left to right) Uncle Joe (played by Capt. Harry McMullen) and Frank Rutledge Jr. (W. D. Jobson) before the war. Junior turns out to be the villain of this play, *The Drummer Boy, or the Battle of Shiloh*. These images were taken at a studio (thought to be Gordon & Wilson's Indianapolis Photographic Temple of Art), presumably during (or immediately before or after) playwright Samuel Muscroft's visit to Indianapolis to direct his play with the local Grand Army of the Republic (GAR) organization and other citizens at the Metropolitan Theatre, June 10–20, 1868. (All images accompanying this essay were originally in sepia tint and are from the Robert Gordon Album, c. 1868, 1906, Manuscript and Visual Collections Department, P0474, William Henry Smith Memorial Library, Indiana Historical Society, Indianapolis.) Courtesy of the Indiana Historical Society.

Figure 2. (Left to right) Tom Elliot (Robert Gordon), Mart Howard (Sam Muscroft, playwright/director), Johnny Howard, the drummer boy (Master Eugene Taylor), and Will Smith (Lafe Robinson). Johnny is murdered by one of the "rabid" Confederates in the prison during this scene. Courtesy of the Indiana Historical Society.

The Drummer Boy was one of many amateur plays written by/for Union veterans and the Grand Army of the Republic (GAR) organization in the decades following the war. Some theatre historians have provided important insights into these amateur plays. Rosemary Cullen refers to these texts as "chronicle plays" that were "virtually indistinguishable retellings of the events of the Civil War" with "a number of obligatory scenes."[5] Jeffrey Mason calls the authors "professional or semiprofessional hacks" and the products "formulaic," though he goes on to show that there is more to the texts than the seeming "ludicrous naïveté and clumsiness of dramaturgy."[6] He further claims that these

Figure 3. (Left to right) Will Smith, Master Eugene Taylor, Robert Gordon, Sam Muscroft. Johnny the drummer boy is shot by Frank Rutledge in prison in the playtext, contrary to the caption. Considering the short production period and the chaos that probably accompanied coordinating hundreds of locals, it is not unlikely that Robert Gordon might have mislabeled things—or that Muscroft might have changed aspects of the play. Of course, these pictures were taken in a studio, so this is clearly not an exact representation of the stage performance—though some of the tableaux and costumes were undoubtedly similar. Courtesy of the Indiana Historical Society.

plays worked with melodrama conventions and "tended towards reduction and simplification," with "a point of view presented as northern or as generically American, a strategy that appropriated the South and denied the history of sectionalism."[7] David Mayer examines these amateur plays in the context of D. W. Griffith's theatrical influences and the Civil War on the popular stage, calling the plays "simplistic and partisan" and "clumsy melodrama," as well as "boastful and crude."[8] These scholars situate the GAR plays in a progressive model that moves from amateur to professional, rightly linking some tropes from the texts (such as intersectional romances and spy narratives) with later commercial hits—William Gillette's *Held by the Enemy* (1886) and *Secret Service* (1895), Bronson Howard's *Shenandoah* (1888), or David Belasco's *The Heart of Maryland* (1895).

While Mason in particular devotes a substantive amount of pages to unpacking the mythology of the common soldier and outlining the general tendencies of the GAR plays, the ubiquity and importance of amateur drama in the formation of Civil War memories has yet to be given ample consideration. Prior to the touring circuitry of the Syndicate and the mass commercial hits of the late nineteenth century, amateur theatrical productions staged by/for Grand Army of the Republic posts and other amateur associations were the primary consumption points of Civil War memories on the theatrical stage.[9] These plays, as suggested above, are indeed redundant: there is an intersectional complication (within or among families or between lovers), a celebration of masculine honor and loyalty, a strong Union agenda, and fairly predictable plot lines. One critic's summary of an 1873 production of *The Color Guard* could be applied to the entire genre: "The plot of the play, for such it must be called, is very slight."[10] These aesthetic caveats aside, the practice and performance of these plays have been overlooked and not fully contextualized within the GAR's function and status throughout the late nineteenth century.

In this essay, I describe how the "business" of remembering the war on the amateur stage created multiple sites of memories for local audiences, where hegemonic and exclusionary tactics were infused into Civil War narratives. In calling performances "sites of memories," I argue that these performances are akin to Pierre Nora's *lieux de mémoire* and are invested with ideology, political capital, and power.[11] Though there are nearly forty Civil War–related texts languishing in various archives that might have been performed by GAR and amateur groups, I make reference to only twenty plays with confirmed performances.[12] It is only via performance that these texts become "sites of memories," actively produced, invested with time and representational practices and ideology, and consumed as part of larger cultural processes of remembering the war. Furthermore, I argue that the claims to "authenticity" embedded in these productions and in the very structure of melodrama held real juridical consequences in shaping popular mental conceptions on a local level, as an onslaught of legislation throughout the late nineteenth century buttressed the privileges of white citizenship.

A Charitable Business

Theatre was part of the overall "incorporation of America" in the postwar years, and the business of Civil War memory and the amateur theatre market intertwined robustly throughout the late nineteenth century.[13] The Grand Army of the Republic actively participated in the business of remembering the war and creating sites of memories. The GAR was one of many fraternal organizations in the postwar era, but was notable for holding great political sway during various moments prior to the turn of the century—and for staging plays as part of its many charitable projects.[14] Theatrical activities appear to have been clustered around and marketed to specific localities, which reflected the structure both of the Civil War–era Union army and the GAR posts.[15]

Because so many of these productions were staged under the auspices of charity, amateur theatricals allowed performers "to engage in morally questionable behavior while maintaining an outward display of propriety," as Eileen Curley points out.[16] She believes that postwar charity productions had a "dual purpose for participants—fund-raising and leisure entertainment."[17] The casting of amateur participants as bourgeois philanthropists also allowed them to indulge in theatre, a previously suspect leisure activity; thus, amateur theatre became an emergent form of socially sanctioned performance.[18] With nearly 7,000 GAR posts appearing throughout the former Union states during the postwar decades, there were ample opportunities for veterans and residents to reinforce or claim bourgeois status by performing charitable deeds in a historically disreputable form.[19]

While major metropolitan posts had a better chance of drawing in larger audiences, many of these plays were written under the auspices of a smaller regional post (often in the Midwest) before becoming part of a circuit of amateur performance and/or text publication.[20] Publishers sensed a market and created various series of affordable dramatic texts, such as Ames's Series of Standard and Minor Drama or French's Standard Drama. These series not only offered detailed instructions (including elaborate stage diagrams for the amateur player confused by the designation "stage left," costume notes, and scenic plots), but also included general guidebooks as theatre moved out of living room parlors and onto community stages. Clearly authors and publishers hoped that these plays would become popular among GAR and amateur producers: for example, the author of the nine-character *Midnight Charge* promises readers that the play "might be rendered on a small stage, with only a few actors, with pleasing effect."[21] The materials further assure the players that many of the more spectacular scenes (with live horses and elaborate drills, etc.) could be omitted, in hopes that "our efforts may meet the wants of the G.A.R. and the public in general."[22] To appeal to particular communities, some playwrights, such as A. D. Ames and C. G. Bartley of *The Spy of Atlanta*, left references to merchants blank so that the actors could insert local names.

In the case of authors Ames and Bartley, O. W. Cornish (*Foiled*), Edwin A. Lewis (*Newbern; or, the Old Flag*), George T. Ulmer (*The Volunteer*), W. Hector Gale (*The Loyal Heart of 1861*), and Samuel Muscroft, the playwrights appeared in and/or directed their own plays.[23] While there is no immediate evidence that other playwrights did the same, it seems safe to say that GAR plays provided opportunities for amateur playwrights and for itinerant actors seeking to capitalize on the market. In a set of reminiscences published in the *New York Times* in 1934, Harry Miller—a seventy-year-old owner of an agency in Manhattan that "sends out directors and costumes for the presentation of amateur shows" at the time of the interview and a "survivor of those ancient days"—specifically recalled the ubiquity of *The Drummer Boy* in terms of the economics of amateur productions: "The smart actors usually carried with them a package of plays, just to be safe. If they were stranded they put on an amateur performance under the auspices of some local groups and raised enough cash to go home. They'd have...'Ten Nights in a Bar-Room' for the W.C.T.U., 'The Drummer Boy of Shiloh' for the G.A.R."[24] Thus, even staging plays for charity could provide lucrative business opportunities, especially for those catering to a market created by a powerful political organization.

The cast was most often amateur—a mix of both veterans and other local amateur actors, with an occasional professional actor or two appearing in some productions. Since almost every GAR play includes a romance and features tableaux where the women of the town present the flag to the recruits, the female members of the local theatre societies would have been necessary to fill out these obligatory scenes, as women were excluded from the GAR. The *carte de visite* scrapbook of 36th Indiana Infantry veteran Robert Gordon lends further insight into aspects of GAR performances.[25] The photos and newspaper articles included in his scrapbook give a sense of the local investment in such productions (it merited a visit to the local photography studio to document the occasion [figs. 4–10]), the tableaux presented, and the popularity of such entertainments.[26]

CIVIL WAR MEMORIES

Figure 4. Robert Gordon, Union veteran. Courtesy of the Indiana Historical Society.

Figure 5. Robert Gordon as Tom Elliot, a farmer "going to town to enlist." Many of the GAR plays presented "common men" of the land and farmers' sons as the heroes; recruitment scenes were standard. Courtesy of the Indiana Historical Society.

CIVIL WAR MEMORIES

Figure 6. Robert Gordon as Tom Elliot in his Union soldier garb. Courtesy of the Indiana Historical Society.

Figure 7. Robert Gordon as Tom Elliot, wounded at Shiloh. The only representation of Shiloh is actually in act 3 (not act 4, as is handwritten on this print), and Tom Elliot's character had no speaking lines, nor was he mentioned in the stage directions. It is plausible that the stage was littered with bodies for affect during a battle tableau, often mentioned in newspaper reviews and scripts. Courtesy of the Indiana Historical Society.

Figure 8. Robert Gordon as Tom Elliot in Andersonville Prison (act 4 in the playtext). Courtesy of the Indiana Historical Society.

Figure 9. Robert Gordon as Tom Elliot, returned home on furlough (presumably at the end of the war, as it is in "act 6"). His friend Mart Howard (played by Sam Muscroft) did not make out as well, having lost an arm upon their return home in the play. Courtesy of the Indiana Historical Society.

Figure 10. At no point does a masquerade appear in the script, nor was it mentioned in the reviews of this Indianapolis production. It is unclear if this was part of the show at all, or if Mr. Gordon was taking advantage of his time in a studio. Courtesy of the Indiana Historical Society.

Gordon played Tom Elliot in Samuel Muscroft's *The Drummer Boy* at the Metropolitan Theatre in Indianapolis, June 10–20, 1868. Laura Cooke had seen *The Drummer Boy* only days earlier in Sandusky.[27] Muscroft appeared as the hero Mart Howard in both productions, as did the child actor "Master" Eugene Taylor, playing the drummer boy, suggesting a rather quick rehearsal period with the Indianapolis group. Memories of the production published in a local newspaper in 1906 confirm that all the participants other than Muscroft and Taylor were residents of Indianapolis. The ticket prices for the Muscroft production were within the means of most middle-class households: though these productions clearly did not cater to the lower income bracket (as did the later "ten-twent'-thirt'" shows"), prices were not so high as to prohibit entrance to many middling sorts.[28] Newspaper ads for later GAR productions in the late nineteenth century suggest that these tickets continued to be affordable for the middle class.

The writer of the 1906 reminiscence claims that "200 veterans of the Grand Army of the Republic, assisted by over 100 ladies of the city" staged the 1868 Indiana production "for the benefit of the widows and orphans of deceased soldiers."[29] The Ohio production lists around fifty cast members, with other residents appearing in tableaux and providing music—clearly a large production as well. Such large casts seem to have been common for most productions staged by GAR posts with "fifty or a hundred familiar townsmen" and "ladies who composed the tableaux."[30] Tableaux were included in every extant script of GAR dramas and, considering the repetition of "obligatory scenes" mentioned by Cullen, the sorts of scenes and tableaux depicted in Gordon's album would have been familiar to audiences by the mid-1870s, when such shows had become common in local communities and larger cities. When *Newbern* appeared at the Concordia Opera House in Baltimore in 1887 under one of the co-author's direction, it included "50 Young Ladies in Beautiful Tableaux," as well as a "Chorus of 100 Voices," accompanied by "scenes in camp and on the march."[31] When *Allatoona* was staged at New Yorks' Eagle Theatre in 1877, the ad for the show boasted that there would be 300 soldiers appearing, between the GAR and the New York State National Guard.[32] While it is conceivable that the ads might have exaggerated the numbers participating, it is clear that many GAR posts and residents invested significant time and interest into these events, regardless of the post's size or the area's population density.

When piecing together the scraps of evidence, it is apparent that the GAR plays were popular sites of war memories within a booming amateur market. Due to the unique nature of the GAR plays—they were staged by/for veterans of the very war being represented—the "real" history of the war factors greatly into the business of remembering and historicizing the conflict.

Sites of the Allegory and Real War History

Laura Cooke, with her observation of *The Drummer Boy* being "true to life," demonstrates her fascination in the "culture of imitation" that Miles Orvell identifies as emerging in the United States of the late nineteenth century.[33] Each amateur production, with silent or explicit claims to veracity, entered the fray over the war's cause(s) and meaning(s), as the battle to determine what the war was actually *about* was in its formative years; while also catering to the "culture of imitation" and the public desire for realistic-seeming constructions of the war. Mason tends to focus solely on the allegorical elements of these plays in his rendering of the amateur dramas, claiming that these "crude attempts" at plays "were in fact endeavors to create completely unequivocal allegory."[34] He goes on to argue that "realism trades on its ambiguity, but those designing the veterans' myth sought absolute clarity in their (re)construction of events and participants, and the meaning they hoped to impart. A realistic technique would have confused the message, so the playmakers, like the temperance dramatists before them, employed exegetical representation to deliver the most explicit possible message."[35] These amateur dramas were indeed often described as allegories in titles or in reviews, and were part of a larger trend in popular depictions of the war in newspapers, illustrations, monuments, and novels that represented the Union triumph within the rubric of allegorical Christianity.

The GAR amateur dramas were cobbled from elements of allegory and melodrama, and even if the playwrights were not strictly deploying "realistic techniques" in a dramaturgical and structural sense, the playwright, producers, and marketers of these texts repeatedly lauded the narrative realism of the plays' contents and incorporated realistic elements. These attempts at authenticity—particularly the claims to staging the "real" history of the war—cannot be ignored. By claiming that the dramatic representations on stage represent a real, authentic, and true depiction of wartime events, the political and ideological investments in these sites of memories are implicitly endorsed by the performers and the audience alike.

The players would read testaments of veracity in the first few pages of the play-texts, where there is often some kind of dedication or an explicitly stated link between the author and the war that "authenticates" that particular representation.[36] Some ads highlight the role of GAR posts in the production, or, as one for *The Union Spy* appearing in San Francisco in 1891 claimed, the performance was "a most wonderful experience unanimously indorsed by the G.A.R."[37] Others are simply dedicated to a GAR post, as if this dedication in and of itself were confirmation of the "truth" presented in the play text.[38] In addition, some of the scenes—particularly battle scenes, drill scenes as the recruits are prepared, camp life, or the filthy conditions of the Confederate prison—fed into the need for "lifelike imitation," allowing the audience a glimpse into military life and the veterans a chance to reenact their past experiences. A review for an amateur benefit production of *The Drummer Boy* at Chicago's Opera House suggests that it is "based upon familiar scenes in the life of a soldier," and these "familiar scenes" crop up in the GAR plays consistently.[39] There are camp songs, orders, detailed battle maneuvers, sign/countersign rituals, among other realistic elements. The amateurs in this same production were said to have "very neat and skillfull [sic] military" drills.[40] Militia and guards were sometimes included to bestow a more pronounced authentic experience. When *In the Enemy's Camp* appeared at the Holiday Street Theatre in Baltimore in June 1895, a reviewer was thrilled by the 4th Regiment of the Baltimore National Guard, which "marched upon the stage in great shape last night during the third act." This "novel spectacle of real militia upon the stage" made the audience demand that they "march back again, even though it interrupted the progress of the play."[41] *Newbern, or the Old Flag*, produced by the Dushane GAR Post in 1887, featured "an exhibition drill by Dushane Post Guard" that "elicited much applause."[42] Every night during the week-long run, various companies from Maryland regiments would compete for a fifty-dollar prize for the best execution of military drills. The occasional appearance of historical figures like General Lee, General Grant, and a host of other military leaders gave audiences the thrill of seeing war heroes impersonated onstage, while suggesting that a historical rendition was underway.[43] Many more plays incorporate actual battles or physical sites related to the war. Imprisonment in Libby or Andersonville—the notorious Confederate prisons, where 30,000 Union soldiers died—is a fairly regular feature.

The realistic elements, narrative techniques, and assertions of authenticity make implicit claims to the war's causes and "meaning(s)." The refrain of "preserving the Union" is the primary motivation for the war in GAR dramas. The Union cause places the concept of nation and the inviolability of the nation-state as the central motivating factor of the war.[44] In *Allatoona* secession is a "monster,"[45] and the hero of *The Dutch Recruit* says he will "defy you or any force you can bring to force me to raise a hand against the glorious old Stars and Stripes."[46] The patriarch of *The Drummer Boy* tells his Southern visitors that "our only hope is in the perpetuation of our Union. A division or secession, call it by what name you will, is disastrous."[47] The South Carolina Unionist hero and *The Loyal Heart of 1861* calls secessionists "traitors," and secession the "act of a viper that poisons with its venomous sting the hand that has nourished it."[48] The Union cause even acquires divine providence, as a Southern loyalist in *Our Heroes* declares: "This country ain't going to be divided, no how—for God has made it the grandest country on the face of the earth!" While he speaks, a tableau of the goddess of liberty, with the US flag, children, and loyal Union soldiers, opens before the Confederate recruits.[49]

The view of republicanism that the GAR proposed was that of a "virtuous nation" that had "come through the war purified of the blot of slavery and ready to lead the rest of the world into the sunshine of universal democracy."[50] In the GAR plays the abolition of slavery was an added bonus of the war's conclusion, not the primary motivating factor.[51] In fact, slavery is not directly cited as a cause of the war: tableaux repeatedly allegorize "liberty" or "democracy" as a goddess, rarely featuring those who would be emancipated by the war's close. In *Allatoona*, the Southern heroine invokes slavery and asks if the Northern hero will do "the bidding of a lot of fanatical abolitionists" who "want only to slay her people." She asks, "is it natural we should like a people who inaugurate expeditions like John Brown's, and send them among us to incite our slaves to murder and to deeds far worse?" The hero can only offer his patriotism as rebuttal, side-stepping the topic at the heart of her accusations: "Helen, I have always endeavored to avoid this subject when speaking with you. A true soldier knows but one people, one government, and one flag."[52] The Southerner in the first scene of *Lights and Shadows*, leaving his New York sweetheart to go fight, says that he will "assist my people in chastising these insolent abolitionists." The Yankee who looks to take his place says that his "sentiments...are to defend the old flag, and to assist in putting down the rebellion."[53] Even in postwar representations, it is implied that abolitionists were radicals, since the heroes rarely adopt antislavery rhetoric.

When slavery does enter the dialogue, it is often part of a jab at Southern "honor" or masculinity. John Brown is invoked again at the opening of *The Union Spy* as a Southern student accuses his Northern colleagues of being "Northern abolitionists and John Brownites." When his Northern counterpart says it was a "fair election" and they should honor the outcome, a more heated argument ensues. The Northern Sleeper argues for a country "not...blighted with the black curse of slavery," saying that slavery allows "*chivalrous* Southerners" to "debauch your servants and sell your own children. What chivalry!" The enraged villain can only counter that the Yankees used slaves "as long as it would pay, and when it wouldn't, you sold them to us."[54] As the encounter leads to blows, vows of revenge, and stomping on the Confederate flag, the Northerners lapse back into saying that the "bleeding country needs our help" to restore the Union.[55]

Within the many calls for national preservation and such patriotic/allegorical displays, the exclusionary tactics of the GAR are implied. In the GAR plays, the performances of black and ethnic characters have more serious repercussions, bound up in the local and national movements to reify the privilege of white middle-class masculinity in a fractured and—moving into the Progressive Era—expanding US empire.

Melodrama and Nostalgic Spaces

It is fitting that these GAR playwrights used melodrama to depict a nation in peril on stage, since—as Peter Brooks argues—melodrama "reenacts the menace of evil and the eventual triumph of morality made operative and evident."[56] Linda Williams expands on Brooks's formulation of melodrama, noting that it "begins, and wants to end, in a 'space of innocence,'" whether this is an actual space of innocence or a "nostalgia for a virtuous place."[57] The space of nostalgia pursued in the GAR dramas is not necessarily just the idyllic Northern village in which most of the plays begin and end, but it is instead the *reunited country* that is the ultimate utopian space of innocence.

This reunited country is distinctly masculine and the main impediments to achieving the space of innocence are the Southern elites and their sympathizers. John A. Logan, a politician and veteran instrumental in crafting the GAR and its ideology, determined that the "main threat to this yeoman's paradise was 'class distinction,' both in the slaveholding South and at 'aristocratic' West Point"—not slavery.[58] Though not always depicted onstage, the reenfolding of the white middle-class Southerner into the embrace of the unified nation is the key to achieving this space of innocence.

Even when the melodramatic villains (copperheads or Southerners) came from a lineage of patriotic service, their judgment was clouded by their antiabolitionism. The Confederates are consistently characterized as impulsive and overly passionate, displaying the most unmanly excesses of anger and illogicality: with or without the aristocratic implications, all the Confederate villains are indicted on this charge of steroidal emotions. Even one of the Southerners in the opening West Point scene in *Allatoona* admits that those from "the South are by nature an impulsive people."[59] Deploying distinctly dishonorable conduct within the perceived codes of acceptable war behavior, the Confederates often display dishonesty, malice, and maniacal hatred toward their helpless captives by torturing or shooting them. Conversely, the Confederate villains are spared, jailed in comparatively agreeable conditions (compared, that is, to the conditions depicted in Confederate prison camps), and treated with justice and benevolence (even if that same justice dictated a death sentence). Worse yet, the villains at times have to be saved by the hands of a woman.[60]

Unlike popular melodramas where romance is foregrounded, the women in these amateur plays—whether Southern women ultimately conquered by their Northern sweethearts (as in most cases), or Northerners who eschew their Confederate lovers/husbands for the Union cause—mostly serve as a sort of measuring mechanism alongside which the depravity of the Confederate villain can be compared. For this reason, the women in the amateur plays are given a certain amount of agency in their devotion to the Union cause, but ultimately remain ancillary to the military focus. These female characters eventually acknowledge the errors of their—and, by extension, the Confederacy's—ways and recognize the superiority of the Union cause. The villain of *The Color Guard*, for example, causes the heroine to make a statement that highlights the political devaluation of women occurring in many of these plays. Though he is a "Southern man in feeling…a *yes* from your lips would lead me to fight in any cause. The faintest hope of your love would make me respond to-morrow to Lincoln's call." This egregious declaration of intent is countered by the livid Lucy: "No, sir, I despise you. Your words confirm my worst fears of your utter want of principle. I can respect the Southern people who act honestly out of their errors; but a man whose sword hangs upon a woman's word, when great principles are at stake, should not be trusted even by his friends."[61] Other amateur texts replay similar scenes wherein the villain lacks agency, honor, and emotional control—the hallmarks of masculinity.[62]

Once this emasculated villain is disposed of, the space of innocence can be achieved. The "nostalgic" aspect of this GAR space is perhaps most clearly articulated in representations of nonwhite and/or ethnic characters. Every extant play features at least one Dutch, Irish, or African American character, and these players perform a greater function than simply letting an actor try his hand at a comic type. The ethnic and racial representations in these plays also take on different connotations than the complex "fear and fascination," class fomentation, and cultural borrowing that Eric Lott reads in blackface minstrelsy. These instances of cross-ethnic or cross-racial performance are set within wartime narratives of incredible violence and nation rebuilding. Within this context, the GAR sites of memory make implicit claims about who is worthy to participate in citizenship.[63] Considering the demographic makeup of the GAR and of the plays, it is possible to read the texts as a sort of white male nostalgia for the time when African Americans were still slaves or were blindly loyal to the Union emancipators, and when thick-accented Germans and drink-loving Irishmen provided reliable ethnic humor—in contrast to the new wave of Eastern European immigrants entering the United States in the 1880s.

While Stuart McConnell claims that the GAR was one of the most progressive organizations of the nineteenth century due to its color-blind policy of admission—and this is true in comparison to other U.S. organizations—the GAR was by no means an all-inclusive, desegregated, democratic fraternal group. The status and treatment of African American veterans varied from post to post in the GAR, at times denying black men an important platform for juridical and social acceptance. Donald Shaffer reveals the gap between the policy on paper and the actual practice of the GAR, noting that many African American veterans were blackballed by admissions voting policies. Whites-only posts were established in some Southern states, and black veterans were not allowed to establish their own posts there. There were debates among black and white veterans as to whether or not posts should be segregated: in reality, most posts experience de facto segregation regardless of the official policy.[64] In addition, though the GAR had members of German and Irish extraction, such groups were often contained within urban posts, geographically limited due to the "residential segregation in the American metropolis" throughout the postwar decades.[65] Since the GAR never allowed veterans of later US wars to join its ranks, the organization remained locked in a demographic stasis: there was a veritable explosion of immigration toward the end of the nineteenth century, but GAR plays performed in the 1880s and beyond represented the more limited diversity of decades past.[66]

The exclusionary tendencies of the GAR reflect larger national juridical processes. Immediately after the war and in anticipation/protest of the passage of the Thirteenth, Fourteenth, and Fifteenth Amendments, Southern state legislatures passed Black Codes severely curtailing the basic rights of the newly emancipated population—in what legal scholar Ian Haney López would see as the beginnings of a "self-perpetuating pattern" where "race becomes real becomes law becomes race."[67] Socially endorsed segregation and the imposition of racial categories in everyday practice eventually became legislated inequality—thus reifying such categories. Further attempts at equality on a federal level—such as the passage of the Civil Rights Act of 1875 that tried to enforce equality in the public sphere, which was then overturned by the Supreme Court in 1883—were swiftly dismantled or blocked by states or courts. Likewise, immigration laws were enacted throughout the postwar decades to try to define what it meant to be "white" and a "citizen" of the country.[68] Haney López argues that "racial categories exist only as a function of what people believe,"[69] and it is here that the danger embedded in the representations of the "Other" in popular culture becomes clearer. Popular depictions of ethnic and racial characters as inferior systematically deny the humanity of the real person, thus protecting and reinforcing whiteness via social and legal exclusion.

In amateur performed sites of memory, examples abound to suggest that many nonwhite/nonnative people should be excluded or have limited participation in the reunited nation. These stage types often fight among each other in the plays—precluding any sort of solidarity. Many deploy violence in "unsuitable" ways (like Confederate villains), but they cannot expend such energy in actual defense of the Union. Although, as mentioned above, slavery is rarely invoked as a cause of the war, the Irish and Dutch characters mention it in a comic vein to mask cowardice: "I vouldn't go down dere and vight mit dose niggers of you vould gife me der whole Goffermant," according to Sockery Schneidlebecker in *The Confederate Spy*.[70] Several of the Irish and German stage characters are fond of drink, they bumble military maneuvers (an ethnic character ineffectively leading a drill is featured in several plays), and many—particularly Herr Sockery—are quite obsessed with food. Barney of *The Volunteers* tells his Irish sweetheart Bridget, "Oi'm going to die foighting for the nagurs," then repeatedly proceeds to run and hide or find some reason to return to camp as battle begins.[71] Fritz, one of *Our Country's Defenders!*, is assured by another enlistee that he is "fearfully brave, especially where there is a charge to be made on pretzels and lager."[72]

The most credible evidence that nonwhite and ethnic characters are not truly enfolded into the Union cause is that many do not show an inherent loyalty to either side but—in the case of the Irish and German—can be bought as mercenary soldiers, like those in *The Color Guard* or in *The Rebel's Last Shot*, among others. Often these characters, and especially African Americans, base loyalty on a personal sense of obligation or servitude to a single character and reinforce their represented inferiority. The rare ethnic characters who express patriotism in the GAR plays, such as Dietrich in *The Dutch Recruit*, are routinely emasculated in other ways: Dietrich falls asleep and lets a Confederate soldier escape, has to dress like a woman to aid the hero, and even his killing of the villain Frank Duncan, who is attempting to rape the heroine Maude, is rendered dishonorable. "How you like dot, Misdur Guerrillas?" Dietrich asks the dying man; and Maude tells the hero Harry, late to the scene, that she is "thankful that you did not stain your hands with his blood."[73] Thus, the rare heroic feat is often framed as a happy accident rather than the outcome of a truly masculine endeavor. Clearly, all the behaviors exhibited by the ethnic types fall well outside of the realm of acceptable, masculine behavior: they ascribe the war to simplistic causes like fighting for the "nagurs" rather than the Union, thus failing to adopt the preservationist mission of the GAR. Cowardly, prone to excess of appetite (lust, drink, or food), with a lack of loyalty to the Union, the Bradys, Barneys, and Sockerys are viable targets for comedy in the midst of the trauma and tragedy of war.

Whether depicted as loyal Uncle Toms, comic minstrels, or a mixture of the two, no political agency is afforded to African American characters when they appear.[74] Ultimately these characters reiterate the supposed superiority of white identity and antebellum racial codes. It is telling that three of the plays contain an almost identical scene, wherein African American characters discuss their involvement in the war. In *The Dutch Recruit*, Uncle Ned asks another slave, Sam, if he's going to "fite" for "your massa, missus, and de old plantation."

SAM: Look heh, Uncle, you've seen two dogs fitin' ober a bone?
UNCLE NED: Yes
SAM: Dat's de Nof an' Souf fitin' ober us. Now Uncle, did you eber see de bone fite?[75]

A similar dialogue appears in *Harry Allen*, but the hero Harry asks Sam, the slave of their Southern guests, if he'll enlist. Sam has inexplicably covered himself in flour in order to hide, asking, "Me go for a soger? I guess not." When Harry asks why Sam will not enlist, he replies with a query:

SAM: Now, look a here, Massa Harry, did you ebber see two dogs fighten ober a bone?
HARRY: But what's that got to do with it?
SAM: Well, Massa Harry, did—you—ebber—see—de bone get up and fight?
HARRY: I don't remember that I ever did.
SAM: I guess not. Now you boys can be dogs and I'll be de bone, dat am de innocent cause of all dis fuss.[76]

An even closer rendition of this dialogue occurs between Zeb and the Irish Ike in *Lights and Shadows of the Great Rebellion*.[77] Shortly after this exchange, Zeb and Ike share a comic exchange trying to lay claim to a bottle of booze, until Dutchey shows up and also tries to steal it. The "Sams" and "Zebs" (and other young African American male characters) who could possibly be involved in the war's causes or its battles declare their innocence and absolution: as mere objects that dogs are fighting over, all the black characters are literally devoid of life and agency. The "Sams" and "Zebs" make a declaration that the whites in these plays routinely discount: that slavery is somehow at the root of "all dis fuss." This notion is regularly cast aside in the amateur plays, and it becomes clear that only the misinformed minstrel characters have this "distorted" perception. They cannot begin to grasp the complexities of the matter at hand.

The comic stage types who appear often display the sort of humor and physicality typical of minstrel shows. These characters fight, participate in comic business, and often exhibit the dialect and malapropisms of stump speeches. For instance, Jumbo in *The Midnight Charge* steals chickens, plays the banjo, brawls with Confederate villains and ethnic characters alike, and promotes his singing group the Pumpkin Blossom Club in the Union camp. Jeff in *Our Heroes* feigns readiness to participate in the war, since his "gran'-fadder fell fightin' in the reb'lutionary struggle"; but Jeff fell more recently (and clearly not in keeping with his heroic lineage) "when I had de row wit dat odder nigger." Instead, Jeff's participation in the war is relegated to "malufactrer of hard tack chowder for de troops."[78] Other African American characters are likewise granted limited participation in the war through emasculating or dehumanizing depictions. For example, Clay in *The Confederate Spy* overhears a Confederate plot while hiding under the sofa in a Southern parlor, but the Union general struggles to understand Clay's convoluted minstrel meanderings, declaring Clay is "getting things mixed."[79]

The GAR's limited corroboration of African American masculinity is crystallized in the few scenes where blacks are allowed to bear arms—and do not prove to be up to the task. Zeb in *Lights and Shadows* fights both the German and Irish characters for booze, holding them at gunpoint to procure a bottle. The same happens when Sam/Zeb captures the Confederate villain, who encourages him to drink and seizes Zeb's weapon. The inebriated Zeb gives up, deciding instead to steal some poultry, since "Niga know more about chickens, dan dey do about war."[80] Pete in *Allatoona* exposes a Confederate plot to the Union general and saves the young hero. The general tells the hero that "you owe your life to this faithful negro." His ex-master swears, "Curse the infernal niggers!" "Cuss away, massa, cuss away," Pete replies, "but it won't do no good, massa." The appellation of faithful is of particular importance here: still denied a name in his heroism, Pete is relegated to a "faithful negro," who has correctly transferred his loyalty to the Union. It is only once he is deemed a "faithful negro" that he is given a weapon; he appears to be a poor soldier, merely mimicking the movements of those surrounding him.

The pathos-inducing, Uncle Tom–derived, emasculated elderly slave often displays the most pronounced kind of loyalty. As a contraband—one of those nebulous designations given to fugitive or freed slaves during wartime—Pete fights at the close of the play, serving as a foil to Uncle Ben, who waits on General Corse. Ben is a contraband too, preparing food and singing spirituals for the

Union general, his "massa," while informing the good General that "de bondman must be free" when Corse asks if he ever grows discouraged. Ben is passive, taking a bullet while he scouts for sharpshooters unarmed at the play's close, loyal to the general's orders until his death: his freedom is circumscribed and ultimately denied within the rubric of black subservience. Old Joe in *The Union Spy* shares Topsy's genealogy, having "no brudder, no sister, no fader, no mudder, no nothin' but Joe. When you see Joe, you see all there is of us."[81] At one point, Joe holds his Confederate ex-master at gunpoint and demands dispatches from General Lee. Instead of receiving any credit for this heroic action, Old Joe utters a string of malapropisms while attempting to acquire the dispatches, and his new "massa," the Union spy Sleeper, hands the dispatches to Grant without any mention of Joe's role. When Sleeper is wounded and captured on the battlefield, Old Joe can only weep.

On the rare occasion when African American characters are depicted without minstrel trappings, there are still serious impediments to their advancement in the world of these amateur plays. Jim in *The Old Flag* represents the ignorant minstrel type, believing his master's claims that the Yankee generals subject all the blacks they capture to execution—they are "roasted alive—burned to a crisp."[82] Jim's misconceptions are corrected by Sam, a fugitive slave (not scripted in dialect) who aids his ex-master Union spy with elaborate plans, and is crucial in a direct and tangible way to the Union's success. When Sam is captured by the Confederates and they attempt to execute him so others will "see how niggers are served when they aid our enemies," a white woman intercedes and deflects the gun-wielding arm, saving the life of the African American man much as she saves the disgraced and emasculated Confederate soldier in other GAR plays.[83]

The stage Irish, German, and minstrel types in the GAR plays were nothing new to the US theatre. What is more interesting is how those nonwhite or nonnative persons who contributed to the war effort are so easily marred by the application of comic stage traditions and ultimately marked as being unfit for citizenship. Attempts to define and limit citizenship were part of larger national developments, led by the dominant Anglo-Saxon population to "establish white supremacy" with "a systematic and effective drive…that mirrored developments in the South" after Reconstruction.[84] The gendered, racial, and ethnic play's repercussions on the amateur stage invested the Anglo-Saxon intersectional masculine reunion with power and value on a local level—contributing to a nationwide exclusionary project and white hegemony.

BETHANY D. HOLMSTROM

True Reconciliation

Laura Cooke's emotive notations in the margins of her program in June 1868 capture the early process of a nation trying to heal. The "awfully sad" and "true to life" deaths and the tableaux of patriotism and freedom would become an exercise in national mourning—by the close of the nineteenth century, such memories were no longer circumscribed by sectionalist loyalties. In fact, the politics of the GAR plays fell somewhat out of vogue by the 1880s. In anticipation of William Gillette and his company performing *Held by the Enemy* below the Mason-Dixon line in November 1890, the *Atlanta Constitution* printed a Northern critic's thoughts on the production: "Dramas founded upon the events of the late civil war, of the character of 'The Color Guard,'... 'The Drummer Boy of Shiloh,' and others of a similar type, have lost their drawing quality. They appealed too much to sectionalism and kept alive the bitter feelings engendered by the war, painted the horrors of prison pens and lost sight of the fact that there were heroes on both sides—men brave and good, women pure and patriotic.... The author...[has] so equally divided the honors between the 'blue and the gray' that, whether in New Orleans or Boston, the play is certain of a hearty reception."[85] Even if the GAR by and large opposed the memorialization of the Lost Cause, ex-Confederate soldiers were welcomed to the Blue-Gray reunions of the 1880s as part of the dulling of these "bitter feelings," leading to what McConnell calls a "love feast of reconciliation."[86]

However, GAR plays continued to be staged into the twentieth century, even as the veterans grew wizened and some critics declared the rhetoric of the texts shrill. With the ruling of *Plessy v. Ferguson* in 1896, "separate but equal" became the law of the land, and the earlier attempts by Radical Republicans to establish an equal citizenry were quashed. With the passage of legalized segregation laws throughout the nation, the limits to mental conceptions of democracy were demarcated. As new immigrant populations entered the country and were encountered via imperial pursuits like the Spanish-American War, courts scrambled to fix and protect that fickle construct of "whiteness" throughout the Gilded Age and Progressive Era. In the midst of the civic and legal upheaval of the postbellum years, there was a nostalgic desire for a fictional space of innocence, a perfect union, and a world that no longer existed. The melodramatic mechanisms of GAR plays ensured that sectionalism was ultimately eliminated, and that the common white soldier was welcomed home. Indeed, even if some critics could not see the political work being done beyond the resuscitation of "bitter feelings," the GAR plays had already begun to set the table for the "love feast" well before the Blue-Gray reunions and commercial war plays of the

1880s. The inner workings of the GAR and the amateur sites of war memories that its veterans performed—with the investments in class representations, the allegorical and thrilling realistic elements, and the rendering of nonwhite and nonnative peoples as comic types rather than participants in the war's history or American citizenship—allowed performers and audiences to create and consume war memories that ultimately celebrated a whitewashed space of nostalgic innocence, presented within a comforting world of hierarchies past.

Notes

I would like to thank Judith Milhous and James Wilson at the CUNY Graduate Center for their feedback on earlier versions of this article. This work also benefitted from the ASTR 2010 working session "Power and Performance: War on Stage" in Seattle. Thanks to journal editor Elizabeth Reitz Mullenix for her comments and suggestions.

1. M. John Lubetkin, *Jay Cooke's Gamble: The Northern Pacific Railroad, the Sioux, and the Panic of 1873* (Norman: University of Oklahoma Press, 2006), 3.
2. *The Drummer Boy*, program, Sandusky, Ohio, 1868, in Papers of the Barney, Cooke, McClew, and Neilson families, 1820–1895, Accession #7786-x, Special Collections Department, University of Virginia Library, Charlottesville. From a comparison of the handwriting in the program to that in other letters from Laura in the family records, it seems almost certain that she is indeed the author of the comments.
3. The advertised Great Western Band began playing at "4 min of 8. music commences. we are quite tired of waiting + are glad—it makes me sad + dear knows I am sad enough already without that." She also thought that the portrayal of the Goddess of Liberty in the closing act 1 tableau was "charming."
4. Samuel Muscroft, *The Drummer Boy; or, The Battle Field of Shiloh* (Mansfield, OH: L. D. Myers, 1872), 23.
5. Rosemary L. Cullen, *The Civil War in American Drama before 1900: Catalog of an Exhibition* (Providence: Brown University Library, 1982), 24, 28.
6. Jeffrey Mason, *Melodrama and the Myth of America* (Bloomington: Indiana University Press, 1993), 162–63.
7. Ibid., 178.
8. David Mayer, *Stagestruck Filmmaker: D. W. Griffith and the American Theatre* (Iowa City: University of Iowa Press, 2009), 123–24.
9. I use the designations "amateur" and "GAR" plays interchangeably. The GAR was one of the largest organizations performing these plays, but many other amateur dramatic associations (those with veterans and not) staged these texts. I do not mean to imply that these texts were performed exclusively by the GAR when referring to them as such, but the materials were often explicitly marketed or dedicated to this organization.
10. "The Color Guard," *New York Times*, September 2, 1873, 5.
11. Pierre Nora, "Between History and Memory: Les Lieux de Mémoire," *Representations* 26 (Spring 1989): 7.

12. I reference only those plays with confirmed productions, because without proof of performance the potential consumption of these memories cannot be ascertained. Rosemary Cullen documents anywhere from thirty to forty extant texts that could have been plays explicitly marketed for the GAR. See Cullen, "A Checklist of American Civil War Drama: Beginnings to 1900," *Performing Arts Resources* 12 (1987): 135–55. Fourteen of the plays read for this essay can be found in the English and American Drama of the Nineteenth Century microform collection, Butler Library, Columbia University, New York; A. D. Ames and C. G. Bartley, *The Spy of Atlanta* (Clyde, OH: A. D. Ames, 1879); S. J. Brown, *In the Enemy's Camp; or, The Stolen Despatches* (Boston: Walter H. Baker & Co., 1889); O. W. Cornish, *Foiled; or, A Struggle for Life and Liberty* (Chicago: Dramatic Publishing Company, c. 1871); J. H. Dawson and B. G. Whittemore, *Lights and Shadows of the Great Rebellion, or the Hospital Nurse of Tennessee* (Clyde, Ohio: A. D. Ames, 1885); David Hill, *The Pride of Company G; or, The Volunteers* (Boston: Walter H. Baker & Company, 1897, c. 1892); Judson Kilpatrick and J. Owen Moore, *Allatoona* (New York: Samuel French, 1875); James S. Rogers, *Our Regiment* (Boston: Alfred Mudge & Son, 1884); Muscroft, *The Drummer Boy; or, The Battle Field of Shiloh*; L. W. Osgood, *The Union Spy; or the Battle of Weldon Railroad* (Woburn, Mass.: Parker's Amateur Player, 1871); John B. Renauld, *Our Heroes* (New York: Robert M. De Witt, 1873); W. Ellsworth Stedman, *The Confederate Spy* (New York: Samuel French, 1887); W. Ellsworth Stedman, *The Midnight Charge* (New York: Samuel French, c. 1892); J.T. Vegiard, *The Dutch Recruit; or, The Blue and Gray* (Clyde, OH: A. D. Ames, 1879); Veteran of the War for the Union, *The Union Sergeant; or, the Battle of Gettysburg* (Springfield, MA: George W. Sargent, Publisher, 1873). Hathi Digital Trust provides the texts of Joseph Barton, *Harry Allen, The Union Spy* (Lansing, MI: W. S. George & Co., 1873); A. R. Calhoun, *The Color Guard* (Providence: Millard, Gray & Simpson, Steam Printers, 1872); Charles Foster, *The Rebel's Last Shot; or, The Gunmaker's Bride!* (New Haven, CT: Hoggson & Robinson, 1871); Greenleaf S. Tukey, Walter E. Simmons, & Philipp W. Golliff, *Our Country's Defenders!* (Boston: Rockwell & Churchill, 1873); G. W. Walker and Edwin A. Lewis, *The Old Flag: Or the Spy of Newbern* (Hartford, CT: Soldier's Record Print, 1870). The final text surveyed here, W. Hector Gale, *The Loyal Heart of 1861* (Oneida, NY, 1898), resides in the Harris Collection of American Poetry and Plays, John Hay Library, Brown University, Providence, RI.
13. Alan Trachtenberg, *The Incorporation of America: Culture and Society in the Gilded Age* (2007; rpt. New York: Hill & Wang, 1982), 3–4.
14. Historian Stuart McConnell confirms that the GAR was created by Illinois Republicans as "*both* a charitable and political organization…but the political side of the order was not proclaimed publicly." See Stuart McConnell, *Glorious Contentment: The Grand Army of the Republic, 1865–1900* (Chapel Hill: University of North Carolina Press, 1992), 25. Charity was one of a triumvirate of tenets of the GAR—loyalty and fraternity being the other two. The organization did not subscribe to donating large sums of money. The limited, supplementary amounts bestowed upon veterans, widows, and orphans were part of a larger masculinist project of encouraging independence—construed as a direct correlative of manliness—rather than fiscal dependence. The "fraternity" a veteran could expect was circumscribed in the realm of charity: a veteran's brother would help, but only if no one's liberty and masculinity were compromised due to this act. To be viable capitalist contenders, the veterans could not receive consistent, large handouts from their brethren. See McConnell, *Glorious Contentment*, 136.

15. Soldiers were recruited out of geographically defined areas for the most part, serving with members of their home community. This local pride manifested itself during and after the war: on the battlefield, in the final Grand Review after the war's close in Washington, D.C., and in the GAR posts. Though relocated veterans could join posts in their new area, the sense of localism was widely prevalent—and many veterans identified regionally. See McConnell, *Glorious Contentment*, 10.
16. Eileen Curley, "Tainted Money? Nineteenth Century Charity Theatricals," *Theatre Symposium* 15 (2007): 52–53.
17. Ibid., 57.
18. Within the amateur plays explored in this chapter, the women are not typically the main characters or dramatic foci. The romantic storyline is often secondary to the military one, which undoubtedly allowed women acting in the dramas to maintain a sense of propriety. Women performing for charity was one thing—performing for wages as an occupation was quite another. See also Curley, "Tainted Money?"
19. McConnell found 6,928 GAR posts throughout the North, but he also makes an important qualification: in 1890 when the GAR had record roster numbers (409,489 members), the GAR represented fewer than half of the one million living veterans in 1890. See McConnell, *Glorious Contentment*, 54, 206.
20. It so happens that, toward the end of the nineteenth century, one of the largest blocs of veteran soldiers was in the Midwest. See Patrick J. Kelly, "The Election of 1896 and the Restructuring of Civil War Memory," in *The Memory of the Civil War in American Culture*, ed. Alice Fahs and Joan Waugh (Chapel Hill: University of North Carolina Press, 2004), 182.
21. Stedman, *The Midnight Charge*, 2.
22. Ibid.
23. In his play, Edwin Lewis directed the Dushane GAR Post No. 3 in January 1887. See advertisement, *The Sun*, January 12, 1887, 1. Major George T. Ulmer appeared in *The Volunteer* in Washington, D.C., in 1891. See "On and off the Stage," *Washington Post*, September 21, 1891, 4. The other listings appear in the cast lists of the play texts. Ames was quite popular in his work with amateur groups and traveled all around the Midwest and into New England to both play roles in texts published by his press catering to the amateur market, and to direct/instruct the amateur players. See Hope P. Litchfield and Roger E. Stoddard, "A. D. Ames, First Dramatic Publisher in the West," *Books at Brown* 21 (1966): 97–99.
24. Bosley Crowther, "The Not So Grand Old Theatre," *New York Times*, April 29, 1934, X1. *The Drummer Boy* was one of the best-known and often-presented amateur war dramas, being staged even into the twentieth century by amateur players. A GAR post in Boston produced the play as late as December 1901 as a benefit, and the "large audience did not hesitate to say that it was one of the best entertainments every given by this oppular [sic] organization." See "Reproduced Stirring Scenes of the Civil War," *Boston Daily Globe*, December 12, 1901, 2. It appeared again in Boston in June 1902 as a benefit for a GAR fund as well, but this time it was staged after a GAR encampment. See "Fusiliers' Night," *Boston Daily Globe*, June 18, 1902, 9.
25. Carte de visite albums were a very common self-created representation of middle-class status. See Andrea Volpe, "Cartes de Visite Portrait Photographs and the Culture of Class Formation," in *The Middling Sorts: Explorations in the History of the American Middle Class*, ed. Burton J. Beldstein and Robert D. Johnston (New York: Routledge, 2001), 160.

26. Robert Gordon Album, c. 1868, 1906. Manuscript and Visual Collections Department, P0474, William Henry Smith Memorial Library, Indiana Historical Society, Indianapolis. Many thanks to Susan Sutton at the Indiana Historical Society for her help in procuring these images.
27. *The Drummer Boy*, program. The Sandusky production ran June 2–4.
28. In Sandusky, a ticket to the gallery was 25 cents, and 50 cents for general admission; the Indianapolis production was more expensive and seemingly more spectacular than the Sandusky production in terms of its large amount of participants. Admission for the Indianapolis show was 50 cents, with private boxes for $5 and reserved seats at 75 cents. Just as a means of comparison: many skilled job workers (bricklayers, carpenters, painters, plumbers, etc.) in the Northeast earned between $3 and $3.90 a day in 1868. Farmers earned $1.50 in comparison. Many theatre tickets in the 1860s and 1870s in New York City were between 50 cents and $1.50. The later ten-twent'-thirt' shows (typically melodramas) were popular and affordable, with seats starting at ten cents. These offerings appeared throughout the 1890s and into the early twentieth century. See Scott Derks, ed., *The Value of a Dollar: Prices and Incomes in the United States, 1860–1989* (Detroit: Gale Research, 1994), 11–18.
29. Surprisingly, the program for the Sandusky production does not mention any charitable ends.
30. Litchfield and Stoddard, "A. D. Ames," 99.
31. Advertisement, *Sun*, January 12, 1887, 1.
32. Advertisement, *New York Herald*, October 21, 1877, 4.
33. Miles Orvell, *The Real Thing: Imitation and Authenticity in American Culture, 1880–1940* (Chapel Hill: University of North Carolina Press, 1989), xx.
34. Mason, *Melodrama and the Myth of America*, 163.
35. Ibid.
36. For instance, a letter from General John Corse—who fought in the real battle of Allatoona and is portrayed in the play of that name—affirms that the battle was "very correctly represented," and the authors avow that "many of those who were prominent in the battle…pronounce it as not only deeply interesting, but, so far as consistent, *historically* correct." Judson Kilpatrick and J. Owen Moore, *Allatoona* (New York: Samuel French, 1875), 4. English and American drama of the Nineteenth Century microform collection, Butler Library, Columbia University, New York. These sorts of claims appear in several plays texts.
37. Classified advertisement 9, *San Francisco Chronicle*, February 6, 1891, 8.
38. Of course, these testaments appear more often when the play was not authored or co-authored by an actual veteran.
39. "Amusements," *Chicago Tribune*, November 1, 1870, 4.
40. Ibid.
41. "Militia on the Stage," *Sun*, June 6, 1895, 8. It is unclear if the actors that appeared in this particular drama were amateurs or professionals, but the 4th Regiment presented clearly amateur actors on the stage.
42. "Public Amusements," *Sun*, January 18, 1887, 4.
43. For instance, Generals Grant and Lee appear in *The Union Spy*. Along with John Corse, *Allatoona* includes Generals Sherman and Slocum, *The Spy of Atlanta* both Generals Sherman and McPherson, and *The Midnight Charge* lists General Geary in its cast.

44. Gary Gallagher devotes an entire study to articulating the importance of "Union" in the mid-nineteenth century, a "political sense" which has since "disappeared from our [contemporary] vocabulary." See Gallagher, *The Union War* (Cambridge, MA: Harvard University Press, 2011), 3.
45. Kilpatrick and Moore, *Allatoona*, 9.
46. Vegiard, *The Dutch Recruit*, 15.
47. Muscroft, *The Drummer Boy*, 8.
48. Gale, *Loyal Heart*, 9.
49. Renauld, *Our Heroes*, 17.
50. McConnell, *Glorious Contentment*, 192–93.
51. Jeffrey Mason likewise notes that the playwrights use the "comic darky" to "dissociate their work from any critique of slavery or any claim that slavery inspired the Union commitment to the war." See Mason, *Myth and Melodrama*, 169.
52. Kilpatrick and Moore, *Allatoona*, 9.
53. Dawson and Whittemore, *Lights and Shadows*, 6.
54. Osgood, *The Union Spy*, 5.
55. Ibid., 6.
56. Peter Brooks, *The Melodramatic Imagination: Balzac, Henry James, Melodrama, and the Mode of Excess* (New Haven, CT: Yale University Press, 1995), 15.
57. Linda Williams, *Playing the Race Card: Melodramas of Black and White From Uncle Tom to O. J. Simpson* (Princeton, NJ: Princeton University Press, 2001), 28.
58. McConnell, *Glorious Contentment*, 198.
59. Kilpatrick & Moore, *Allatoona*, 7.
60. An example that combines many of these villainous unmanly features: the Yankee sweetheart of a Confederate spy begs to get her lover's sentence commuted to a Northern prison seconds before his court-martial execution is to be carried out in *Our Regiment*. The scenes of the Yankee prison at Fort Warren in the play make it seem a veritable vacation compared to the fetid conditions in Libby, where the Yankee hero resides. These Confederates in Fort Warren complain about the meal of "bread, coffee, sugar, crackers, and cold meat" with all the appropriate utensils—"it is wholesome enough, to be sure; but I should think they might vary it a little with fruit, and some kind of fish or fowl"—as the Union captives in Libby are beaten to death and denied even a crust of bread or sip of water. Rogers, *Our Regiment*, 30.
61. Calhoun, *The Color Guard*, 9–10.
62. In the same vein the villainous Confederate spy of *The Midnight Charge* is exposed as a philandering liar by his abandoned ex-wife, who has donned a nun's habit as a disguise and pleads for his life at the close of the play. The sister of *The Confederate Spy* convinces her Union lover to save her brother, and the spy himself swears loyalty to the Union before breaking down and sobbing into a handkerchief.
63. Eric Lott, *Love and Theft: Blackface Minstrelsy and the American Working Class* (New York: Oxford University Press, 1993), 25.
64. Shaffer characterizes the status of black veterans in the GAR as the position of "second-class members," with only a few managing to achieve high positions within several posts. See Donald R. Shaffer, *After the Glory: The Struggles of Black Civil War Veterans* (Lawrence: University Press of Kansas, 2004), 158.
65. McCullough, *Glorious Contentment*, 55.

66. From 1880 on, immigrants arrived progressively more from southeastern Europe rather than the northwestern regions. As new waves of immigrants from Eastern Europe—quite unlike their German and Irish predecessors and rendered even more "foreign" in popular discourse—came to the United States during the latter part of the nineteenth century, the rhetoric of nativism escalated in the courts and government chambers. Whereas, in 1882, only 13 percent of new immigrants were from southeastern Europe, the early twentieth century saw 80 percent of incoming immigrants from the same region. See Desmond King, *Making Americans: Immigration, Race, and the Origins of the Diverse Democracy* (Cambridge, MA: Harvard University Press, 2002), 50.
67. Ian Haney López, *White by Law: The Legal Construction of Race* (New York: New York University Press, 2006), 133.
68. King, *Making Americans*, 51. King also mentions the "irony" that "restrictionist politics often consisted of the most recently accepted immigrants"—the Irish, German, and other northwestern Europeans—"to delay the new generation."
68. Haney López, 103.
70. Stedman, *The Confederate Spy*, 10.
71. Hill, *The Volunteers*, 5.
72. Tukey et al., *Our Country's Defenders!*, 26.
73. Vegiard, *The Dutch Recruit*, 49.
74. No black female characters appear in the amateur plays with proof of performance.
75. Vegiard, *The Dutch Recruit*, 9.
76. Barton, *Harry Allen, The Union Spy*, 10–11.
77. Dawson and Whittemore, *Lights and Shadows of the Great Rebellion*, 9. Mason likewise mentions one instance of this scene in his analysis. However, the appearance of some version of this scene in numerous play-texts suggests that the real contributions of black men to the war were often slighted in the GAR plays. See Mason, *Myth and Melodrama*, 169.
78. Renauld, *Our Heroes*, 11.
79. Stedman, *The Confederate Spy*, 39.
80. Dawson and Whittemore, *Lights and Shadows*, 22.
81. Osgood, *The Union Spy*, 8
82. Walker and Lewis, *The Old Flag*, 4.
83. Ibid., 43.
84. Desmond S. King and Stephen G.N. Tuck, "De-centering the South: America's Nationwide White Supremacist Order after Reconstruction," *Past & Present* 194 (February 2007): 214.
85. "The Theater This Week," *Atlanta Constitution*, November 16, 1890, 8.
86. Stuart McConnell found that there were around twenty Blue-Gray reunions with GAR involvement in the 1880s, with the "love feast" in full effect by the mid-1890s among white Northerners and Southerners. See McConnell, *Glorious Contentment*, 190. This "love feast" mentality is in keeping with what David Blight notes as the collapse of reconciliationist tendencies on Civil War memories, creating the "superstructure of Civil War memory," with a "base" constituted by "white supremacy in both its moderate and virulent forms. See David W. Blight, *Race and Reunion: The Civil War in American Memory* (Cambridge, MA: Harvard University Press, 2001), 361.

Corporeal *Disasters of War*
Legibilities of "Spain" and the Jewish Body in Helen Tamiris's *Adelante!*

—LISA JACKSON-SCHEBETTA

> With Goya a new standard for responsiveness to suffering enters art…While the image, like every image, is an invitation to look, the caption, more often than not, insists on the difficulty of doing just that.
> SUSAN SONTAG, *REGARDING THE PAIN OF OTHERS*

> The civil war now raging in Spain has brought Goya's *Disasters of War* to [an] intense second life. Through them we see deeper into the present suffering in Spain than we could in newspaper photographs.
> A. HYATT MAYOR, "GOYA'S 'DISASTERS OF WAR'"

Between 1810 and 1820, Francisco de Goya created *Disasters of War* in response to Napoleon's invasion of Spain. Each of the eighty-five etchings explicitly depict wartime atrocities (rape, dismemberment, castration, torture, massacre). Goya captioned each print with cryptic phrases: "This is bad." "With reason—or without." "Poor mother." When first published in 1863 by the Royal Academy of Fine Arts in Madrid, the series appalled British and U.S. critics as psychotic filth and served for others as yet further evidence of the Black Legend, of just how cruel and degenerate the Spanish could be. The etchings found a receptive English-speaking audience, however, after World War I, an audience that grew larger during the Spanish Civil War, 1936–1939. In 1936, the Spanish military revolted against the Spanish Republic, democratically elected in 1931. The western democracies adhered to a policy of nonintervention throughout the conflict, leaving the Republican side dependent on Communist Russia and, to a lesser extent, Mexico. The Nationalists, in contrast, benefited from the support of Italy and Germany, borne out in arms, airplanes, money, and bodies. Despite official U.S. policy, as deaths mounted in Spain and fascism's hold on Europe grew, Republican sympathy in the United States gained momentum. Spanish Republicans conjured popular resistance to Napoleon as a precedent to their current plight, an ideological move that featured Goya's images, the well-known *Third of May 1808* and *Second of May 1808* as well as the *Disasters*. In the United States, Goya's series was republished in 1938 as a newly potent invective against the atrocities of global fascism in which Spain figured as the key battleground.

The publication of the *Disasters* in 1938 could be read as but one more contribution to the representations of wounded, displaced, dead, and dying bodies that circulated through the international imaginary of the Spanish Civil War. It is not difficult to rattle off such images: Jay Allen's account from Badajoz, Pablo Picasso's *Guernica*, Robert Capa's *Falling Soldier,* and the violence of air raids, mass graves, and executions documented in newspapers and photography and imagined on screen and stage. What is unique about the *Disasters* is that they found their way onto a national stage in the United States: Helen Tamiris staged Goya's work in the dance piece *Adelante!* (meaning "onward" or "forward"), presented by the Federal Theatre Project (FTP) in April 1939. The presence of Goya in the work has yet to be examined by scholars. In this essay, I argue that Goya's etchings influenced the aesthetics of the dance, its dramaturgy, and the historiographical bent of its politics. In *Adelante!,* Tamiris ostensibly presented a story of Spain as told through the memory of the dying body of Republican soldier José, but Tamiris was not only documenting the corporeal disasters of war that were littering Spain. Tamiris's disasters of war, built upon both Goya's and Spain's, staged a revision of Iberian Jewish history in order to issue a call to arms, not for the Spanish but for the American Republic. Continued U.S. inaction against the anti-Semitism of fascism, *Adelante!* declared, compromised America's legitimacy as a democracy in a global world.

Tamiris's activism in American modern dance, her passion for organizing, and her instrumentality in the Federal Dance Project and the Federal Theatre Project have been addressed by Elizabeth Cooper (1997, 2004), Mark Franko (2002), Susan Manning (2004), and Ellen Graff (2007). Tamiris's work on *Adelante!,* in particular, has been amply documented by Cooper (2004) as an example both of Tamiris's political activism and of censorship practices at the Federal Theatre Project, anxious as they were about the Spanish and antifascist content of the piece.[1] My project here is to add to *Adelante!'s* history by exploring in detail how Goya's images resituate the corporeal legibility of the piece. Goya's presence in the piece, I argue, reveals that *Adelante!'s* indictment of U.S. nonintervention depended upon a reexamination of the historical and ideological relationships between U.S. histories of antifascism, Jewishness, and Spain.

Corporeal Legibility: Badajoz, Goya, Tamiris

In March 1931, Spain elected a democracy.[2] The king and his supporters fled. The Second Republic instituted reforms against the Church, the military, and the aristocracy. Yet leftist factions in the government and the country chafed against one another as alliances splintered and reformed. Resistance to the Republic from the right likewise increased; military leaders began looking for support outside of their country. Strikes, demonstrations, armed uprisings, and repressions multiplied. Tensions increased until, as noted above, the military revolted against the government in July 1936. Monarchists, clergy, and landowners supported the offensive. The Nationalists expected a rapid victory, but the Republicans managed to resist. In November 1936, the People's Army of Madrid, bolstered by Communist support, held off the Nationalist advance. Madrid, the capital of the Republic, would not be brought to her knees until March 1939.

During the Spanish Civil War, both Nationalists and Republicans presented themselves as fighting for a "true" Spain. For the Nationalists, Spain had been forged in the glory of the Catholic Empire. Their Spain was deeply threatened by the 1931 elections. For the Republicans, Spain had been legally elected by its people. Their Spain was nascent. Both sides, from 1936, claimed they were protecting *their* nation from foreign invaders and both used history to do so. While Nationalists conjured their true Spain as wrought through the purges of Ferdinand and Isabella's *Reconquista*, Republicans hearkened back to "the most well known resistance myths in Spanish history"—including the Spanish resistance to Napoleon from 1808 to 1813, the very subject of Goya's *Disasters* series.[3]

In 1808, Napoleon Bonaparte sought to place his brother, Joseph, on the Spanish throne, an act that would have placed Spain firmly within Napoleon's empire. Napoleon (not unlike the Nationalists) planned a rapid victory; Spain was a poor nation and its army should not have been a match for the French. Yet the Spanish managed to resist. What had been planned as a regional battle became a six-year civil war. Though the French were beaten in 1814, war and its attendant atrocities—or disasters, as Goya would have them—engulfed Spain. Robert Hughes writes that it was Goya's "fate and genius to become the epic poet of this process, with his etchings called *Los desastres de guerra—The Disasters of War* (e.g., fig. 1)—and his two great paintings of the first uprising against

Napoleon's troops, on May 2–3, 1808."[4] Goya, in his sixties, was living in Madrid in May 1808. He also traveled to Zaragoza in October. Zaragoza's resistance to the French became legendary. The citizens forced Napoleon's army to enter the city "house by house; every collapsed bunker became a barricade, every cellar a bunker, every pile of rubble a sniper's post."[5] Republican propaganda "re-appropriated" the "sieges of Zaragoza and Girona, the Spanish victory at Bailén (1808), and, above all, Madrid's popular uprising against French troops on May 2, 1808…in order to stress the parallels between those nineteenth-century representatives of the Spanish popular classes and the twentieth-century fighters belonging to working class organizations."[6] The narrative of "the people united against tyranny" appealed to Republican sympathizers the world over.

Though Republican rhetoric echoed general popular front and antifascist slogans, Republican propaganda found it easy to explicitly disseminate linkages between the resistance to Napoleon, Goya, and the Spanish Republic. The female resistance fighters of Zaragoza (depicted in Goya's *Disasters* plate no. 7, *What courage!*) resonated with the *milicianas* of the Republican side of the Spanish Civil War, reported on throughout international newspapers in 1936. The People's Army of Madrid could be seen as but a reincarnation of the men and women charged upon by French troops in the Puerta del Sol in May 1808. Images of civilian cityscapes transformed to barricades, as in Zaragoza, were iterated across Spain in 1936, from Madrid to Barcelona. Republican posters and news articles presented "Madrid's defenders as typical eighteenth century villagers dressed in the fashion that painter Francisco de Goya used to portray these

Figure 1. Goya, "And there's nothing one can do about it."

sorts of people."[7] Thus was the Republican-Nationalist civil war coupled with a war for history. Republican sympathizers from around the world, including those in the United States, picked up on both.

For leftists and antifascists in Europe and the Americas, Spain became the first nation to manage viable armed resistance to fascism. In the theatre world of the United States, previous isolationists and antiwar voices—including high profile figures such as Archibald MacLeish and Irwin Shaw—turned toward advocating for intervention on behalf of Republican Spain. In March 1935, *New Theatre* published a special antiwar issue. Just over a year later, the magazine completely changed course. Ben Ossa and Angel Flores introduced the September 1936 issue of *New Theatre* with an introductory essay entitled: "Spain, 1936—The Theatre in Arms!" Dancer and writer Agna Enters's article in the same issue attempted to narrate the fight for the Republic among artists and laborers. To do so, she called upon history. On page one she included five images sketched in pen and ink: a matador, lifting his hat victoriously; a farmer, standing despondently with hoe in hand; a flamenco dancer; a large-bodied miner with blunt features, lugging two pails; and a peasant figure on a blindfolded horse, evocative both of Sancho Panza and the bullfighting ring. On the facing page, the same figures appeared, but each held a rifle. Their bodies strained toward an unseen enemy and their expressions were hardened. The Panza figures sheltered behind the dead body of his horse, using it as barricade. The two sets of figures faced each other: *two* Spains, a traditional Nationalist Spain and a resistant Republican Spain, readied for a battle to the death.[8]

As Susan Sontag argued in 2003, "With Goya a new standard for responsiveness to suffering enters art."[9] The explicit representations of the *Disasters* point toward a certain reality that "things like this happen." Hughes moves one step further and figures Goya's *Disasters* as a form of documentary journalism. It is fitting, then, that images of historical bodies should serve as *New Theatre*'s first rallying cries for the Republic. Corporeal disasters, among which Goya's *Disasters* counted, formed the very basis for representations of the Spanish Civil War, its material and its historiographical battles. The body count in the Spanish Civil War, as Caroline Brothers details, was uniquely documented by an increasingly mediatized world of radio broadcast and photojournalism coupled with vociferous propaganda operations.[10] In the first months of terror, the urban battle sites and the iterative destruction of air raids inducted the global imagination into a new vision of civilian warfare, as Helen Graham argues.[11] Both Nationalist and Republican sympathizers used bodies to propagandize their Spain. In support of Nationalist Spain, the American Catholic press publicized the looting and desecration of churches. Newspapers showed photographs of coffins razed from churches, their contents spilled out alongside decaying bodies of nuns left in piles on church steps.[12] The leftist press, including agencies organized for Spanish relief, used images of dead children, mute and grisly testaments to the callous power of the Nationalist war effort. Republican press offices regularly mailed packages of photos of air raid victims and decimated cultural treasures, such as art museums and libraries, to would-be sympathizers outside Spain. It is such a package that Virginia Woolf has on her desk in *Three Guineas*.[13]

Though journalists on both sides of the war admitted to exagrating for effect, an archival problem that continues to plague historical accounts of the Spanish Civil War, the facticity of Jay Allen's report of Badajoz remains uncontested.[14] First published in the *Chicago Tribune*, Allen's account, in Graham's words, "catapulted" Spain "into headlines."[15] As such, it functioned as an early contribution to conceptualizations of the Spanish Civil War, helping to further link the corporeality of the Spanish Civil War to that of Goya's *Disasters* in American imaginations. Badajoz fell to the Nationalists on August 14. Allen arrived a week later. Pools black with blood and rotting corpses besmirched the town. The victors continued to round up any who had resisted. Allen witnessed Nationalist troops stop a man in the street and yank his shirt open to search for the tell-tale sign of his Republican sympathies: a bruise on the shoulder, earned from firing a rifle over and over. Nationalists took all arrested offenders to the bullring to face machine guns. "After the first night," wrote Allen, "the blood was supposed to be palm deep on the far side of the lane. I don't doubt it. Eighteen hundred men—there were women, too—were mowed down there in some twelve hours." It is Allen's final sentence that is, in its understatement, most arresting. He writes: "There is more blood than you would think in eighteen hundred bodies."[16] The simple sentence is an observation rather than a gratuitous flourish. It is an attempt to put the unimaginable into words. The statement—the summation—is like a caption to the preceding image. Its tone is not unlike those Goya attached to his *Disasters of War*. Although the prints had been created over a hundred years earlier, Spain was "again experiencing those 'Disasters of War'" in 1936. The prints, as well as the painter, "acquire[d] a certain tragic timeliness."[17]

William M. Ivins Jr., curator of prints at the Metropolitan Museum of Art, wrote about the series for the Museum's *Bulletin* twice, in 1924 and 1928, to address the lamentable absence of the *Disasters* from the public eye. The Met had held, for "several years," a bound volume of the eighty-five prints, but no mention of them had ever appeared in the *Bulletin*. Per Ivins's argument, this oversight was due to the history of their critical reception in Europe. At the first printing of the *Disasters*, art critics of repute denounced Goya as "proof positive of the low estate to which Spanish artistry and taste had fallen in Spain at the end of the 1700s," a hearkening to the meta-narrative of the decadence and decline of Spain's Golden Age.[18] In 1867, another critic dismissed *Disasters of War* as particularly "debased and degraded," while another "reportedly" burned the images in impetuous shock at their content. Ivins concluded that *The Disasters of War*, "stout stomached things," were unsurpassed in their depiction of "rank humanity" and "hard grounded reality."[19] Ivins wrote again about the etchings in 1928, when upon their exhibition in New York he concluded, "Time with its softening hand has at last made this great artist palatable to those of tender stomachs and academic minds. To the robust he has always appealed."[20] Perhaps Ivins was thinking that the experience of World War I, the mass casualties combined with the implacable presence of war, also contributed to the change in the *Disasters*' reception. Ten years later, the same year that Tamiris began planning her dance piece about Spain, and one year after Picasso completed his black-and-white *Guernica*, the prints reached yet a wider circulation.

In 1938, two years into the Spanish Civil War, Oxford University Press/Phaidon republished the entire series of the *Disasters of War* in response to public demand for the images.[21] "Reproduced in actual size" and priced at $1.50, the volume was intended "to make conveniently available material for which there is a demand in every library."[22] The 1938 collection could not but conjure images of the Spanish Civil War, the civilian aspects of its violence, and the images of profound corporeal disaster consumed throughout Europe and the Americas. In the series, violence takes place not within the heat of battle, but near its end, off to the side, among civilians as much as soldiers. Goya had not dreamt up aerial warfare, but in print 41, "They Escape through the Flames," civilian women and children flee a smoke-filled sky, a horizon eerily prescient of cityscapes charred by flame and bomb. Plates 32, 33, 37, and 39 are all scenes of torture and dismemberment. In plate 37, a naked, armless man is impaled on the ragged branch of a tree. "This is still worse" is the simple caption to the image. Print 34 shows a dead priest, a crucifix grasped tightly in his lifeless fingers. In print 67 looters carry away a statue of the Virgin Mary. Thirteen of the eighty-five prints depict masses of corpses. No print is captioned "There is more blood than one would think in eighteen hundred bodies," but Allen's summation of Badajoz fits in nonetheless. The series was indeed "tragically timely." For Tamiris, the timeliness inspired a unique vision of the *history* of Spain. If Spanish Republicans reached back to 1808 to contextualize the corporeality of their current fight, Tamiris reached further, challenging U.S. nonintervention in Spain, Spanish Nationalists, and global fascism with a revision of Iberian history that began before 1492.

Tamiris mapped Goya's images onto the dramaturgical, visual, and corporeal aspects of *Adelante!* "The entire ballet," she wrote in the scenario for the dance, "should remind one of Goya's black and white drawings." There was no mention of Goya in the program. Neither did John Martin of the *New York Times*, who saw and reviewed the dance twice, nor the reviewers for the *Daily Worker*, *New Masses*, or *Dance Observer* make any note of Goya. Yet the *Disasters of War* were present throughout the scenes of the dance. Tamiris described her vision for the set as minimal and stark: a bare stage, with a backdrop and legs of "white going into grayish and black tones." There would be a moveable gauze curtain and dancers would wear leotards, all in tones of gray, black, and white. The colors were "important." They "heighten[ed] the *goyaesque* effect."[23] While I cannot say whether Tamiris owned a copy of the Oxford/Phaidon *Disasters*, from her scenario notes it is clear that she was conversant with the images. Additionally, though *Adelante!* was her only dance about the Spanish Civil War, she had worked with Spain in her dances before, suggesting that the nation, its history, and its geography had been familiar to her for at least a decade. It is highly plausible that she would have come across Goya's work.[24]

The idea of mass death and the image of accumulated corpses, palpably present in *Disasters*, informed the dramaturgy of *Adelante!* from its opening moments. Tamiris adapted the opening spoken text from a published collection of Spanish Civil War poetry. In the original poem, the final line reads: "A peasant's voice replies: 'I know who went by here.'" In Tamiris's adaption, the line became "*Corpses of peasants* cry '*We* know who went by here.'" Additionally, in scene 2, Tamiris staged a clutch of courtiers "balancing stylized heads on long poles which they twirl playfully" (fig. 2). José was to be "horrified yet fixed by."[25] These grisly horrors conjured the staring decapitated heads perched on branches and trees in print 39 ("What a feat! With dead men!") of the *Disasters of War*. In another scene José falls in love. Tamiris's description of the scene is as follows: "José and Elena. A dance of youth and love. During this scene the audience is told of how José and Elena love each other, how he went off to war (this is accomplished by breaking the idyllic movements of the two with an onrush of a group of soldiers who enact a short scene of battle, *fall in combat and are left as corpses on the stage*). Elena and José continue their dance, sadly. José realizes that he must go off to war and leaves Elena dancing alone. This section ends on a note of tragedy and pathos. A roll of drums recalls Elena to the war and *focuses her attention on the dead men on the stage*."[26] The latter part of the scene was completed amidst piles of corpses. Pauline Tish, who danced in the piece, remembered that the final sequence was played "with the presence of corpses on stage."[27] *Adelante!* iteratively embodied the corporeal idiom

CORPOREAL DISASTERS OF WAR

of Goya's *Disasters*; multiple plates showcase jumbles of corpses. Though John Martin of the *Dance Observer* did not mention Goya, he experienced some of the atmosphere Tamiris intended. He described the piece as a "phantasmagoria of Spain" in which every scene was "shot through with presence of war and death," an echo of the mise-en-scène of *Disasters*, however unintentional.[28] On his second viewing, Martin's impression did not change. *Adelante!* was a "death ridden panorama of Spain...[and] over it all hangs an air of the fantastic and the nightmarish."[29] Owen Burke described the final dance of the piece as "following defeat on defeat and death on bewilderment."[30] The reviewers may not have explicitly articulated Goya's presence in the piece, yet their commentary conjured him. Tamiris's rendering of Spain further resonated with a public whose imagination of Spain was, through newspapers, propaganda, art, photography, and radio, populated with dead and dying bodies. This was the Spain documented and publicized by Jay Allen's account of the events of Badajoz in August 1936. From November 1936 to March 1939, as Alun Kenwood writes, Madrid became "the center of the world" for Republican sympathizers, "the forge of a new humanity and new consciousness: a symbol of heroism, martyrdom and antifascist struggle."[31] The theatre- and dance-viewing public eagerly consumed performances about Spain. *Adelante!* was originally scheduled for a one-week run. Its success warranted an extension of an additional week—despite the fact that by the time the piece opened, the Republic had lost.

Adelante!'s popularity and Tamiris's repeated references to Goya speak to her fluency not only with Goya's images but with the historiographical stakes pinned to them for the past, present, and future of Spain. Through Goya, I suggest, Tamiris presented the vision of a monstrous present and the possibility of a worse future through a unique refiguring of Iberia's past. The death surrounding José was not only that of the Spanish Civil War, but that of an anti-Semitic Inquisitorial Spanish past resurrected in fascist Europe, threatening the world and unchecked by the United States.

The "Peasants' Brigade": Fascism, Anti-Semitism, and the (Il)legitimacy of the American Republic

Most of the prints of Goya's *Disasters of War* depict legible human suffering, however horrific, in the form of rape, torture, dismemberment, stabbing, shooting. A few of the prints render monstrous forms or nightmarish figures.[32] Print 71, "The carnivorous vulture," contains a huge bird, wings spread, eyes rolling. A group of people cower behind it. In print 74, a large wolf-like creature writes with pen and paper. Humans minister to him. Perhaps they see him as a human, rather than a beast, or perhaps they are so blinded by the disasters of war that they can no longer determine what is human and what is animal. "Contrary to the General interest," print 71, depicts a human-demon hybrid figure, with clawed fingers and toes and huge bat-wing ears. He is calmly reading and pontificating. Humanity is under threat, but the menace is not only from beasts: it is from humans, too, those capable of atrocity and the others who support them, or stand idly by, dumbfounded or terrified. A number of these images resonate with other nightmare themes and religious iconography in Goya's work. For American modern dance and audiences in the 1930s, such images and the message contained therein must have conjured the threat of an Aryan fascism, enacted in the warfields of Spain, yes, but consolidated in the concentration camps peppering German territories.

Well known in the annals of dance history is Martha Graham's refusal to perform at the International Dance Festival, part of the 1936 Olympic festivities in Berlin. "I would find it impossible," she wrote in response to the invitation, "to dance in Germany at the present time. So many artists whom I respect and admire have been persecuted, have been deprived of the right to work for ridiculous and unsatisfactory reasons, that I should consider it impossible to identify myself, by accepting your invitation, with the regime that has made such things possible. In addition, some of my concert group would not be welcome in Germany."[33] A number of Graham's dancers, including Lily Mehlman and Jane Dudley, were already involved with New Dance League efforts to mount a campaign to boycott the Berlin games. Tamiris, Doris Humphrey, Charles Weidman, Anna Sokolow, and Lincoln Kirstein, among other well-known people, joined the Berlin boycott.[34]

As Graff, Foulkes, and others have pointed out, for many modern dancers born of Jewish immigrant parents and raised on classes and performances at the Henry Street Settlement, Lower East Side dance studios, and, later, the 92nd Street YMHA, antifascism was an urgent facet of the perpetual fight against anti-Semitism. The first United States Dance Congress, held in May 1936 in New York, passed a number of resolutions regarding the priorities of the dance community in America. Of fourteen resolutions, number four was a statement against fascism: "The Dance Congress resolves that its members, in the interest of a free and uncensored growth of the dance, go on record as being opposed to war, fascism and censorship and to all efforts that foster such retrogressive policies."[35] In May 1937, Tamiris helped facilitate an alliance of the Dance Association (of which she was chair at the time), the New Dance League, and the Dance Guild. The new organization, called the American Dance Association (ADA), elected Tamiris as president. Antifascism figured in the constitution, in terms similar to those of the Dance Congress. For Tamiris and her fellow dancers, the Spanish Civil War presented an opportunity to localize and ground antifascist convictions in an immediate geography: between 1937 and 1939 at least twenty dances of varying length premiered specifically in response to the Spanish Civil War.[36]

Although Tamiris's only piece exclusively devoted to the Spanish Civil War was *Adelante!*, she regularly participated in pro-Republican efforts. The first project of the ADA was a benefit for Spanish Loyalists, in cooperation with the Medical Committee to Aid Spanish Democracy, on May 23, 1937, at the Adelphi Theatre. The event was supposed to take place on the last night of the convention, a plan that indicates the centrality of the benefit and of Spain to the organization's commitment to antifascism. *The Dance Observer* summed up the evening as full and varied, "almost too varied for one evening's consumption."[37] Performers included Miriam Belcher's New Dance Group, Anna Sokolow's Dance Unit, Sophia Delza, Lasa Galpern, Lily Mehlman, Ruthanna Boris, Polonco, and Tamiris. Tamiris, in the middle of performing her wildly successful *Negro Spirituals*, contributed two older dances to the evening: *South American Dance* and *Impressions from the Bullring*. Mehlman, Delza, and Sokolow performed recently created pieces specifically about Spain. Tamiris had not yet completed a dance on the Spanish Civil War, but her choice of pieces for the evening's program attest to a desire to sympathize with Spain, through her body, and she chose material appropriately themed. In addition to the first Dances for Spain organized by the ADA in May 1937, Tamiris also appeared at four other Republican benefits between 1937 and 1939, including a December 1939 benefit for Spanish refugees. By the time she began rehearsing *Adelante!*, Tamiris was well acquainted with Spain, its civil war, and the historical and ethnic-religious facets of the conflict.

Writing in 1941, Margaret Lloyd described *Adelante!* as "cover[ing], in vivid stage pictures, a deal of historical background, on which, for a peasant, the soldier seemed remarkably well informed."[38] José's understanding of Spanish history and its use in the Spanish Civil War reflected Tamiris's. *Adelante!* began with José, a soldier of the "Peasant's Brigades," facing his execution. His "Beloved," Elena, embraces him. The soldiers shoot, José falls, and the narrator speaks: "In the last moments left him…all of Spain presses upon him" and "he sees all of Spain, old and new."[39] The "dream" commences: eight episodes follow in which historical and contemporary representations of Spain alternate with José's recollections of his own life. As Lloyd put it, he "remembered the Renaissance, the Inquisition, the elegance and decadence of the court, as well as

{ 45 }

personal history of love and death, marriage and war."[40] Although the narrator begins the sequence by intoning "back through the ages," the scenes do not progress chronologically, and it is not always clear which scenes take place in the past and which in the present. Tamiris juxtaposed episodes of action to create a gestic effect that dramatized the history of Spain in immediately dialectical terms. The result is not the history of Spain, but a revision of that history, rendered for Tamiris's audience in the very legible terms of corporeal disaster, as described above.[41]

In scene 5, Tamiris's historical revision enacted explicit political intervention. José dances "with a group who are going through a simple ceremony of prayers... He approaches the altar and walks right through it. The mourners continue and the dance is climaxed by the appearance of José's body limned against the background of a large crucifix."[42] Broadly, the image of José on a cross may have communicated his martyrdom, not dissimilar to Capa's *Falling Soldier* or the Nationalist shooting of Federico García Lorca, whose death was invented and reinvented on the left as a symbol of the martyrdom of the Republic. The image of the crucifixion was also a repetition of the same image used by Tamiris in *Negro Spirituals*. Peter Becker, Tamiris's brother, recalled to Pauline Tish that in *Negro Spirituals*, Tamiris "wanted to show that Christ was actually a human being. That was very important."[43] Again broadly, in *Adelante!* the image may have been intended to function similarly: the messiah, if indeed such a being existed, was only a man of flesh and blood. The peasant soldier is as likely a candidate as a holy infant ordained by God. Yet, within *Adelante!* it is unclear to what religion José belongs. Tamiris states that the entire history of Spain passes before José's eyes—and in such a history questions of political, religious, and religious-ethnic identity carried significant weight.

Spain's official religion for over four hundred years had been Catholicism, purchased through the expulsion, conversion, and repression of Jews and Muslims. In 1931, the Republican government set about to redress the hegemonic economic and political power of the Catholic Church. The government declared a separation of church and state and freedom of religion. Streets names were secularized; religious education in public school was made voluntary; Church property was nationalized. The Republic, thus, worked to decrease the presence of the Catholic Church. By walking through the altar, José mirrors these efforts and renders the church powerless. On the one hand, his interaction with the altar represents the more radical wishes of the leftists of Spain. Yet, limned against a cross, José both displaces Christ and replaces him with a Spanish volunteer of the Spanish Brigade. He could be a Communist of no religion. He could also be of a past, vanquished religion. Naum Rosen, writing on "The New Jewish Dance in America" in 1934, extolled the inspirational source provided by Jewishness, "not the dances that Jews do, but dancing that suggests and portrays that which is particularly Jewish."[44] One of these particularly Jewish qualities for Rosen was that of the wandering Jew, traipsing through history and among geographies and peoples, an image that is resonant with the journey José takes in *Adelante!* in his subconscious moments before death.

The plausibility of José's Jewishness is further supported by his membership in the Peasant's Brigades. By using the name the "Peasant's Brigade" Tamiris avoided using the politically charged monikers of Loyalist, Republican, International Brigades, or People's Army. Still, for anyone familiar with the meaning of any of these names or their associated politics, the Peasant's Brigade would have signified as Republican, either part of or allied with the International Brigade. The IB consisted of approximately 50,000 volunteer soldiers from over fifty countries, recruited and funded by the Communist International. A large contingent of Jewish volunteers from around the world convened in Spain. Of the estimated 2,700 Americans who volunteered, 30 percent identified as Jewish. In a letter home, one Jewish American volunteer declared he was fighting in the best "Maccabean tradition." Another felt his fight was against a "modern inquisition," a fight that would both vindicate the past and secure a future.[45] Ben Leiden, the first American aviator killed in Spain, was heralded as a hero of the Jewish people who died for his antifascist convictions. He was honored with a parade and rally in New York. Tamiris's audience could easily associate a soldier in the Peasants' Brigade with the American Jewish volunteers for Spain. Through José, Tamiris affiliated the International Brigade/Peasant's Brigade with an American Jewish fight against fascism. In doing so, she also effectively expunged Republican Spain of its Iberian anti-Semitic history, a move that consequently indicted the United States. Tamiris's audience would have apprehended the associations: religious and religious-ethnic identity, particularly Jewishness, infused the Spanish Civil War and its representation in both Spain and the United States.

In the United States, anticommunist, pro-Nationalist contingents were also often anti-Semitic, built upon and fueled by the Red Scares and anti-immigration sentiment of the 1910s and 1920s. The Jewish population, thanks to an influx of immigration to the United States between 1881 and the First World War, "was big enough to make a sizeable target."[46] The Immigration Acts of 1917, 1921, and 1924 restricted immigration to the United States. The government instituted national quotas. Proponents of the new laws saw them as ways to protect the United States from undesirable populations, a means to keep would-be enemies out and to oust foreigners already within American borders. By 1933, with the rise of fascist powers in Europe, anti-Semitism grew more public and vocal in the United States. Between 1933 and 1940, Donald Strong counted 121 new anti-Semitic organizations. These groups, ranging in size and power from Father Coughlin's National Union for Social Justice to the Christian Front to the Pacific Coast's Silver Shirts to the local chapters of the Paul Reveres and Orders of '76, regularly characterized "Jewish Reds" as threats to American culture and security in universities, neighborhoods, and places of employment. Within modern dance, Jewishness was both championed and maligned. So many leading moderns were Jewish women that it is perhaps not surprising that the Dance Congress of 1934 should prioritize antifascism. Yet Martin and Lloyd, leading dance critics, condemned the politics of the Congress. Lloyd declared that "if the left wingers continue to run the whole show, as they did this one, they will only succeed in turning the remaining liberals into fascisti."[47] As Foulkes argues, these criticisms may have been tinged with anti-Semitism. Ruth St. Denis and Ted Shawn restricted the numbers of "foreign blooded" dancers in their group. Doris Humphrey and Charles Weidman praised their Jewish dancers but did so with tones of anti-Semitic stereotypes, regaling the "emotional intensity" and economic shrewdness of the "race."[48]

For Tamiris, her fellow antifascists in modern dance, and her Jewish collaborators and colleagues, the Nationalist version of Spain, built on Catholic history and aligned with Germany and Italy, could not, would not, accommodate Jews. The Republican version of Spain, with its leftist, democratic, Communist, and antifascist ties, promised a nation of tolerance and equality, one that neither Jewish dancers nor the Jewish volunteers for Spain were finding safeguarded in the United States. Tamiris's sensitivity to the religious and ethnic-religious aspects of her work and the Spanish Civil War played out further still. Throughout her source material and notes, she crossed out all references to Moors. In Spanish history and the Spanish Civil War, Catholicness and Jewishness went hand in hand with Moorishness and Muslims. Franco's "Moorish" troops inspired conflicted feelings in both Nationalists and Republicans. Ferdinand and Isabella had purged the Muslims as well as the Jews. The Moor was sometimes depicted as particularly ferocious and lecherous by Republican sympathizers, as a kind of kin with old Spain, though not explicitly described as such. The Nationalists, for their part, gave Moorish soldiers Christian and Catholic medals as rewards for their service, creating a theatrical veneer of religious acceptability through props. By absenting the Moors, Tamiris also absented Spain and permitted its Catholic, Jewish, Fascist, and Communist politics to play out in an alternative geography—that of America—in the minds of her spectators. The piles of corpses, borrowed from Goya, spread from Spain, through Europe, and to the United States in Tamiris's dance.

As noted above, one of the key ways in which the Nationalist sympathizers publicized their efforts in Spain was in terms of a holy war, a crusade the likes of which had not been fought since the time of Ferdinand and Isabella against radicals, communists, anarchists, and Jews.[49] Not all U.S. Catholics were pro-Nationalist, nor were all pro-Nationalists anti-Semitic. Still, as Dominic Tierney documents, "Catholics were the backbone of the pro-Nationalist movement in the United States," a fact that necessarily played into President Roosevelt's official policy on Spain. Between 70 and 80 percent of American Catholics had voted for Roosevelt in 1936; politically affronting that demographic was unthinkable for the president.[50] The lobbying power of the Catholic Church affected Roosevelt's handling of American policy on the Spanish Civil War. It also impacted the Federal Theatre Project. Barry Witham points out that "although there were clerics like Archbishop Rummel in New Orleans who were supportive of the Theatre Project, there was also suspicion on the part of the Church that federally sponsored theatrical presentations on a national basis should be thoroughly scrutinized for their moral and political content."[51] Pro-Nationalist Catholic influence was felt from the Oval Office to the desks of Federal One (the Federal Project Number One, the collective name for several projects in the Works Progress Administration that included the FTP). Evidence suggests that Tamiris's revision of Spanish history in terms of religious and ethnic-religious identity was indeed noticed and engendered objections.

As Cooper has detailed, both Hallie Flanagan and the Federal Theatre Project under her direction, as well as the Federal Dance Project, queried the content and politics of *Adelante!* Broadly, the FTP could not, given its mission statement and its governmental funding, justify a stance for either side of the Spanish Civil War. Flanagan instructed Tamiris to emphasize the "human tragedy of war" and to abstract the Rebel (Nationalist) and Loyalist salutes. Furthermore, a pro-Spanish Republic dance piece would have provided yet more fodder for allegations concerning the presence of Reds on the Project. Cooper points out that the documentary record surrounding *Adelante!* provides no direct evidence of a Catholic-centered controversy. Yet, Paula Bass Perlowin, who danced in *Adelante!*, recalled that the Catholic Church exerted pressure on Flanagan to cancel the production.[52] If we consider how strongly religious and religious-ethnic identity figured in both pro-Nationalist and pro-Republican circles in the United States, the plausibility of Perlowin's claim increases. Additionally, Flanagan advised Tamiris to consult a Catholic priest in order to ascertain the authenticity of the gestures in the church scene (scene 5, described above).[53] Flanagan's suggestion indicates that Catholic organizations might scrutinize the dance piece. If those organizations were anti-Loyalist and/or anti-Semitic, the

Project could be criticized for any number of things: for political bias, possibly, but also, and perhaps more damningly, for anti-Catholicism manifested by inaccurate gestures, articulated by a Jewish body, in favor of a Communist cause. Flanagan further asked Tamiris to cut a scene that satirized military generals—the generals would have read as Franco. A scene mocking him, by extension, might have also been seen to ridicule Catholicism.

When *Adelante!* opened, its program contained the usual disclaimer: "The viewpoint expressed in its productions in not necessarily that of the WPA [Works Progress Administration] or any other agency of the government." The Play Advisory Board of the Federal Theatre Project had planned to submit *Adelante!* for the New York World's Fair in 1939 to position Tamiris as an example of American artistry. In May, upon the closing of *Adelante!*, the board decided to abandon the plan, "in view of the consideration that the dance was decidedly not American."[54] But that decision was reversed and *Adelante!* was performed at the WPA Buildings of the World's Fair after all.[55] The piece was cut to an hour. Which scenes—which un-American aspects—were excised is unclear. The generals? The church? Or, were small excisions throughout the piece made? The un-American content of the dance might have been any number of things, as innocuous as Spanish rather than American characters, as threatening as pro-Loyalist, pro-Communist sympathies and implicitly politicized religious content, or as volatile as charging the United States with shirking a domestic and international responsibility to defend and uphold democracy against anti-Semitism and fascism.

Wending through Goya's *Disasters of War* is the message that, when faced with tyranny, the people will fight. In Goya's plate 7 ("What courage!"), the image likely intended to immortalize the women of Zaragoza, a woman stands behind a cannon on top of a pile of sliding corpses, brandishing a knife at an unseen attacker. When Tamiris planned *Adelante!* in the fall of 1938, Republican Spain, though suffering, was still holding out against the Nationalists, still brandishing the knife atop its corpses. In March 1939, the Spanish Civil War was over. The Nationalists had won. Global fascism had staked yet another claim with the fall of the Spanish Republic. And yet the living characters at the end of dance still chant "Adelante!," meaning "Onward!" or "Forward!" The American Republic had yet to take its stand. The disasters of Goya provided Tamiris with the corporeal language to challenge, through the history and present of Spain, the future of America's commitment to antifascism and global democracy.

Figure 2. Production photo of *Adelante!*, courtesy of George Mason University Special Collections, Fairfax, VA.

Notes

I would like to thank Jill Lane, Neil Doshi, and Tara Rodman for feedback on a 2011 draft of this article delivered at the American Society for Theatre Research working group "Global Topographies" in Montreal. Thanks also to Jeanmarie Higgins and Sarah Marsh for additional feedback. The epigraphs in this chapter come from: Susan Sontag, *Regarding the Pain of Others* (New York: MacMillan, 2003), 45 and A. Hyatt Mayor, "Goya's 'Disasters of War,'" *Art*, November 1936, 710.

1. Tamiris is well known for her political visibility in American modern dance; she worked tirelessly for dancers' rights, part of which included her crusade to convince the Federal Theatre Project to create a separate Dance Project in New York. Dance was originally included with theatre, but, due in large part to Tamiris's efforts, Federal One, the name for arts-oriented group projects under the WPA that included the FTP, conceded that a separate dance project would more effectively serve unemployed performers in both fields.

    Cooper articulates how Tamiris was seen by contemporaries as a "non-conformist" aesthetically, devoted to artistry but also at odds with prevailing dance theories of her day. See Ellen Graff, *Stepping Left: Dance and Politics in New York City, 1928–1942* (Durham, NC: Duke University Press, 2007); Mark Franko, *The Work of Dance: Labor, Movement and Identity in the 1930s* (Middleton, CT: Wesleyan University Press, 2002); Elizabeth Cooper, "Dances about Spain: Censorship at the Federal Theatre Project,"

{ 51 }

Theatre Research International 29, no. 3 (2004): 232–46; Elizabeth Cooper, "Tamiris and the Federal Dance Theatre, 1936–1939: Socially Relevant Dance amidst the Policies and Politics of the New Deal Era," *Dance Research Journal* 29, no. 2 (Autumn 1997): 23–48; Susan Manning, *Modern Dance, Negro Dance: Race in Motion* (Minneapolis: University of Minnesota Press, 2004).

2. The history of the Second Republic and the Spanish Civil War is deeply complex and fraught. My exceedingly brief overview of the events between 1931 and 1936 is merely intended as the most basic context. There is no shortage of history books penned on the Spanish Civil War. A particularly comprehensive publication is Helen Graham, *The Spanish Republic at War 1936–1939* (Cambridge: Cambridge University Press, 2002).
3. Xosé-Manuel Núñez Seixas, "Nations in Arms against the Invader: On Nationalist Discourse during the Spanish Civil War," in *The Splintering of Spain: Cultural History and the Spanish Civil War*, ed. Chris Ealham and Michael Richards (Cambridge: Cambridge University Press, 2005), 48.
4. Robert Hughes, *Goya* (New York: Alfred A. Knopf, 2004), 265.
5. Ibid., 275.
6. Núñez Seixas, "Nations in Arms," 49.
7. Ibid.
8. Ben Ossa and Angel Flores, "Spain, 1936—The Theatre in Arms!" *New Theatre* (September 1936): 1; Agna Enters, "Spain Says 'Salud!'," *New Theatre* (September 1936): 7–8.
9. Sontag, *Regarding the Pain of Others* (New York: Macmillan, 2003), 45.
10. Caroline Brothers, *War and Photography: A Cultural History* (London: Routledge, 1997).
11. Graham, *The Spanish Republic at War*.
12. *Images of the Spanish Civil War*, ed. Ann Wilson (London: Allen & Unwin, 1986), 52.
13. Virginia Woolf, *Three Guineas* (Boston: Houghton Mifflin Harcourt, 2006).
14. For a detailed examination see Phillip Knightley, "Commitment in Spain 1936–1939," in *The First Casualty: From the Crimea to Vietnam: The War Correspondent as Hero, Propagandist and Myth Maker* (New York: Harcourt, Brace and Jovanovich, 1975), 191–241. See also, for example, Larry Rother's article in the *New York Times* concerning Capa's photograph: Larry Rother, "New Doubts Raised over Famous War Photo," *New York Times*, August 17, 2009.
15. Graham, *The Spanish Republic*, 112.
16. Jay Allen, "Blood Flows in Badajoz," in *From Spanish Trenches: Recent Letters Home from Spain*, ed. Marcel Acier (New York: Modern Age Books, 1937), 7. The story was first published in the *Chicago Tribune*.
17. Gilbert Chase, "Goya, in Whose Great Art All Spain Was Embraced," *New York Times*, October 30, 1938, 3.
18. William M. Ivins Jr., "Goya's Disasters of War," *Metropolitan Museum of Art Bulletin* 19, no. 9 (September 1924): 220.
19. Ibid., 220, 223.
20. William M. Ivins Jr., "A Goya Exhibition," *Metropolitan Museum of Art Bulletin* 23, no. 10 (October 1928): 232.
21. It is from this edition that I take my print numbers. The etchings were printed from the original copper plates in 1937, the last time the copper plates were used. Francisco de Goya, *The Disasters of War: 85 Etchings Reproduced in Actual Size* (Vienna: Phaidon Press; London: George Allen and Unwin, 1937).

22. John Shapley, review of *Francisco de Goya's Disasters of War*, *Metropolitan Museum of Art Bulletin* 20, no. 2 (June 1938): 230.
23. Helen Tamiris, *Adelante!* scenario (1939), Unpublished ts., Helen Tamiris Collection ca. 1939–1966, Folder 107, New York Public Library for the Performing Arts, 1 (emphasis added). Though Tamiris did not name the *Disasters of War* series in the treatment for the dance, it is the most plausible inspiration for her from Goya's corpus. For the content and black, gray, and white palette of the dance, Tamiris could have used Picasso's *Guernica*, touring through Europe in 1938 and arriving in the United States in 1939. What *Disasters* provided for Tamiris that *Guernica* could not was a series of images that emphasized—in iteration—the legible corporeality of war, a theme in which Tamiris was consistently interested. She had sculpted the events of war through human bodies before. In 1935 in *Harvest*, Tamiris used her dancers' bodies as both cannons and ballast. *Dance Observer* complained: "After human projectiles have been fired from a human cannon (the latter depicted…by a female foursome), nothing can surprise or shock, for nothing matters." Mary P. O'Donnell, "Tamiris," *Dance Observer* (December 1935): 100.
24. Tish recalls, however, that there were "suggestions of bullfighting." As she further recalled, "Large circle dances of the peasants used elements of folk dancing. In one of them the entire company danced the essence of a Spanish jota, with its complex rhythms and accented heel beats, using one of Tamiris's classroom phrases that resembled a matador's thrust." See Pauline Tish, "Remembering Helen Tamiris," *Dance Chronicle* 17, no. 3 (1994): 327–60. Lloyd holds that in many sections of the dance, "stylized suggestions of the Spanish idiom were embossed on the modern." Margaret Lloyd, *The Borzoi Book of Modern Dance* (New York: Alfred A. Knopf, 1949), 146.
25. Helen Tamiris Collection, 1–2. Regarding the text, the pages within the New York Public Library's Tamiris papers appear to be torn from a published book but contain no bibliographic information. When performed, the piece mixed dance with pantomime, and music with text. There was a narrator as well as a chorus. Tamiris pulled, edited, and adapted text from a published collection of contemporary Spanish poets—including Angel Lázaro and Rafael Albertí—in English translation.
26. Helen Tamiris Collection, 2–3, emphasis mine.
27. Tish, "Remembering Helen Tamiris," 357.
28. John Martin, "Federal Theatre Gives *Adelante*," 26.
29. John Martin, "The Dance: 'Adelante'; Second Thoughts on the WPA's Production at Daly's," *New York Times*, April 30, 1939, 180.
30. Owen Burke, "Tamiris in 'Adelante!,'" *New Masses*, May 16, 1939, 36.
31. Alun Kenwood, "Art, Propaganda and Commitment: Hispanic Literature and the Spanish Civil War," in *The Spanish Civil War: A Cultural and Historical Reader*, ed. Alun Kenwood (Oxford: Berg Publishers, 1993), 33.
32. Goya's original title for the series was "Fatal Consequences of the Bloody War in Spain with Bonaparte." Critics divide the series into three parts: war, famine, and allegorical *caprichos* (literally, whims or caprices, a term Goya used in reference to imagined scenarios across his work).
33. Cited in Russell Freedman, *Martha Graham: A Dancer's Life* (New York: Clarion Books, 1998), 80–81.
34. The Spanish Republic organized the People's Olympics in July 1936, as an alternative to the Berlin games, in protest and opposition. The Republic thus set itself up as *the*

preeminent place to enact antifascist struggles in corporeal form. The People's Olympics never took place due to the outbreak of the Civil War, however.

35. "Resolutions" (of the First National Dance Congress and Festival), *Dance Observer* (June–July 1936): 64.
36. Agna Enters presented two pieces in 1936: *Red Malaga* and *Spain Says Salud*. In 1937, Martha Graham presented *Immediate Tragedy* and *Deep Song*. The same year, José Limón created *Danza de la muerte* at Bennington's summer festival. The piece contained ensemble numbers as well as "three satiric solos": one for generals, one for landlords, and one for the church, the three "causes of the destruction in Spain" (Lloyd, *The Borzoi Book*, 203). Anna Sokolow performed *Slaughter of Innocents-Madrid 1937*; Jane Dudley and Sophie Maslow gave *Women of Spain* and *Evacuación*; Sophia Delza danced *We Weep for Spain—We March for Spain*; Miriam Belcher performed *Advance Scout—Lincoln Battalion 1937* and *Flower Festival Madrid 1937*; and Lily Mehlman created *Spanish Woman*. In 1938, Ida Soyer contributed *War Face*; Ted Shawn, *Women of Spain*; Lester Horton, *Pasarémos*; Lillian Shapero, *Dance for Spain—No Pasarán*; and Nadia Chilkovsky, *Suite for Defense—of Soviet Union, of Spain*. In 1939, Horton presented *Madrigal Doloroso*, Ruth Page created *Guns and Castanets*, a restaging of *Carmen* during the Spanish Civil War, Pauline Koner presented *Legenda—Tragic Fiesta*, and Tamiris, of course, gave *Adelante!*
37. "Dances for Spain," review of "Dances for Spain," *Dance Observer* (June–July 1937): 69.
38. Lloyd, *The Borzoi Book*, 145.
39. Helen Tamiris Collection, 2.
40. Lloyd, *The Borzoi Book*, 145.
41. *Adelante!* comprised a series of eleven scenarios/suites, nine of which were staged as occurring between the shooting of José and his death. Reviewers agreed that these nine scenes took place in the mind of José. From the scenario, Tamiris intended the nine scenes to be staged as José's "subconscious," like a "dream." She wanted a gauze curtain moved around the perimeter of the stage, on a circular track, along with a number of dancing, twirling bodies, to signify the transition from consciousness to dream world. The same transition movement, repeated after scene 9, brought José back to "the reality of the execution."
42. Helen Tamiris Collection, 4.
43. Tish, "Remembering Helen Tamiris," 334.
44. Naum Rosen, "The New Jewish Dance in America," *Dance Observer* (July–June 1934): 51.
45. Albert Prago, "Jews in the International Brigades," in *Our Fight: Writings by Veterans of the Abraham Lincoln Brigade, Spain 1936–1939*, ed. Alvah Bessie and Albert Prago (New York: Monthly Review Press with the Veterans of the Abraham Lincoln Brigade, 1987), 96, 98.
46. Donald S. Strong, *Organized Anti-Semitism in America: The Rise of Group Prejudice During the Decade 1930–1940* (Washington, DC: American Council on Public Affairs, 1941), 15.
47. Julia L. Foulkes, "Angels 'Rewolt!': Jewish Women in Modern Dance in the 1930s," *American Jewish History* 88, no. 2 (June 2000): 255. See also Foulkes, *Modern Bodies: Dance and American Modernism from Martha Graham to Alvin Ailey* (Chapel Hill: University of North Carolina Press, 2002).
48. "Angels 'Rewolt!," Foulkes 255–56.

49. For an examination of the complicated Moroccan Jewish response to Nationalist anti-Semitism, see Isabelle Rohr, "The Use of Anti-Semitism in the Spanish Civil War," *Patterns of Prejudice* 37, no. 2 (November 2003): 195–211.
50. Dominic Tierney, *FDR and the Spanish Civil War: Neutrality and Commitment in the Struggle That Divided America* (Durham, NC: Duke University Press, 2007), 63–64.
51. Barry Witham, "Censorship in the Federal Theatre," *Theatre History Studies* 17 (June 1997): 10.
52. Cooper, "Dances about Spain," 242.
53. Ibid.
54. Cited in ibid, 242–43.
55. Henry Gilfond, "*Adelante*," *Dance Observer* (May 1939): 218.

A Doughgirl with the Doughboys

Elsie Janis, "The Regular Girl," and the Performance of Gender in World War I Entertainment

—DEANNA TOTEN BEARD

The May 31, 1918, issue of the recently launched military newspaper *Stars and Stripes* featured a notice about the christening of two new 155mm "Big Bertha" field cannons by the American Expeditionary Forces (AEF): "Following the gallant custom of the French Artillery, the boys of Battery B of our own F.A. Regiments decided to name their guns after those whom they considered the outstanding figures among the patriotic women of American history."[1] These artillery guns were some of the mightiest in France and were christened with the intention of inspiring future soldiers and honoring their namesakes. The two patriotic women chosen for this honor were Betsy Ross, who "made for General Washington the first American flag," and Elsie Janis, who "made the first hit of the A.E.F."[2] American vaudeville star Elsie Janis (1889–1956), known as "The Regular Girl," was one of the most popular entertainers of the early twentieth century. Born in Ohio, Janis was on the variety stage by the age of three and a noted musical comedy star by sixteen. Famous for her light songs, acrobatic dancing, and uncanny impersonations, she charmed audiences in the United States and headlined popular revues in London and Paris. She was also a best-selling writer, nationally syndicated columnist, film producer, and movie star, as well as the first female announcer on nationwide radio. For all these successes and celebrity, Elsie Janis largely defined herself by the period she spent entertaining troops in World War I. Her epitaph at Forest Lawn Cemetery in Glendale, California, reads simply, "Sweetheart of the A.E.F."

At a time before the creation of the USO, and without the assistance of the

YMCA or the Red Cross, Elsie Janis organized and funded her own mission to entertain and support Allied soldiers. Commissioned as a general in the U.S. Army by General John J. Pershing for her service as an entertainer, Janis was esteemed by the men she visited. An enthusiastic *Stars and Stripes* editor (possibly Alexander Woollcott, who is listed on the masthead for the newspaper) noted: "Elsie Janis is as essential to the success of this Army as a charge of powder is essential in the success of a shell."[3] This explosive analogy—together with the naming of the artillery gun after Janis—suggests that the troops perceived Janis as highly capable and even forceful. She was not simply another woman in need of male protection. Colorful nicknames given to her by the military, such as "Playgirl of the Western Front"[4] and "Doughgirl,"[5] further reveal the unorthodox position Janis occupied in this wartime world of men. It was a position Elsie Janis made for herself through careful management of her identity. She claimed new territory by establishing herself as the soldiers' colleague, a doughgirl with the doughboys, through her performances, her choice of clothing, her interactions with the men offstage, and her self-reporting to a reading public. This article explores Janis's balancing of conventionality and audaciousness to create of an effective and significant persona for her wartime activity. Special attention is paid to Janis's use of male impersonation in her theatre work so as to better understand her subversive gender representation. The article also briefly considers the concurrent practice of cross-dressed entertainment by soldiers in order to examine relationships between the image of "The Regular Girl" Janis presented and the archetype used by the male soldiers in their performance of stage "girls."

Germany declared war on France and Belgium on August 3, 1914, and a few months later Janis was already overseas entertaining wounded British troops. By late 1916, Janis was spending more time in London hospitals visiting Allied soldiers than in the theatre. "We spent six weeks in London," she recalls of the summer of 1916, "during which time I did not play at all, but sang every day and all day to the poor Tommies who had already been at it nearly two years."[6] Once the U.S. entered the conflict in 1917, Janis increased her work for the war cause: "I started in at home, recruiting, playing benefits, and doing a very 'war-mad' act in vaudeville, singing patriotic songs, etcetera, and telling everyone I was going to France."[7] She made her way "Over There" and began performing for wounded American troops in hospitals as well as for active soldiers at their camps near the battlefields. Through these years, she also periodically starred in musical comedies in London, performed as a vaudeville headliner, and acted in silent films. As a *Stars and Stripes* article commented in notably militaristic language, "From time to time she will make a raid on the commercial theater but only for brief excursions, and only to replenish the larder and store up enough funds for her to take once again to the greatest circuit of them all."[8] Janis paid her own way on this personal mission, choosing not to work directly with agencies such as the YMCA or the Red Cross for fear they would want to control her itinerary.

Janis traveled throughout France and Belgium with a pianist and her mother/manager, the commanding Jennie Bierbower. They drove vehicles lent to them by the U.S. military; General Pershing even gave Janis the use of a Cadillac with AEF Headquarters insignia.[9] She performed on everything from large stages to improvised arrangements of tabletops to truck beds. "Her audiences ranged from small groups to large assemblies of 6000 to 8000 men, and she thought nothing of performing many times in one day."[10] Visits began with Janis shouting to the men "Are we downhearted?" to which they would robustly respond, "No!" The act "included her imitations, dancing, a number of songs, and sometimes a closing with a number of cartwheels. Elsie was already an expert with a lariat, which she used effectively in her imitation of Will Rogers."[11] Among her other impersonations in the act was a number in which she mimicked George M. Cohan singing "Over There" and then morphed into her own voice performing her original adaptation of the song: "Over Here." A highlight of the act was Janis leading the men in rousing singalongs of popular music, usually selected by the soldiers themselves. Lee Alan Morrow, in his chapter on Janis in Kimberley B. Marra and Robert A. Schanke's *Passing Performances*, uses the term "kid sister"[12] to describe the friendly companionship she offered the soldiers. "Kid sister" suggests the raucous fun Janis appeared to provide, yet that archetype lacks the power attributed to her in contemporary accounts. Indeed, it has always been difficult to find the best way to classify and categorize the kind of woman Elsie Janis represented.

In her 1932 autobiography, *So Far, So Good*, Janis recalls how her wartime act and her popularity seemed strange to the French leadership to whom she applied for permission to travel. "From the fuss that the fellows made over me, I'm sure they thought I must be at least the American edition of Bernhardt. Imagine their surprise when my performance consisted of telling stories filled with hells and damns,[13] singing in a voice that was only mediocre, making the men sing with me, a refined little ditty entitled, 'Oh, You Dirty Germans, We Wish the Same to You!' swinging legs that were long but far from the French idea of comeliness, and finishing with cartwheels!"[14] Here, as in many parts of her memoirs, Janis calls attention to her unidealized behavior and appearance. She was cheerful and lithe but not a picture of the ultra-feminine American icon of the Gibson Girl. Martha Banta, in her book *Imaging American Women*, establishes a variety of late nineteenth and early twentieth-century American female types in popular culture, including three discrete varieties of the beloved American Girl: the Beautiful Charmer, the New England Woman, and the Outdoors Pal.[15] Janis, with her athleticism and moxie, seemed to exemplify Banta's "Outdoors Pal," a pretty girl who could be adventurous while staying safely feminine. In *Vaudeville, Old and New: An Encyclopedia of Variety Performers in America*, Frank Cullen offers a description of Janis that reinforces this image. As Cullen notes, "When not entertaining the boys, the otherwise ladylike Elsie might be found on her knees shooting craps with them… She was a gal pal not a pinup, although she was attractive."[16] Janis was very careful to be "otherwise ladylike," as discussed below, because it helped to achieve her goals. Cullen's comment is most interesting because it is typical of the way Janis is often described, including in this article, in terms of both what she is ("a gal pal") and what she is not ("a pinup").

A key feature of Elsie's Janis's public persona for her wartime work was her tactic of balancing conventional clothing and nonconforming behavior. Janis was accustomed to donning trousers for her professional stage work, which, as noted, included cross-dressing and impersonations of male stars such as Will Rogers and George M. Cohan. Yet when entertaining the troops, Janis always presented herself in a standard costume that was conventionally and conservatively female: a long blue skirt and sweater, crisp white blouse, and blue hat.[17] There were certainly more alluring ways for Janis to dress even by the modest standards of the 1910s, but she elected not to call attention to herself as a sex object. Janis might have opted to dress more daringly in a men's suit or military uniform, as she did on stage both before and after the war; but she did not choose to flaunt gender roles with her clothing while entertaining the troops. Instead, Janis wore a costume that signified femaleness, though not sexual availability, and then used that traditional appearance as license to behave in ways that challenged assumptions about traditional women's behavior. In fact, Janis also resisted conforming to the female caregiver archetype by not offering herself as a maternal figure or nurse to the men she entertained. It was, rather, her own ever-present mother, Jennie Bierbower, who performed nurturing duties on the visits. Bierbower sat with the men, held their hands, wrote letters home for them, and generally provided motherly comfort.

In her clothing and behavior, Janis declared what she was (a woman) and what she was not (a girlfriend or a mother). She was adamant that what the men needed from her was to be spoken to "like pals, not lauded and treated like heroes."[18] So she cast herself as their comrade and therefore as something of their equal. Neither an "Outdoors Pal," "gal pal," nor "kid sister," Janis made herself a comember of the AEF, a woman who was one of the company of men. A March

1918 *Stars and Stripes* article seemed to accept this identity, declaring in its boldfaced title, "Elsie One of Us While War Lasts."

Janis's own commentary in her memoirs reveals some of the particular ways that she positioned herself as the men's colleague. In *The Big Show: My Six Months with the American Expeditionary Forces*, Janis tells a story about the soldiers requesting that she lead a singalong of the popular AEF parody "The Pay Roll," a ditty sung to the tune of the "The Battle Hymn of the Republic." The chorus includes these lyrics (as Janis writes):

> All we do is sign the pay roll,
> All we do is sign the pay roll,
> All we do is sign the pay roll,
> And we never get a G-- d----- cent![19]

Janis recalls that the men hesitated to finish the lyrics with a woman present. But she shouted, "What's the big idea? I know that song and if you can sing it to yourselves you can sing it to me, I'm in the A.E.F."[20] The public singalong was an act of communion with the soldiers and reinforced her unofficial membership among their ranks. Janis's declaration, "I'm in the A.E.F.," even if an apocryphal addition for the sake of the memoir, clearly establishes an affiliation with the men for her reading public. The memoirs also strategically include the note that Janis herself does not condone the offensive phrase "God damned." However, she writes, hearing it sung in unison by "two thousand huskies who have faced hell and are looking for more" is so pleasant that she is sure "it would never be counted as a regular 'swear' by the great Judge of all transgressors."[21] This nod to conventional morality, like her clothing choices, achieves a skillful balance by bolstering Janis's presentation of her feminine respectability in order to minimize the potential controversy of her soldier-like language.

Janis's memoirs also present numerous examples of her audacious behavior without notes of mitigation, revealing her tendency toward gender exceptionality. An anecdote about firing the massive field cannon christened "Elsie" is exemplary. "Now, Miss Janis, kill a few Huns," she recalls the general instructing her when she got behind the big gun. She describes the thrill when she "stood to attention and waited for my orders," as well as the pride she felt in firing the massive weapon. "They told me I was the only *woman* who had fired regular hundred and fifty-five power hate into Germany."[22] Stories of Janis as the only woman in many war situations can be found throughout her memoirs, as well as in the news stories printed about her in the era. The American public enjoyed hearing about Janis's activity, but they received her adventures differently from the news of other women who were transgressing into the all-male world of war.

Unlike wartime nurses who were at least engaged in a traditional female occupation, women ambulance drivers in the war, though rare, were seen as unfeminine in their choice not only to drive but also to enter dangerous situations. British and American women could not serve in the armed military, though some cross-dressed and enlisted; perhaps most famous was the case of English journalist Dorothy Lawrence, who served ten days in the 179th Tunneling Company as "Denis Smith."[23] The American reading public during the war was especially fascinated with stories about the Russian "Battalion of Death," an all-female military group led by commander Maria Botchkareva.[24] As Kimberly Jensen notes in *Mobilizing Minerva: American Women in the First World War*, "Articles about [the Battalion of Death] appeared in major newspapers and journals such as the *New York Times* and the *Literary Digest*, in suffrage and antisuffrage journals, and in major women's magazines such as the *Delineator*, *Good Housekeeping*, and the *Ladies' Home Journal*."[25] Such curious and frequently scandalous tales of women warriors fueled the contentious national conversation about women's place in wartime service, women's gun use, and traditional gender roles. Yet Janis appears to have been universally accepted and lauded for her exceptional activity. This success seems due in large part to her skillful balancing of bold behavior with expressions of feminine sensibilities and patriotic affection for the soldiers. Janis's nonconforming activities such as shooting craps with men and firing their guns could be read as an outgrowth of feelings that were appropriate for a woman and, once again, her distinctly feminine clothing choices seem to have prevented social anxiety about her gender identity.

In her stage career, as in her mission of wartime service, Janis problematized her presentation of self, calling attention simultaneously to what she was and what she was not. Her playful subversion of male and female representation is seen in her mimicry of men such as Rogers and Cohan and in other gender-bending performances. For example, in George Ade's 1909 musical comedy, *The Fair Co-Ed*, Janis played the only girl attending an otherwise all-male school, Bingham College. When Janis's character appears at a school dance cross-dressed as a male cadet from a nearby military academy, she unintentionally attracts romantic attention from all the Bingham students' girlfriends. Janis cross-dressed again in her London debut, *The Passing Show of 1914*. Arthur Butt wrote a number for her called "Florrie Was a Flapper," which Elsie would later call "the best song I ever sang." The song was meant to be performed by Janis as Florrie. A few days into rehearsal, however, she announced her intention to sing "Florrie Was a Flapper" in full *male* evening dress, playing a man commenting on a girl he had known."[26] Such gender bending had certainly been seen on the vaudeville stage before; noteworthy British and American male impersonators in the early twentieth century included Della Fox, Vesta Tiley, and Florenze Tempest. The popular act of British entertainer Hetty King (1883–1972) blended cross-dressing and war themes much like Janis; King was "featured as a saucy sailor boy with such songs as 'I'm Going Away,' whose lyrics recount the trials of the handsome sailor with too many girls in every port."[27] Janis would not likely have found the same degree of acceptance for her own gender-ambiguous performances such as "Florrie Was a Flapper" were it not for the well-established use of the device in mainstream, family entertainment.

Theatre audiences had grown accustomed to transvestism in vaudeville, and most seem to have experienced cross-dressing as a reinscription of the natural differences between the male and female rather than as a challenge to traditional gender roles or normative heterosexuality. The public as well as the popular press did not choose to label Janis as deviant or dangerous. This is interesting considering her close acquaintance with lesbian actress Eva Le Gallienne, whom she called "an invincible friend" and with whom she worked on the postwar variety show, *Elsie Janis and Her Gang in a Bomb Proof Revue*.[28] Produced by Florenz Ziegfeld and Charles Dillingham with songs by a slew of popular writers and a book by Janis herself, the show ran for six weeks from December 1919 to January 1920.[29] In act 2 of the revue, Janis—dressed as a male French soldier—partnered with Le Gallienne in a number that featured the female duo dancing a foxtrot that transformed into a tango and then finally metamorphosed into a waltz. Later in the act, "Elsie, still dressed as the soldier, sang to four maidens (dressed to represent the Allied nations) 'I Love Them All a Little Bit.'"[30] The song by famed composer Dan Kildare and his partner Harvey White had appeared first in the London revue *Hullo, America* in November 1918. The homoeroticism of these cross-dressing performances by Janis is often used to corroborate other evidence that she may have been a lesbian.[31] However, press in the era suggests that mainstream audiences did not read her inversion of gender roles as socially threatening, perhaps because she was so often playing for humor or because she had established herself as a mimic very early in her stage career.

In fact, imagery of Janis in men's clothing was acceptable enough to be used to sell sheet music. The best-selling music for "Après La Guerre," another song Janis popularized in *Hullo, America*, was illustrated by a picture of the singer in a modified British officer's uniform with a Sam Brown belt and a beret (fig. 1). Like Dorothy Lawrence, who had to disguise herself as a man to enlist, Janis is wearing a male uniform. However, unlike Lawrence, there is no attempt at deception about the cross-dressed figure's sex; Janis's name, already internationally famous, is emblazoned in large orange lettering on the cover art. The song's lyrics speak to the hopes of postwar life:

A DOUGHGIRL WITH THE DOUGHBOYS

Figure 1. Cover of sheet music for "Après la Guerre."

Après la guerre!
There'll be a good time everywhere!
Beaming mothers, smiling misses,
Just a world of love and kisses.
After the war,
We shall be happier than before,
And the girl who tried your life to wreck
And turned you down three times, by heck,
Will execute the chicken reel and fall upon your neck
Après la guerre.

These words, which humorously conjure images of the mothers and lovers waiting back home for the doughboys, could imply either a male or female speaker. Janis took good advantage of this openness and used it to assert herself as belonging with the soldiers. Her image in a man's uniform aligns the singer with the soldiers longing for home rather than with the women on the home front. This echoes the sentiments in Janis's song "Over Here," which proudly used the word "we" for the singer and the soldiers: "Send the word—send the word, we are here and we are working!" Janis could not be clearer about her self-created role as a member of the soldiers' own company.

{ 63 }

The iconography on the sheet music for Janis's "Just a Little after Taps" further establishes her collegial identity with the men. This time a more conventionally feminine image of Janis is used while the words of the song indicate a heterosexually male narrative voice:

> At reveille you seem to me,
> Like the morning flowers dew,
> When assembly sounds
> O'er the camping grounds
> I'm still thinking dear of you.
> Through our hiking and drills,
> You're the one thing that fills,
> My thoughts without a lapse.
> But the time I love you most of all is just a little after taps.

The song, which was also featured in *Hullo, America*, is sung from the perspective of a soldier reflecting on the girl he left at home, thus offering an opportunity for Janis to once again identify with the men as a fellow war-worker and, maybe, to surreptitiously express her desire for women. The illustration for the sheet music is a popular image of Janis with a bright smile and a metal army helmet perched jauntily on her head of girlish curls (fig. 2). The M-1917 helmets, also known as Brodie helmets, were required gear for World War I soldiers and were an easily distinguished icon of the doughboy. Janis certainly wore one for safety as she traveled among soldiers, but her use of a Brodie helmet in publicity imagery was designed to demonstrate her active engagement near actual warfare. While "Après La Guerre" and "Over Here" make it clear that Janis is a fellow war-worker, "Just a Little after Taps" and the image that accompanied its sheet music suggest that Janis was very much like the men she visited, close enough to not only wear their clothing but to also feel their feelings.

In the forward battle areas frequented by Janis, she had the opportunity to witness all-soldier musical entertainments put on by the men and for the men. On one occasion, when Janis and her mother were visiting Major General John F. O'Ryan and his 27th Division, the company theatrical troupe presented their own show for the celebrated guests. A feature of the entertainment was a small chorus of men in women's clothes. Janis recalls, "After dinner he said, 'Now Mrs. and Miss Janis, we realize that you have been working hard, so we have planned a little recreation for you.' They then put on one of the best shows I ever saw. The 'leading lady' was John Roche, since those days a film luminary and at one time my leading man. When they finished I gave my performance and believe me I had something to follow!"[32] Considering Janis's own cross-dressing on stage and her tendency toward gender play in performance, it is fascinating to imagine

Figure 2. A familiar image of Elsie Janis with a steel Brodie helmet.

her in the audience of this war-side revue. The performers of the 27th Division, an AEF unit composed of members of the New York National Guard, may have been professional soldiers but they were hardly amateur entertainers.[33] As a New York City–based division, the troupe included a number of experienced commercial actors, singers, and dancers. In 1918, while stationed for training at Camp Wadsworth in Spartanburg, South Carolina, the men of the 27th Division were encouraged by Major General O'Ryan to create the all-soldier musical revue *You Know Me, Al!* that they performed in Spartanburg to sell-out crowds.[34] The soldiers then transferred the show to Broadway and Washington, DC.[35] Even after the 27th Division deployed to Europe, Major General O'Ryan encouraged theatrical entertainment among the soldiers. In the Flemish area where the soldiers made camp, O'Ryan reorganized the artistic team responsible for *You Know Me, Al!* to perform a variety show on a temporary stage erected in a field. The new variety show became popular not only with the 27th Division but also with soldiers passing through the area on the continual flow in and out of battle. As was typical for military variety shows, the performance included men who sang and danced as women. Dressed in long country frocks and with their

Brodie helmets disguised as bonnets, the soldiers offered their own fictionalized and theatricalized image of the American girl. On the day of Janis's visit, the soldiers presented their construction of femininity not just for one another, but for a performer who was herself an expert at gender impersonations.

We know some details about the variety show Janis likely witnessed because O'Ryan provided photographs of the theatrics in his memoirs. There were certainly musical duets, dance numbers, and blackface minstrels. O'Ryan's record of the show includes photographs of the cross-dressing performers. "The four 'leading ladies' of the Divisional Theatrical Troupe: Privates Krebs, Crawford, Pauly and Burns," the general writes. "Note the hats—they are the regulation steel helmets."[36] The "girls" are dressed as milkmaids and are being serenaded by Janis's former musical revue cast mate, Jack Roche, in a number called "Wait Till the Cows Come Home," which depicts the unsuccessful advances of a young man to an industrious and chaste farm girl. The collection also includes a photograph of "the same 'ladies' minus their stage make-up,"[37] four strapping young men in their standard uniforms. The record O'Ryan leaves behind in his *Story of the 27th* reveals pride in the men's performance, including their humorous cross-dressing. The general's description of Flemish children's reactions to the soldier's variety show exemplifies his understanding of the power of the performers: "At first they gazed in almost dumb wonderment at the nonsense of the clowns, or the dancing of the 'girls,' and listened intently to the divisional jazz band and the popular Broadway songs. After a week or two they got to know the leading men and leading 'women' of the troupe, and great was the pride of the little urchins when during the day their friendly greeting was returned by one of these great personages." The cross-dressing performance evidently did not make the general or other soldiers uncomfortable, probably because they had become accustomed to transvestism in popular theatre. "Aware of the illusion in progress, spectators perceived the 'play' presented for their entertainment," writes Martha Banta of cross-dressing in vaudeville. "The fact that the performers' actual sex was different from the costumes, gestures, and lyrics meant that detours were taken along the route from perception to conceptualization. But all was safe for society as long as the impertinence of these theatrical acts stayed within the conventions that structure 'fantastic socialization.'"[38] The ridiculous "girls" of the 27th Division did not challenge gender roles or otherwise disrupt the military culture; they did not suggest that anything needed to change in the life of men and women offstage.

The performance of gender that Janis created for her persona as a wartime entertainer, while similar on surface to the soldier's playful cross-dressing, was asserting something entirely different. She was physically present as a woman among the soldiers, dressed in a distinctly feminine costume, but behaving like "one of the boys" without exaggeration or grotesqueness. Her presentation of self skillfully overlapped the male and the female, causing both genders to share space simultaneously. Janis placed herself as close as possible to the soldiers, casting herself as one of them in both her personal interactions and through her act. In doing so, she avoided being seen as one of any number of expected and clichéd female types by the soldiers who, she acknowledged, were eager to put the idealized American girl on a pedestal: "One of the most wonderful things in the A.E.F. was the absolute and undying respect the American soldiers had for the American girl. They put them on a pedestal that grew and grew with each succeeding day the boys spent in France. The more he saw of other women, the more he boosted the girl at home, until she was almost too high to be human."[39] Instead, she asserted herself as the soldiers' colleague who shared their experiences of war as a near equal. By staying firmly on the ground—near the trenches, camp huts, and field hospitals of the men's wartime world—Janis avoided the limitations women face when placed on pedestals and thereby offered another model for women in the emerging modern American society.

Reflecting back on her period of voluntary service with the Allied troops, Elsie Janis remarked on the particular joy of a memento from the 27th Division: "I have been presented with a medal by General O'Ryan from the New York boys of the A.E.F. I've flooded the stage of the Globe Theatre, where it was presented to me, with tears not because I got a medal but because engraved on it were the words, 'In loving and grateful appreciation.' The loving is what got me. I don't want anyone to thank me, but I do hope they mean it when they say *'loving'*... Just why they should give me a medal for spending the happiest days of my life with a lot of *regular guys*, I don't see."[40] Janis was "The Regular Girl" amidst a lot of regular guys. She achieved this by skillfully balancing feminine orthodoxy in her clothing and respectability in her reported attitudes with bold, unconventional behavior that imitated the activities and even sensibilities of male soldiers. The position Janis occupied with the men is revealed in the rhetoric of one soldier writing home to his sister after a visit from Janis: "She made us realize what we left behind, but not with regret. Each one individually felt as though he had been patted on the back and urged forward. You went away loving her, knowing she was with you."[41] Thus Janis's performance of gender provided a unique woman's presence in the wartime world of men. She was not their mother, nurse, or sexual partner, but she was with them as a provisional co-member of the AEF. Elsie Janis fostered sincere camaraderie between herself and the men, forging a collegiality that may have helped promote new postwar attitudes about social roles for the sexes in American culture.

Notes

1. "Betsy Crashes, Elsie Smashes—Artillery Battery Names Its Guns for Two Patriotic Women," *Stars and Stripes* 1, no. 17 (May 31, 1918): 1.
2. Ibid.
3. "Elsie," *Stars and Stripes* 1, no. 6 (March 15, 1918): 4.
4. "Elsie One of Us While War Lasts," *Stars and Stripes* 1, no. 8 (March 29, 1918): 7.
5. "'Don't Forget Me,' Elsie's Order," *Stars and Stripes* 1, no. 32 (September 13, 1918): 6.
6. Elsie Janis, *The Big Show: My Six Months with the American Expeditionary Forces* (New York: Cosmopolitan Book Corporation, 1919), xi.
7. Ibid.
8. "Elsie One of Us While War Lasts," 7. On one such occasion when Janis left the war area to do a show in London, she wrote an open letter that was published in the *Stars and Stripes*:

    My dear boys—Each and every one, Hello! and au revoir for the present. I am in London about to make some money. You all know how difficult it is to find over there, and I have not found any for seven months. I shall be thinking of you and pulling for you. To those who I have met and had the honor of singing for I say, keep the pep that you had when I saw you. To those I did not see I say, I'm sorry, but I will get you yet. Don't forget me. Good luck to you all. Get a Hun for me, and if you want anything that I can get for you, write to me, Palace Theater, London. You see, I shall not be very far away from you all and the big show. Always your friend, Elsie Janis. P.S. Love from Mother.

    From "'Don't Forget Me,' Elsie's Orders," 6.
9. Lee Alan Morrow, "Elsie Janis: A Compensatory Biography" (Ph.D. diss., Northwestern University, 1988), 198.
10. Ibid.
11. Allen G. Debus, "Elsie Janis: From Ohio to the Front Lines in France and Back Again," liner notes from "Elsie Janis: Sweetheart of the A.E.F .," by Elsie Janis, Basil Hallam, Owen Nares, Stanley Lupina, and Will West (*Sweetheart of the A.E.F.* St. Joseph, Ill: Archeophone, 2009), 10.
12. Lee Alan Morrow, "Elsie Janis: A Comfortable Goofiness," in *Passing Performances: Queen Readings of Leading Players in American Theatre History*, ed. Kimberley B. Marra and Robert A. Schanke (Ann Arbor: University of Michigan Press, 1998), 163.
13. Janis said, "When I first started in this work I was considerably handicapped in telling a good story because I did not use some of our stronger adjectives. But, one day I heard a chaplain say: 'Boys, we should make Henry Ford a chaplain in the United States army because he has shaken the hell out of so many people.' Ever since then I have felt I could do so too." Quoted in Morrow, "Elsie Janis: A Compensatory Biography," 203–4.
14. Elsie Janis, *So Far, So Good: An Autobiography* (New York: E. P. Dutton, 1932), 198–99.
15. Martha Banta, *Imaging American Women: Idea and Ideals in Cultural History* (New York: Columbia University Press, 1987), 46.
16. Frank Cullen, *Vaudeville, Old and New: An Encyclopedia of Variety Performers in America* (New York: Routledge Press, 2007), 562.
17. A *Stars and Stripes* article called this costume her "one-dress wardrobe, a plain

18. Morrow, "Elsie Janis: A Compensatory Biography," 210.
19. Janis, *The Big Show*, 186.
20. Ibid.
21. Ibid., 187.
22. Ibid., 73.
23. For more on this subject, see Dorothy Lawrence, *Sapper Dorothy Lawrence, the Only English Woman Soldier, late Royal Engineers, 51st Division 179th Tunneling Company, B.E.F.* (London: John Lane, The Bodley Head, 1919).
24. For more on the subject, see Laurie Stoff, "They Fought for Russia: Female Soldiers of the First World War," in *A Soldier and a Woman: Sexual Integration in the Military*, ed. Gerald J. DeGroot and C. M. Peniston-Bird (London: Longman Publishers, 2000).
25. Kimberly Jensen, *Mobilizing Minerva: American Women in the First World War* (Urbana: University of Illinois Press, 2008), 64.
26. Morrow, "Elsie Janis: A Comfortable Goofiness," 159.
27. Banta, *Imaging American Women*, 270.
28. Le Gallienne was known to be lesbian by the theatre community and was seen as "notorious" by the public. Nonetheless, Janis describes their friendship unapologetically: "When she came on a Saturday, I told the door man to let her come in, and Eva Le Gallienne walked into my life, where she remains today. The same quality that made me stand in the rain and talk to her makes her now actress, directress, founder of the New York Civic Repertory Theatre and, better than all, invincible friend!" (Janis, *So Far So Good*, 133).
29. There was also a 1922 version of the revue—with neither Elsie Janis nor Eva Le Gallienne in the cast—produced by Janis herself and titled *Elsie Janis and Her Gang in a New Attack*, featuring music, lyrics, and book entirely credited to Janis.
30. Morrow, "Elsie Janis: A Comfortable Goofiness," 164.
31. In 1930, Janis married a younger actor named Gilbert Wilson. "There are indications that this was a 'bearded' arrangement that signaled not only Janis's final emergence from her mother's chaperoning but a reversal of the star-making dynamic, as she attempted in fierce motherly fashion to manage her husband's acting career much as Jennie had managed hers… He never ascended to theatrical greatness, but he did become one of [Noel] Coward's party companions. Janis also socialized independently, appearing at one gathering clad in male riding attire on the arm of the notoriously libidinous actress Marilyn Miller." "Elsie Janis," *The Gay and Lesbian Theatrical Legacy: A Biographical Dictionary of Major Figures in American Stage History in the Pre-Stonewall Era*, ed. Billy J. Harbin, Kimberley B. Marra, and Robert A. Schanke (Ann Arbor: University of Michigan Press, 2007), 217.
32. Janis, *So Far, So Good*, 223.
33. The 27th Division was the only National Guard unit to be converted to Regular Army during the First World War.
34. For more on O'Ryan and the 27th Division, see my chapter "Performance, Preparedness, and Playing with Fire: Major General O'Ryan and U.S. Military Theatricality in the World War I Era," in *Public Theatres and Theatre Publics*, ed. Robert Shimko and Sara Freeman (Cambridge: Cambridge Scholars Press, 2012).

35. The more famous World War I soldier show, *Yip, Yip, Yaphank*—with music by Irving Berlin—played at the same Broadway house, the Lexington Theatre, later that same year. *Yip, Yip Yaphank* began in July 1918 at Camp Upton's Liberty Theatre before moving on to the Century Theatre and finally to the Lexington in September 1918. The show included military drills choreographed to Berlin's music and featured popular songs such as "Oh! How I Hate to Get Up in the Morning."
36. John F. O'Ryan, *Story of the 27th* (New York: Wynkoop, Hallenbech, Crawford, Company, 1921), 202.
37. Ibid.
38. Banta, *Imaging American Women*, 275.
39. Janis, *The Big Show*, 224.
40. Ibid., 222–223.
41. Morrow, "Elsie Janis: A Compensatory Biography," 200.

Staging Hibernia

Female Allegories of Ireland in *Cathleen Ní Houlihan* and *Dawn*

—TANYA DEAN

> Did that play of mine send out
> Certain men the English shot?
> W. B. YEATS, "MAN AND THE ECHO," 1939

In the midst of the Irish uprisings of the late nineteenth and early twentieth centuries, a subsidiary war was being fought on a cultural front. In tandem with the movement to liberate Ireland from British sovereignty, a parallel crusade was gaining momentum, one that sought to assert Ireland's artistic independence from what was felt to be Britain's malign cultural domination. Within this artistic revolution, theatre was used by notable groups like the Irish Literary Theatre and *Inghinidhe Na h-Éireann* (Daughters of Ireland) as a prime battleground to reassert national authority over depictions of the "real" Ireland and the Irish, and to offer an alternative to the (mis)representations of Irishness emanating from a colonial force. To this end, W. B. Yeats and Augusta Gregory's play *Cathleen Ní Houlihan* and Maud Gonne's *Dawn* both featured anthropomorphic incarnations of Ireland as a female character. In this essay I examine the context in which the two plays were written, and their dramaturgical and political use of the allegorical female figure. I believe that this trope was employed both in conversation with Irish mythological tradition and in reaction to derogatory representations of Ireland in foreign popular arts and media. I also consider these works within the framework of the roles and representations of women as part of the Irish nationalist agenda.

The foundation of the Irish Literary Theatre in 1898 was partially predicated on the desire of the founders to use the stage as a medium for a proud self-definition of the "true" Irish character. In the manifesto written by William Butler Yeats, Lady Augusta Gregory, George Moore, and Edward Martyn at Gregory's home in Coole in 1897, they state: "We propose to have performed in Dublin in the spring of every year certain Celtic and Irish plays, which whatever their degree of excellence will be written with a high ambition, and so build up a Celtic and Irish school of dramatic literature. We hope to find in Ireland an uncorrupted and imaginative audience trained to listen by its passion for oratory, and believe that our desire to bring upon the stage the deeper thoughts and emotions of Ireland will ensure from us a tolerant welcome, and that freedom to experiment which is not found in theatres of England, and without which no new movement in art or literature can succeed."[1] This was intended both as an action of revolution—ushering in a new era of cultural as well as national independence—and a counterstrike against what the founders considered to be the proliferation of negative colonial representations in the theatre. The Irish Literary Theatre's founding charter goes on to say that this performance project will prove "that Ireland is not the home of buffoonery and easy sentiment, as it has been represented, but the home of an ancient idealism. We are confident of the support of all Irish people, who are weary of misrepresentation, in carrying out a work that is outside all the political questions that divide us."[2]

However, a little context: it is worth noting that Yeats, Gregory, and Martyn's paean to the "uncorrupted and imaginative" Irish audience they planned to cultivate and satisfy was, in reality, a slightly snobbish fiction. In *A History of the Irish Theatre, 1601–2000*, Chris Morash wryly notes the irony of the group's origins: "In a sense, the Irish Literary Theatre came into being by imagining an empty space where in fact there was a crowded room."[3] Ireland (and Dublin in particular) enjoyed a thriving theatrical tradition in the late nineteenth century. Melodramas by playwrights like Dion Boucicault (produced by both indigenous and imported companies) that engaged in the so-called "buffoonery and easy sentiment" of the archetypal "stage Irish" play were highly popular and profitable on national tours and in Dublin theatres like the Queen's Royal Theatre. In fact, the Royal, established in 1884 under the management of the English entrepreneur J. W. Whitbread, declared itself the "Home of Irish Drama." Enthusiastic and vocal audiences from across classes would queue up for an opportunity to cheer the heroes, boo the villains, and comment loudly upon the action. As far as the general audience was concerned, these melodramas were not misrepresentations. Indeed, the plays often traded heavily on the weight of the work's purported authenticity. A playbill for Boucicault's *The Colleen Bawn* described the play as "Founded on a true history First told by an Irishman and now Dramatized by an Irishman"[4] and further claimed that "Ireland, so rich in scenery, so full of romance and the warm touch of nature, has never until now been opened by the dramatist. Irish dramas have hitherto been exaggerated farces, representing low life or scenes of abject servitude and suffering. Such is not a true picture of Irish society."[5]

But the cheerful stereotypes and popular appeal of playwrights like Boucicault was anathema to Yeats, Gregory, Moore, and Martyn. Despite the Irish Literary Theatre's declaration of confidence in the "support of all Irish people," in reality the company was tailoring its work for an elite audience who they felt would appreciate their political and cultural principles. In 1899, in the company's periodical *Beltaine*, Yeats explained that his works were written for "that limited public which gives understanding," and he would "not mind greatly if others are bored."[6] And when the Abbey Theatre was opened in 1904, it lacked a certain egalitarianism in its architecture: the traditional sixpence seats in the upper galleries of its rival Dublin theatres (that offered the opportunity for working-class audiences to enjoy a variety of performances) were conspicuously absent. The Abbey ticket prices were originally fixed at three shillings for the stalls, two shillings for the reserved seats in the balcony, and a shilling in the pit (twice the price of the sixpence seats in the other theatres). The lease drawn up by tea heiress Annie Horniman (who was a vital investor in the Abbey Theatre) explicitly stipulated that "the prices of the seats can be raised, of course, but not lowered…to prevent cheap entertainments from being given."[7] While the Irish Literary Theatre may have been "confident of the support of all Irish people," the original ticket prices served to implicitly exclude a significant portion of the Dublin theatregoing demographics. So it is worth keeping in mind that the foundation of the Irish Literary Theatre was not a response to a widespread national call for "true" theatrical representation, but rather a select group using the stage to promote their own nationalist and artistic ideals.

However, despite these somewhat elitist aesthetic ambitions, the Irish Literary Theatre did not work in isolation. In its desire to debunk misrepresentations and repatriate the authority of authenticity, the Irish Literary Theatre was part of a larger movement seeking to use art as a revolutionary force in the struggle for independence. In 1900, a sociopolitical women's group called *Inghinidhe Na h-Éireann* (Daughters of Ireland) was formed to provide an avenue for women to participate in the nationalist agenda (as the majority of the political and paramilitary organizations were for men only). The English-born Irish revolutionary Maud Gonne (with whom Yeats was besotted) was elected president. Similar to the Irish Literary Theatre, *Inghinidhe Na h-Éireann* believed that the battle for Irish independence had to be fought on cultural as well as political fronts. Among their core tenets, they pledged:

- to encourage the study of Gaelic, of Irish Literature, History, Music, and Art, especially among the young, by the organizing and teaching of classes for these subjects.
- to discourage the reading and circulation of low English literature, the singing of English songs, the attending of vulgar English entertainments at the theatres and music hall, and to combat in every way English influence, which was doing so much injury to the artistic taste and refinement of the Irish people.[8]

In order to raise funds for their education program, members of *Inghinidhe Na h-Éireann*, aided by Frank and Willie Fay, staged *tableaux vivants* showing scenes from some period in Irish history or illustrating some legend or patriotic melody.

In 1902, *Inghinidhe Na h-Éireann* formed a small dramatic company called The National Players for those members interested in acting, which included such later Abbey performers as Maire Nic Shiubhlaigh, Sara Allgood, and Maire O'Neill. Gonne taught drama classes for the group when she was in Dublin. This little group produced full-length plays only occasionally then, but its objective was to encourage young Dubliners to write for the stage and to establish the nucleus of a national dramatic company that would run in conjunction with nationalist organizations in the city. In 1902, W. G. Fay's Dramatic Company was founded, comprising members from the Ormond Dramatic Society and from *Inghinidhe Na h-Éireann* and the National Players. Frank Fay told Yeats, Gregory, and Gonne of their efforts and Yeats offered his play *Cathleen Ní Houlihan* (which, he later acknowledged, was written in collaboration with Gregory), to fill out the program of their debut. Gonne was persuaded to take the title role, and the Irish National Dramatic Company produced it with *Inghinidhe Na h-Éireann* at St. Teresa's Hall, Clarendon Street, on April 2, 1902.

Cathleen Ní Houlihan was perfect for the purposes of the fledgling company; it was a short poetic drama, with a single set (a peasant's cottage in Killala in 1798) that dramatized "Ireland's call" to young patriots. On the eve of his wedding, young Michael Gillane is beguiled into abandoning his fiancée, Delia, and his family in order to dedicate his life (and, most likely, his death) to helping the mysterious old woman, Cathleen, reclaim her "land that was taken from me…my four beautiful green fields."[9] The "four green fields" were a clear analogy for the four provinces of Ireland (Ulster, Munster, Leinster, Connacht), and the "Poor Old Woman" served as the anthropomorphic incarnation of Ireland, demanding in stenorian tones for all patriotic young men to answer the call to arms. She openly admits that the price paid for allegiance may well be their lives, but claims that in spite of this, true sons of Éire will still answer the call. "They that have red cheeks will have pale cheeks for my sake, and for all that, they will think they are well paid."[10] The distraught Delia and the Gillane family watch Michael follow the mysterious woman out of the cottage to join the revolt; when asked if he saw the old woman walking down the path, their younger son Patrick innocently replies, "I did not, but I saw a young girl, and she had the walk of a queen."[11] In this triumphant offstage metamorphosis, Cathleen Ní Houlihan—the "Poor Old Woman"—and, by extension, Ireland are rejuvenated by the restorative power of the dedication and bravery of revolutionary men. So pervasive and popular was Yeats's and Gregory's creation that they were to present it as part of a triple bill with Yeats's *On Baile's Strand* and Gregory's *Spreading the News* on the opening night of the fledgling Abbey Theatre in 1904.

In creating this stage allegory of Ireland as woman, Yeats and Gregory may have been delving into their shared fascination with Irish myth and legend in order to create a character that combined aspects of many elements of the recurrent trope of the "sovereignty goddess." In their introduction to *Gender in Irish Writing*, Toni O'Brien Johnson and David Cairns discuss the three incarnations of this archetype, all of which share characteristics with the stage Cathleen Ní Houlihan. First, there is the pre-Christian anthropomorphic goddess at the center of the *banfheis rígi* ritual, or the "marriage of kingship," whereby the king sought physical union with the land in the form of a woman. This protean goddess could appear as a youthful beauty or an aged hag (*cailleac*), depending on the adequacy of the king who "married" her, representing the integral importance of devoted royal stewardship versus feckless leadership to the prosperity of the land. The worthiness of Michael Gillane to take up the burden of military duty to Ireland seems to be intimated by the offstage transformation of Cathleen from poor old woman to regal young girl; in their "union," she/Ireland is reborn. The second embodiment of this trope appears during the medieval period, when mortal manifestations of this goddess appear in the form of amazonian figures like Queen Medbh of Connacht, who mates with a number of kings and whose aggression is a core cause for the epic saga of the *Táin Bó Cuailgne* (The Cattle Raid of Cooley). The final phase, following the suppression of the indigenous Irish culture from the seventeenth century onward, is the emergence in literature and song of an allegorical female figure representing the anthropomorphized Ireland, described in the eighteenth century genre of vision poems (the *aisling*) as the *spéir bhean* (sky woman). Cathleen Ní Houlihan is just one name for this figure's many incarnations, who include Eriú, Fódla, Bana, Roisín

Dubh, and *Sean Bhean Bhocht*/Shan Van Vocht (Poor Old Woman—an epithet that Cathleen Ní Houlihan applies to herself in the play).[12]

Gonne herself felt a very strong relationship to this allegorical figure: in her autobiography, *A Servant of the Queen*, she poetically describes an encounter with this embodied spirit of Ireland that was the turning point that set her on the path toward nationalist activism: "Tired but glowing I looked out of the window of the train at the dark bog land where now only the tiny lakes gleamed in the fading light. Then I saw a tall, beautiful woman with dark hair blown on the wind, and I knew it was Cathleen Ní Houlihan. She was crossing the bog toward the hills, springing from stone to stone over the treacherous surface, and the little white stones shone, marking a path behind her, then faded into the darkness. I heard a voice say: 'You are one of the little stones on which the feet of the Queen have rested on her way to Freedom.'"[13] Yeats shared this belief that Gonne was spiritually connected to the land and the revolution, saying in his memoirs that he thought of her as "in a sense Ireland…the romantic political Ireland of my youth."[14] Indeed, Gonne was so attracted to the notion of a female embodiment of Ireland and to Yeats's play that in 1904 she penned her own dramatic work on similar themes, entitled *Dawn: A Play in One Act and Three Tableaux—Sunset, Night, and Dawn*, which was published in the nationalist newspaper, *The United Irishman*, on behalf of *Inghinidhe Na h-Éireann*.

In her short play, Gonne allegorizes Ireland in the form of the tragic Bride, whose lands have been stolen by a villainous landlord (the Stranger, a melodramatic symbol for the British colonizers). Her neighbor, Old Michael, speaks with her with awe: "Bride, Bride of the Sorrows, it is your service I took, I have been faithful. I thought one time I might have been one of the stones your foot would rest on when you walked to Freedom—when you will drive the Stranger out—but I am too little a stone."[15] As her daughter Brideen dies from starvation, Bride comforts her with the thought of the revolution to come: "The night has been long and dark. It is nearly morning. See, the light is coming, Brideen, *a stóir*…Your eyes are closing now, Brideen, my daughter, but you and I will never be parted…See, Brideen, see the dawn is coming and the red dawn. The river of blood must flow, but there is freedom on the other side of it, and the Strangers are driven away like clouds before the sun. Brideen, it is you and the mighty dead who are driving back the clouds."[16] Her tone is not so much of a grieving mother, but rather of a general sorrowfully reflecting on the necessary sacrifice of a soldier. This tragic death is what spurs the peasants to rise up against the oppression of the Stranger.

In the same manner in which *Cathleen Ní Houlihan* and *Dawn* employed an allegorical female character of Ireland as a dramaturgical tool within a political agenda, the anthropomorphized Hibernia was also a key figure within the sphere of visual political icongraphy played out in the satirical cartoons of publications like *Punch, or the London Charivari*. In *Drawing Conclusions: A Cartoon History of Anglo-Irish Relations, 1798–1998*, Roy Douglas, Liam Harte, and Jim O'Hara analyze the evolution of the pictorial representations of the "Irish problem" in the British media: "Principal *Punch* cartoonists such as John Leech and John Tenniel…were staunch defenders of respectable middle-class values and of Britain's imperial integrity who reserved their most venomous ink for those, such as Irish separatists, who threatened to disrupt both."[17] Exaggerated depictions of race were a particularly potent weapon in the satirical cartoonist's arsenal; from the inception of *Punch* in 1841, the depictions of Irish peasants and rebels grew increasingly bestialized and prognathous, until the image of a grotesque and apelike Fenian rebel would have become a staple for many middle-class readers of the English comic weeklies by the 1860s. These savages were often contrasted with a depiction of Hibernia—another anthropomorphic incarnation of Ireland, this time as the lovely and frail avatar of a nation in soulful feminine distress.

In "The Fenian Pest" in 1866, a classic example of Tenniel's oeuvre from *Punch*, the dainty and terrified Hibernia clings to the arm of her Amazonian sister Britannia, as a savage Irish thug threatens them. Hibernia begs her sibling for aid: "O my dear sister, what *are* we to do with these troublesome people?" Britannia, a veritable Athena of wisdom and strength, grimly responds, "Try isolation first, my dear, and then—" (The cartoon's title is a reference to the cattle disease rinderpest—the recommended treatment for which was isolation, followed by slaughter.)[18] With vicious visual wit, Tenniel is here tapping into the predominant sense of unease in British society at the armed threat of the Fenian campaign for independence. By juxtaposing the depiction of the rebels as subhuman and Hibernia as a quintessential damsel (being protected by her stronger and more capable sister), Tenniel is also evoking classic colonial archetypes, presenting the weak colonized nation in need of the colonizer's superior strength and protection. By presenting an anthropomorphic version of Ireland who is fiercely patriotic and an active inciter of rebellion, Yeats, Gregory, and Gonne were seeking not only to debunk this colonial stereotype, but replace it with a powerful counter-myth.

As Hayden White puts it, "A given culture is only as strong as its power to convince its least dedicated members that its fictions are truths."[19] The choice to mine the myths of Ireland to synthesize a powerful woman as allegory was a consciously political choice as well as an artistic one. John Wilson Foster, in *Fictions of the Irish Literary Revival*, describes the nationalist aesthetic movement of the times: "The Irish Literary Revival of the late nineteenth century sought to redefine the country's present by recalling a past world of nobility and bravery. For writers of the period, recovery of the era of legend was 'recovery of a heroic Ireland.'"[20] In hearkening back to the racial memory of these myths, Yeats and Gregory hoped to create an "enabling myth" that would mine the patriotism of audience members; to evoke a shared nostalgia that would inspire men to restore Ireland to her former glory in a transformation similar to that of Cathleen Ní Houlihan.

The dramaturgy of *Cathleen Ní Houlihan* may seem simplistic in retrospect, but the power of the nationalist rhetoric of this short play to galvanize the revolutionary spirit of its admirers was profound. Among its ardent devotees was the Countess Constance Markiewicz, a female revolutionary who went out to fight with the men of the 1916 Easter Rising and was condemned to death for her part in the Rising (although this was later commuted to life in prison on "account of the prisoner's sex," and she was released in 1917 as part of a general amnesty for those who had participated in the Rising). In a letter from prison she wrote, "That play of Yeats was a sort of gospel to me."[21] One critic asserted that this play (alongside Gregory's *The Rising of the Moon*) "made more rebels than a thousand political speeches or a hundred reasoned books."[22] However, as indicated in "Man and the Echo," Yeats later admitted unease with the "success" of his play's patriotic message. This work exemplified what Susan Cannon Harris, in *Gender and Modern Irish Drama*, describes as the "cult of blood sacrifice" that permeated the rhetoric of the Irish uprising, and was a recurrent motif in Irish literature and performance through the Irish literary revival: "The martyr is marked as male and the great Other that receives the blood of the sacrifice (whether she is Hibernia, the bog, the Virgin, or the Shan Van Vocht) is marked as female."[23]

These plays were witness to the birth of the indigenous Irish theatre, yet they also served as propaganda texts. In her stage incarnations, Hibernia's passivity has been replaced with something almost frighteningly rapacious; the hunger of the two female characters/nations/deities in *Cathleen Ní Houlihan* and *Dawn* is depicted essentially as a cry for blood. Their speeches are crafted to appeal on a visceral level, rather than offering considered political dissertation. Both openly acknowledge that they are calling upon "true Irishmen" to die for their cause (rhetoric that is disturbingly close to the ideology of the suicide bomber). They seduce their chosen men with language rather than through sexual allure, and pro-social procreation (symbolized by Michael's impending wedding) becomes secondary to martyrdom (implicit in his decision to follow the putatively female Cathleen) as the more honorable masculine obligation.

Harris discusses how Cathleen's asexuality is an essential part of her power as political allegory: "She cannot afford to 'set out the bed' for her lovers because to represent herself as sexually attainable is to suggest that she might also be violable."[24] The domestic sphere in *Cathleen Ní Houlihan* emphasizes the personal, the pleasurable, the immediate, the material, and the familial. The impending marriage, with its mercantile trappings (the dowry, the pride in the fineness of the groom's suit), is made to seem shortsighted and selfish in contrast with Cathleen's nationalist rhetoric that transcends history.

However, the patriotic tone of *Cathleen Ní Houlihan* is complicated by the contentious historical event during which the action of the play is set. The stage directions for *Cathleen Ní Houlihan* place the action very specifically in the "interior of a cottage close to Killala, in 1798."[25] Both the date and the location are chosen with intent: the final episode of the 1798 Irish rebellion took place in County Mayo. A long-awaited force of slightly over a thousand French soldiers, under General John Humbert, arrived at Killala Bay to support the United Irishmen (led by Wolfe Tone) in raising a revolt in the west. Hence Patrick's triumphant shout of "There are ships in the Bay; the French are landing at Killala"[26] near the play's climax. Yet Killala was a notoriously grim failure in the history of the Irish revolution; the French forces arrived a few months too late to make a decisive difference in the struggle, and they landed in one of the poorest counties with the least republican support. The rebellion failed, and the French were forced to surrender to the combined forces of Generals Lake and Cornwallis on September 8. The French were treated as political prisoners and accorded due courtesy; the Irish rebels were regarded as traitors to the crown and were subject to brutal mistreatment (including the notorious "half-hangings") and execution (the 1798 rebellion was infamous for the atrocities committed on both sides). When Michael walks out the door of his parents' cottage in a daze at the climax of *Cathleen Ní Houlihan*, he is not following her siren's song to a noble victory or even a noble defeat. In actuality, this young man would have been part of an inglorious loss for the Irish forces, and would almost certainly have been subjected to ruthless punishment and most likely execution. When viewed in its diachronic historical aspect, the action of the play is not the recruitment of a patriot, but the last days of a man who would go on serve Ireland as cannon fodder.

Figures like Hibernia and Cathleen Ní Houlihan serve as a key example of Marina Warner's theory of how public representations of women are usually mythic or allegorical, while those of men are of historical figures: "The female tends to be perceived as generic and universal, with symbolic overtones; the male as individual, even when it is being used to express a generalized idea."[27] Much like Britannia, Athena, and the Amazons, these ostensibly feminine figures transcend or neutralize gender rather than defy it. These depictions of fiercely martial anthropomorphic female characters were at odds with the social role mandated for women by the Nationalist cause. Female revolutionary figures like Maud Gonne and Countess Markiewicz and the female-only paramilitary group *Cumann na mBan* (the women's association) gained some prominence (and notoriety) for their roles in the revolution, though these figures were the exception rather than the rule. Gonne in particular tried to buck the shackles of acceptable nationalist feminine behavior and take on a more active role in the revolution; the divorce proceedings following her disastrous marriage to John MacBride, however, destroyed both her reputation and her political effectiveness in the conservative sphere of Irish politics, and led to a ten-year exile in France. The discourse of the Irish nationalist parties was predominantly in favor of prescribing a domestic role for Irish womanhood as part of their charge to create a new nation. The Irish nationalists condemned the suffrage movement for turning Irish women's attention "Englandwards," thus distracting them from their true task of supporting the national cause. *Cumann na mBan* agreed to give absolute priority to the struggle for independence over the achievement of women's rights, lest there be division in the ranks of the nationalist movement.

Part of this repressive attitude toward women was a practical political consideration, as David Cairns and Shaun Richards write: "In political terms, this resistance was grounded in the needs of the parliamentarians to garner support from the majority of Irish electors—the tenant farmers—and in the dictates of the contemporary realities of rural Ireland's familist economy, an especially stringent form of patriarchy."[28] Pro-social behavior for patriotic women was laid out in pamphlets like Mary E. Butler's *Irishwomen and the Home Language*, which cautioned readers that "shrieking viragoes" and "aggressive amazons" were detrimental to the national cause. Instead, woman was to provide roots for the growth of national character: "Woman reigns as an autocrat in the kingdom of her home. Her sway is absolute. She rules and serves simultaneously in the home circle. Not only does she attend to the organization of the practical details, and the supplying of material wants, but the spiritual side of home life is starved or satisfied according as her nature is noble or ignoble… The spark struck on the hearthstone will fire the soul of the nation."[29] The Gaelic League encouraged women to foster the nationalist revolution and a positive Irish character through their control of the domestic sphere.

Warner observes that "the female form does not refer to particular women, does not describe women as a group, and often does not even presume to evoke their natures."[30] In their work in the theatre, Yeats, Gregory, and Gonne were creating a powerful patriotic symbol in the form of an embodied "Mother

Ireland," as part of a cultural campaign to stage indigenous representations of Ireland and the Irish. Yet the pride of place of this female allegorical figure onstage was at odds with how Irish women were sidelined in political thought. Implicitly, these incarnations of Hibernia as Cathleen Ní Houlihan and Bride were limited to serving as a figurehead to rally the troops of the rebellion, valued only in the realm of the symbolic.

Notes

1. Augusta Gregory, *Our Irish Theatre; A Chapter of Autobiography* (London: G. P. Putnam's Sons, 1914), 8–9.
2. Ibid.
3. Chris Morash, *A History of Irish Theatre, 1601–2000* (New York: Cambridge University Press, 2002), 117.
4. Quoted in Townsend Walsh, *The Career of Dion Boucicault* (New York: The Dunlap Society, 1915), 74.
5. Ibid.
6. W. B. Yeats, "Plans and Methods," in *Beltaine: The Organ of the Irish Literary Theatre* 1 (May 1899): 7.
7. Annie Horniman to George Roberts (28 Nov. 1904), Harvard Theatre Collection, Houghton Library, (bms Thr 24), 114.
8. *United Irishman*, 13 October 1900, 8.
9. W. B. Yeats, *Cathleen Ní Houlihan*, in *The Variorum Edition of the Plays of W. B. Yeats*, ed. Russell K. Alspach (New York: Macmillan, 1966), 223.
10. Ibid., 229.
11. Ibid., 231.
12. Toni O'Brien Johnson and David Cairns, *Gender in Irish Writing* (Philadelphia: Open University Press, 1991), 3–4.
13. Maud Gonne, *The Autobiography of Maud Gonne: A Servant of the Queen* (Chicago: University of Chicago Press, 1995), 9.
14. W. B. Yeats, *Memoirs*, ed. Denis Donoghue (London: Macmillan, 1972), 50.
15. Maud Gonne, *Dawn: A Play in One Act and Three Tableaux—Sunset, Night, and Dawn* in *Maud Gonne's Irish Nationalist Writings, 1895–1946*, ed. Karen Steele (Dublin: Irish Academic Press, 2004), 206.
16. Ibid., 210.
17. Roy Douglas et al., *Drawing Conclusions: A Cartoon History of Anglo-Irish Relations, 1798–1998* (Belfast: Blackstaff, 1998), 2.
18. Ibid. Derived from *Fianna* (the name of a legendary band of Irish warriors), "Fenian" was a term used to describe supporters of Irish nationalism. For example, the American branch of the Irish Republican Brotherhood dubbed themselves the Fenian Brotherhood.
19. Hayden White, *Tropics of Discourse: Essays in Cultural Criticism* (Baltimore: Johns Hopkins University Press, 1978), 6.

20. John Wilson Foster, *Fictions of the Irish Literary Revival: A Changeling Art* (Syracuse: Syracuse University Press, 1987), 10.
21. Constance Markiewicz, *The Prison Letters of Countess Markiewicz*, ed. Esther Roper (London: Virago, 1987), 51.
22. Lennox Robinson, Tom Robinson, and Nora Dorman, *Three Homes* (London: Michael Joseph Ltd., 1942), 218. Quoted in George B. Saul, *Prolegomena to the Study of Yeats's Plays* (Philadelphia: University of Pennsylvania Press, 1957), 34.
23. Susan Cannon Harris, *Gender and Modern Irish Drama* (Bloomington: Indiana University Press, 2002), 3.
24. Ibid., 58.
25. Yeats, *Cathleen Ní Houlihan*, 214.
26. Ibid., 230.
27. Marina Warner, *Monuments and Maidens: The Allegory of the Female Form* (New York: Atheneum, 1985), 12.
28. David Cairns and Shaun Richards, "Tropes and Traps: Aspects of 'Woman' and Nationality in Twentieth-Century Irish Drama," in *Gender in Irish Writing*, ed. Toni O'Brien Johnson and David Cairns (Philadelphia: Open University Press, 1991), 130–31.
29. Mary E. L. Butler, *Irishwomen and the Home Language*, Gaelic League Pamphlet (Dublin: 1900), 3.
30. Warner, *Monuments and Maidens*, 12.

Germanification, Cultural Mission, Holocaust
Theatre in Łódź during World War II

—ANSELM HEINRICH

During World War II, the "war in the East," or the *Weltanschauungskrieg* ("war of ideologies"), as the Nazis termed it, was intended to go beyond previous military conflicts.[1] Apart from military and economic objectives, this war was about *Lebensraum*, about acquiring new territories for the "Germanic master race," about the brutal and lasting reshaping of Eastern Europe. As part of this reshaping, "the Nazis conducted a cultural campaign in which theatre…was a major component." This campaign was intended to illustrate serious commitment to the newly acquired territories and their inhabitants.[2]

The Warthegau, a *Reichgau* (a subdivision in an area annexed by Nazi Germany) in central Poland was one such region being incorporated into the Reich. The fact that its German minority was relatively small made it even more important in the eyes of Nazi propagandists to subject the region to a sustained program of "Germanification," in which theatre played a crucial role.[3] The region's industrial powerhouse, Łódź, was Poland's third largest city with a population of 680,095, and in September 1939 it became the "most Easterly major city in Adolf Hitler's Reich." Here, the Nazis intended to "erect a bulwark of German culture in the East based on the unshakeable belief in the victorious and continuing existence of the Third Reich."[4] A central part of this "bulwark" was the foundation of a lavishly funded municipal theatre for the rising German-speaking minority, an undertaking high on the agenda of the Nazi propaganda machine. More than other art forms, the theatre was called upon to encourage "German character [to] flourish" in the East. District president Friedrich Uebelhoer charged artistic director Hans Hesse and his staff with the "consolidation and stabilization" of German traditions and the fostering of German culture. Fittingly for this purpose, the opening production by the *Theater der Stadt Lodsch* ("Lodsch" was the German version of Łódź's name until the Nazis renamed the city "Litzmannstadt") was a German classic: Gotthold Ephraim Lessing's *Minna von Barnhelm*. On occasion of its premiere on January 13, 1940, Mayor Schiffer claimed that the city, which had been founded by the "industriousness and ability" of German merchants over a hundred years ago, was now (rightfully) returning into German hands, after having suffered from an "inorganic and racially inferior" character due to the "influx of a quarter of a million Jews" and "conscious neglect by the Polish state."[5] The theatre, therefore, was suddenly expected to shoulder a responsibility beyond the immediate need to entertain audiences; it also played a crucial role in changing the character of city and region to exemplify the success of the occupiers' wider cultural and political mission. In fact, the success of this mission in the Warthegau was in small measure dependent on the triumph of Łódź's prestigious new German theatre.

In this article I discuss the short history of the German language theatre in Łódź (Lodsch/Litzmannstadt) during World War II and evaluate to what extent the Nazis were able to turn it into a success. I investigate the Nazis' undertakings in quantitative and qualitative terms by looking at attendance figures, funding, and infrastructure, as well as the attempt to produce the "right" kind of repertoire—uplifting, serious, and *völkisch*. (The term "völkisch" derives from the German word *Volk* [people]. It has strong nationalistic, racial, romantic, and folkloric undertones, which, in its emphasising of the "Blood and Soil" idea, combine with an antiurban populism. The völkisch movement was also characterized by anticommunist, anti-immigration, anticapitalist, antiparliamentarian and particularly strong antisemitic undercurrents.) The existing research has largely failed to acknowledge the importance of the arts in the Germanification of large parts of Eastern Europe during the war. Łódź as one of its main urban centers was crucial to this undertaking and thus deserves attention.[6]

Occupation

On September 9, 1939, German forces occupied Łódź, eight days after Nazi Germany's invasion of Poland. Within a few months the whole region was branded *Reichsgau Wartheland* and incorporated into the "Greater German Empire." The city was renamed Litzmannstadt in honor of a German general Litzmann who fought there during World War I, and it was one of the biggest ghettos (for

Jews) in Eastern Europe. Over the following years the Germans tried to establish Łódź as a predominantly German city,[7] expelled parts of the Polish and Jewish population (90,000 Jews and Poles by the end of 1939), and attempted to replace them with Germans. By the end of the war some 400,000 Germans from within Germany (*Reichsdeutsche*) and a further 600,000 Germans from across Europe (*Volksdeutsche*) were resettled in the Warthegau. Theatre played a major role in promoting Germanification in the city. Uebelhoer claimed in September 1940: "To foster German culture is one of our chief purposes in the German East. German theatre art in particular as one of its chief expressions (and represented here by the municipal theatre) is called upon to allow German national traditions, which have been suppressed before, to blossom again and to award this region with the cultural character it deserves."[8] Money was being poured into Litzmannstadt's theatrical undertakings, providing substantial prestige for the Germans. Properties, scenery, and costumes were bought, new staff hired, the theatre building upgraded, and an elaborate system of advertising instigated. The theatre had its own operetta and ballet ensembles, the newly founded professional municipal orchestra was at its disposal, and in early 1942 the city opened a second venue for theatrical entertainment, the *Kammerspiele* (studio) in General Litzmann Street (the so-called *Sängerhaus*). Later that year a dance school associated with the playhouse was founded, and during the 1943–1944 season, the theatre introduced grand opera. In a few years' time the cultural landscape of the city had changed substantially.

Łódź developed into a predominantly Polish city following the departure of sizeable Russian and German minorities by 1918.[9] After the German occupation during World War II, members of the Polish majority became second-class citizens dominated by their German oppressors.[10] The demands on the theatre were clear in this context. It was expected to provide the rising German population with the relevant cultural and propagandistic "ammunition" to establish and assert itself in the "German East."

Germanisierung

Even the German occupiers admitted—albeit only in internal papers—that Łódź was not and never had been a German city—neither politically nor culturally.[11] Nevertheless, the drive to make Łódź German was immediately obvious and carried through with a conviction, brutality, and speed that stunned the Polish population. Although the files of the civic authorities (which have largely survived the war) were written in a matter-of-fact style and used typical administrative jargon, they display some of the occupiers' broadly held beliefs. What shines through is a deep feeling of superiority communicated by a chosen elite who feel justified in colonizing the "wild East."[12] These attitudes were played out in the public arena immediately and without any hint of sensitivity—not even against the German minority who had largely lived peacefully alongside the Polish population and whose German name of the city, Lodsch, was entirely disregarded and only used for the first few months of the occupation. Instead, the name Litzmannstadt was conjured up, even though it had no historical roots there and was forced on the city in April 1940 on Hitler's direct order.[13] The aggressiveness of the occupiers was also illustrated by the name changes for streets. Apart from the new Hermann Göring, Rudolf Hess, General Litzmann, Dietrich Eckart, and Schlageter Streets, even the world famous Łódź thoroughfare Piotrkowska was renamed Adolf Hitler Street.

Turning Łódź into a German city, however, did not stop at name-changes for streets. By early 1940, the Nazis had detailed plans for a massive building program. The city's senior planning officer Wilhelm Hallbauer produced a report on "spatial issues in Lodsch," which he sent to different Reich ministries. One of the driving forces for the building plans was that the Germans considered the quality of housing in Łódź to be unacceptable to them.[14] Their suggestions for changes were radical. The city's main railway station was to be moved from the east to the west of the city, all manufacturing was to be moved to the outskirts (a substantial part of the city's manufacturing base was located in the city center or nearby), and the Polish population was to be moved out of the city center and "crammed into other bits of the former city." The planners intended to build a whole new suburb for the incoming German population toward the west of the new railway station, which was to house "approximately 25,000 people," and for which entire areas needed to be torn down. Plans quickly evolved and *Gauleiter* (Regional Director) Greiser soon suggested that the new suburb should hold up to 100,000 people. A new main road "of two kilometers length" would connect the railway station with the old city center. At the one end of this new axis were the city chambers and a new building for the National Workers' Association (*Arbeitsfront*), and at the other a massive new "People's Hall" (*Volkshalle*) for 12,000 people. Figures and plans seem to have been changed almost at will and without any consideration for the existing infrastructure and the residents involved. Even planning experts in Berlin, not normally known for their modest approach to town planning, were baffled and suggested to Greiser that he might want to consult the German railways first before moving railway stations around.[15] Greiser and his team, however, had already started substantial building, and widespread demolition in inner-city districts had begun at the end of 1939. New inhabitants from the Reich were tempted into the city, and companies were lured to the East with promises that they would be able reinvest profits made in the Reich free of taxes in the Warthegau region.[16]

The official statistics looked impressive: while the city's overall population decreased, the German minority rose steadily from 80,000 in 1939, to 129,000 in 1942, and to 135,000 in 1943.[17] The percentage of Germans in the wider Warthegau region had increased similarly from 6.6 percent in 1939 to almost 23 percent in 1944.[18] Monthly statistical reports documented Litzmannstadt's radical development in order to illustrate it as a "success" story for local, regional, and national authorities. The reports also reflected tremendous growth—in electricity and gas consumption, in the number of people owning a radio or a car, in the number of people using the trams and saving their money at the Sparkasse bank, and in the number of books in the city library and in their circulation. In April 1942 Litzmannstadt had twelve cinemas with 7,000 seats and monthly audiences of around 335,000.[19] New city guides were needed for this expanding "German" city, and the official *Publikationsstelle Berlin-Dahlem* was quick to commission new publications.[20] In 1942 the German UFA film company even produced a feature-length propaganda film entitled *Łódź Turns into Litzmannstadt* (*Aus Łódź wird Litzmannstadt*) written by Hans F. Wilhelm, to document the radical transformation.[21] It almost seemed as if the German occupiers wanted to found an entirely new city, a fortress against the "uncivilized hordes in the East," an outpost of German culture.[22] The large ghetto toward the north of the city center did not play any part in the planning exercises, although by 1942 it housed almost 250,000 people. Corresponding to the Nazis' fondness for euphemisms, the ghetto was almost exclusively referred to as *Litzmannstadt Nord*, as if it were a suburb like all others.[23]

The Arts

From the beginning, the arts played a crucial part in what the Nazis perceived as their cultural "crusade" in the new Litzmannstadt. The exhibition *German Art in the East* (*Deutsche Kunst im Ostraum*), which took place from late 1940 to early 1941 in the city's art museum, is just one example of how closely linked art and politics were supposed to be.[24] Newly found institutions such as the *Deutsches Volksbildungswerk / Volksbildungsstätte Litzmannstadt* (the Center for Public Education) or the events organized by the *Kreiskulturring*, as well as the municipal office for cultural affairs (*Städtisches Kulturamt*), acted as additional means to create and foster a distinctly German cultural community. Events were held entirely in German (Polish citizens were not even admitted) and often featured guests from the *Altreich* (Germany's 1939 borders) or international stars. Concerts organized by the *Kreiskulturring* between 1942 and 1944, for example, featured conductors, soloists, and ensembles from Berlin, Hamburg, Vienna, and Rome, and soloists included such internationally renowned stars as the pianist Wilhelm Kempff or the violinist Wolfgang Schneiderhan, and conductors such as Eugen Jochum and Count Hidemaro Konoye from Japan.[25] In the summer of 1943, the *Volksbildungsstätte Litzmannstadt* organized approximately ten events per month and offered language classes, lectures, screenings, and concerts. Their work was deemed particularly important, as it promised to bring together Germans who had already lived in Łódź before 1939 and the new arrivals, as Gauleiter Greiser claimed. Mayor Werner Ventzki summed up what German popular education meant during this war. The main goal of the *Volksbildungsarbeit* was "to communicate to all German nationals the knowledge about the national treasures and cultural assets the war was being fought over. The better you know your nation's language, history, and culture, the more you will be steeped in its importance and its historical mission. At the same time you will be able to appreciate that this war is being fought for nothing less than the eternal safeguarding of everything German."[26] Also in the summer of 1943, a series of big sporting events raised money for the *Winterhelfswerk* (winter relief organization) with soccer games, children's parties, parachute show jumping, gymnastics, cycling, boxing, and swimming. These events were accompanied by a cultural program as well.[27] Overall, the amount of money spent on cultural affairs in general was staggering: Litzmannstadt received its own professional municipal symphony orchestra, as well as a municipal music school and a new dance college attached to the civic theatre. Further plans included a Museum of Natural Science, a Museum of Anthropology, a Museum for Science and the Arts, and a number of art galleries.[28]

Before the German occupation, however, and contrary to Nazi claims, Łódź had been anything but a cultural desert. It boasted a rich and multilingual performance tradition with subsidized theatres, variety playhouses, and circuses featuring performances in Polish, Russian, German, and Hebrew. The city's three main playhouses, *Teatr Miejski*, *Teatr Polski*, and *Teatr Popularny*, produced popular entertainment as well as more challenging fare. The municipal *Teatr Miejski*, for example, staged elaborate productions with professional actors in a repertoire consisting not only of Polish plays but also plays by Shaw, Scribe, Sardou, Shakespeare, Schiller, Galsworthy, Strindberg, Hauptmann, Ibsen, and Gogol.[29] For the years 1934, 1935, and 1936 the theatre produced an average of 400 performances annually with rising attendance figures reaching 152,000 in

1936.[30] During the 1938–1939 season the *Teatr Miejski* employed two artistic directors, seven directors and producers, nine administrative staff, one dramaturge (*doradca literacki*), and no fewer than fifty-five actors.[31] This was a major theatre and, judging from its size alone, one that could have rivaled almost any municipal playhouse in Germany.

Despite later Nazi claims to the contrary, the German-speaking minority largely appreciated the work done by the Polish language theatre. For example, on the occasion of the retirement of Kazimierz Wroczyński (who had been the director of the Teatr Miejski between 1923 and 1925 and again between 1933 and 1939), the German newspaper *Neue Lodzer Zeitung* on behalf of the German *Verein der Theaterfreunde in Łódź* extended "cordial words of farewell," stating that "Wroczyński has made a great contribution to Lodz's theatrical life… Although he suffered a financial fiasco this is not really his fault but is due to the particular situation in Lodz and a general atmosphere which is not conducive to producing great theatrical art."[32] Only three months later, the city was occupied by German forces amid claims it was in desperate need of artistic renewal after years of cultural neglect.

Foundation of the German-Language Municipal Theatre in Łódź

Łódź was not unlike many other conquered cities across Europe where the German occupiers sought to erect their own theatres as a sign of confidence, commitment, and permanence. After a number of guest performances by the ensemble of the Breslau municipal theatre in autumn 1939, the German language *Theater der Stadt Lodsch* opened its doors in January 1940.[33] It was situated in Moltkestraße, off the main thoroughfare *Piotrkowska* in central Łódź, and seated 747 people. The opening production was performed by the German language theatre company of the Baltic city of Reval on January 13, 1940, and it was this company under the direction of Hans Hesse that became Litzmannstadt's standing theatre ensemble.

So far this account of events suggests a straightforward and planned development that Nazi propagandists were able to use to their advantage. Looking behind the scenes proves more complex. The files reveal that in the weeks and months preceding the opening performance, chaos reigned. Immediately after the German occupation of Łódź, it seemed as if the existing German amateur dramatic society (*Thalia Theater-Verein*) would continue to offer theatrical entertainment. Then, in mid-October, a newspaper article promised an "immediate re-opening" of a German theatre, but gave no indication as to when this might happen and whether this would be a receiving or a standing theatre. The Breslau company was then invited to give a number of guest performances, and by the end of October a municipal theatre seemed in the offing—but not growing out of the local *Thalia* ensemble. This group, instead, was given no role in the future developments apart from the thankless task of "supplying the new theatre with a substantial audience." On December 7 the press suddenly announced that a contract with the Reval company under Hans Hesse had been signed, and that (despite the fact that the beginning of the season was as yet unconfirmed) "the artists will be arriving in Łódź tomorrow morning."[34] This abrupt turn of events surprised not only the city's population, but the regional authorities as well. On December 8, Hesse asked the regional propaganda office in Poznań (Posen) to book hotel accommodations for the whole troupe and announced that rehearsals would start immediately. Vossler, head of the regional propaganda office, had not previously been informed about the arrival of the company and sent a furious telefax to his superiors in the Berlin Propaganda Ministry the next day asking for clarification. Vossler had no idea where the company would be going to perform; he did not even know where to put them up.[35] Łódź's new cultural dawn could hardly have been more chaotic.

After the theatre opened in January 1940, local, regional, and national authorities closely monitored it and were keen to receive notes of successes; of particular concern were repertoire and attendance figures. Hesse constantly reminded the German-speaking population that going to the theatre was an obligation for every good German—most clearly expressed by buying a season ticket. These "reminders," however, tended to be far from subtle. In fact, potential patrons were almost bullied into fulfilling their "obligation." After all, it was supposed to be their duty to play their part in the expansion of German culture in the East.[36] At the of the 1941–1942 season, for example, the theatre's management published a special edition of the program notes, which not only contained a review of the season about to conclude, but also featured a preview of the 1942–1943 season in connection with an "invitation" to take out a season ticket.[37] Łódź city archives still hold seven issues of this special program note—indicative of its print run, for the entire city administration seems to have been flooded with these flyers—sometimes even several times. The office for cultural affairs exerted substantial pressure on colleagues in other departments by distributing circulars that staff members had to sign.

What is noteworthy in connection with these program notes is that they looked strikingly similar to those of other German theatres at the time. They featured advertisements by local (German) businesses, photos of members of the ensembles, theatre anecdotes and biographies, dramaturgical pieces concerning particular productions (and largely written by the theatre's chief dramaturge), articles concerning the theatre's history, inserts with the week's repertoire, and, last but not least, a substantial political section. This section featured statements and sometimes whole speeches by leading politicians, as well as photos both of national, regional, and local party representatives. After the opening of the theatre in early 1940 until the beginning of the 1940–1941 season, program notes appeared quite spartan; from September 1940 onward, however, they were much more elaborate and grand both in quantitative and qualitative terms, which seemed only fitting for an important outpost of Germanic culture in the East.[38] The programs increasingly reported on the activities of similar stages in annexed and occupied territories and featured articles concerning the activities of theatre companies operating behind the front lines. Throughout Germany at large, the political tone of the programs diminished over the course of the war.[39] What remained was an emphasis on the canonical classical literature with many articles on Goethe, Schiller, and Grabbe, among others.

The image of the German artist who is fighting the same war as the German soldier but with different means—an ideal frequently referred to by Hitler and Goebbels and a popular motif in paintings and sculpture—seemed to ring true in the East. It was a message, too, that was constantly hammered home by cultural politicians, practitioners, and party leaders in occupied Eastern Europe. In a special program note published just before the 1940–1941 season, dramaturge Hanns Merck claimed that even in wartime, theatre performed a special role in Germany.[40] Actors eagerly followed in the footsteps of the soldiers and moved into the captured emplacements. Their mission was not an entirely artistic one anymore but had become political. These artists were charged to foster the German national spirit in the conquered territories. In Łódź, Merck went on to claim, "in this Polish Manchester, hitherto a dirty city of obtrusive Jewish character, they are faced with particular circumstances." The theatre, therefore, was not only meant to be an expression of the superior German culture that had rightfully occupied Eastern Europe; it was also charged with uplifting, encouraging, and equipping the German minority population with the necessary ammunition to continue a different struggle once the army had moved on. The German minority was also asked to educate those Germans moving to Łódź, for example from the Baltic, who had not been exposed to German culture before. It was, therefore, not only the theatre, which had a particular political function to fulfil in Łódź, but also its audience.

ANSELM HEINRICH

Repertoire, Audiences, Funding

To successfully play its role in the propaganda war, the choice of a heroic, Germanic, and uplifting repertoire was crucial. Mayor Schiffer demanded that "the German theatre in Lodsch must develop into a fortress of German spirit and German culture here in the east of the Reich." The press was equally ecstatic—and equally demanding: "It is a matter of course for a German theatre, which has to fulfil such an important cultural mission, that only those dramatic works can be considered which are products of a truly German mind." Hesse was happy to oblige, and claimed that the theatre had a central role to play in the Germanification of Łódź: "The actors and their artistic director had to defeat the Polish-Jewish heritage first before being able to approach the world of poetry. They carried out pioneering work, like everyone else who arrived at Łódź in 1939, in order to turn a city with a substantial German population in former central Poland into a truly German city."[41] The missionary function of the theatre seemed best served by focusing on the classical dramatic canon. Not surprisingly, the theatre produced Shakespeare's dramas (*Measure for Measure*, *As You Like It*, *Hamlet* [as late as November 1943]) as well as works by Friedrich Schiller (*The Robbers, Wallenstein's Camp, Don Carlos*), Heinrich von Kleist (*The Broken Jug*), Gotthold Ephraim Lessing (*Emilia Galotti*), and Friedrich Hebbel (*Maria Magdalena*). The theatre performed Johann Wolfgang von Goethe's epic *Faust I* in a production staged seven times in ten days in late April and early May 1943.[42] Apart from the classics, the theatre also incorporated nationalistic and *völkisch* plays into its repertoire—plays that were particularly supported by the Propaganda Ministry. In May 1942 the theatre produced Eberhard Wolfgang Möllers's *Das Opfer* (*The Victim*), a production accompanied by intense media coverage,[43] as well as Hermann Burte's *Katte* and Felix Dhünen's *Uta von Naumburg*.

In a typical week, April 12–19, 1942, the theatre offered fourteen productions at its two venues, the main house theatre and the studio. Apart from a dance production by its own ballet ensemble (which was performed three times during this week), the theatre offered Shakespeare's *Measure for Measure* (four performances), three contemporary comedies by Waldemar Frank, Heinz Steguweit, and Felix Lützkendorf (with four performances between them), and two operettas (three performances)[44]—a respectable showing, one might think. The theatre seemed to take its cultural mission seriously. In October 1943, the theatre premiered Emmerich Nuß's comedy *Dissonances*. Hesse faxed the Leipzig publishers of this play afterward to relay the happy news that it had been a huge success and "received 28 curtain calls at the end." As late as November 1943 the theatre offered a "week of premieres" with four different plays.[45]

In addition to the "correct" choice of repertoire, audience figures were of vital importance. The popular success of its theatre was crucial for the Nazi regime, and records in attendance figures were constantly used in its propaganda. Failing to attract large audiences would not only have contradicted claims of a true "national theatre" (*Volkstheater*), but would also have compared unfavorably to the years prior to the German occupation when, according to the Nazi propaganda, audiences had been pitiful. To attract the desired record attendances, the theatre offered a mix of individually sold tickets, season tickets, block bookings, and reductions for particular groups (members of the armed forces were admitted at prices reduced by 30 or 40 percent). Block bookings were offered to organizations such as *Kraft durch Freude* (*Strength through Joy*— which offered eight different schemes of block bookings to its members), the police force, the city administration, the postal service, the job center, the state railway, the Hitler Youth and other party organizations, and national offices such as the customs authority, the board of trade, and the revenue office. There were also closed performances for injured soldiers and for schools.[46] The system of reductions and concessions was so widespread, in fact, that the ordinary full ticket prices, which ranged from Reichsmark (RM) 0.70 to RM 4.50, were hardly ever paid by anyone. But income, even profit, seemed a secondary concern in this system; more important was the fact that the theatre managed to draw in the crowds.

Crucially for the city's cultural ambitions, theatre audiences did indeed rise. Between 1941 and 1942 the increase was close to 30 percent. Utilization reached 80 percent, and at closed performances even over 90 percent.[47] In the first half of 1942 the theatre seemed to have turned a corner with monthly audiences averaging 25,000. The newly opened studio (*Kammerspiele*, seating capacity of 479), which unashamedly and almost exclusively concentrated on light-hearted fare, completed an increasingly successful picture for the Nazi propaganda—at least in terms of quantity. During the first half of 1942 the studio presented an average of twelve shows per month, attracting some 5,000 patrons.[48] In the same season, the theatre management introduced operetta to its portfolio, which further increased its popularity. In early 1942 operetta performances achieved ticket sales of 93 percent,[49] and in late 1942 the theatre was operating at near capacity. In October, it staged fifty-six performances, in December sixty-four, and it reached monthly audiences of up to 35,000.[50] Although slightly lower, audience figures in late 1943 generally held up with utilizations of well over 80 percent.[51] Overall, audiences rose from 190,000 in 1940–1941 to almost 300,000 in the last two seasons, and the number of performances went up from 330 to 572 in the same timeframe.[52]

Without its elaborate system of closed performances and concessions, however, the theatre would never have attracted these record numbers. For example, during February 1941 (a typical month) the theatre offered one classical drama, one contemporary drama, and five comedies. Out of thirty-one performances, twenty were reserved as closed performances (eight of which were for KdF [*Kraft durch Freude*: "Strength through Joy"], but also for the armed forces, SA [*Sturmabteilung*: "Storm Troopers"], Hitler Youth, police, the women's association [*Frauenschutzbund*], and city administration). Out of overall audiences of 17,500, closed performances accounted for 13,500.[53]

For the purpose of securing these audiences, the new theatre was generously funded out of municipal, regional, and national funds. The municipal subsidy rose substantially from RM 562,000 in 1941 to RM 831,000 in 1942. Moreover, Litzmannstadt received substantial sums from the central government. This was unusual, as most civic theatres in Germany were almost exclusively subsidized out of municipal pots. In fact, this decentralization was a hallmark of the German arts funding system. The theatres in the "German east" were different, though. Here, it was not only city councils that paid substantial amounts of money but also regional and national authorities. Already in late January 1940, for example, Mayor Schiffer asked the Propaganda Ministry for almost RM 60,000 as a contribution toward the costs of running the theatre. And he did not ask for the money politely—he demanded it ("transfer the money as soon as possible"). It seems that the city's officials knew full well that they were in a strong position when it came to financial support from Berlin, due in particular to Litzmannstadt's status as a "beacon" of German culture in the East—a model city. By March 1940 the theatre's renovation had already cost RM 105,000 (paid for by the city) and another RM 230,000 was needed from elsewhere. Schiffer declared that for 1940/41 the overall theatre budget was going to be RM 600,000, and that he hoped ministry and region (*Gau*) would contribute RM 200,000 each.[54] In September 1940 Schiffer asked for a subsidy of RM 250,000 from the Propaganda Ministry, a sum of previously unheard of proportions, and less than a month later he received the notification that the ministry was prepared to pay the full amount.[55] Still, the hole in the theatre's budget grew. Between September 1940 and late March 1941 the theatre was in the red by a staggering RM 553,000. Undeterred, city officials kept asking for more. For 1942 they wanted an increase in national subsidies of 100 percent, RM 400,000 instead of the already generous RM 200,000 they had received the year previously. Additionally, they asked for RM 300,000 for a new theatre building. The head of the Reich theatre chamber within the Propaganda Ministry, Rainer Schlösser, cautioned Reich Minister of Propaganda Joseph Goebbels against these enormous sums, and the annual subsidy remained at RM 200,000, but Goebbels agreed to contribute RM 150,000 from a "special fund" to the building costs. This means that the theatre in Litzmannstadt in 1942 received a phenomenal RM 350,000 in Reich subsidies. The other theatres in the region were equally pampered. The main theatre in Poznań (the *Gautheater Posen*) in 1941 received RM 400,000, and the traveling ensemble of the *Landesbühne Gau Wartheland* was in receipt of RM 50,000. It may not be surprising that Litzmannstadt's administration got carried away. In December 1942 Mayor Ventzki wrote to ask for a Reich subsidy of RM 450,000 for 1943. These sums proved too much for the Propaganda Ministry, who paid RM 170,000 in 1943—still a substantial sum, however.[56]

Parallel to rising subsidies for the current theatre operation, the city planned for a brand new theatre building, particularly as the existing theatre building was inadequate for the staging of grand opera. A site was acquired in 1941, the project reached the planning stage at the end of that year, and construction seems to have started soon after that.[57] The new theatre apparently made use of an older structure (in the vicinity of the existing playhouse on Moltke street). The new building was never finished, however; only the shell construction was finished in 1943. However, on July 1, 1943, work on the site was halted as the building project was no longer deemed of strategic importance for the duration of the war.[58]

In terms of personnel, the theatre was equally spoiled, and its staffing numbers were quickly brought up to a level comparable to those in theatres in any large German city. At the beginning of the 1940–1941 season, the company consisted of twenty-nine actors, one artistic director, one scene designer, two dramaturges, three directors, one conductor, one costume designer, and two administrative staff members. At the end of the following season, in July 1942, the theatre's size had increased substantially. At a time when many German theatres had to cut down in size and and save resources in view of the war effort, the Litzmannstadt theatre continued to grow. Management and senior artistic staff comprised sixteen people, and in addition there were another thirteen staff members in administration, forty-eight actors, twenty singers in the theatre's own professional chorus, fourteen dancers plus an associated dance school, and nine technical staff members.[59] In August 1940 Litzmannstadt received its own fully funded municipal orchestra for the first time in the city's history—another propaganda coup for the regime, or so it seemed, particularly as the Nazis consistently claimed that the city's musical life during the 1930s had been characterized by "popular music of Jewish-Polish-American persuasion."[60] The new musical director, Adolf Bautze, now headed a professional orchestra of fifty-two (which soon afterward reached its full capacity of eighty-five musicians), playing a series of symphony concerts alongside the musical provision for the theatre. The orchestra, too, was in receipt of municipal as well as Reich subsidies that rose to RM 100,000 in 1943.[61] In 1944—after opera had been added to the theatre's repertoire—the theatre still employed twenty-three actors, fifteen opera soloists, thirty chorus members, eleven dancers, plus a municipal orchestra of fifty musicians, three conductors, one pianist, and two chorus coaches.[62] In fact, the theatre's size compared favorably to some of the more established municipal theatres, and toward the end of the war it outstripped many of them.[63]

Salaries, too, compared favorably to other regional German theatres—and they rose exponentially within a very short period of time. When the theatre opened in January 1940, the average monthly salary of the actors was RM 350.[64] Half a year later the average salary had risen to almost RM 500,[65] while during the 1941–1942 season the average salary for an actor had risen to RM 600, and some of the soloists in the musical theatre received up to RM 1,400.[66] On top of this increase, every employee received allowances and extra payments (including a so-called "development bonus"), which could amount to up to RM 100 extra per month.[67] At the Westphalian theatre of Bielefeld, for example, a typical monthly salary for an actor at the same time was just RM 365, half of what their colleagues in Litzmannstadt earned.[68] Overall salary costs for actors, singers, and musicians rocketed from RM 200,000 in 1940 to RM 666,000 in 1942—more than some Reich theatres received as their total annual subsidy.[69]

However, rising subsidies did not go unnoticed in the general public, particularly in a city where living conditions were significantly below the national average and money was desperately needed to improve infrastructure, quality of housing, and local amenities. As if to counter the criticism, the theatre's program notes featured an article by A. E. Frauenfeld, who justified municipal expenditure on theatres.[70] Frauenfeld claimed that having a publicly funded civic theatre was a major asset for any city and had a substantial economic impact. To illustrate the value he proposed to look at a hypothetical case—a municipal theatre in a city of 100,000, with a capacity of 1,000, 150 staff, and a budget of RM 500,000, of which "between a third and half would be paid by the city as subsidies." Assuming a realization of 70 percent (which seemed realistic) he arrived at annual audiences of 300,000—a substantial figure apparently intended to convince even the staunchest Philistine of the importance of a publicly funded theatre. Even aside from the fact that this model did not discuss the repertoire (as we have seen, a crucial issue in Litzmannstadt) there are two problems with it: first, the sum of RM 500,000 was quickly outstripped as funding needs rocketed out of control, and second, the theatre was never able to make up 50 percent (or even 30 percent) of its financial needs itself; the income generated by the box office was significantly lower. Therefore, both civic and national funding was substantially higher.

Despite the changing fortunes for Nazi Germany as the war went on and the front drew nearer, Litzmannstadt's theatre continued to be in receipt of substantial subsidies and performed its propagandistic role. Looking ahead to the 1943–1944 season, Hesse boasted about the successful *Faust* production mentioned above, which would compare favorably to the best the big Reich theatres had to offer.[71] In addition he planned three world premieres for the 1943–1944 season, for which a poster was designed to attract season ticket holders.[72]

Overall, the statistics are staggering. In spring and early summer 1944 the studio presented an average of twenty shows and attracted monthly attendances of 10,000—double what they were two years prior. In June 1944, the municipal theatre still staged twenty-five performances that attracted some 15,000 people.[73] The cultural propaganda seemed to have worked, and the Nazis had made their theatre a success.

Problems and Inconsistencies

Despite the grand proclamations, however, a closer look particularly at the theatre's early period reveals that it only achieved "a fraction of what it had hoped and planned for."[74] It was clear that despite the bold announcements, the theatre's first few months had not fulfilled the high expectations. As if to buoy himself and his colleagues, dramaturge Hanns Merck announced that at least they had made a start—only a small consolation given the function this playhouse was meant to fulfill both to educate the German population and to stand as a bastion of German culture in the East. At the beginning and well into summer 1940, audiences had been dismal. After a bleak January monthly audiences peaked at 17,000 in February but after that fell consistently to below 9,000 in June.[75] This was a disaster, both in terms of their own expectations but also, more importantly, in comparison to audiences attracted by the former Polish municipal theatre. The *Teatr Miejski* had achieved almost three times these figures in the preceding year.[76]

Even more problematic in relation to the theatre's grandiose claims was the reality in terms of its repertoire. Contrary to expectations of a high art program dominated by classical drama and serious political plays in order to cultivate the city and educate its population, the fare actually produced at Litzmannstadt was quite pedestrian. As the theatre was under close scrutiny by party officials and cultural politicians, its dramaturge was at pains to justify its mundane repertoire: "In Litzmannstadt it is important to reach out to audiences, who are partly still negotiating their way in a new environment, which so far has been largely alien to German theatre. [The theatre, therefore,] has to offer a mixed fare, and one which is palatable to people of every age, every class; personnel who are only temporarily stationed here and people who have moved here from all areas of the Greater German Empire."[77] Merck's comments are a desperate attempt to defend a choice of program that increasingly relied on light entertainment and avoided the classical canon as too heavy. In April 1942, for example, the *völkisch* drama *Uta von Naumburg* by Felix Dhünen sold only 362 tickets, and Shakespeare's *Measure for Measure* attracted only 101 patrons its first night.[78] The failure of the *völkisch* repertoire in particular hurt cultural politicians. Almost none of the officially celebrated new political drama was produced in Litzmannstadt—no plays by the German playwrights Hanns Johst (the Nazi Poet Laureate), Siegmund Graff, Ernst Bacmeister, Curt Langenbeck, Paul Ernst, or Hans Bethge.[79] Even worse was the dichotomy between high demands and actual output concerning the studio theatre, which, according to announcements by the theatre management on the occasion of its opening, was envisaged to stage the classics in particular.[80] This classical canon, however, was nowhere to be found on the studio's stages.

Local commentators were shocked. The theatre critic of the *Litzmannstädter Zeitung*, Gustav Röttger, did not buy Merck's desperate attempts to sell the focus on entertainment as part of the "education process" in a largely uncivilized Eastern city. "Endowed with substantial sums out of municipal pockets the theatre has become everyone's friend due to some good achievements. In future, the goal will be, above all, to look after the dramatic ensemble and repertoire. It has to become a bulwark of the German character, a site of great art, which, far exposed in the East, can never only entertain, but must become presentable and prestigious in a way which it is not quite at the moment."[81] Not surprisingly, city officials were not amused, either, and in their voluminous 1943 administrative report reminded everyone of the theatre's function: "Since Schiller and Richard Wagner we appreciate the importance of the theatre as a national place of education and culture. In the *Litzmannstadt* region good theatre more than anything is called upon to fulfil this function and to become the enunciator of German art and spirit."[82] The report made it clear that the theatre must not become a "place of sheer amusement or superficial interests." And then, at the end of this long preamble the report stated that Litzmannstadt's theatre "on the whole" moved "in the right direction"—hardly a ringing endorsement.[83]

The reasons for the meager attendance at productions of classical drama were manifold, but their poor quality seems to have been one of the prime causes. Concerning the production of Goethe's *Urfaust*, for example, the press stated that the actors "tried very hard to give their best," which when it comes to press reviews in Nazi Germany is pretty close to calling it a failure.[84] And despite Shakespeare plays being regular features in the repertoire, their performances must have been dismal. City officials arrived at the conclusion that "for Shakespeare the time has not yet come in Litzmannstadt"—a damning verdict.[85] But it was not only the classical canon that proved problematic. Even allegedly less demanding pieces, for example, Max Halbe's *Strom* (*Stream*), failed—and even under the direction of Hesse himself. The actors had performed "as best they could" and excelled in those parts that "did not require too much intellectual depth."[86] Commentators criticized the theatre for avoiding the serious contemporary repertoire and asserted that—contrary to claims by the theatre management—Litzmannstadt audiences did not "necessarily demand lightweight plays."[87]

Issues of artistic standards and quality also concerned the municipal orchestra. It quickly dawned on local cultural politicians that large subsidies did not necessarily translate into great performances. The official 1943 administrative report, for example, certified the orchestra's "diligent work." Musical director Bautze, too, did not seem to have been a successful choice, and several official reports mention that he had only conducted choirs before.[88] Not surprisingly, the theatre's first attempts at opera during the 1942–1943 season attracted a lukewarm reception. Puccini's *Tosca* was "noteworthy" and as an experiment "quite successful."[89]

Concerning ticket sales, too, the situation was not as rosy as the propaganda made people believe, particularly in the early years. The weekly balance sheets the theatre had to provide the city administration (and which were not published) are a useful indicator to gauge the popular success of the theatre. The theatre's biggest client in terms of ticket sales was *Kraft durch Freude* (KdF; in English, Strength through Joy), the leisure-time organization that booked whole performances for their members. In a typical week in May 1940, for example, almost half of the weekly takings of RM 1,400 were guaranteed by KdF (RM 600). The theatre, however, faced two problems in connection with this system of block bookings. First, this system put organizations such as KdF in a very strong bargaining position. For example, KdF hardly ever paid their dues on time; in fact they regularly paid only a fraction of what they owed the theatre. Second, the apparent success with large organizations and block bookings disguised that fact that regular box office takings were often abysmal. During the week mentioned above, ticket sales were sometimes as little as RM 150 for an evening performance.[90]

The precarious financial situation did not go unnoticed. As late as February 1944 the National Accounting Office (*Rechnungshof*) carried out an audit to check the proper deployment of national subsidies.[91] The detailed report raised a number of issues and questioned the way the city had recorded income and expenditure in its books; it even considered asking for the repayment of some of these subsidies. The Accounting Office criticized inflated salaries both at the theatre and the orchestra and particularly in view of the immense pressures on the city's finances and the increasing deficits in the theatre's budget. Indeed, some of the honoraria must have raised a few eyebrows among the wider public had they been known. A Berlin guest conductor, for example, who stayed three weeks in Litzmannstadt to conduct *Tosca* and who was asked to write a report to assess whether local audiences were "ready" for grand opera, received the princely sum of RM 4,000, almost three times the monthly salary of Hans Hesse. Although musical director Bautze headed the symphony orchestra, he did not conduct the orchestra when it played in the theatre even though this was common practice at other venues. Instead, the city appointed an additional conductor to conduct musical theatre, although Bautze was "hardly overworked."[92] The orchestra musicians, too, received extra payments on top of their normal salary—something that according to the Accounting Office was not covered by existing employment law. These extra payments were all the more surprising since the orchestra as a whole was hardly on sound financial footing. In 1940, for example, the orchestra's expenditures of RM 246,100 stood in sharp contrast to its box office gross, which only amounted to a meager RM 18,300—in other words, it only managed to recoup 7 percent of the subsidies it received.[93] Interestingly, this discrepancy occurred despite the fact that the orchestra offered a popular program, which avoided too many "difficult" contemporary pieces and should have drawn large crowds. Indeed, the Accounting Office criticized the orchestra's programming, as this did not feature the required number of contemporary orchestral works and largely played it safe. Instead of the required share of 33 percent, *Litzmannstadt*'s orchestra only managed 15 percent. In its report, the National Accounting Office concluded that some key conditions for the national subsidy had not been met and that the municipal authorities should be asked to pay back some of the money, or indeed all of it—a devastating blow to the ambitions of Litzmannstadt's cultural politicians.

Conclusion

To establish a German-speaking theatre in Litzmannstadt was a matter of the highest priority for the German authorities in the Warthegau and beyond. In his "model Gau," Gauleiter Greiser regarded the performing arts as an important "weapon in ethnic struggle," especially highbrow German culture, which he saw as infinitely superior to "gauche Polish entertainment."[94] The sums pumped into Litzmannstadt's theatre both by the municipal authorities and central government were truly astounding. Until late 1944, the theatre was deemed to be operating at the front line of an aggressive Germanification of the city and the wider region. In this respect the demands put on the theatre were almost impossible to achieve. On the one hand, cultural politicians expected a program of classics as well as *völkisch* and nationalistic drama, for which a mass audience proved difficult to find. Two substantial theatre spaces with 479 and 755 seats, respectively, needed to be filled in a city whose German-speaking population even by 1944 was still relatively small. Spaces, too, were far from ideal, with limited views of the stage from some seats, poor heating and drafts, basic performance conditions, and a simple stage technology. On the other hand, the presentation of comedies and farces, which did attract larger audiences, hardly related to political demands. In any case, the municipal authorities closely monitored audience figures, and the city's statistical office was keen to receive monthly balance sheets. It complained if these did not arrive on time and made sure the calculations added up. In the end, and despite the vast amounts of money poured into the venture, the playhouse fell into oblivion after the city's liberation in early 1945. The theatre and its audience had simply gone, and no traces were left. The Polish majority reclaimed and once again dominated the city's culture.[95] The Nazis had clearly failed in their cultural and geopolitical ambitions in Litzmannstadt, despite their reporting to the contrary, and the theatre could be seen as exemplifying this fiasco.

However, concluding on this note of failure is insufficient, as it would mask the real horror. The fact that Litzmannstadt's theatre entertained large audiences with a simple repertoire at bargain prices illustrates the validity of Hannah Arendt's dictum of the "banality of evil."[96] Audiences including SS personnel, *Wehrmacht* servicemen, police and Gestapo staff, members of the ghetto administration, and other people directly involved in the Holocaust enjoyed light entertainment, civilized comedies, and Viennese operetta. They appreciated informative program notes that avoided serious political issues and instead presented theatrical anecdotes, production photos, and inconspicuous adverts for local businesses. The contrast between civilized entertainment and genocide could hardly be starker, yet in Litzmannstadt culture and Holocaust coexisted in close proximity, geographically and ideologically.[97] The grand opening of a new dancing school on September 16, 1942, for example, took place only days after the infamous *Gehsperre Aktion*, during which 12,000 Jews (and in particular children, the elderly, and the infirm) were sent to their deaths in the extermination camp at Chełmno. And in February 1943 Litzmannstadt's municipal theatre presented Ino Wimmer's *Litzmannstädter Bilderbogen* (*A Picture Book from Litzmannstadt*) under the title *Bitte, alles einsteigen!* (*All on Board, Please*) with a tram as a prominent feature in the production.[98] The link to the deportations from Łódź's Radogast (Radogoszcz) train station must have been obvious to the audiences; maybe the intention of this humorous revue was precisely to make light of the connection. The theatre's artistic director proudly announced in summer 1943 that this show, which came across "fresh with local color," had been performed twenty-five times in the studio between February and the close of the season in June.[99] More research is needed in this area, not least to question a discourse that continues to struggle with Arendt's claim. Suzanne Marchand in a 1998 review article, for example, asked whether arts and culture under the Nazis were "banality or barbarism."[100] Such approaches establish a problematic dichotomy and fail to grasp the situation in places like Litzmannstadt where the banal can hardly be separated from the barbaric.

Notes

1. Research for this article was made possible through a research grant from the Royal Society of Edinburgh. I am indebted to Professor Małgorzata Leyko and Dr. Karolina Prykowska-Michalak for their support during my stay in Łódź. Archival research was carried out at the two locations of the Archiwum Państwowe w Łodzi, the German federal archives in Berlin Lichterfelde (BArch) and the University of Łódź. I would like to thank Dr. Elwira Grossman (University of Glasgow) for her comments on an earlier version of this article, and for correcting mistakes in the Polish spelling. Unless otherwise stated, all translations are my own.
2. William Abbey and Katharina Havekamp, "Nazi Performances in the Occupied Territories: The German Theatre in Lille," in *Theatre under the Nazis*, ed. John London (Manchester: Manchester University Press, 2000), 262–63.
3. *Gauleiter* Arthur Greiser envisaged a total transformation of the Warthegau's "infrastructure, architecture, landscape, and public memory" to make it German (Catherine Epstein, *Model Nazi: Arthur Greiser and the Occupation of Western Poland* [Oxford: Oxford University Press, 2010], 231).
4. Mayor Schiffer on the opening night of the German theatre on January 13, 1940

GERMANIFICATION, CULTURAL MISSION, HOLOCAUST

(Archiwum Państwowe w Łodzi, Zbiór Teatraliów Łódzkich 21/58, Programy przedstawień teatralnych teatrów łódzkich z okresu okupacji [1940–1943]), 6.

5. Archiwum Państwowe w Łodzi, Zbiór Teatraliów Łódzkich 21/58, Programy przedstawień teatralnych teatrów łódzkich z okresu okupacji [1940–1943], 6, 23.

6. Małgorzata Leyko's article on Łódź theatre during the Second World War is the only publication on the topic so far, although she does not interpret the theatre in its wider context (Małgorzata Leyko, "Das deutsche Theater in Lodz in den Jahren 1939–1944," in *Polen und Europa. Deutschsprachiges Theater in Polen und deutsches Minderheitentheater in Europa*, ed. Horst Fassel, Małgorzata Leyko, and Paul S. Ulrich [Łódź/Tübinben: University of Lodz Press, 2005], 123–147). Of all the studies of theatre under the Nazis, only Bogusław Drewniak, *Das Theater im NS-Staat. Szenarium deutscher Zeitgeschichte 1933–1945* (Düsseldorf: Droste, 1983) and Hans Daiber, *Schaufenster der Diktatur. Theater im Machtbereich Hitlers* (Stuttgart: Neske, 1995) deal with theatre in occupied territories, but they only mention Łódź in passing—if at all.

7. Even though the demographic mix of Łódź was constantly shifting, the majority of its citizens during the mid-nineteenth century were Germans or people of German origin. In 1839, for example, 80 percent of the population was German, and by 1897 the figure still stood at 40 percent. After the First World War the German population steadily declined.

8. Friedrich Uebelhoer, "Zum Geleit," *Theater zu Litzmannstadt. Spielzeit 1940/41, programme note no. 1*, 2.

9. See Archiwum Państwowe w Łodzi, Akta Miasta Łodzi 28510, 1.

10. The curfew for Polish citizens began at 9 p.m. and lasted until 5 a.m. A German newspaper article applauded: "From 9 p.m. Litzmannstadt is reserved for the Germans!" and its author promised with similar enthusiasm that the ghetto would soon be history. Instead, "in a little while the same tram will travel through well-presented beautiful squares, and nothing will remain of the Getto apart from the memory, some old photographs" (*Litzmannstädter Zeitung*, February 26, 1941).

11. See BArch R55/20389, 26 (letter by Stadtkommissar Schiffer to the propaganda ministry dated February 16, 1940). After the First World War only 7 percent of Łódź's population was German (see Karolina Prykowska-Michalak, "Die deutsche Dilettanttenbühne in Lodz im 20. Jahrhundert," in Fassel, Leyko, and Ulrich, *Polen und Europa*, 114).

12. A detailed 250-page administrative report published in 1943 stressed the "enormous efforts" of the occupiers to establish the arts in an "uncultured" city. The first task was to "eliminate" all the "alien, in particular all Jewish influences" (*Verwaltungsbericht der Stadt Litzmannstadt 1939–42*, Archiwum Państwowe w Łodzi, Akta Miasta Łodzi 28595, 165).

13. The German-language newspaper had difficulty keeping up with all the name changes. Originally named *Freie Presse*, it changed its name to *Deutsche Lodzer Zeitung*, then *Lodzer Zeitung*, *Lodscher Zeitung*, and finally *Litzmannstädter Zeitung* from May 1940.

14. The planners stated that on average 5.8 people lived in a single room, and that most flats only had one bedroom. In large parts of the city there was no running water and no sewage (see BArch, R4606/3366).

15. See ibid.

16. *Litzmannstädter Zeitung*, February 26, 1941.

17. The overall population had decreased to 481,000 in 1943, of which an impressive 28

percent were now German (see *Verwaltungsbericht*, Archiwum Państwowe w Łodzi, Akta Miasta Łodzi 28595, 54).

18. See Epstein, *Model Nazi*, 192.
19. The number of people owning a radio set rose from 19,300 in January 1941 to 27,500 a year later. Car ownership rose from 764 in January 1941 to 1,161 a year later. The library's stock increased from 18,100 books in May 1941 to 34,100 a year later, and the number of its patrons jumped from 8,000 to 15,600 (see Archiwum Państwowe w Łodzi, Akta Miasta Łodzi 28961, 89, 98, 144, 168).
20. See BArch, R153/300, BArch, R153/630.
21. The film, which even contained a few scenes from the Ghetto, was finished in 1944 and was meant to enter cinemas in autumn that year.
22. The progress of the "Germanification" of city and region was closely monitored by the authorities and summarized in regular reports (*Volkspolitische Lageberichte*) (see Archiwum Państwowe w Łodzi, Akta Miasta Łodzi 31772).
23. It was not until June 1940 that the *Litzmannstädter Zeitung* published a detailed article about the ghetto. Under the heading "250,000 Jews govern themselves" (June 9, 1940), the newspaper produced a long article which compared the ghetto's inhabitants to the "parasitic plant ivy...which entwines around the oak tree [but] is destined to die." The paper assured its readers that the founding of the ghetto was "only a temporary interim solution on the way to the final settlement of the Jewish question." It concluded, "We are convinced, however, that in contrast to the ivy the fate of the Jew is that he is unable to die in a beautiful and dignified way."
24. See Archiwum Państwowe w Łodzi, Zbiór Teatraliów Łódzkich, 21/57, Repertuary przedstawień teatralnych teatrów łódzkich z okresu okupacji [1940–1945], 1. See also *Litzmannstädter Zeitung*, January 6, 1941, and several other articles concerning this particular exhibition over the next few days and weeks. There were a number of similar exhibitions over the following years.
25. See Archiwum Państwowe w Łodzi, Zbiór Teatraliów Łódzkich, 21/55. Afisze programowe koncertów z okresu okupacji niemieckiej/Litzmannstadt 1942–44, 1–2, 12.
26. Quote from the mayor's preface to the forty-page "summer schedule" of the *Volksbildungsstätte Litzmannstadt* (Archiwum Państwowe w Łodzi, Zbiór Teatraliów Łódzkich, 21/60, Materiały różne—teatry łódzkie z okresu okupacji).
27. Archiwum Państwowe w Łodzi, Zbiór Teatraliów Łódzkich, 21/55, Afisze programowe koncertów z okresu okupacji niemieckiej/Litzmannstadt 1942–44, 11.
28. See Archiwum Państwowe w Łodzi, Akta Miasta Łodzi 28595, 166.
29. See Archiwum Państwowe w Łodzi, Zbiór Teatraliów Łódzkich, 21/46, Recenzje teatralne i wycinki z łódzkiej prasy polskojęzycznej, 71. See pictures of productions, program notes, and press cuttings throughout this file. See also Archiwum Państwowe w Łodzi, Zbiór Teatraliów Łódzkich, 21/20, Teatry miejskie w Łodzi, Repertuary przedstawień teatralnych sezonu 1938/39.
30. Archiwum Państwowe w Łodzi, Akta Miasta Łódzi 29056, 16a, 16b, 18.
31. See Archiwum Państwowe w Łodzi, Zbiór Teatraliów Łódzkich, 21/33, Łódzkie Teatry Miejskie, Wydawnictwo Łódzkich Teatrów Miejskich 1937–1939.
32. Article published on June 2, 1939 (Archiwum Państwowe w Łodzi, Zbiór Teatraliów Łódzkich, 21/46, Recenzje teatralne i wycinki z łódzkiej prasy polskojęzycznej, 125). The mutual respect between the German and the Polish theatre in Łódź went back further.

GERMANIFICATION, CULTURAL MISSION, HOLOCAUST

In autumn 1911 the German-speaking *Thalia-Theater* held a charity performance in aid of Polish actors who had suffered from their theatre's destruction by fire earlier that year. There was also a considerable crossover of audiences, including a significant number of Jewish patrons at the *Thalia-Theater* (see Artur Pełka, "Deutsches Theater in der Dreivölkerstadt Łódź—die Direktion Adolf Kleins am Thalia-Theater [1909–1914]," Fassel/Leyko/Ulrich, *Polen und Europa*, 78).

33. See *Litzmannstädter Zeitung*, October 17, 1939.
34. See *Litzmannstädter Zeitung*, October 14, October 29, and December 7, 1939.
35. BArch, R55/20389, 263–65.
36. See Archiwum Państwowe w Łodzi, Zbiór Teatraliów Łódzkich, 21/57, Repertuary przedstawień teatralnych teatrów łódzkich z okresu okupacji [1940–1945], 29.
37. For this and the following see Archiwum Państwowe w Łodzi, Zbiór Teatraliów Łódzkich 21/58, Programy przedstawień teatralnych teatrów łódzkich z okresu okupacji [1940–1943], 73.
38. The size of the program notes was only reduced during the 1943–1944 season (Archiwum Państwowe w Łodzi, Zbiór Teatraliów Łódzkich 21/58, Programy przedstawień teatralnych teatrów łódzkich z okresu okupacji [1940–1943], 94–99).
39. See Anselm Heinrich, *Entertainment, Education, Propaganda: Regional Theatres in Germany and Britain between 1918 and 1945* (London: University of Hertfordshire Press / Society for Theatre Research, 2007), 193.
40. Archiwum Państwowe w Łodzi, Zbiór Teatraliów Łódzkich, 21/58, Programy przedstawień teatralnych teatrów łódzkich z okresu okupacji [1940–1943], 2. For the following please compare with this program note, too.
41. *Litzmannstädter Zeitung*, January 14, 1940; Walter Jacobs in *Litzmannstädter Zeitung*, January 15, 1940; *Litzmannstädter Zeitung*, July 25, 1943.
42. Archiwum Państwowe w Łodzi, Zbiór Teatraliów Łódzkich, 21/56, Repertuary przedstawień teatralnych teatrów łódzkich z okresu okupacji [1940–1945].
43. See, for example, program note 20, 1941–1942 season (Archiwum Państwowe w Łodzi, Zbiór Teatraliów Łódzkich 21/58, Programy przedstawień teatralnych teatrów łódzkich z okresu okupacji [1940–1943], 68).
44. Archiwum Państwowe w Łodzi, Zbiór Teatraliów Łódzkich, 21/56, Repertuary przedstawień teatralnych teatrów łódzkich z okresu okupacji [1940–1945].
45. See BArch, R55/20389, 345, 358.
46. Archiwum Państwowe w Łodzi, Zbiór Teatraliów Łódzkich, 21/56, Repertuary przedstawień teatralnych teatrów łódzkich z okresu okupacji [1940–1945].
47. These figures are for January 1942 (see Archiwum Państwowe w Łodzi, Akta Miasta Łodzi 28961, 87). Figures for the following months substantiate this trend (see pp. 125, 156, 169, 206, 236).
48. Archiwum Państwowe w Łodzi, Akta Miasta Łodzi 29056, 51–56, 59–64.
49. Archiwum Państwowe w Łodzi, Akta Miasta Łodzi 28595, 179.
50. See Archiwum Państwowe w Łodzi, Akta Miasta Łodzi 28961, 244, 251, 259. See also Archiwum Państwowe w Łodzi, Akta Miasta Łodzi 29056, 82–101.
51. Archiwum Państwowe w Łodzi, Akta Miasta Łodzi 28961, 264.
52. See Leyko, *Das deutsche Theater in Lodz 1939–1944*, 136.
53. Archiwum Państwowe w Łodzi, Akta Miasta Łodzi 29056, 10.
54. See BArch, R55/20389, 220; BArch, R55/20389, 8; BArch, R55/20389, 14–16.

55. BArch, R55/20389, 43. In the *Altreich*, theatres could apply for financial help from the Propaganda Ministry, too, but these extra payments never reached six-figure sums (see Heinrich, *Entertainment, Propaganda, Education*, 102).
56. BArch, R55/20389, 45, 90, 124, 195. For 1944 the mayor asked for RM 250,000 and again received RM 170,000 from the Ministry (see Heinrich, *Entertainment, Propaganda, Education*, 234).
57. For a detailed budget concerning the building cost see BArch, R55/20389, 223–27.
58. The project used the existing building of a former Polish theatre, which was located on Moltkestr. 94/98 (Archiwum Państwowe w Łodzi, Akta Miasta Łodzi 31602, 217).
59. See last program note of the 1941–1942 season published in July 1942 (Archiwum Państwowe w Łodzi, Zbiór Teatraliów Łódzkich 21/58, Programy przedstawień teatralnych teatrów łódzkich z okresu okupacji [1940–1943], 73).
60. Archiwum Państwowe w Łodzi, Akta Miasta Łodzi 28595, 171.
61. See BArch R55/215, 125.
62. See BArch R55/20389, 219–20.
63. The theatre in the Westphalian city of Hagen, for example, during 1942/43 employed little more than half the number of staff (see Hagen City Archives, Ha1/9272).
64. Archiwum Państwowe w Łodzi, Akta Miasta Łodzi 31601, 2–3.
65. Archiwum Państwowe w Łodzi, Akta Miasta Łodzi 31601, 25.
66. Archiwum Państwowe w Łodzi, Akta Miasta Łodzi 28531, 205–6.
67. Archiwum Państwowe w Łodzi, Akta Miasta Łodzi 31601, 144.
68. See Bielefeld City Archives, Städtische Bühnen und Orchester, no. 1678.
69. BArch R55/20389, 219. See also Archiwum Państwowe w Łodzi, Akta Miasta Łodzi 28531, 216.
70. The article was featured in issue no. 9 of the 1940/41 program notes (see Archiwum Państwowe w Łodzi, Zbiór Teatraliów Łódzkich 21/58, Programy przedstawień teatralnych teatrów łódzkich z okresu okupacji [1940–1943], 35).
71. *Litzmannstädter Zeitung*, July 25, 1943.
72. Archiwum Państwowe w Łodzi, Zbiór Teatraliów Łódzkich, 21/58, Programy przedstawień teatralnych teatrów łódzkich z okresu okupacji [1940–1943], 88.
73. Archiwum Państwowe w Łodzi, Akta Miasta Łodzi 29056, 69–71, 76.
74. Archiwum Państwowe w Łodzi, Zbiór Teatraliów Łódzkich, 21/58, Programy przedstawień teatralnych teatrów łódzkich z okresu okupacji [1940–1943], 2.
75. Archiwum Państwowe w Łodzi, Akta Miasta Łodzi 29056, 25–30.
76. Attendance figures were as follows (rounded): 19,000 for January, 29,000 for February, 30,000 for March, 22,000 for April, 17,000 for May, 22,000 for June, and 19,000 for July (see Archiwum Państwowe w Łodzi, Akta Miasta Łodzi 29056, 46).
77. Archiwum Państwowe w Łodzi, Zbiór Teatraliów Łódzkich, 21/58, Programy przedstawień teatralnych teatrów łódzkich z okresu okupacji [1940–1943], 2. Similarly *Litzmannstädter Zeitung*, March 17, 1940.
78. Archiwum Państwowe w Łodzi, Akta Miasta Łodzi 29056, 51–56.
79. See Leyko, *Das deutsche Theater in Lodz 1939–1944*, 143–44.
80. *Litzmannstädter Zeitung*, January 14, 1942.
81. *Litzmannstädter Zeitung*, March 24, 1940.
82. Archiwum Państwowe w Łodzi, Akta Miasta Łodzi 28595, 176.
83. Archiwum Państwowe w Łodzi, Akta Miasta Łodzi 28595, 177.

84. *Litzmannstädter Zeitung*, March 24, 1940.
85. Archiwum Państwowe w Łodzi, Akta Miasta Łodzi 28595, 181.
86. *Litzmannstädter Zeitung*, October 7, 1940.
87. *Litzmannstädter Zeitung*, August 20, 1942.
88. Archiwum Państwowe w Łodzi, Akta Miasta Łodzi 28595, 172–74.
89. Archiwum Państwowe w Łodzi, Akta Miasta Łodzi 28595, 180.
90. Archiwum Państwowe w Łodzi, Akta Miasta Łodzi 28531, 217–19 (the week in question was May 3–9, 1940).
91. For this and the following see BArch R55/20389, 213–22. For the Accounting Office's report on the orchestra see BArch R55/215, 124–32.
92. BArch R55/215, 124.
93. See BArch R55/215, 124–28 (also for the following).
94. Epstein, *Model Nazi*, 232, 247.
95. See Leyko, *Das deutsche Theater in Lodz 1939–1944*, 146–47.
96. Hannah Arendt, *Eichmann in Jerusalem: Ein Bericht von der Banalität des Bösen*, 3rd ed. (Munich: Pieper, 2008), 56.
97. The theatre was only a few hundred meters away from the ghetto.
98. Archiwum Państwowe w Łodzi, Zbiór Teatraliów Łódzkich, 21/56, Repertuary przedstawień teatralnych teatrów łódzkich z okresu okupacji [1940–1945]. Wimmer was one of the directors in the theatre.
99. *Litzmannstädter Zeitung*, July 25, 1943.
100. Suzanne Marchand, "Nazi Culture: Banality or Barbarism?," *Journal of Modern History* 70 (March 1998): 108–18.

Resistance to War

Carl Zuckmayer's *Des Teufels General*

—GENE A. PLUNKA

During the Third Reich, German resistance was minimal because defiance of the Nazis was synonymous with treason. Furthermore, the suppression of all opposing political parties, including the Social Democrats and Communists, and the removal of dissenters to German concentration camps by the late 1930s made resistance quite difficult. Nevertheless, several individuals felt that an expression of opposition to a totalitarian dictator who had led them into war and allowed evil to flourish was necessary. This essay focuses on resistance of the German military both to Hitler's rule and to the abyss of war into which he led the German nation. I demonstrate that in Carl Zuckmayer's play *Des Teufels General*, his protagonist General Harras embodies the spirit of resistance to Hitler's Reich. Zuckmayer also offers rationales for individuals to oppose a diabolical regime that leads its citizens into an unjust war. In other words, this essay argues that Zuckmayer's play demonstrates how theatre can function as a forum for thoughtful debate about the moral and ethical reasons to oppose totalitarian governments that instigate wars.[1]

Zuckmayer was born in 1896 in Nackenheim on the Rhine and spent much of his middle-class childhood in Mainz. His grandfather on his mother's side was a Jew who later converted to Catholicism, the religion that Zuckmayer was born into and embraced throughout his life. When World War I broke out in 1914, the patriotic seventeen-year-old enlisted; subsequently, he achieved the rank of lieutenant. After his war stint, he enrolled briefly from 1918 to 1919 at the University of Frankfurt and then studied at the University of Heidelberg in 1919.[2] Zuckmayer later abandoned his studies to turn to writing, and in 1925 he went to Berlin to work in Max Reinhardt's Deutsches Theater. There he began a prosperous career and won the Kleist Prize, typically awarded to encourage talented novice playwrights; he married that year, had his enormously successful comedy, *Der fröliche Weinberg* (*The Merry Vineyard*), staged at the Theater am Schiffbauerdamm, and, in 1929, won the Georg Büchner Prize and the Heidelberg Festival Performance Prize. *Der fröliche Weinberg*, replete with cliches that parodied all walks of German life, was so successful (except among the "moral" National Socialists) that Zuckmayer's realistic style, deemed to be in the tradition of Gerhart Hauptmann, was believed to bring an end to expressionism in Germany. His 1931 satire on the military, *Der Hauptmann von Köpenick* (The Captain of Köpenick), perhaps his most critically acclaimed play, brought on Nazi wrath that implicated Zuckmayer as a pacifist. After Hitler rose to power in 1933, Zuckmayer's plays were banned, so Zuckmayer, who never joined the Nazi Party, took his family to live in his country home near Salzburg, Austria; while in Austria, he wrote several novels, two plays, some poetry, and a few screenplays. After the Anschluss, Zuckmayer fled to Switzerland in 1938, and to the United States one year later. He labored briefly as a screenwriter for Warner Bros. in Hollywood and then leased a dilapidated farmhouse in a rural area of Vermont that reminded him of his former home in the Rhineland. After the war, Zuckmayer worked as a civilian employee of the American government assigned to writing reports on the postwar cultural situation in Germany and Austria. In postwar Europe, Zuckmayer was the most widely performed playwright in West Germany other than Brecht. He continued to write plays and won major awards for his efforts: the Gutenberg Plaque (1948), the Goethe Prize (1952), the Vienna Culture Prize (1955), the Literature Prize of the Rhenish Palatinate (1957), and the Insignia of the Order Pour le mérite for Science and Art (1967). He was also awarded honorary doctorates from Dartmouth College (1956), the University of Bonn (1976), and the University of Vermont (1976). He passed away on January 18, 1977, in Visp, Switzerland.

In December 1941, while in Vermont, Zuckmayer read an American newspaper article about the death of his old wartime friend, pilot Ernst Udet, a World War I ace and winner of the Iron Cross who had years later become chief of the Air Force Supply Service of the German Army.[3] The newspaper reported that Udet (who actually committed suicide) suffered a fatal flying accident while in service to the Reich and was given a state funeral. In his autobiography, *A Part of Myself*, Zuckmayer recalled that when he last saw Udet, in 1936, his comrade, already a high-ranking officer in the Luftwaffe, lamented, "Shake the dust of this country from your shoes. Clear out of here and don't come back. There is no more decency here."[4] Udet would have left, too, except for the fact that he was so enamored with flying that he could not abandon it and therefore resigned himself to serving a corrupt regime. Upon learning that his friend was given a state funeral, Zuckmayer conceived the idea for *Der Teufels General*, with the notion that "state funeral" would be the last words of the play. During a three-week period in January 1943, he had developed an outline for the play and wrote its first act without ever having to change a word of it afterwards. Zuckmayer got distracted with farm work, but after hearing of the attempted assassination of Hitler on July 20, 1944, he became motivated to finish the play.

After he had written it, Zuckmayer realized that the play had minimal chances for production in West Germany, where collective amnesia about the war permeated the society and where the Allies were skeptical of his nostalgic glorification of German militarism that could conceivably arouse new nationalistic sentiments and a venting of frustration against the occupied forces. Literary critic Siegfried Mews recalls, "It is understandable that the allied occupation forces did not look favorably upon a play that seemed to offer too sympathetic a portrayal of a Nazi general."[5] Thus, *Des Teufels General* had its debut in Zurich at the Schauspielhaus, on December 14, 1946, in a production directed by Zuckmayer's longtime confidant Heinz Hilpert.[6] The play was so popular that it remained in production in Zurich for sixty performances. Hilpert, who cast the great German actor Gustav Knuth as Harras, went on to direct the West German premiere of the play in Frankfurt at the Stock Exchange in late November 1947. The running time of the original play was five and a half hours; Hilpert cut one-third of the dialogue, which made for a more manageable production. From 1947 to 1950, *Des Teufels General* was given 3,238 performances throughout West Germany (the East Germans adamantly refused its production, claiming that the play glorified the fascist military hierarchy), making the play the most frequently performed and most debated drama written by any German playwright during the postwar period.[7] From 1947 until he collapsed from a heart attack in late January 1948, Zuckmayer went on tour throughout Germany, discussing the controversial play at student meetings, youth group sessions, and union halls; the text was adopted as standard reading in many of the German secondary schools. Moreover, the play was hotly debated by German critics, many of whom found Oderbruch's sabotage of German airplanes to be repulsive.[8] In 1963, because of its controversial subject matter about German moral responsibility that still lingered years after the war and was exacerbated by the Eichmann trial in 1961, Zuckmayer withdrew the play from the stage; three years later, he revised the final act to develop Oderbruch's character in more detail, toning down his single-mindedness, allowing him to have more of a troubled conscience and feel guilt about the death of Eilers, and permitting Harras to give his friend valuable moral instruction.

RESISTANCE TO WAR

In 1955, German director Helmut Käutner made a black-and-white film version of *Des Teufels General* starring Curt Jürgens as Harras and Marianne Koch as Diddo; the film's screenplay, penned by Georg Hurdalek and Käutner, was faithful to Zuckmayer's original text, although cuts had to be made to shorten the film to less than two hours.[9] While the play has continued to be popular in Germany (Frank Castorf staged a revival at the Volksbühne in Berlin during 1996), there have also been a few notable productions elsewhere. In London, during autumn 1953, Trevor Howard gave one of the more memorable performances as Harras at the Savoy Theatre. Alan Scarfe can also be commended for his portrayal of Harras at the Dallas Theater Center in January 1979 in a production staged by Harry Buckwitz, who had directed the play's first run in Munich.[10]

When the Nazis came to power in 1933 and through much of the rest of the 1930s, Hitler was quite popular among German citizens. He had provided the Germans with a sense of pride and patriotism after the humiliation of the Versailles Treaty, reestablished political stability, and restored economic prosperity after the high inflation rates of the Depression. Hitler was also viewed as a master statesman who rearmed the German military and created a new balance of power in Europe, allowing the modern Germany to rise from the ashes after its descent following World War I. Even the Nuremberg Laws were accepted by the majority of anti-Semitic German citizens who believed that the Jews could never assimilate into German society and certainly were overrepresented in politics, finance, commerce, and culture during the overtly liberal Weimar Republic. Most Germans agreed that the conservatism of the Nazis allowed for a balance that would control the excesses of the Weimar Republic, including the increased presence that Jews had in all spheres of German life.

Hitler's foreign policies in the late 1930s, which initially created resistance from the military, were proven to be calculated gambles that eventually made the Führer more powerful among German citizens. Many military officers became resisters when Hitler announced plans to invade Czechoslovakia; they feared that Hitler's actions would draw Germany into a new war, at least with France, Czechoslovakia's ostensible supporter. These men, such as director of counterintelligence Wilhelm Canaris and chief of staff Ludwig Beck, saw visions of World War I again, with the same ensuing results due to a military that seemed unprepared for war. However, the Sudeten crisis appeared to be benign, as Hitler's Wehrmacht (the united armed forces of Germany) swept through Austria and Czechoslovakia, mostly to crowds cheering their arrival. When resisters such as Beck and General Franz Halder protested the invasion of Poland in 1939 and then the 1940 invasions of Denmark, Norway, France, and the Low Countries, claiming that these nations had not provoked Germany or threatened its security, Hitler's popularity proved them to be in the minority. He knew that the United States was not ready militarily to enter into a war, and the other major power that he feared, the Soviet Union, was kept at bay by having signed a nonaggression pact with Germany. The German citizenry was awed at Hitler's military successes, and thus high-ranking officers who protested were viewed as whiners or defeatists. Even the invasion of Russia in June 1941 was regarded as a necessary action—a justification of the fundamental values of the Reich against worldwide Bolshevism. Furthermore, opposition to Hitler's policies was not only considered to be outside the mainstream of German public opinion, but was also viewed as treason.

Despite the widespread support of National Socialism during the 1930s, there were a few dissenters. General Beck, chief of the general staff of the Army, considered Hitler to be reckless and perfidious, arguing that annexation of Czechoslovakia would lead to a war with France.[11] Beck resigned his position on August 27, 1938, after his initial attempts at both submitting memoranda of protests and applying international pressure failed. Beck's successor, Franz Halder, viewed Hitler as a criminal because of his efforts to instigate war. Hoping to murder Hitler and establish a coup d'état, Halder's plans were aborted after Hitler successfully managed to invade Czechoslovakia without the danger of war. As historian Peter Hoffman explains, by 1939, "Halder was busy with the war against Poland and the other generals involved lacked…the opportunity, the time or the will to do anything."[12] In truth, Halder's allegiance to military authority prevented him from taking direct action to have Hitler assassinated or removed through direct revolt. However, the most vocal resister was Dr. Carl Goerdeler, who, as mayor of Leipzig, refused to hoist the swastika flag at city hall and adamantly opposed the removal of a statue of Felix Mendelssohn (who was a Christian himself but whose parents had been born Jewish) at the city orchestral hall. Goerdeler complained that the Nazis rejected German history, insisted on blind obedience, and relied on brute force in their quest for totalitarian power. On April 1, 1937, Goerdeler resigned his post as mayor of Leipzig.

The widespread negative view of the Reich substantially increased among German citizenry after Kristallnacht (November 9, 1938), thus fueling the resistance movement in Germany. Kristallnacht resulted in the murder of ninety-one Jews, the arrest and subsequent deportation of between 25,000 and 30,000 Jews to concentration camps, the deliberate burning of 267 synagogues, and the ransacking of thousands of homes and businesses. This night of terror precipitated the penultimate phase of National Socialism's racial program, the Final Solution, which meant genocide. From this moment on, resistance became more prevalent because the citizenry began to realize that the Nazis failed to live up to the principles they had originally established. The corrupt nature of the ruthless regime, with its totalitarian abuse of power and its display of mass brutality, conflicted with the notion of an ethical society, a pure Christian and spiritual Germany in which individuals could prosper bereft of the elements that had originally tainted the materialistic Weimar Republic. Historian Theodore S. Hamerow notes the strife present in military quarters after Kristallnacht: "Even some members of the officer corps who had appeared indifferent to Hitler's assumption of direct command over the armed forces expressed shock, at least in their private conversations, letters, and diaries, at the brutality of the anti-Semitic riots."[13] Germans who championed justice, decency, and morality now condemned the actions of their brethren that they believed superseded the Nuremberg Laws.[14] German citizens who envisioned National Socialism as the embodiment of patriotism were now forced to question their allegiance to a regime that had become ruthless in persecuting those who displayed any dissenting opinions about the tenets of the Reich. Others were concerned that the totalitarian German nation had lost its credibility abroad.

The resistance movement accelerated by December 1941, when the United States was on the brink of entering the war and when the Russians successfully defended Moscow against the advances of the Wehrmacht. Once the Russians forced the Germans to retreat, the balance of power clearly shifted in the war. During this time, news of the atrocities committed by the Germans in the Nazi-occupied Eastern territories was becoming notorious and further shocked the German public. Meanwhile, the Reich attempted to Nazify all authority, purging all uncooperative officers from the ranks and relieving the diplomatic corps of its autonomy. In short, resisters who favored the overthrow of the German government realized that Hitler's disastrous foreign policies spelled the defeat of the empire—another repeat of World War I and perhaps another Treaty of Versailles lurking in the future. Thus, the welfare of the Fatherland was clearly at stake; the Nazis had compromised the security of the nation, and so opposition to the government became a patriotic gesture and less a treasonable one. The basic goal of resistance became more a defense of the national interest rather than a fear of the consequences of military defeat. Hamerow asserts, "Clearly, although the Allies would never agree to negotiate with Hitler, they might be willing to consider a compromise settlement with an anti-Nazi government in Germany."[15]

One such resister was Claus von Stauffenberg, the mastermind of the July 20, 1944, assassination attempt on Hitler. A devoted follower of National

Socialism in the early part of his military career, Stauffenberg, who consistently championed justice and decency, became distraught with Nazi policies after Kristallnacht, complaining that the atrocities went far beyond the intent of the Nuremberg Laws. After beginning his army career as a lieutenant in 1930, Stauffenberg was part of the First Light Division that invaded the Sudetenland and later attacked Poland in 1939. As part of the Sixth Panzer Division that occupied France in 1940, Stauffenberg was rewarded with the Iron Cross. After witnessing the mass murder of Jews during his tour of duty in the Soviet campaign during 1942, he became disenchanted with Nazi policies. During late 1942, when the Nazi defeat seemed imminent, Stauffenberg, advocating not only for the sake of the Fatherland but also for the moral spirit of Germany, joined the resistance. Newly promoted to lieutenant colonel of the general staff, Stauffenberg had access to Hitler's briefing meetings. Young and impetuous, Stauffenberg was willing to do what more seasoned officials such as Goerdeler, Beck, and Halder might discuss but would not act upon. Stauffenberg realized that an assassination attempt on the Führer would be a suicide mission, but he was now willing to martyr himself in a symbolic act that would oppose the moral evil endemic to the Third Reich. The bomb that Stauffenberg planted in the briefing room at Hitler's retreat at Wolfschanze, near the East Prussian town of Rastenburg, did not kill the Führer.[16] After the investigation by the Gestapo, Stauffenberg was tried along with his coconspirators and then shot; during the trial, he assumed full responsibility for the coup. His last words, "Long live holy Germany," indicated his patriotism and his commitment to purging the Fatherland of an insidious evil that had tainted the nation's morality.

In 1936, when Zuckmayer had asked his friend Udet why he did not abandon his career as a high-ranking officer in the Luftwaffe, the latter responded, "I'm completely sold on flying. I can't disentangle any more. But one of these days the devil will fetch us all."[17] Zuckmayer's protagonist, General Harras, modeled after Udet, working for Hitler, the devil, became the protagonist for the title of the play: *The Devil's General*. The apocalyptic subtitles of the three acts—"The Time Bomb," "Stay of Execution or The Hand," and "Damnation"—suggest that trouble is brewing, that time has been allocated for resolution, but hell awaits. The notion of the German people selling their souls to the devil, Faustlike, is palpable throughout the play. As scholar Alan Robertshaw astutely realizes, "The answer given by the play is presumably that Hitler, as the devil, is beyond redemption, whereas Harras, as his servant, can perhaps, like Faust, ultimately be saved."[18] The conflict, then, revolves around the notion of what aviators such as Udet and Harras could do to resist the temptations provided by the devil; in the larger context, the play focuses on what individual resisters could do to oppose

RESISTANCE TO WAR

a diabolical force that had enslaved their nation. Thus, Zuckmayer initially dedicated the play to "dem Unbekannten Kämpfer" (the unknown combatants) who died with Stauffenberg in the aftermath of the sacrifice of their lives made during the virtually suicidal July 20 assassination attempt.[19] These resisters accepted the guilt and took action to free their beloved Germany from a devil who was leading the country to its ruin. I will argue that Harras's suicide is a gesture in accord with the grand defiance of those Germans who sacrificed their lives in the resistance movement, thus leading a guilty man who has aligned himself with the Nazis to place his fate in God's hands.

To make the play appeal to a diverse postwar German audience, Zuckmayer's dilemma was twofold: he needed to find a suitable form for the play, and he had to refrain from stereotyping German society during the Third Reich. To solve the dilemma of the most suitable form for the play, Zuckmayer relied on his talents as a realist playwright. The play has the traditional three-act structure with which audiences were familiar, and the form is firmly embedded in the objective realist tradition that ostensibly sought Truth through an exploration of everyday characters, modern settings, and conventional dialogue; the only hint of abstraction is the five-fanned beams of light that, in act 2, morph into fingers representing the tight grip that Hitler has on the nation and concomitantly the fingers of God that exacerbate Harras's feelings of guilt. Zuckmayer's forte was that he could represent a diverse cross-section of German life during the Nazi reign. As Roy C. Cowen has observed, every geographical area of Germany is represented in the play: Pfundmayer is from Bavaria, the pilot Hastenteuffel lives in Westphalia, Writzky hails from Berlin, Hansen represents northern Germany, Mohrungen and Hartmann are Rhinelanders like Zuckmayer himself, Baron Pflungk is referred to as an "old Saxon," and Oderbruch has his roots in Silesia.[20] Zuckmayer, the master of working with German dialects, knew that his audiences would be enamored with their understanding of the subtle differences in the language spoken throughout Germany. Moreover, Zuckmayer created a cross section of German society by portraying characters from all classes and all walks of life—from waiters (Detlev) to generals (Harras), from the working class (Oderbruch) to wealthy industrialists (von Mohrungen). Furthermore, Zuckmayer was determined to show that National Socialism affected persons from all ages, from the young (Hartmann, Anne Eilers, Pootsie, and Diddo) to the middle-aged (Harras, Olivia Geiss, and Oderbruch) to the older generation (Korrianke). In fact, Zuckmayer has much in common with Anton Chekhov, whose plays carried widespread appeal because he wrote about people from all classes and all ages.[21]

Aside from the firmly committed National Socialists (Hartmann, Pootsie, and Schmidt-Lausitz), the minor characters in the play fully represent the diverse opinions of the general German populace toward National Socialism during late 1941, when the drama takes place. As a matter of fact, German audiences were amazed that a playwright who had been living abroad during the war could so readily and accurately capture the sentiments of the German personae; spectators could easily identify with at least one, and sometimes several, of the characters portrayed on stage. Mohrungen, the opportunistic upper-class industrialist who is president of the procurement office for raw materials, believes in surrendering his honor and will to Germany in order to help the Führer save the world from Bolshevism; he is typical of the German entrepreneurs of the 1930s who succumbed to the Nazi allure. Colonel Friedrich Eilers, the young, idealistic war hero and leader of a fighter squadron, realizes that killing is wrong yet submits, as a good soldier typically did in Nazi Germany, blindly and obediently to the will of the Reich, which, he rationalizes, will result in peace once the war is won. His wife, Anne, is a well-respected, quiet, elegant mother of two children, not atypical of most German women who were subordinate to their husbands during the Nazi regime. Herr Detlev, the waiter, spies for the Nazis out of self-preservation: like many obedient Nazis, he has a family to support. Olivia Geiss, whose passion for acting equates with Harras's love of flying, agrees to capitulate to Goering's demands to perform primarily Wagner's operas, and although her artistic freedom has been compromised, she is willing to submit to the Nazis in order to remain on stage with her dreams. Finally, there is Baron Pflungk, a diplomat of the Foreign Ministry who despises the "plebeian" agenda of the National Socialists yet realizes that his service to the Reich means advancement, which he very much cherishes. This selection of diverse characters demonstrates how effective the Nazis were in subjugating all types of people into accepting the Party mentality. If the demonic had been running rampant in Germany, then it had infected people from all stratifications.

One must understand that since all other political parties except for the Nazi Party were outlawed during the Reich, every German character in the play is a Nazi; however, only Schmidt-Lausitz, Pootsie, and Hartmann are stalwarts of National Socialism. Doctor Schmidt-Lausitz, the Minister of Culture, is reminiscent of Zuckmayer's nemesis, Dr. Goebbels, who was largely responsible for banning Zuckmayer's plays after 1936. Schmidt-Lausitz says to Harras, "In me you see a mortal enemy. You are quite correct. There isn't room enough under the sun for us both."[22] Schmidt-Lausitz, with his ties to the Gestapo, understands that Harras is not fully supportive of the regime. Schmidt-Lausitz teases Harras by comparing him to Erich Maria Remarque, the pacifist writer who so irritated the Nazis, and then calling Remarque a Jew. When Harras reminds Schmidt-Lausitz that Remarque was not Jewish, Schmidt-Lausitz attacks Harras personally: "Remarque of Ullstein. Whoever associates with Jews is himself a Jew" (927). Schmidt-Lausitz knows that Harras has been trying to smuggle Jews out of the country; the comment about Ullstein, the publishing company that in 1933 stopped serializing Zuckmayer's novella *Eine Liebesgeschichte* due to the Nazi protest against the author's pacifism, is particularly pertinent to the comparison of Zuckmayer and Remarque. Dr. Schmidt-Lausitz was a poorly paid writer before the war, much like Goebbels, who majored in the humanities before fully immersing himself into National Socialism. As critic Margot Finke writes, "Zuckmayer considered such unimportant, intellectually mediocre people with a great need for recognition to be the best executors of National Socialist policies because the system offered them the desired upward mobility for their dirty work."[23] By including an academic as an ardent Nazi, Zuckmayer depicts how National Socialist ideology had influenced even the most intelligent German citizens.[24] Schmidt-Lausitz, the mediocre academic, has been enlightened by the Nazis, who can provide ordinary citizens with power and glory; even Schmidt-Lausitz's double name suggests a preference for aristocratic nomenclature. Schmidt-Lausitz becomes the personification of Nazi terror (a *Laus*, the German word for "louse")—the small bureaucrat who glorifies in terrifying others under the auspices of the powerful Gestapo. He turns Harras over to the Gestapo for questioning and then, following the interrogation, gives the general ten days to find the saboteur in Oderbruch's unit.

To downplay the idea that the Nazi Party consisted only of ambitious men, Zuckmayer attempted to show how the tenets of National Socialism penetrated all walks of life by creating the ideal female Nazi as a counterpart to the evil of Schmidt-Lausitz. Pootsie von Mohrungen (Anne Eilers's sister), having lost her mother at an early age, has been raised by her father and by the Party, thus becoming a fanatical Nazi. Trained in the Hitler Youth and now ready to enter the League of German Girls (Bund deutsches Mädel), Pootsie has been fully indoctrinated into National Socialist ideology and is planning to accept a leadership position in the Party after she completes her course that includes a lecture series on Nietzsche's philosophy: the value of suffering in the life of the nation. Pootsie is thus trained to sacrifice her will for the sake of Nazi Germany. She is empowered to become a mother for the Fatherland and stoically admits, "When I have a baby there won't be any anesthesia. It's going to be a matter of suffering wide awake and screaming till the seams burst" (942–43). Consistently wearing her tight Hitler Youth uniform that reinforces how her conformity has dehumanized her, Pootsie, devoid of scruples, mouths Party cliches as an automaton without the ability to think for herself. Zuckmayer critic Ausma Balinkin remarks that Pootsie's given Germanic name, Waltraut, identifies her with the

Germanic notion of strength and power, the blood-and-guts cult of National Socialism.[25] To Zuckmayer, she is a sad indictment of Nazis without a will of their own, who have become dehumanized victims of a demented ideology.

Pootsie is not only indoctrinated and thus lacks empathy for others, but is also a threat to others. Acting as the archetypal Lilith, she demonically tempts the moral Harras into accepting his calling as a Nazi. Pootsie admires Harras as a brave pilot but shuns him when his morality allows him to tear down the facade of National Socialism. When Harras does so in front of Pootsie, she can only respond in the way she was trained: "You talk like a Jew" (943). Rocking back and forth on Harras's war memorabilia in his Berlin apartment, Pootsie is essentially fetishizing Nazi iconography that represents her ideal notion of the warrior mentality that she so dearly covets. She tempts Harras to regain his warrior mentality and join the Nazi Party, noting that power is freedom: "You're no Jew and no Communist. You know you can't fight it. Don't be a fool! You have blood, race, spirit. You were born to rule, to grasp, to possess" (948). When Harras defers, refusing to be tempted by satanic forces, Pootsie reveals that when she was hiding in the closet, she overheard Harras's plans to smuggle Jews to safety and thus threatens to destroy him. Harras expels her from his apartment by chasing her with a whip.

One might imagine that through the portrayals of hard-core fascists such as Schmidt-Lausitz and Pootsie, Zuckmayer has stereotyped all such dedicated Nazis during the Third Reich. Audiences viewing the activities of Schmidt-Lausitz and Pootsie would recognize that they inhabit an unflattering, vicious world of spying on their neighbors, hiding in closets to overhear conversations, and informing on one's brethren; they reflect the appalling reality of life under the Nazis. However, the inclusion of Lieutenant Hartmann in this group breaks the stereotypical mold. Hartmann has the soul of the resisters who attempted to assassinate Hitler in 1944; he, like so many Nazis loyal to Germany, had doubts about the efficacy of National Socialism after Kristallnacht and even more so in December 1941, when the play takes place and the Nazis had committed atrocities in Eastern Europe. Zuckmayer seemed to have tapped into the national malaise, for after the postwar productions of *Des Teufels General* throughout West Germany, he admitted, "I received several hundred letters that began: 'I am your Lieutenant Hartmann.'"[26]

Hartmann seems to have been the idealistic "pure Aryan" that the Nazis love to recruit. He turns out to be a daredevil pilot who volunteers for missions, has boundless energy, is intelligent, respects his superiors, and is athletic. Feeling abandoned after his father died in World War I, Hartmann found a new home among comrades in the Hitler Youth and then in the officers' training school; from there, he went on to become a pilot in the Eilers Squadron. He was told that his duty was to be a crusader for the nation. However, as Lutz Weltmann infers, Hartmann became disenchanted after discovering that war was not a chivalrous adventure but was instead more like the slaughter of the innocents.[27] He is plagued by doubts about the purity of his Nazi mission in the East, and he feels that the ideals that he learned as a member of the Hitler Youth have been compromised, perhaps even destroyed. Hartmann tells Harras that in Łódź, "they shot at defenseless people as a joke, they laughed when the victims whimpered with fear—they—I can't say it, General. That isn't part of war or goals or ideals. There is no justification for what they did" (953). Like so many Germans who believed in the original intentions of the Nazis (stressing racial purity but not murder of undesirables), Hartmann became disillusioned with the Reich once it abandoned those principles. Hartmann is conflicted that he once thought of himself as a crusader for the new Reich and admits his dilemma to Harras: "But how can a new thing become strong and good if it begins by unleashing the lowest and meanest in human beings? How can anyone stand life in this new age if it begins with straight murder?" (953). Pootsie comments that Hartmann cannot dance; in other words, he has lost the ability to be happy, which is anathema to Zuckmayer. After being convinced by Harras that there is divine justice, Hartmann becomes the perfect candidate to turn to the resistance, work with Oderbruch, and thus carry on the activities abandoned by his role model Harras after he martyrs himself. As Anthony Waine has noticed, his surname suggests "hard man" (Zuckmayer, writing in Vermont, would have understood the English meaning), yet, after his conversion, he becomes one whose heart now rules his former warrior's head.[28] At the end of the play, we suspect that his conversion is complete when he joins Oderbruch in reciting the Lord's Prayer after witnessing Harras's fatal accident.

After having created a microcosm of German society during the Third Reich, visibly represented in the lengthy act 1 set in a high-class restaurant, Zuckmayer's second dilemma was to endear his protagonist, General Harras, to German audiences. Using his friend Udet as the model for Harras, Zuckmayer created a larger-than-life charismatic figure who is loyal, honest, witty, intelligent, charming, humorous, considerate, moral, boisterous, and experienced; moreover, he is masculine enough so that he is admired by the men yet enough of a bon vivant and raconteur so that women are immediately attracted to him. Harras also shares kinship with Zuckmayer himself (Zuckmayer and Udet, both born in 1896, had so many personality traits in common, as well as similar interests and histories, that they remained close friends). Moreover, both had a zest for living, which, as Ian C. Loram has pointed out, stems from "an unshakable belief in the dignity and worth of the human being."[29] Finally, both Harras and Zuckmayer were essentially humanists who believed in the secular piety of mankind that was disrupted by the Nazis. No matter how diabolical the political regime may be, Zuckmayer, and his alter ego Harras, ultimately believe that change can be accomplished only through the goodwill of individuals.

Throughout the play, Harras, despite being the devil's general, possesses many virtues.[30] Although he never joined the Nazi Party, Harras admits his fraudulence in serving the Nazis, thus surrendering his soul because of his love for flying. Edward M. V. Plater notes, "When Zuckmayer's hero shows in this way how much he has thought about the moral bankruptcy of Nazism and the moral untenableness of his position, one is reminded how reprehensible his role has been and continues to be."[31] As a hedonist, Harras appears to be above the political fray. While reproaching industrialists such as von Mohrungen for profiting from their alliances with the Nazis, Harras seems to excuse his own complicity with the regime by falling back on his love of aviation. Yet Harras does have good intentions, often helping the victims of Nazi persecution. He has smuggled Jews to safety across the border. Harras befriends the painter Schlick, who is ostracized in Germany because of his now-divorced Jewish wife. Disallowed from exhibiting his paintings in the Reich, Schlick has become a degenerate alcoholic. Harras also shelters the American journalist Buddy Lawrence, who has been ordered to leave Germany and has been under surveillance by the Gestapo; this aid to an American is a gesture that Hitler would find repulsive on the eve of his archenemy Roosevelt's entry into the war.[32] Harras also has a deep antipathy toward the Nazis and their racist ideology, refusing to give the Hitler salute to match Schmidt-Lausitz's gesture, thus defying the Gestapo: "Those boys don't fool me. And if I can step on their toes, I do it with pleasure" (920). The play primarily focuses on the various epiphanies that Harras goes through to move from his self-indulgent machismo of being the devil's general who lives for his passions to a more humane understanding of the importance of assuming responsibility for resisting the crimes of the Reich.

The first major change in Harras's outlook on life comes when he fails to extricate Bergmann from Germany to avoid Nazi persecution. Bergmann, the Jewish surgeon who is a friend of opera singer Olivia Geiss, was already sent once to Buchenwald. After being brutalized for six months in the concentration camp, Bergmann ended up in a hospital. Harras agrees to fly Bergmann and his wife to safety in neutral Switzerland. The plan never comes to fruition because the Bergmanns decide to commit suicide by consuming poison rather than cause difficulties for Harras. The double suicide is a gesture that deeply affects Harras, who has been merely condescending toward the Nazis but has not actually taken responsibility for their crimes against the Jews. Harras begins to realize his pitiful lack of responsibility when he hears the fate of the Bergmanns, explaining to Olivia, "We're guilty for what's happening to thousands of people we don't know and can never help. Guilty and damned for all eternity. Permitting viciousness is worse than doing it" (940).

The second epiphany, one that leads Harras to a spiritual awakening, occurs during his conversation with Hartmann in act 3. After recounting the horrors of war that he has witnessed in the Eastern territories, Hartmann asks Harras if God exists. Harras begins by stating, "I don't know Him but I have looked the devil in the eye. That's how I know that there must be a God" (954). Hartmann is losing faith, but Harras bolsters him by saying, "Believe, Hartmann—go ahead and believe confidently in divine justice! It will not betray you" (954). If Harras believes what he says to Hartmann, then he must accept damnation for his guilt and for lack of responsibility for the war crimes of which he is now aware. As Henry Glade perceptively notes, Harras has indeed previously forfeited his soul to the devil.[33] Harras now calls into question his self-indulgent behavior and even his sarcastic remarks against the regime, which, up until this point, have seemed harmless until Hartmann sheds light on the atrocities being committed by the Germans. Plater comments, "The lesson the Hartmann story contains—that it is morally indefensible to let evil happen without doing all that one can to stop it—is essentially the same as that demonstrated by the story of General Harras."[34] Thus, this sense of moral idealism that ultimately shapes the resistance is equated, at least in Harras's mind, with a spiritual sensibility.

The third epiphany occurs in act 3 when Anne, the wife of Colonel Eilers, confronts Harras and blames him for the death of her husband. Anne argues that Eilers, who died in a plane accident, sacrificed himself for a just cause. She contends that history led her husband to believe idealistically that the horrors of war typify what one must endure to rebuild a more prosperous society for the future, explaining to Harras, "We thought that everything new had to be born in pain and blood" (955). Anne accuses Harras of refusing to take responsibility for an unjust war and allowing others to die for a cause that he understood was corrupt, reprimanding him by stating, "You put on a great show of courage with your sarcasm and lukewarm doubt. What good is that to anybody? You are a part of the rottenness. You are guilty of every murder committed in the name of Germany. You stink of death!" (955). Harras, who earlier admitted that "permitting viciousness is worse than doing it," tries to defend himself, but his argument with Anne's logic, the justification for his *weltanschauung* (worldview), serves to awaken his dormant conscience. When he says to Anne, "Can you stand before the Divine Judge yourself—and say: 'I believed in the good, I didn't know about the bad?' How could you ever have believed in a cause whose stinking rottenness burned your nose every day?" (955), he is echoing the spiritual awareness that he tried to instill in young Hartmann instead of exonerating himself. Harras, whose love for aviation and for the masculine virtues of the hedonist warrior cum technocrat is perpetuated by service to the Nazis, now begins to see his life as a sham. As scholar Anthony Waine comments, "The destruction of Harras' male ego goes hand in hand with the unmasking of a society which is destructive and self-destructive."[35] This obsession with technology, flying, and the aesthetics of warfare has become an ersatz religion to Harras, unfortunately blinding him to meaningful spiritual insight and the assumption of constructive responsibility for the actions of his superiors. In this scene with Anne, Harras begins to move further away from his nostalgic role-playing in a macho career as warrior of the state and assumes the vestiges of individual responsibility.

The last conversation that creates the impetus for Harras's assumption of responsibility is with Oderbruch, his chief engineer and close friend. Harras, Oderbruch's superior, is responsible for aircraft security, but it is Oderbruch who supervises the aircraft parts used in the manufacturing of the planes. By not reporting a fault in the planes' steering construction and thus inevitably sabotaging the aircraft, Oderbruch's actions have led to the death of Harras's friend Eilers. Oderbruch defends his stance, arguing that resistance is the only means to defeat Germany, for if Hitler wins the war, the nation is lost: "There is no other way. We need the defeat—We must help it with our own hands. Only then can we rise up again, cleansed" (956). Realizing that resistance is not only suicidal but also equivalent to martyrdom, Harras questions Oderbruch's motives. Oderbruch pauses and then responds, "Gregory the Great said: 'The martyr alone is nothing, but he who knows why he suffers, his testimony is stronger than death.' We know why" (957). Oderbruch becomes the catalyst that tempts Harras spiritually by telling him that his soul is at stake: "Justice is the uncompromising ruling law in which spirit, nature, and life are subservient. When it is fulfilled—it is called freedom" (957). Henry Glade extrapolates the meaning of Oderbruch's philosophy to Harras: "Justice, to Oderbruch, is a natural eros-type of inexorable law in all creation, and its ultimate manifestation is man's fulfillment of the natural impulses which are here imbued with moral significance."[36] Herbert Lederer astutely remarks about Harras, "In the final analysis, it is his feeling of personal responsibility for the death of his friend and comrade Eilers which brings him to the full realization of his guilt, his knowing and willing participation in the evil around him."[37] This final encounter with Oderbruch thus leads Harras to a more moral acceptance of the divine justice that will liberate the conflicted general.

Schmidt-Lausitz has given Harras a ten-day deadline to discover the saboteur. At the start of act 3, when Harras is in his last day to choose, he has several options. He could turn Oderbruch over to the Gestapo, engage in the resistance with his friend and possibly join their base in Switzerland, or flee with young Diddo Geiss, who is starry-eyed over the mature war hero. Harras sympathizes with Oderbruch's goals to resist the Nazis, but sabotaging airplanes will result in the murder of more innocent pilots like Eilers. Besides, Harras admires the war mentality and bravery of pilots (the dinner party at the fancy restaurant in act 1 celebrates Eilers's military success), so it would make no sense for him to murder them. Anthony Waine's claim that Harras is a lone wolf whose individualistic style and machismo temperament thus prevent him from allying with the resisters seems far-fetched.[38] Harras is not enslaved to the cult of masculinity; instead, he demythologizes himself as he recognizes that as an integral part of being a successful aviator, he was abused by a corrupt nation. His humanitarian nature has surfaced through the various epiphanies, and so he categorically rejects turning in Oderbruch to the Gestapo or evading responsibility if he were to reinforce his ego by fleeing with Diddo.

Oderbruch does not represent the true spirit of German resistance to the Nazis. Oderbruch became a resister because he was ashamed of being German. Moreover, his acts of sabotage resulting in the deaths of innocent aviators, essentially substituting one type of fanaticism for another, were considered to be treason, especially by West German audiences viewing the play after the war.[39] Others argued that Oderbruch personified an abrogated war effort because of the way the Nazis were stabbed in the back by their own soldiers; this view only reinforces nostalgia for the purity of a corrupt Nazi regime.[40] Oderbruch's rationale for resistance—the notion that the death of Eilers is an unavoidable loss that must be faced in the larger scheme of liberating his country from tyrants—was too hardened and cynical for most audiences. Henry Glade sums up the problem that West German audiences had with Oderbruch's philosophy: "To Oderbruch, the end justifies the means, making him the very epitome of a totalitarian spirit."[41] Thus, Oderbruch's idealism appeared to be misguided to most postwar audiences.

In contrast to Oderbruch, Harras seems to personify the mentality shared by the resisters of the 1944 assassination attempt on Hitler. With Stauffenberg's last words in mind, "Long live holy Germany," we can appreciate Harras's persona as a resister. Like the 1944 resisters who were proud patriots, Harras, as a loyal Luftwaffe general, loves his country. Harras gravitates to individuals who profess their love for Germany, such as Buddy Lawrence and Lieutenant Hartmann. When Hartmann admits that his genealogy from the Rhineland may be tainted with the possibility of Jewish ancestry, Harras, reflecting Zuckmayer's own love of the German heartland, tells the lieutenant to take pride in a region of Germany that produced such great talents as Goethe, Beethoven, and Gutenberg. Harras, the moral Christian, the champion of justice and decency, is much like the 1944 resisters who saw hope in the original tenets of National Socialism but became disenchanted with the Party when those goals were subverted after Kristallnacht.[42] When Lawrence says to Harras that he loves the Germans, Harras responds, "Me too. To the point of hate. Just like an actor who loves and hates the character he plays, the role to which he has been sentenced—love and hate" (946). Zuckmayer, forced into exile by the Nazis who banned his plays, shares Harras's love-hate relationship with Germany and identifies with the 1944 resisters who loved their country yet saw it in decline and felt obligated to act. Staying in contact with his few friends when he was in exile, Zuckmayer writes of his fellow Germans: "Many of them looked askance at me because of my obstinate faith in a different Germany, in a true German spirit which, I insisted, must not be equated with the Nazi filth."[43]

Zuckmayer takes responsibility for Hitler's rise to power. In his autobiography, Zuckmayer laments that German intellectuals contented themselves with laughing at Hitler, the housepainter and paperhanger who looked like a barber, spoke poor German, and, with his bombastic style and meager education, could not be taken seriously as a potential leader.[44] Zuckmayer writes, "Hardly anyone thought that the threats against the Jews were meant seriously. Even many Jews considered the savage anti-Semitic rantings of the Nazis merely a propaganda device, a line the Nazis would drop as soon as they won governmental power and were entrusted with public responsibilities."[45] Zuckmayer understands that at the time when the play occurs, during December 1941, after the ravages of Kristallnacht have taken place, after reports about the genocide in the East were documented by soldiers such as Hartmann, and on the eve of America's entry into the War (911), soldiers such as Harras were morally obligated to resist such a corrupt regime.

Harras's flight in the defective M41–1304, and thus his self-imposed suicide/martyrdom, serves several purposes. First, just as Zuckmayer himself felt guilty about the intellectuals whose lack of responsibility toward the Nazis allowed them to flourish, Harras's suicide serves to expiate his own guilt for being the devil's general. Jennifer Taylor suggests that by identifying Hitler with the devil, Zuckmayer virtually exonerates Harras from personal responsibility.[46] On the contrary, resisters who viewed Hitler as the devil did not assume that the evil was merely a temporary phase in the history of German society; instead, they acted to destroy the evil. Second, Zuckmayer's play stays true to the historical framework that precipitated the writing of the play: Udet's own tale of suicide that was essentially a protest of a corrupt Reich. Third, Harras's suicide is consistent with his role as a Christlike redeemer who sacrifices himself to divine justice in order to reestablish mercy for his beloved country. In his essay about Zuckmayer, Murray B. Peppard notes, "In this play it is a subordinate who betrays his superior for the sake of a higher principle than that of personal loyalty."[47] Moreover, as one who is responsible for the safety of the aircraft and therefore Schmidt-Lausitz's chief suspect for the sabotage, Harras, through his sacrificial suicide, shields his friend Oderbruch of any liability, at least temporarily. Fourth, the humanitarian Zuckmayer embodies his protagonist with a suicide that coincides with his own humanistic perspective. Rather than murder his fellow pilots through sabotage, which is the path Oderbruch takes, Harras's suicide is another form of resistance from a humanist who listens to his own conscience. Finally, Zuckmayer's portrayal of Harras taking responsibility for his own actions in the form of suicide as a statement against a totalitarian regime vindicates the resisters who, sacrificing themselves in the suicidal assassination attempt, latently remind us of a better Germany in which heroic, decent citizens were capable of dying for a noble cause. Surely, Zuckmayer considers Harras's suicide to be a means of reclaiming his dignity and self-respect after prostituting himself to Hitler. Zuckmayer and Udet, both World War I pilots, would agree that losing one's life in a combat aircraft is a fitting way for a soldier to die with honor. As Mariatte C. Denman has observed, "Harras's final air stunt is reminiscent of those heroic acts performed in WWI with a sense of pride, self-reliance, and independence."[48]

The last words of *The Devil's General*, "State funeral, with full military honors" (958), spoken in honor of Udet, were the starting points that led Zuckmayer to write the play. The funeral also refers to the death of the state—a regime that has lost those qualities of honor, decency, humanism, and spirituality that Zuckmayer can only nostalgically remember as having once existed in his beloved country. *The Devil's General* becomes a paean to those resisters who, like General Harras, took responsibility for their actions instead of making excuses for widespread ruthlessness and depravity that corrupted a nation. Moreover, the play is significant as a focal point for debate about the moral and ethical reasons for resisting corrupt governments that instigate unjust wars. Finally, Zuckmayer's play, which, when produced after the war, became a watershed that established debate about German responsibility during the Third Reich, defends the notion that despite the exposure to years of overwhelming propaganda, individuals who can think for themselves can still be humanists.

Notes

1. Whereas previous criticism on the play focused on Zuckmayer's cult of masculinity in the German military (see Anthony Waine, "Carl Zuckmayer's *Des Teufels General* as Critique of the Cult of Masculinity," *Forum for Modern Language Studies* 29, no. 3 [1993]: 257–70), Harras's conversion from hedonism to an ethically motivated life filled with religious overtones (see Henry Glade, "Carl Zuckmayer's *The Devil's General* as Autobiography," *Modern Drama* 9 [May 1966]: 183–90), the identification of Harras as a combatant with diabolical forces (see Jennifer Taylor, "The Dilemma of Patriotism in German Plays of the Second World War," *New German Studies* 9, no. 3 [1981]: 181–92), or an argument for a nostalgic sense of the glories of Germanness before the country was tainted by the values of the Reich (see Mariatte C. Denman, "Nostalgia for a Better Germany: Carl Zuckmayer's *Des Teufels General*," *German Quarterly* 76, no. 4 [2003]: 369–80). My study differs from previous criticism by advocating that the play provides a forum for resistance to totalitarianism.
2. Joseph Goebbels was at the University of Heidelberg at the time, completing his doctoral work in eighteenth-century Romantic drama. Later, Goebbels criticized Zuckmayer's pacifism and accused him of writing comedies that mocked German life. Goebbels had a major hand in getting Zuckmayer's plays banned when the Nazis staged book-burning rallies after 1933.
3. After World War I, Udet founded an aircraft construction company in Munich and then became a stunt pilot who dazzled audiences in Germany, Western Europe, and the United States. In 1933, he introduced the Stuka, a high-speed dive bomber, to Lufthansa. Despite the fact that he had never joined the Nazi Party, he was appointed head of the Luftwaffe Technical Office in 1936 and was promoted to Generalluftzeugmeister in 1938. Ultimately, the Nazis blamed him for faulty aircraft production and for the failure of the air war in the Battle of Britain. On November 17, 1941, he committed suicide in Berlin, but the Nazis covered up the shooting by calling his death a flying accident and giving him a state funeral. For details about Udet's life, see Herbert Lederer, "The Drama of Ernst Udet: A Nazi General in Eastern and Western Perspective," in *Theatrum Mundi: Essays on German Drama and German Literature Dedicated to Harold Lenz on His Seventieth Birthday, September 11, 1978*, ed. Edward R. Haynes (Munich: Wilhelm Fink, 1980), 175–84.
4. Carl Zuckmayer, *A Part of Myself*, trans. Richard and Clara Winston (New York: Harcourt Brace Jovanovich, 1970), 381.
5. Siegfried Mews, *Carl Zuckmayer* (Boston: G. K. Hall, 1981), 83.
6. Throughout the course of his career, Hilpert directed nine of Zuckmayer's sixteen plays. Zuckmayer and Hilpert first met in 1925, the year the latter directed *Der fröhliche Weinberg* in Berlin; the play went on to be successful in Frankfurt and then throughout smaller cities in Germany. Hilpert's wonderful direction also contributed to the success of *Der Hauptmann von Köpenick* when it was staged at the Deutsches Theater in Berlin during 1931. Actually, Zuckmayer had written *Des Teufels General* with Hilpert in mind as the director. For details about the collaborations between Zuckmayer and Hilpert, see William Grange, *Partnership in the German Theatre: Zuckmayer and Hilpert, 1925–1961* (New York: Peter Lang, 1991).

7. Ibid., 122–23.
8. For a summary of the critical debate concerning the play, see Alan Robertshaw, "The Downfall of General Harras: Carl Zuckmayer's *Des Teufels General* and Its Critical Reception," *Modern Languages* 66, no. 4 (1985): 242–47; and Hans Wagener, *Carl Zuckmayer Criticism: Tracing Endangered Fame* (Columbia, SC: Camden House, 1995), especially 83–104.
9. For a comparison of the film version and the play, see Edward M.V. Plater, "Helmut Käutner's Film Adaptation of *Des Teufels General*," *Literature/Film Quarterly* 22, no. 4 (1994): 253–64.
10. For a review of this production, see Reinhold Grimm, "Harras in Dallas," *Brecht Jahrbuch* (1980): 201–5.
11. Peter Hoffmann, *German Resistance to Hitler* (Cambridge, MA: Harvard University Press, 1988), 78.
12. Peter Hoffmann, *The History of the German Resistance, 1933–1945*, trans. Richard Barry (Cambridge, MA: MIT Press, 1977), 113.
13. Theodore S. Hamerow, *On the Road to the Wolf's Lair: German Resistance to Hitler* (Cambridge, MA: Harvard University Press, 1997), 224.
14. There is ample evidence to suggest that anti-Semitism in Germany increased during the years immediately preceding the rise of National Socialism. In the aftermath of World War I, Jews were blamed as the internal enemy that caused the German defeat that resulted in the humiliation of the Treaty of Versailles. Jews also became linked both with the moral decline of the country during the decadent years of the Weimar Republic and with the financial collapse of Germany during the Depression. The Nazis were able to associate Jews with the Bolsheviks, the enemies of fascist government as well as the alleged threats to the Nazi utopia of a pure racial state. German citizens readily accepted the fact that the Nazi Party platform was intricately bound to anti-Semitism. Thus, in the 1932 presidential elections (which was the last "poll" taken of the degree of anti-Semitism in the country, since there was no voting conducted between 1933 and 1945), 36.8 percent of the population voted for Hitler and the National Socialist German Workers Party. In short, anti-Semitism in Germany became the norm in the 1930s, and even many Jews who acknowledged that reality were only too glad to cooperate with the Nazis in making emigration plans. However, there is no evidence to suggest that, although German citizens readily accepted anti-Semitism as the norm, they felt the same about genocide.
15. Hamerow, *On the Road*, 319.
16. For details about the abortive assassination attempt, see Hoffmann, *German Resistance to Hitler*, especially 117–25; and Hoffmann, *The History of the German Resistance, 1933–1945*, 397–411.
17. Zuckmayer, *A Part of Myself*, 382.
18. Robertshaw, "The Downfall of General Harras," 245.
19. Denman, "Nostalgia for a Better Germany," 372. In particular, Zuckmayer cites Theodor Haubach, Wilhelm Leuschner, and Count Hellmuth von Moltke, all of whom were hanged as coconspirators with Stauffenberg.
20. Roy C. Cowen, "Type-Casting in Carl Zuckmayer's *The Devil's General*," *University of Dayton Review* 13, no. 1 (1976): 83.
21. The major difference between Zuckmayer and Chekhov, who were writing realist plays

about life in Germany and Russia, respectively, is that Chekhov was aiming for a more universal appeal whereas Zuckmayer clearly had a German-Austrian audience in mind.

22. Carl Zuckmayer, *The Devil's General*, trans. Ingrid C. Gilbert and William F. Gilbert, in *Masters of Modern Drama*, ed. Haskell M. Block and Robert G. Shedd (New York: Random House, 1962), 935. All subsequent citations are from this edition and are included within parentheses in the text.
23. Margot Finke, *Carl Zuckmayer's Germany* (Frankfurt am Main: Haag and Herchen, 1990), 201–2.
24. In 1966, Zuckmayer publicly lamented the fact that intellectuals procrastinated too long before 1933 to stem the rise of National Socialism. See Michael H. Kater, "Anti-Fascist Intellectuals in the Third Reich," *Canadian Journal of History/Annales Canadiennes d'Histoire* 16, no. 2 (1981): 263.
25. Ausma Balinkin, *The Central Women Figures in Carl Zuckmayer's Dramas* (Bern: Peter Lang, 1978), 95.
26. Zuckmayer, *A Part of Myself*, 402.
27. Lutz Weltmann, "Two Recent Plays," *German Life and Letters* 2 (1948–1949): 161.
28. Waine, "Carl Zuckmayer's *Des Teufels Generall*, as Critique of the Cult of Masculinity," 268.
29. Ian C. Loram, "Carl Zuckmayer—German Playwright in America," *Educational Theatre Journal* 9, no. 3 (1957): 183.
30. The name Harras probably derives from Friedrich von Schiller's 1804 play *Wilhelm Tell*. According to legend, in the fourteenth century, William Tell murdered the brutal Austrian bailiff Albrecht Gessler who forced Tell to shoot an apple off his son's head. Rudolf der Harras, Gessler's adjutant, was portrayed as a sympathetic soul even though he was "the devil's general." In act 1 of *The Devil's General*, strangely enough, Harras is asked to shoot a wine glass off a young officer's head.
31. Plater, "Helmut Käutner's Film Adaptation of *Des Teufels Generall*," 259.
32. Hitler consistently demeaned Americans as being weak, particularly Roosevelt, whom he called "Rosenfeld" to suggest that the American president had an affinity for Jews (he had appointed some Jewish people to cabinet positions) and to insinuate further that he was secretly Jewish or had Jewish ancestry (which were untrue).
33. Glade, "Carl Zuckmayer's *The Devil's General* as Autobiography," 59.
34. Plater, "Helmut Käutner's Film Adaptation of *Des Teufels Generall*," 262–63.
35. Waine, "Carl Zuckmayer's *Des Teufels General* as Critique of the Cult of Masculinity," 259.
36. Glade, "The Motif of Encounter in Zuckmayer's Dramas," 187.
37. Lederer, "The Drama of Ernst Udet: A Nazi General in Eastern and Western Perspective," 178.
38. Waine, "Carl Zuckmayer's *Des Teufels General* as Critique of the Cult of Masculinity," 264.
39. For example, see Sheila Rooke, "Carl Zuckmayer," in *German Men of Letters*, vol. 3, *Expressionism and After*, ed. Alex Natan (London: Oswald Wolff, 1964), 218; Robertshaw, "The Downfall of General Harras," 243; and Wagener, *Carl Zuckmayer Criticism*, 86–104, passim.
40. Robertshaw, "The Downfall of General Harras," 242.
41. Glade, "Carl Zuckmayer's *The Devil's General* as Autobiography," 58.
42. There was a long history of anti-Semitism in Germany. During the early part of the twentieth century, much was written in Germany, including many dissertations, about the

false notion that the Jews refused to assimilate into German society. Anti-Semitism became the norm in Germany during the twentieth century. As a result, during the early and mid-1930s, many Germans and Jews mutually agreed that Jewish emigration from Germany was a noble goal. However, moral Christians in Germany did not subscribe to the notion that anti-Semitism should result in genocide. In other words, they agreed that if the Jews could not assimilate, they should emigrate; murder was never publicly discussed. In short, Zuckmayer's play forces the majority of German citizens to question their own judgments during the Third Reich.

43. Zuckmayer, *A Part of Myself*, 378.
44. Ibid., 319.
45. Ibid., 320.
46. Taylor, "The Dilemma of Patriotism in German Plays of the Second World War," 188.
47. Murray B. Peppard, "Carl Zuckmayer: Cold Light in a Divided World," *Monatshefte* 49, no. 3 (1957): 126.
48. Denman, "Nostalgia for a Better Germany: Carl Zuckmayer's *Des Teufels General*," 377.

"Imposing the Standards of Boston on Japan"
Kasutori Performance, Censorship, and the Occupation

—DAVID JORTNER

At the end of the Second World War, the Allies had an enormous rebuilding task ahead of them in Japan. Much of the nation lay in ruins, the economy was in shambles, and the Americans feared Communist expansion in Asia if Japan was not rebuilt. As a result, while the fighting stopped with the Japanese surrender, the American military and American foreign policy continued a propaganda war in order to win the "hearts and minds" of the Japanese populace and move them away from wartime fanaticism.

The Allied Occupation of Japan (or, more accurately, the American Occupation of Japan, as the Occupation, or *Senryō*, was an almost entirely American endeavor) is accurately described as "The Confusion Era" by noted cultural historian Mark Sandler. The theatre world in Japan during the Occupation (1945–1952) was no stranger to the issues of confusion and control. From the regulation of kabuki to the attempted transformation of the *shingeki* (modern realist) stage, the history of Occupation theatre is filled with stories of censorial confusion, Japanese theatrical evasions and resubmissions, and cultural misunderstandings between American censors, Japanese officials, and theatre artists.

One of the most interesting theatrical subjects to examine in light of this confusion is the genre of erotic performance. Erotic performance, or what I term (after historian John Dower) *kasutori* performance, not only tested the limits of expression but also confronted American censors with issues of morality, freedom, and control. Japanese lawmakers and police also attempted to exact censorial control over this art form but their concerns often clashed with postwar American ideology. One of the many difficulties American forces faced was that the type of moral control called for ran counter to the stated Occupation goals of freedom of expression and commerce. Thus, U.S. censors were uncomfortable with demanding an American morality for the Japanese populace, while other officers felt that one of the censors' roles was the elimination of "indecent" performances. Essentially, the American postwar military attempted to uphold contradictory goals, although they were sometimes unaware of the dueling nature of their mandates. A study of kasutori performance perhaps best exposes these competing ideologies.

Issues of censorial and military control, civilian freedoms, eroticism and sexuality, and cultural imposition are wrapped into the discussions about erotic performance during the Occupation. This essay explores the different genres of *kasutori* performance, looks at the censorship structures in place in both Japanese and American contexts, and highlights the places wherein the two censorship structures came into conflict. The issue of "eroticism" is examined through contemporary views (on both sides) toward erotic material. Kasutori performance challenged Occupation authorities, not just in conventional means (militarily or morally) but philosophically. Indeed, rather than being seen as an interesting footnote, kasutori performance is an excellent case study into the contradictions of Allied policy. American authorities were often in ideological conflict with each other during the Occupation; they wanted to use the theatre to promote freedom and democracy while at the same time enforcing a moral code. This was the case even as SCAP (Supreme Command for Allied Powers) personnel fought among themselves over what these terms and ideas meant. Moreover, the addition of local Japanese censorship laws and the stated Occupation goal of moving the Japanese toward self-governance also conflicted with the declared idea of "freedom" and required SCAP intervention. Kasutori performance showcased the contradictory impulse inherent in occupation, especially the Occupation of Japan. The Americans wanted to promote freedom but control content; they desired and sexualized the Japanese as they simultaneously sought to impose and promote Western morality on the theatre.

Before delving into Occupation policy it is important to understand the divisions within the General Headquarters (GHQ) of SCAP. There were two primary agencies charged with very different missions at GHQ. The first of these was the Civil Information and Education Division (CI&E), whose job involved reeducation and the promotion of democratic ideals. In SCAP documents, it is often CI&E that calls for the promotion of shingeki and textual changes to classical scripts in order to bring the theatre in line with SCAP policy. The other division was the Press, Pictorial and Broadcast (PPB) division of the Civil

Censorship Detachment (CCD), whose job was the elimination of those works found objectionable by Occupation authorities. Essentially, CI&E had the propagandistic job of encouraging the theatre to produce "democratic" plays and wanted to use the theatre to promote the American agenda; essentially this was a form of "positive" censorship that aimed at reforming the theatre along approved American ideologies. In contrast, CCD was tasked with the discovery and elimination of objectionable material. In addition, CCD had the power to prevent a production or script from moving forward or to command a cessation of a currently produced work. Essentially, they were "negative" censors whose role was the elimination of objectionable work. These two branches essentially were the result of the dual nature of SCAP censorship. As SCAP's own "History of the Nonmilitary Activities of the Occupation of Japan" claims: "Guarantees of freedom of speech, expression and opinion, which the Supreme Commander was directed to assure for the new Japan entailed the removal of militarists and ultranationalists from positions of influence, the abrogation or modification of laws and regulations which conflicted with occupation objectives, and the encouragement of the people to *desire individual freedoms* and to respect fundamental human rights. Minimum controls and [the] censorship of films were authorized and freedom of thought was to be fostered by the dissemination of democratic ideals and principles through all available media of public information."[1] According to the report, freedoms were necessary, but freedoms could only be created through censorship. This inherent contradiction would cause dissension not only between SCAP and the Japanese theatre, but also between divisions within SCAP itself. Moreover, both CI&E and CCD were divided into geographical zones, with Tokyo as Zone I, Kyoto/Osaka as Zone II, and so on. Since Zone I was the primary headquarters of SCAP and the PPB, it had the authority to overturn decisions made at lower levels. In essence, any script in Japan had to navigate both positive (CI&E) and negative (CCD) censors in both their home region and Tokyo.

Censorship procedures also shifted and changed during the years of the Occupation; this added to confusion for American censors, Japanese officials, and theatre producers. In the first few years of the Occupation (until around 1947) SCAP practiced what was known as "precensorship." Essentially, every script was sent to CCD for approval before it could be staged; this resulted in CCD having between 2,000 and 4,000 scripts to examine per month.[2] These scripts were predominantly spot-checked by native Japanese speakers who would flag any inappropriate material for further examination; in 1946 and 1947 these violations were primarily of a political nature. After the native Japanese speaker had examined it, the scripts went to CCD officers for the decision to approve, alter (that is, modify a word, words, or sentence in the text), or suppress the script.

Despite the large numbers of staff, the precensorship system was clearly untenable. Theatrical producers disliked that it slowed down the amount of productions possible, and CCD was overworked. In 1947 SCAP began to shift to a system of postcensorship, where spot checks were undertaken on work that had already been already staged. In addition, CCD investigated claims of violations made by either local police or even by concerned Japanese citizens. However, the nature of live theatre often meant that CCD arrived after the production had closed; in such cases they could do little other than to bring the offending author/producer in for chastisement. Both CI&E and CCD filed numerous reports on their activities during both the pre- and postcensorship era; these reports detailed theatre work even when SCAP declined to undertake any censorial activity.

On paper, the above systems would seem to work and mesh well in order to create a streamlined system of censorship. However, in reality numerous problems plagued SCAP authorities. CI&E and CCD fought over propriety and turf and their respective missions. In addition, theatrical producers felt constrained by the process, feeling that the censorship procedures (especially in the early years of the Occupation) led to extreme bottlenecks. Moreover, the system presupposed that theatrical producers would be willing to abide by regulations instead of avoiding them; while in certain cases (such as the well-known kabuki and shingeki theatres) this was not an issue, other smaller theatres often ignored censorship restrictions/procedures for the sake of convenience or profit. The officials who conceived of these procedures were familiar with a Western theatrical paradigm, and alternative or marginal performance genres such as kasutori presented them with challenges for which regulations left them unprepared.

John Dower sees erotic performances as a part of what he terms "kasutori culture" after the alcoholic drink of the same name (*kasutori shōchū* is a beverage that lent its name to a genre of pulp, erotic, and escapist literature after the war known as *kasutori bunka* [kasutori culture].) Kasutori culture, according to Dower, "flourished into the 1950s and left a gaudy legacy of escapism, titillation and outright sleaze—a commercial world dominated by sexually oriented entertainments and a veritable cascade of pulp literature."[3] Kasutori work included novels, films, pulp magazines, and stage shows. Generally these works celebrated indulgence, humor, and a lack of authority, and an end to traditional societal norms of moral behavior. Moreover, during the Occupation kasutori came to be seen as "honest" due to its frank depictions of the above. In fact, as Dower notes, "Thanks to the pulp publications...life on the margins became intertwined with theories of decadence as the only true honesty and authenticity... In some of these formulations, sex, degeneracy, and 'love' even became equated with 'revolution.'"[4] Therefore, kasutori art and literature were not understood as merely examples of decadence, but important markers of postwar freedoms. Although most kasutori publications and performances attracted little critical notice, the work tended to be both profitable and pervasive in the Occupation years.

Despite this fact, analysis of kasutori performance is notably absent from Western scholarship. Most writing about these "decadent" forms focus on literature, especially novels and pulp magazines. In the theatre, most writings on censorship focus on the more traditional kabuki theatre or the modern shingeki stage. Analysis of kasutori performances are sporadic, either focusing on the genre as an example of freedom under "democracy," or on the titillating aspects of sexual performance. Because so little critical analysis of this art form exists, I first examine and outline three genres within the category of kasutori performance.[5] These genres, although different in style and form, each involved the titillation of the audience, the presentation of the sexualized body, a concern with commercial success, and an interest in sensational stories and events both from the Occupation present and the past.

The first genre of erotic entertainment was the *gakubuchi nūdo shyō*, or nude frame picture show. The nude frame picture show, was, as its name implies, the re-creation of great works of art (predominantly Western) in tableau vivant style. The first of these performances, entitled *The Birth of Venus*, was staged in 1947 by Hata Toyokichi and was a popular success. Dower writes, "Lines of male devotees of Western art...extended from the performance hall down five flights of stairs and out into the street."[6] *The Birth of Venus*, interestingly enough, did not feature nude performance but rather "a statuesque half-Russian young woman named Nakamura Shōko, who draped gauze over her bosom and loins."[7] Later productions in this style were more explicit. A SCAP theatrical log sheet of the erotic review *La Bomba*, staged at the Teitoza Gokai Gekijō in December 1947, describes "scene 3–A semi-nude woman with breasts exposed, poses beside a tree in a tableau vivant" and "Scene 18—An enlarged hundred million yen bill is seen on the stage but a semi nude woman, breasts exposed, is fitted in the cut-out portion of the lady."[8] Another logsheet from April 1948 notes, "A play entitled *Teitoza's Beauty Album* (*Teitoza Meiga Album*) submitted by the Teitoza group in Shinjuku, contains four nude scenes. During the four scenes, which are similarly staged, two different women appear in a picture frame with bared breasts. Each scene lasts for approximately two minutes."[9] These performances eventually dropped the "art" motif, and merely had young women stand partially exposed in a scenario while the audience looked on.

The show *Spring Dance*, for example (*Haru no Odori*), while generally a dance review piece, did contain a tableau entitled "four erotic scenes. Four girls will appear in quick succession with bared breasts."[10] Dower claims that shows such as this favored actresses with "unusually white skin": "The latter quality was a virtue in the old, traditional canons of personal attractiveness, although now…an obvious overlay of bringing one closer to the Caucasians."[11] The gakubuchi nūdo shyō is thus seen not only as a form of erotic entertainment but also as a site of cultural contestation/construction in the postwar period; not only were Western works of art emulated and "performed" for a predominantly Japanese audience, but they also featured actresses known for their "whiteness," thus connecting the Japanese performers to the Occupation troops. Dower is correct in suggesting that use of "whiteness" is linked to Japan's traditional beauty aesthetic of "paleness."[12] However, it was also seen as sexually desirable and a way for Japanese audiences to reestablish a sense of control and voyeurism over their American occupiers.

In *Embracing Defeat* Dower suggests the gakubuchi nūdo shyō was the progenitor of other forms of erotic entertainment, especially the striptease show. The striptease or burlesque show (the two terms were often used interchangeably by SCAP) was the second genre of kasutori performance. Dower writes that "the strip show soon (1947) made its debut with a rather tame revue called *Tokyo Follies*, which climaxes with dancers striking a pose, reaching behind their backs, and unhooking the tops of their costumes."[13] Striptease and burlesque quickly became popular, making stars out of featured performers and spreading throughout the country.[14] These shows had a variety of structures, from musical revues to shows with comic skits, jokes, and nudity, to outright striptease shows. Striptease and burlesque shows were both relatively cheap to produce, attend, and thus fairly profitable during the Occupation years. For example, the 1947 performance of *Man's World* by the Tokyo Follies Troupe was criticized by SCAP as "one of the best examples of bad burlesque yet reviewed. Cheap and routine in its skits, there is no excuse for the production except its low admission price—20 yen."[15]

Nudity, as well as low admission costs, contributed to these shows' popularity. A CI&E comment page from 1947 discusses the production of *Log of the Cruise of the Dream Islands* (*Dorimoto Kokaiki*) presented by Kokusai Geinosha. During the section of the show known as *Festival of Breasts* (*Chifusa no Saiten*), "a gauzy scarf was stripped from the raised arms of a Japanese girl posing on a pedestal revealing her naked except for a G-string for a brief period before she left the scene."¹⁶ SCAP describes audience response: "Public reaction was swift and for every one of the three shows per day the dance was played to capacity houses (In the Japanese sense that there is not even standing room)...newspaper reporters wrote slyly of young boys in the audience 'filled with ecstasy' and of 'freedom' in this day of democracy"¹⁷ (fig. 1). The implication that the freedoms of the Occupation are somehow manifest in the popularity of the striptease is fascinating; it provides a possible unforeseen reason for the underlying popularity of kasutori-era performances. Freed from wartime austerity and militarist control, the burlesque performance could be seen not only as erotic escapism but also as a means of self-expression.

Figure 1. Actress Maeyuki Sachiko (center), backstage at the Naniwa Theatre for the show *Dorimuto Kokaiki* (*The Log of the Cruise to the Dream Islands*), produced by Kokusai Geinosha in 1947 in Osaka. Publicity photo submitted to the *Osaka Nichi-Nichi* newspaper. Courtesy of the National Archives and Records Administration, College Park, MD.

The third form of kasutori performance was the erotic or salacious play. Primarily staged in the shingeki format, these plays mirrored the pulp novels of the kasutori era in their portrayal of the most shocking, erotic, and sensationalist stories the writers could create. Titles from this style of production include *Hidari Jingoro's Yoshiwara Amusement* (*Hidari Jingoro Yoshiwara*, 1947), *Abe Sada, A Woman of Sensual Desire* (*Abe Sada*, 1947), *Rejuvenation Room* (*Kaishun Sitsu*, 1948), *Lost Virgin* (*Rosuto Vahjin*, 1948), *Decameron Love Affair* (*Renai Decameron*, 1948), and *A Woman's Life* (*Onna no Ikko*, 1949). *Lost Virgin* provides an

KASUTORI PERFORMANCE, CENSORSHIP, AND THE OCCUPATION

excellent example of the kind of performance discussed. The synopsis of the play in SCAP files reads:

> Flapper, a stubborn young woman who desires to have sexual relations with men, prays to Saint Mary to protect her from becoming pregnant. However, her father who is a doctor objects to his daughter losing her virginity. After much quarrelling, an operation is performed to remove her hymen, and thereafter she begins to flirt with many men.
> Later she meets a detective whom she loves, but who doubts her chastity.
> Proudly she leads him to a safe where her precious hymen is safeguarded, but to her surprise finds it stolen. So the detective goes on a search, and one day finally discovers her hymen blown into a balloon floating in the air.
> After returning the hymen he marries her.[18]

The play was produced by the Moulin Rouge Troupe and performed at the Shinjuku theatre. It was not just the sexual content (here played for humorous effect) that linked this to kasutori culture; the presence of a love story and detective fiction also linked it to the genre.

Similarly, the play *The Woman Burglar's Confession* (*Joto Zange*) offers another example of these sexualized plots. A SCAP report noted a "female burglar chief offers herself to her three male accomplices, who, under the influence of liquor, are desirous of raping the daughter of the owner of the house into which they have broken. The woman burglar, who feels sorry for the girl, takes off her outer dress and clad only in a chemise pulls down her drawers."[19] The play was produced by the Terajima troupe of Tokyo and performed on or around January 2, 1948. Both *Lost Virgin* and *Woman Burglar's Confession* have all the hallmarks of kasutori theatre: an obsession with sex and sexuality, crime, and romance. In many ways, works such as *Woman Burglar* echo many of the noir themes of the 1930s and 1950s; the main difference between them is the overt sex and sexuality as well as the presentation of nudity in the kasutori plays. Very little scholarship in English or Japanese exists about kasutori works due to their sexual nature; what is written focuses on individual story tropes (often in later Japanese theatre and film) and not on the texts or genre as a whole.[20]

The style, content, and nature of these shows were not new to Japan. Japanese theatre dealt with political and moral censorship for a long time before the Occupation. The Japanese theatre had a long history of official and unofficial government control, with prohibitions on certain Edo-era bunraku and kabuki plays, especially those which were deemed too sexually suggestive or those which implied governmental officials or activities were being conducted in bad faith. The Meiji era (1868–1912) also allowed for the censorship of stage productions deemed to be "injurious to public morals"; often this phrase was used to refer to those plays that rewarded vice or presented morality counter to "Japanese values."

However, with the rise of the Japanese Shōwa government in the 1930s, censorship restrictions gained strength. Plays at this time were most often censored for political reasons, especially those that questioned the Emperor system, advocated for leftist causes, or criticized the war effort. On a local level, stricter censorship went into effect in 1940, when all theatre managers and companies had to submit scripts for approval to the Information bureau (Jōhō Kyoku). The government wanted the theatre to promote wartime goals and would censor plays and productions it felt were too critical. In 1944, the government enacted Regulations for the Control of Theatrical Production, creating a national level of censorship in addition to the existing local ones.

After the war, Japanese censorship laws changed with the adoption of the new Constitution and (especially) the presence of SCAP authorities. Political censorship was definitely the purview of SCAP; however, SCAP, while overtly censoring many works (especially in the first few years of the Occupation) also pushed for creative freedom and freedom of expression for the stage. In order to encourage this latter goal, SCAP (at least initially) left the issue of moral censorship to the Japanese government. For example, the proposed production of *The Woman Burglar's Confession* met with this reply from Don Brown, censor for CI&E, who simply stated, "We don't approve of it, but the police will probably step in."[21]

Nonetheless, the freedoms promoted by SCAP conflicted with moral censorship codes, and the resultant confusion led to an explosion of erotic performance forms during the Occupation years. Moral censorship codes fell under the purview of local police, who either exceeded or ceded their authority. Although Japan created several postwar censorship laws, the confusion surrounding understanding, application, and enforcement of these laws left many of the decisions on obscenity in the hands of SCAP. Moreover, since SCAP censorship was primarily conducted on a local basis, productions not considered objectionable in some areas were closed and/or censored in others. In addition, both CI&E and CCD had their own censorial concerns and missions, and often these brought them into conflict with local authorities. Finally, SCAP agencies also had to balance moral controls with their mission of noninterference; documents illustrate a desire for moral instruction among SCAP members that went against the overall mission of restoring control of the theatre to the Japanese.

After the war the Japanese government created a new constitution. Article 21 proclaimed that "no censorship shall be maintained." However, this law clashed with the tradition of local censorial control of material deemed morally unsuitable by authorities. In his article "Obscenity, Pornography and the Law in Japan," scholar James Alexander claims that "government authorities typically used public hygiene laws to restrict the sale and distribution of obscene material under Article 175 of the revised 1907 Criminal Code."[22] This section of the criminal code states, "A person who distributes or sells an obscene writing, picture or other object or who publically displays the same shall be punished with imprisonment…or a fine."[23] Article 175 did not specify what was deemed obscene, allowing for each region to determine its own community standards. Clearly, with Article 175, there were enough Japanese legal structures in place to suppress material deemed obscene.

SCAP documents indicate, however, that the fine was often not a significant deterrent. One of the first records of police involvement in the control and censorship comes from the CI&E weekly report from August 7, 1947. Under the heading "Liberal Shows," the report states: "According to the Bunka Tsushin (Cultural Press service) of 4 August, 1947, the attraction 'Young Man and Model,' presented by the Daiei Theatre in Chiba City with the model appearing completely in the nude was the 'show of the century,' until the model and the director of the show were arrested, fined 15 Yen and told to perform hereafter in at least some form of garment. This is the first known case of police intervention regarding 'liberal shows' in post war Japan."[24] The noted ¥15 fine was small and clearly failed as a deterrent. For example, a fine of 15 or 20 yen to an actress was significantly less than what (reputedly) they could make by appearing in these types of performances. According to a newspaper article from the June 30 issue of *Jiji* entitled "Nude Shows Big Attraction," "Any dancer that is willing to appear on the stage stripped and in the manner her enterpriser wants is receiving from 900 to 1000 yen per week for her part. All she has to do is step out into the spotlight and pose."[25]

Enforcement of obscenity laws was also a site of confusion and contestation between local police, theatre producers, and SCAP authorities. Generally, police problems fell into one of three areas: outright corruption on the part of the officers, a concern by SCAP that any censorship action would be construed as a return to the "thought police" of the war years, or pressure from the American censors to allow for freedoms while at the same time the expectation (again from SCAP) that the police would control obscenity. As a result of these situations, SCAP authorities were drawn into dealing with erotic performances, despite a lack of desire to do so.

Theatre producers went to SCAP because there had been several instances of police abuse of authority, especially in the surveillance and control of erotic performances. Many theatre producers resisted the reinstallation of "police boxes," special seating reserved for police (in order to make sure obscenity regulations were being obeyed). However, in January 1948 the Tokyo Metropolitan Police Board announced the restoration of mandatory "police boxes" in theatres in Tokyo. A March 1948 SCAP memo describes the use of police boxes. It states: "While on censorship duty to the theatres, it has been noticed that several theatres including the Rokku, Ikeburo Cultural, and Moulin Rouge Theatres, have special seats, conspicuously built within the theatre. There have been reports that police and firemen are seen constantly in the theatres and sometimes bring along friends, whose admission is of course gratis. Erotic shows according to theatre owners draw the greatest number of police, who reportedly sit through entire performances."[26] Theatre producers, understandably, were dismayed at the loss of revenue (from a loss of saleable seats) while police considered these structures necessary. However, one can question if the supplied tickets were either police abuses or (perhaps more likely) producers' bribes given to allow erotic performances to continue.

As a result of this police pressure, theatre producers turned to SCAP for help in controlling what they viewed as abuses of authority. The Theatre Exhibitors Association asked SCAP to intervene on their behalf, citing the rising cost of tickets and productions. SCAP agreed with the theatre producers and convinced the Metropolitan Police Board to put the police box plan on hold. However, SCAP ended their report with the following warning to the Theatre Exhibitors Association: "The Japanese conferees…were advised that the CI&E interest in this situation is one of cooperation in any effort to maintain freedom of expression in the theatre; that it is no way to be construed as supporting any resistance on the part of exhibitors…it is urged for the dozenth time [sic] that the managers themselves clean up unfavorable conditions…unless this is done, they can expect only to have the police intrude at the risk of usurping such complete powers of control over performances that the censorship and other forms of restrictive supervision which were only eliminated by SCAP order will be none-too-subtly restored."[27] SCAP's contradictory censorial views are on display here: they eliminated the police boxes while simultaneously reasserting the right of the police to interfere in the theatre.

There was deep concern among SCAP officials that police abuse may have a deleterious effect on Occupation goals. An August 30, 1948, memo by W. L. Thompson of CI&E states that "a new law had been passed which deals with immorality and salaciousness in publications and public exhibitions, and the police have every right to step in. The discussion ensued that great care must be taken in police intervention to insure no impression being given to a revival of 'thought police.'"[28] The possibility of the reappearance of "thought police" would become a major focus for SCAP and allow many kasutori producers to bypass Japanese censors.

The "thought police" issue was the theme of a conference between CCD and members of the Miyagi Prefectural Social Education Section in Sendai in March 1948. According to the records of the conference, the Japanese government requested that theatre producers send them scripts for censorship before being sent to CCD in order to check for obscenity. They were reminded of SCAP's policies for submitting scripts for censorship only to SCAP and told that no unapproved play could be performed. CCD, clearly feeling that the Miyagi authorities had overstepped their boundaries, told them about "the desire of the Allied powers that no permanent internal system of censorship be allowed to flourish in Japan. Misawa and Mochizuki understood that a move such as theirs could easily lead to a rejuvenation of former police and Home Ministry controls over the theater."[29]

As a result, even with plays deemed obscene by Japanese authorities, the Americans sometimes chastised the police for their enforcement of the laws. One example of this is the case of the play *Adultery* (*Kanin*) in November 1948. According to SCAP's summation, "'Adultery' is an erotic play about a jealous husband, his nymphomaniac wife, an impotent demobilee, his nymphomaniac wife, a gay blade who flirts with the above two women, and a fisherman. The result is a mixture of sex."[30] According to SCAP, on November 9 the Japanese police and a public prosecutor, after watching the performance, brought Katayama Riki (the author and director), Murata Tadashi (the theatre manager), and the cast of *Adultery* to the Asakusa police station for questioning for approximately four hours.[31] The result was that the Daito Theatre pulled any further performances of the play.

Looking at the case of *Adultery* with this in mind, one can see the possible reasons for SCAP's reservations. The police raid may have been acceptable, but given the memories and awareness of "thought police," SCAP certainly was concerned with the four hours of questioning that followed. The *Adultery* account indicates that things mainly worked as SCAP wanted: the police stepped in and enforced Japan's moral censorship code. However, according the SCAP memo, CCD viewed this action not as a legal and correct, but as "interference." SCAP claimed the censorship of *Adultery* was "the second time the police has directly interfered with the legitimate theatrical activity in Asakusa."[32] This conclusion to the SCAP memo raises a host of questions, most notably why SCAP termed such action to be "interference" and how they deemed a play, which they admitted was salacious, to be "legitimate." Because the SCAP saw in the police raid a hint of the old "thought police" ways, they deemed the raid "interference" in order to quash any suggestion of ideological control.

At the same time, SCAP wanted to clean up the Asakusa region. Proof of this attitude is seen in a memo from August 1948, "Police Intervention in Extreme Erotic Plays." Willard Thompson brought in H. S. Eaton to find a way to eliminate kasutori performances from the Asakusa area, noting that "the threat of police intervention has worn itself out."[33] Erotic theatre performance in this case shows the contradictory impulses within SCAP: the goal of eliminating erotic performances from Asakusa, while desirable, was seen as less important than avoiding the idea of thought police. While SCAP lamented the low quality of performances in the area, they also were afraid of the perception of "thought police." Although SCAP often tried to avoid the issue, these contradictory impulses put the entire issue of kasutori performance in front of SCAP authorities.

Another reason SCAP was forced to engage with eroticism was the use of SCAP "approval" or rhetoric of "freedom" as permission for the avoidance of local obscenity laws. One example of this comes from producer Takano Hiroshi and the play *Moderu Shou* (*Model Show*). Produced in Sapporo in 1949, *Model Show* came to the attention of SCAP authorities based (in part) on a newspaper article in the *Minato Shinbun*. Takano was called into SCAP offices and, according to reports, was "verbally reprimanded for using censorship approval of his obscene show as the basis for evading prosecution under Japanese laws."[34] Takano's wife was also brought in and reprimanded, and he was provided with a copy of the Pictorial Code for reference. Finally, Takano was made to sign the following statement: "While this troupe (*Model Show*, comprised of 21 members) was touring Hokkaido for performances from 15 April 1949 I was called to PPB Broadcast Station, Sapporo on 29 April 1949 and was instructed by the Censor that censorship approval does not constitute exemption for penalties for presentation of obscene material. I was also explained as to pictorial censorship regulations. I have fully understood the instructions and hereby pledge myself to abide by the censorship regulations of the Allied authorities so as to not repeat violations thereof in our future performances."[35] Essentially, Takano was forced to engage in a form of *tenkō* by the American authorities. Tenkō was the forced, public, ideological recantation forced upon socialists, communists, and other political dissidents by the militarist Japanese regime before and during the war years. In many ways, including the signed statement of allegiance and the reprimand of both Takano and his wife, SCAP's actions resemble those practiced by the militarists. Undoubtedly, SCAP was unaware of the connection, but, as many in the theatre community were forced to commit tenkō (notably director Senda Koreya), the SCAP's actions would have a chilling effect. SCAP was more interested in protecting its own reputation than in recreating tenkō or reestablishing militarism. However, in essence, it was a form of de facto censorial control.

SCAP also encountered producers who used Occupation goals as excuses for staging erotic performances. These producers often used the rubrics of freedom of expression or artistic freedom in order to claim legitimacy for their work. One of the more interesting cases of this was the production of *Male Prostitute in Grove* (*Kansho no Mori*) scheduled for performance at the Rokka-zu theatre in 1949. The play, which dealt with the lives of sexual purveyors and deviants in Tokyo, was an "atrocity" according to Thompson. Thompson noted that "Mr. Nakazawa defended his choice of plays by saying this will expose these characters who lurk about Ueno Park and therefore he is doing a great service. (This line of reasoning was expressed more some months ago when a theatre manager defended naked shows as a means of *emancipating men*)."[36] Thompson used CI&E's advisory powers to encourage rewrites, and reported that "Mr. Nakazawa said there would be some rewriting of the script and no repeat on this type of play."[37] CI&E's "positive" censorship is on display here; while they don't ban *Male Prostitute*, their suggestion that Nakazawa would rewrite the script served as an effective mode of censorial control (without having the negative connotations of actual censorship). SCAP often used its powers to encourage better productions (both politically and artistically), but in this circumstance it appears as if moral content also came into play.

Another example of SCAP's contradictory impulses came from its desire to promote accuracy and "truth" in advertising as well as its wish to control obscenity. One interesting example of this comes from SCAP's involvement with the marketing of kasutori performances. CCD was concerned with what they termed "Indecent Advertising" of salacious shows, and in 1947 went so far as to examine the "salacious content" in shows that contained "posters classified as erotic."[38] A 1947 memo reads, "Poster advertising erotic theatrical production 'Festival of Venus' (Venus Matsuri) portrays a girl clad only in a bouquet of flowers. It is intimated that beautiful, youthful nude females can be seen at the performance."[39] However, the examiner's note at the bottom of the memo raises the question of whether CCD objected to the eroticism in the poster/performance or whether it felt this was false advertising. The memo states that "attendance at the performance revealed that the nakedness advertised could be seen for a brief moment at the end of the play; it did not seem beautiful or youthful."[40]

Thompson and CI&E also took issue with "Indecent Advertising." In August 1948, Thompson sent a note to Mr. Ogasawara, the manager of the Nippon *shōgekijō* (little theatre), regarding the advertising of the show *Gate of Flesh*

(*Nikutai no Mon*).[41] The note describes the "a series of 12" by 15" photographs of naked women in various scenes of the play, displayed on billboards on the street."[42] The memo records how Thompson was "informed that the play itself was bad enough and should not have been permitted, but putting such photos on the streets of Tokyo was definitely out."[43] Thompson also brought the matter to the attention the chief of the Toho Theatre Department. Although SCAP disapproved of the production of *Gate of Flesh* on moral grounds, it did not prohibit the play; however, SCAP did order the removal of all "indecent" advertising and promotion materials. Therefore, it can be inferred that the primary objection to the "indecent" advertising was not only the content but its placement in full view of the public. This example demonstrates the vagaries of SCAP policy: the play (with its eroticism) was allowed because it was behind closed doors, yet advertising in the public sphere was more strictly controlled. (This may partially be because reports often indicated that the advertising was far more suggestive than the performances themselves. A *Jiji* article noted this: "Some theatres are employing advertisements that are far from what is really shown on the stage but people will go in just for the sake of getting a 'cheap thrill.'")[44] Essentially, the erotic marketing materials may have alerted SCAP to plays that otherwise would have been ignored. For Japanese producers, the "enticement" effect of the advertisements had to be balanced with the possibility of attracting unwanted SCAP or police attention.

There were also inconsistencies and policy disagreements within the two SCAP censorship agencies, and this led to misunderstandings and conflicts within the censorship authorities. Thompson and CI&E were fairly active in using their advisory capacity to control and transform erotic performances. As mentioned earlier with *Male Prostitute in Grove*, CI&E occasionally stepped into the censorship arena by advising theatre producers and playwrights to either clean up/rewrite erotic material or to remove it from production altogether. Thompson also arranged several meetings with producers and playwrights to encourage the removal of "obscene material" in favor of plays more geared toward SCAP objectives. For example, in 1948 he met with several theatre producers in order to convince them to clean up performances in Asakusa. The record of that meeting states that "the managers of (five) theatres…which had been billing erotic shows regularly were summoned by Will Thompson…and asked that they withdraw erotic shows (of the Breast display type) from their theatre program. They were told that CIE did not approve of these erotic performances particularly in the shady Asakusa and Shinjuku area. They were not under compulsion but apparently, the managers were convinced that these liberal shows were unhealthy for the Japanese public."[45] One wonders, of course,

KASUTORI PERFORMANCE, CENSORSHIP, AND THE OCCUPATION

what "convinced" the theatre managers; undoubtedly, being called into CI&E headquarters and lectured to by Thompson convinced them it was in their best interests to stop showing such material.

Despite these actions, Thompson still felt SCAP was not doing enough to control eroticism and salacious plays. He went as far as to call a meeting with the CCD, where he took the agency to task for failing to censor productions on a moral basis. According to a CCD report of the meeting, Thompson's "entire discussion was extremely rambling, incoherent and vague," and he "considered CCD an incompetent collection of idlers" who were "doing nothing to justify its existence."[46] Specifically, Thompson seemed outraged not over "anything political"; rather, "he would cite only two (plays) both of which involved moral questions (*Gate of Flesh* and *Encyclopedia of Night*)."[47] Upon being told that both plays had been passed by Don Brown, Thompson's superior, Thompson remarked, "I know—you call Don Brown two or three times every day on the telephone. It's the silliest thing I have ever heard of. Brown hasn't been to a theatre in two years. He doesn't know what's going on. He tells you to pass this stuff, and then I get called down on it all day long."[48] The disagreement (at least in Thompson's eyes) was not about political censorship but about obscenity; Thompson (as seen with the memo on *Male Prostitute*) was an advocate for a greater hand in moral censorship for the Japanese theatre at this time.

The above memo also shows dissension and opposing views within CI&E. Thompson clearly disagreed with Don Brown, the primary CI&E review officer for obscenity. Brown did not support the content of kasutori performances, but he adhered fairly strictly to CI&E written policy regarding such work. Brown articulated that policy:

a. He felt that unless the nudity were of a nature which makes the entire production erotic and incites the audience to sensuality, CI&E would not desire suppression.
b. He felt that real control for such material rests with the Japanese government under the penal code.
c. CI&E would feel that the suppression of nudity could evoke the charge of imposing a "puritan code of morals" on the Japanese.
d. CI&E would "object to ruthless elimination" of a large number of individual nudity scenes.[49]

Brown put his concerns more succinctly in a June 1947 memorandum: "What we object to is imposing the standards of Boston on Japan."[50] Brown acknowledged a different role for censorship in Japan. While other censorship officers wished to re-create the American stage overseas, Brown illustrated an awareness of the cultural differences between the two nations and outlined the role of the censors in attempting to maintain that cultural heterodoxy.

The difference between Thompson's and Brown's views on obscenity are striking. Contradictory impulses on eroticism, however, are not surprising when placed in the context of how Americans viewed the Japanese, especially Japanese women. There was a contradictory view of Japanese women during this time. While openly espousing an equality doctrine that emphasized the ability of women to take political and economic leadership roles in the new Japan, the American view of the Japanese woman also echoed traditional Western orientalist views of the East. In this latter view, Asian women were (and arguably still are) seen as a mixture of sexualized and naive, innocent and mercenary, present and available, while at the same time forbidden and exotic.

This orientalist view was seen in GI cartoonist Bill Hume's popular representations of Japanese female/American male interactions in a comic titled *Babysan* (also the name of its main character). Hume's comic was printed weekly in the Far East edition of *Navy Times* and collected and printed as a text in 1953 (with the suggestive subtitle "A Private Look at the Japanese Occupation"). The conflicting American impulses regarding Japanese eroticism are documented in this book. While there was a desire for morality among SCAP authorities, there was also a strong attraction to the stereotype of a sexualized Japanese woman. The book's back cover describes the orientalist discourse of the work. Hume writes, "Babysan is not a travel-bureau impression, nor is she to be found in movie travelogues. She is a phase of Japanese-American life hitherto untouched—a phase that will keep the reader roaring with laughter. She is a symbol of the Japanese impact on young Americans who suddenly find themselves surrounded by oriental culture."[51] Babysan is presented in the work as sexually available, intellectually innocent, and materialistic. Babysan is clearly a sexual being, evidenced by her display of "naturally brown" skin (an alluring trait for the American GIs), her sexual teasing and refusal (as well as the navy man's confusion about how to untie a kimono), and the Hume's drawings of postcoital scenes. Babysan is also inimically connected to the idea that she is available for "purchase." Hume's text clearly states that Babysan is not a prostitute, but "she brings the sunshine into her boyfriend's life and expects, naturally enough, to be rewarded for her efforts." The accompanying cartoon on this page has Babysan complaining (in a postcoital scenario), "Why you all the time bring candy—why never *okane* (money)?"[52] Finally, Babysan is seen as simultaneously manipulative (as when she asks for money) but also intellectually naive (in one panel she asks, "Missouri state named after ship—*ne*?"[53]).

KASUTORI PERFORMANCE, CENSORSHIP, AND THE OCCUPATION

Babysan provides a look into the general views of many Japanese women by Occupation soldiers. Although obviously an exaggeration, the fact that Americans not only tolerated but actively promoted such views links this to one of the central concerns over erotic performance: for most Americans, Japan's exoticism was so extreme that sexuality and sexual performance seemed to be the norm. And yet this cultural construction was set against attempts to increase female participation in the political and economic spheres of postwar Japan. Understanding this allows us to see some of the reasons behind the divergent policies and actions toward kasutori performance. Much like their views toward Japanese women at this time, the American censors both wanted to empower the Japanese as well as control them sexually. Torn between antagonistic mandates, SCAP exerted a form of postcolonial orientalist control while it promoted an ideal of freedom that carried with it inherent moral conflict.

It is tempting to see kasutori performance as nothing more than a side note in the fascinating history of Occupation theatre, but to do so is a disservice to the information it provides. Like the Parisian Left Bank of the 1920s, this "decadent world" was also a refuge for artists and intellectuals. While never artistically successful, some kasutori works did break through into the mainstream (notably the play *Gate of Flesh*, which was adapted into a 1964 film of the same name by Suzuki Seijun). Still, these works allowed for theatre producers to stage profitable plays at a time when both the classical kabuki and modern shingeki theatres tended to lose money for a variety of complex reasons, from a lack of performing venues to an American mandate to stage "democratic" plays. Moreover, the conflicts, misunderstandings, and contradictory impulses present in control of kasutori serves as an excellent case study as to the intersections between power, culture, and politics. SCAP had, from its outset, a twofold mission that created confusion and chaos even among established kabuki and shingeki companies; the additional layers of Japanese governmental regulations, American morality, and theatre producers' desires all increased the censorial misunderstandings surrounding kasutori performance. SCAP never clearly defined its role in controlling eroticism on the Japanese stage, and as a result regulations and policies were ambiguous and fluid; they varied under different individuals, divisions, and situations. These discussions resulted in a multitude of positions, varying even within SCAP itself, which caused even greater confusion, both for theatrical producers and for SCAP officials. Despite these restrictions, contradictions, and controls, erotic performance was extremely popular in Japan during the Occupation. For many Japanese, "erotic" performance was a sign of freedom from wartime restrictions, thus achieving one of the Occupation's goals for the theatre. Kasutori producers used the legal and social confusions present in the

Occupation to stage works for quick profit, but their work also stood as a marker of sexual liberation and social change, creating a performed resistance not only to American control but also to "conservative" Japanese Shōwa-era values and laws. Kasutori performance, therefore, was more than just a sideshow in Japanese theatre history. Rather, it should be seen as perhaps one of the first outpourings of freedom and a forum for artists, producers, and playwrights to test the limits of expression in an environment of confusion, experimentation, and decadent performance.[54]

Notes

1. *General Headquarters: Supreme Command for Allied Powers: History of the Nonmilitary Activities of the Occupation of Japan: Theater and Motion Pictures* (National Archives Monograph Publication MP 65 Roll 4), p. 1 (emphasis mine).
2. James Brandon, "Myth and Reality: A Story of Kabuki during American Censorship 1945–1949," *Asian Theatre Journal* 23, no. 1 (2006).
3. John Dower, *Embracing Defeat: Japan in the Wake of World War II* (New York: W. W. Norton, 1999), 148.
4. Ibid.
5. Dower is an important source for information regarding Occupation culture. However, in his massive history of the Occupation he only devotes ten pages or so to kasutori culture; much of that space is focused on literature with only a few notes on performance. Moreover, he does not explore my third category (erotic plays) of kasutori performance at all.
6. Ibid., 152.
7. Ibid.
8. Faubion Bowers, PPB Theatrical Division Log Sheet, December 30, 1947: SCAP Record Group 331, National Archives at College Park, College Park, MD.
9. Ibid., April 7, 1948.
10. Faubion Bowers, PPB Log of Stories Referred to or Checked with SCAP section, March 17, 1947: SCAP Record Group 331, National Archives at College Park, College Park, MD.
11. Dower, *Embracing Defeat*, 152.
12. Pale skin has numerous cultural signifiers in classical (and in some cases contemporary) Japanese culture. Pale skin indicates wealth, high class, and status. Note the application of white powder to the face in Edo-era Japanese culture and the continued popularity of Caucasian and Eurasian models in Japanese marketing today. For more examples or information see Wagatsuma Hiroshi, "The Social Perception of Skin Color in Japan," *Daedalus* 96, no. 2 (1967): 407–43, and Ashikari Mikiko, "The Memory of the Women's White Faces: Japaneseness and the Ideal Image of Women," *Japan Forum* 15, no. 1 (2003): 55–79.
13. Dower, *Embracing Defeat*, 153.
14. Ibid., 154.

15. George Gercke, CI&E Weekly Report, July 26, 1947: SCAP Record Group 331, National Archives at College Park, College Park, MD.
16. CCD Comment Sheet, August 5, 1947: SCAP Record Group 331, National Archives at College Park, College Park, MD.
17. Ibid.
18. *Rosuto Vahjin* Synopsis, October 25, 1948: SCAP Record Group 331, National Archives at College Park, College Park, MD.
19. Faubion Bowers, Log of Stories Refereed, December 12, 1947: SCAP Record Group 331, National Archives at College Park, College Park, MD.
20. For example, see notes about the historical and fictionalized Abe Sada in Christine Marran, *Poison Women: Figuring Female Transgression in Japanese Culture* (Minneapolis: University of Minnesota Press, 2007), and the numerous critical writings on Suzuki Seijun's 1964 film adaptation of *Gate of Flesh*.
21. Faubion Bowers, Log of Stories Refereed, December 12, 1947, SCAP Record Group 331, National Archives at College Park, College Park, MD.
22. James Alexander, "Obscenity, Pornography and the Law in Japan: Reconsidering Oshima's *In the Realm of the Senses*," *Asian-Pacific Law & Policy Journal* 4 (2003): 154.
23. Ibid.
24. CI&E weekly report: August 7, 1947: SCAP Record Group 331, National Archives at College Park, College Park, MD.
25. "Nude Shows Big Attraction," *Jiji* press translated document (undated): SCAP Record Group 331, National Archives at College Park, College Park, MD, 12. Even if one doesn't accept the *Jiji* report as true (and there is, I think, some question as to its accuracy) and even if the amount is significantly exaggerated, it still suggests that a ¥15 fine would fail to dissuade either audiences or performers.
26. PPB Memorandum for Record: March 24, 1948, SCAP Record Group 331, National Archives at College Park, College Park, MD.
27. George Gercke, CI&E Memo: January 23, 1948, 2: SCAP Record Group 331, National Archives at College Park, College Park, MD.
28. W. L. Thompson, Police Intervention in Extreme Erotic Plays: August 30, 1948, SCAP Record Group 331, National Archives at College Park, College Park, MD.
29. CCD Conference Report #49: March 11, 1948: SCAP Record Group 331, National Archives at College Park, College Park, MD.
30. CCD Memorandum for Record: "Police Interference at Daito Theater in Asakusa," November 9, 1948: SCAP Record Group 331, National Archives at College Park, College Park, MD.
31. Ibid.
32. Ibid.
33. W. L. Thompson, "Police Intervention in Extreme Erotic Plays," August 30, 1948: SCAP Record Group 331, National Archives at College Park, College Park, MD.
34. Y. Goto, CCD Memorandum for Record: May 2, 1949: SCAP Record Group 331, National Archives at College Park, College Park, MD.
35. Takano Hiroshi, "Statement," May 2, 1949: SCAP Record Group 331, National Archives at College Park, College Park, MD.
36. W. L. Thompson, "Play on Sodomy," February 14, 1949: SCAP Record Group 331, National Archives at College Park, College Park, MD.

37. Ibid.
38. CCD memo: "Erotic Posters Advertise Theatrical Presentation," August 20, 1947, 1: SCAP Record Group 331, National Archives at College Park, College Park, MD.
39. Ibid.
40. Ibid.
41. The play is alternately referred to as *Gate of Flesh* or *Flesh Gate* in SCAP documents.
42. W. L. Thompson, "Indecent Advertising," August 18, 1948: SCAP Record Group 331, National Archives at College Park, College Park, MD.
43. Ibid.
44. "Nude Shows Big Attraction," *Jiji* press translated document.
45. CI&E Index Sheet: Synopsis: July 22, 1948: SCAP Record Group 331, National Archives at College Park, College Park, MD.
46. CCD Memorandum for Record "Discussion of Moral Censorship with CIE Representative," August 26, 1948: 2–3 SCAP Record Group 331, National Archives at College Park, College Park, MD.
47. Ibid., 1; SCAP Record Group 331, National Archives at College Park, College Park, MD.
48. Ibid., 2; SCAP Record Group 331, National Archives at College Park, College Park, MD.
49. CCD Check Sheet "Nudity in Small Stage Productions," June 12, 1947: SCAP Record Group 331, National Archives at College Park, College Park, MD.
50. PPB Memorandum for Record "Eroticism at Dai Ichi Toyoko Theatre, Shibuya," 27 June 1947: SCAP Record Group 331, National Archives at College Park, College Park, MD.
51. Bill Hume, *Babysan: A Private Look at the Japanese Occupation* (Tokyo: Kasuga Boeki, 1953).
52. Ibid., 32–33.
53. Ibid., 101. The *ne* is a common Japanese sentence-ending that means "Isn't it?" or "Right?" Hume's Babysan often mixes Japanese and broken English for comic effect.
54. The author would like to thank Yuko Prefume for her assistance on this article.

Locating Fascism by Dislocating War

Stage For Action's *Skin Deep*

—CHRYSTYNA M. DAIL

Aside from the attack on Pearl Harbor, American civilians during the twentieth century remained, for the most part, physically removed from the many sites of war in which the country was involved. Although World War II is often referred to as the least controversial of modern wars, it still had its detractors. Some of these were pacifists and others were anti-interventionists, yet there were also many citizens remaining disengaged because the fighting seemed recondite and distant; these individuals' propensity for engagement was severely weakened by feelings of helplessness.[1] Witnessing war from a distance often leads—after an initial outpouring of support and nationalistic fervor—to feelings of disconnection and even apathy. During World War II an exceptionally well-crafted government propaganda operation helped counteract this potential civilian apathy. Citizens sacrificed material comforts to aid in the war effort. Women were called on in much greater numbers to join the workforce as part of their patriotic duty, and children participated by purchasing war bonds as well as by growing victory gardens. Regardless, many remained largely disconnected from the prodigious social and political implications of the war.

Sensing the malaise U.S. citizens felt about entering another global conflict, theatre artists emerged as some of the most vigilant supporters of World War II. In July 1942, actor Philip Huston wrote in *Equity*, the Actors Equity Association Magazine, "The theatre can be important only where the need for it is important. And some three million khaki-clad arms point to where that need is."[2] The following summer FDR reinforced this in a statement eventually printed in *Billboard Magazine*: "Entertainment is always a national asset; invaluable in time of peace, it is indispensable in wartime."[3] Theatre professionals and government organizations across the country answered the presidential call, and the USO (the United Service Organization—the Treasury Department's entertainment program, founded in 1941), as well as the American Stage Wing with its Stage Door Canteens, rallied to support the troops through theatrics. As patriotic and entertaining as many of these performances were, they rarely traversed beyond engaging surface-level or nationally motivating problems, such as how to economically support the war effort or how to stay healthy while on combat missions. They infrequently addressed how the war impacts individuals or even the future social and economic structure of the United States. In this way, many wartime performances simply widened the geographical and ideological divide between the intentionality of American entrance into the war and how it affected those at home.

Susan Sontag, in *Regarding the Pain of Others*, reinforces this notion of how geographical and cultural distancing exacerbates wartime apathy: "It is because a war, any war, doesn't seem as if it can be stopped that people become less responsive to the horrors. Compassion is an unstable emotion. It needs to be translated into action, or it withers."[4] In 1943 the social activist performance collective Stage For Action (SFA) emerged and argued that action needs to be exercised locally in a productive and tangible way in order to combat a nation full of passivity. Starkly contrasting the relatively anemic government and commercially sponsored entertainments during World War II, Stage For Action was acutely aware of how the war abroad reflected challenges at home and used this pivotal moment both during and especially after the war's conclusion to advocate for social change. This essay explores SFA's performance of *Skin Deep*, revealing the group's ability to theatrically translate the rather esoteric proposition of why we were fighting the war abroad—fascism—by connecting it directly to U.S. social issues at home.

SFA's audiences were racially and religiously integrated and composed of people who did not have the financial means to experience antifascist views on Broadway in plays such as *Decision, Watch on the Rhine*, and *Deep Are the Roots* or who, as civilians, were ineligible to attend Stage Door Canteen and USO plays. SFA performed work illustrating that affronts to race, religion, and civil liberties in the United States mirrored the fascism of Franco, Mussolini, and Hitler, and the organization brought these lessons into the neighborhoods of the very population laboring to support the war.

Artists involved with SFA signed on in order to "bring the message of the dangers of native fascism in America to audiences outside the Broadway area."[5] Native fascism was a war unto its own for leftist artists and progressives during the late 1930s and early 1940s. In *Facts and Fascism*, media and social critic George Seldes defined native fascism as "the combination of social demagogy, corruption and active White terror [at the national level] in conjunction with extreme imperialist aggression in the sphere of foreign politics."[6] The 1936 Sinclair Lewis novel *It Can't Happen Here* about a dictator rising to power in the United States made fascism a household word. The novel warned that any U.S. citizen's belief that one group or race should dominate another was akin to fascist politics in foreign nations. The subsequent Federal Theatre Project adaptation of Lewis's novel, which broke new theatrical ground by opening simultaneously in twenty-one different cities, popularized the term. As the critic Brooks Atkinson wrote, "Thousands of Americans, who do not know what a Fascist dictatorship would mean, now have an opportunity to find out, thanks to Mr. Lewis' energetic public spirit and the Federal Theatre's wide facilities."[7] Fascism emerged, therefore, as the catch-all battle cry and official nemesis of a small but significant population of progressives during the Spanish Civil War.

The Spanish Civil War erupted in July 1936. One month later FDR addressed an audience in the quaint community of Chautauqua, New York, speaking on the subject of peace and reaffirming his commitment to the 1933 "Good Neighbor" policy of opposing armed intervention in foreign affairs. In this same speech the president discussed the impending war in Europe and a time in the foreseeable future in which the United States would no longer be able to watch from the sidelines, reminding his audience "that so long as war exists on earth there will be some danger that even the Nation which most ardently desires peace may be drawn into war."[8] Roosevelt, however, clearly opposed entry into the war in Spain, due to both religious pressures from U.S. Catholics and economic pressure from the powerful oil tycoons of Texaco and Standard Oil.[9] These groups supported the Spanish Nationalists and condemned the Communist-endorsed Republic. But according to opinion polls of the period, over seventy percent of the U.S. population supported—at least rhetorically—the Republic in Spain.[10] By December 1936 (within a month of the Federal Theatre Project's opening of *It Can't Happen Here*), a small number of U.S. citizens had joined the International Brigade in Spain in what became known as the Abraham Lincoln Battalion and "saw action in the battle of the Jarama in February 1937."[11] Ultimately, assistance from Mexico, the Soviets, and the International Brigades proved futile and the Republic was defeated. Therefore, it was not a best-selling novel or its popular theatrical adaptation, reports of human exterminations in Nazi concentration camps, or the loss of U.S. lives in the Spanish Civil War that unified the United

States to take action against global or native fascism. It was an attack on U.S. soil that uniformly motivated the nation toward global intervention.

Heightened anxiety regarding the failure of democracy in Spain, the attack on Pearl Harbor, as well as rising global and native fascism inspired Perry Miller, a young stage and radio actress, to initiate Stage For Action in December 1943. Nazism appalled Miller, as well as her artist and writer colleagues, but they also linked fascism in the United States to bombastic leaders such as Father Charles Coughlin and business mogul Henry Ford, organizations like the American Legion, and, most significantly for SFA's production of *Skin Deep*, the long-standing societal prevalence of race hatred born out of slavery in the United States.

Members of SFA were not alone in linking fascism and racism. The inequitable treatment of nonwhite U.S. citizens negatively impacted desired international relations, especially cooperation with Africa and Asia. In 1944, Swedish sociologist Gunnar Myrdal connected U.S. racism with European fascism, explicating its negative impact on international cultural diplomacy: "Fascism and racism are based on a racial superiority dogma...and they came to power by means of racial persecution and oppression. In fighting fascism and racism, America had to stand before the whole world in favor of racial tolerance and cooperation and of racial equality."[12] But it didn't take an internationally renowned sociologist to link fascism and racism in the United States for performing artists. A popular mobilizing song of the war, written in support of the Double V campaign, was "Freedom Road," by Langston Hughes and Emerson Harper.[13] It includes these lyrics:

> United we stand, divided we fall,
> Let's make this land safe for one and all.
> I've got a message, and you know it's right,
> Black and white together unite and fight.
> That's why I'm marching, yes, I'm marching,
> Marching down freedom's road.
> Ain't no fascists gonna stop me,
> no Nazis gonna keep me,
> From marching down freedom's road.

SFA was especially concerned with the politics of race in the United States and how racial hegemony at home was intensified by war and U.S. imperialism abroad. The group illustrated how cultural domination was a cyclical process and reinforced at every boundary designation: personal, local, national, and global. In their performances, SFA actively created pieces set in liminal or transitional spaces—Homi Bhabha's "interstitial passages"—in order to openly confront notions of racial boundaries.[14] One of the plays the group performed in order to illustrate the bridge between native and international fascism, and therefore to extend the space of war by equating the war front (Nazis) to the home front (racists), was Charles Polacheck's *Skin Deep*.

Facilitated by performances of *Skin Deep*, SFA pinpointed the war for audience members by dislocating it, tearing it away from its geographical and temporal boundaries. *Skin Deep* situated its audiences in a liminal space or interstitial passage, challenging the very notions of 1940s cultural boundaries of race. SFA activated the war for disconnected U.S. citizens and, in doing so, moved beyond responsive, tear-jerking propaganda performances of patriotism. *Skin Deep*, in particular, rent audiences out of their cultural comfort zones, motivating them to envision the home front—even after the war's conclusion—as extension of the war front.

Sensing an intense desire for an appreciable connection to the war, in December 1943 Perry Miller, in association with stage and radio personnel Berrilla Kerr, Peggy Clark, and Donna Keath, launched SFA in New York City to bolster morale and simultaneously raise awareness about native fascism. Funding originally came from private donations and a large benefit performance on April 19, 1944, at the Henry Hudson Hotel, where Eleanor Roosevelt was the guest of honor. Following the benefit, SFA's major funding sources outside of private sponsors were labor unions.

SFA's performances informed audiences about what could be done to help the war effort on the home front and therefore fight fascism nationally, which they believed would have an international impact over time. SFA advocated for wartime issues at a national level not seen since the demise of the Federal Theatre Project in 1939. The group soon expanded from New York City to major metropolitan areas across the United States including Chicago, Washington, D.C., Philadelphia, Detroit, San Francisco, and Los Angeles. SFA was described in newspapers as a group that "dramatiz[es] current problems and [is] patterned after the Living Newspaper technique."[15] A few of the better-known playwrights and performers involved with SFA during its five-year existence included Arthur Miller, Philip Loeb, Abram Hill, Sandra Michaels, Edward Chodorov, Norman Corwin, Will Geer, Paul Robeson, Studs Terkel, Thelma Schnee, and Sam Wanamaker.

The group expanded throughout the 1940s, both in membership and the social problems addressed, but its basic mission during and after the war remained the same. SFA performances were free or very reasonably priced, topical, and inspired personal responsibility from their audiences by focusing on realizable post-show actions. SFA was a vital force for social activism during the 1940s and operated as one of the "opposing currents of dynamic progress and static conservatism...with its militant program...tak[ing] the theatre to the people when the people can't come to the theatre."[16] By the time of Walter S. Steele's July 21, 1947, testimony before the House Un-American Activities Committee labeling SFA as a communist front group, they had initiated a training school in New York City and were funded by, or had direct connection to, a large number of influential Congress of Industrial Organizations (CIO) unions. Implicitly tied to national politics, several members of SFA's Executive Committee served as instructors in the School for Political Action Techniques, which was sponsored by the National Citizens Political Action Committee (PAC) in Washington, D.C. in June 1946. SFA provided the entertainment for the national CIO convention in Atlantic City in November 1946 and sparked the formation of other activist and union supported theatre groups during the late 1940s.

SFA began rehearsals for Polacheck's *Skin Deep* in March 1945. The group officially added the play to its repertoire on April 15, 1945, two weeks before the deaths of Mussolini and Hitler, with at least one performance starring Enid Raphael (a Broadway performer during the 1930s) produced in Harlem in June 1945.[17] In *The Best One Act Plays of 1945*, Margaret Mayorga notes in the introduction to *Summer Fury* by James Broughton that plays dedicated to the prevalence of race prejudice occupied the 1945 season due to "riots develop[ing] when biased people are led to action by mob psychology."[18] Although *Skin Deep* was not published in the Mayorga collection, she considered it "well-done and popular...held by Stage For Action and performed by them in more than twenty-four cities, in schools, union halls, YWCAs, and by organized citizen councils."[19] *Skin Deep* draws on a variety of sources participating in the mélange of early 1940s discourse regarding issues of race. As was typical of SFA productions, scripts went through multiple iterations, adapting to rapidly changing events surrounding a social issue.

Charles Polacheck (1914–2012) was an actor, director, singer, playwright, and music arranger. A member of the touring branch of the Almanac Singers with Pete Seeger and Woody Guthrie, Polacheck participated in People's Songs, Inc. (a sister group sharing office space with Stage For Action) and on May 9, 1946, worked as the stage manager for one of their famous Hootenannies. He arranged songs for Arnold Perl's *Dream Job*, which SFA produced in 1946, and performed these songs with legendary Blues star Brownie McGhee in a Carnegie Hall performance of the play on March 31, 1946. During the 1940s through the 1960s, Polacheck directed and produced television programs such as *Charade Quiz, Captain Video and his Video Rangers, Colonel Stoopnagle's Stoop,*

Voice of Firestone, The Edge of Night, The Far Horizon, Recital Hall, and *Wide World TV.* While his television career blossomed, Polacheck continued his relationship with the theatre, directing in August 1949 the confrontational Brecht piece *The Private Life of the Master Race* translated by Eric Bentley for the People's Drama, Inc., a late 1940s splinter group from SFA. But he tempered this production with safer or at least more centrist work, such as a translation of Puccini's *Gianni Schicchi* (with Herbert Grossman) for television in 1951, and later the same year lending the translation to the Metropolitan Opera for a benefit performance supporting the Free Milk Fund for Babies. In April 1959 Polacheck, known at that point primarily for his television work, produced an evening of Noh plays for an Off-Broadway theatre. Polacheck completed his New York professional theatre career in 1964 by writing a musical version of Oscar Wilde's *Salome.*

Skin Deep was initially inspired by the 1943 pamphlet *Races of Mankind*, which commented on completely incorrect notions of biological differences between people of disparate cultural origins.[20] Authored by Columbia University anthropologists Ruth Benedict and Gene Weltfish, *Races of Mankind* was published by the Public Affairs Committee, Inc., in order to assist in the war effort by "debunking Hitler's racial notions."[21] However, the pamphlet simultaneously served to combat the blatant racism of U.S. segregationists such as Mississippi senator Theodore Bilbo, who was quoted as stating that "one drop of Negro blood placed in the veins of the purest Caucasian destroys the inventive genius of his mind and strikes palsied his creative faculty." Bilbo continued, ranting that interracial relationships result in a "motley melee of miscegenated mongrels," filled with "mestizos, mulattoes, zambos, terceroones, quadroons, cholos, musties, fustics, and dusties."[22] Bilbo's racist epithets, albeit extreme even for the 1940s, were in discourse with contemporary scientific studies of racial difference. So threatening were the revelations in *Races of Mankind* that congressman Andrew J. May blocked the shipment of fifty thousand copies purchased by the army for distribution in military orientation courses. Not long after, the United Service Organization also refused to circulate the pamphlet.[23] The pamphlet was revised at war's end to acknowledge formation of the United Nations and successfully distributed in 1946 by the Public Affairs Committee under supervision of the American Association of Scientific Workers. The pamphlet touts that the "World is Shrinking" because the "greatest fighting alliance of nations in history—the United Nations—has completed the military destruction of fascism." *Skin Deep* was also revised in 1946, incorporating both the changes in the Benedict/Weltfish pamphlet as well as recently alarming events in race relations.[24]

The *New York Times* first took notice of *Skin Deep* when it reported on a performance at a youth conference under the auspices of the Greater New York Federation of Churches on October 20, 1945, at the Marble Collegiate Reformed Church.[25] Less than a month later, on November 9, the integrated cast performed at an Armistice Day program at Benjamin Franklin High School after a outbreak of racial violence in and around the school. Benjamin Franklin High, an all-boys school located in East Harlem, in 1945 had a racial construction of fifty percent Italian American students, thirty percent African American students, and the rest unreported.[26] Dr. Leonard Covello founded the school in May 1941 to "play a central role in the social reconstruction of East Harlem...serv[ing] as a catalytic hub for creating and strengthening social networks and fostering community norms of civility, trust, and reciprocity."[27] This "civility" faced a serious setback on Thursday and Friday, September 27 and 28, 1945, when a student strike demonstration over increased pay for athletic coaches escalated to violence and "street fighting broke out in which knives flashed, stones and bottles were flung from roof-tops."[28] Five hundred students and their guardians engaged in an all-day riot that swarmed to a group of two thousand white and black students battling against plain-clothed and uniformed police officers. Ultimately the riot extended into a weekend of standoffs between Benjamin Franklin students and the police. Five black students were detained at the scene and arraigned later that day for carrying "dangerous weapons," including "knives, an ice-pick, a baling-hook, and a razor." None of the white students, "throw[ing] stones and bottles and assailing [black students] with sticks, bats, and clubs," were arrested.[29]

The greater implications of the fight, the way in which it quickly escalated, and the media coverage spinning the event into a racially charged riot indicated a need for awareness of racial tensions in East Harlem and the rest of New York City. Yet the events at Benjamin Franklin High School in September 1945 were not isolated incidents. Racial tensions were steadily escalating during the early 1940s all over the United States and especially in major urban areas such as Detroit, Chicago, and New York City, and these tensions exploded, despite warnings from prominent religious and political leaders, after the war.[30] In late June 1943, city councilman and eventual sponsor and advisory council member of SFA Reverend Adam Clayton Powell Jr. warned that the 1942 Detroit race riots would soon be replicated in New York City if immediate and proactive attention was not paid to the "whitewashing" of mistreatment in the black community.[31] Challenging the mayor and police commissioner to take responsibility for the rising racial tensions in the city, Powell stated: "If any riots break out here in New York, the blood of innocent people, white and Negro, will rest upon the hands of Mayor Fiorello La Guardia and Police Commissioner Lewis Valentine, who have refused to see representative citizens to discuss means of combating outbreaks in New York. The Mayor says that he is ready. Ready for what? Ready after it is too late? We want to be ready now, beforehand." Despite Powell's warnings and the formation of a subcommittee designed "to handle aspects of a campaign to counteract propaganda designed to foment racial conflicts," the Harlem riots began on August 1, 1943, less than two months after Powell's speech, and resulted in five deaths, four hundred injuries, and property damage estimated at five million dollars.[32] Although Mayor La Guardia and many others denied these were actually "race riots," the events were bred out of general dissatisfaction with the discrepancies in job opportunities, criminal punishment, housing, and recreational facilities between black and white communities.[33]

In June 1944 another prominent leader, Malcolm Ross, chairman of the Committee of Fair Employment Practice, again attempted to draw attention to the racially discriminatory hiring practices in the city. He anticipated the potential racial unrest that would occur when an estimated one and a half million black and Latino veterans did not receive the equitable employment expected in return for serving their country.[34] Ross was attempting in 1944 to push through the original Ives-Quinn Bill, which had been in process for over a year. The Ives-Quinn Bill would establish a permanent antidiscrimination commission in New York state for the purpose of "the elimination of discrimination on racial or religious grounds in the hiring, promotion or the discharge of employees; with enforcing provisions barring labor unions from discriminating in the admission or expulsion of members on racial or religious grounds; and with preventing similar discrimination by employment agencies."[35] However, Governor Thomas Dewey, perhaps fearing damage to his presidential ambitions in the 1944 election if the bill were to pass that year, stalled its movement through the legislature; as a result, nothing regarding fair employment practices that might ease racial tensions was likely until at least the spring of 1945.[36] So when veterans of all races returned and many could not find work in New York City and other large urban centers, racial tensions escalated yet again.[37] Incidents between white and black students in other parts of New York following the Benjamin Franklin riot, and the riot at the high school itself, illustrated relatively clearly that racial tension was threatening the very seams of New York's fragile immediate postwar fabric and underscored the need for a performance such as *Skin Deep*.

Dr. Covello invited SFA to perform *Skin Deep* at the high school because the main action of the play takes place on a bus, and a bus had been the scene of one of the racial "disturbances" in late September. *Skin Deep* was performed to accompany a speech by a black student in the school entitled "Youth Looks

Toward a Decent World Tomorrow"; he received a standing ovation from the audience of 1,100 high school seniors when he called upon the "selfish few to not discriminate against any one group" in attempting to take advantage of postwar opportunities in research and science.[38] Dr. Covello also spoke at the event. He declared race hatred to be the "most serious Atomic Bomb" in their midst and challenged the students to "feel kindness toward other people" to create a better world and "make peace the success it should have been after World War I."[39] These speeches served as the prologue for SFA's performance of *Skin Deep* that day, setting the scene perhaps even more effectively than the stage directions for the production: "Stage For Action composes plays on important subjects for the purpose of combining entertainment with information that will help build a better America... Since we bring these plays to you and don't ask you to come to a regular theatre to see us, we must ask you to imagine all the glamour and expensive scenery of a Broadway play. For instance, the opening scene of the play on the bus. We can't put a real bus on the stage, so we have put these chairs here to represent the bus."[40] The play does indeed begin with a confrontation on a South-bound bus between a black veteran and the white driver with other bus riders becoming involved. There is a college professor on board acting as both mediator and narrator for the performance. He leads the riders of the bus and therefore the audience to various significant landmarks, including a medical tent in the South Pacific during World War II, a blood specialist center, and a psychologist's office in New York City, as well as the Tuskegee Institute. The riders are introduced through these sojourns to an injured white soldier (receiving the blood of a black medic) and the spirits of both George Washington Carver and Adolf Hitler.

The purpose of these trips is addressing stereotypes about different races while also educating audiences about cultural history. At each stop common cultural prejudices of the 1940s regarding racial differences in blood type, brain size, intelligence, and contributions to civilization are debunked, and the riders on the bus ultimately realize that their prejudices are supporting Hitler's overarching message of "hate." At the climax of the play the spirit of Hitler shouts gleefully, "My idea is: HATE! Hate the Jews, hate the Russians; hate the foreigners; hate the Catholics and hate the dirty, stinking, black niggers! And you *do* it. You fall for it. Look what happens in your Tennessee in the town of Columbia. Look what happens in your great state of New York in Freeport, Long Island! That's right. Hate them, jim-crow them, starve them, terrorize them, shoot them, kill them. Be like me. Be supermen. Be NAZIS!"[41]

Although the original version of *Skin Deep* was penned sometime between the initial publication of *Races of Mankind* in 1943 and the outbreak of violence at Benjamin Franklin High in September 1945, a close reading of the extant version of the script informs readers that the play was adapted in 1946 to respond directly to an upsurge in violence toward returning black veterans; especially the 1946 Columbia, Tennessee, race riot. This riot broke out on February 26 following an altercation in a store between two veterans, one black and one white, concerning repairs of a radio owned by the black veteran's mother. Though the historical record is full of discrepancies, it seems that James Stephenson (the black veteran) threw the clerk of the store (the white veteran) through the window for threatening his mother. The Stephensons were arrested for disturbing the peace but released after paying a fifty-dollar fine. Later that day, however, James Stephenson was arrested again under charges of assault with the attempt to commit murder. These charges were brought up by the father of the store clerk. Word of the arrest and subsequent release of Stephenson quickly spread through town. By nightfall a white mob gathered around Mink Slide, the black district of Columbia. The residents of Mink Slide threatened retaliation if the mob attacked. When four white policemen entered the neighborhood that night, the residents of Mink Slide opened fire on the officers, critically injuring one of them. Early the following morning, police officers entered the district "fired randomly into buildings, stole cash and goods, searched homes without warrants, and took any guns, rifles, and shotguns they could find. When the sweep was over, more than one hundred blacks had been arrested, and about three hundred weapons from the black community had been confiscated. None of the accused were granted bail or allowed legal counsel."[42] While under police custody on February 28, two of the black prisoners were shot and killed by their interrogators. All-out hysteria ensued and Governor Jim Nance McCord called out the National Guard to quickly clamp down the violence.

The riot garnered national attention for its severity of violence, which included both civilians and police officers. The Columbia event is especially significant to post–World War II race relations because the defense lawyers in the case, led by Antigua-born Zephaniah Alexander Looby, successfully won acquittals for twenty-three of the twenty-five black defendants charged, despite facing an all-white jury. The case catapulted Looby to fame and earned him the title "Mr. Civil Rights."[43] He continued fighting for civil rights into the 1960s, becoming one of the most respected attorneys in Tennessee.

Skin Deep was not revised in 1946 to highlight the rising career of Looby. The intent was alerting audiences to increases in racial violence toward black veterans and U.S. cultural minorities of all backgrounds following World War II. At the very beginning of *Skin Deep*, Sergeant McGinnis, a black veteran, stops at the front of the bus to speak with the soldier to whom he gave his blood at the Iwo Jima company aid station. The white bus driver, seeing that McGinnis has not moved toward the back of the bus, responds to this "inciting incident":

DRIVER: Get back in the rear of the bus, black boy.
WHITE VET: Why you lousy civilian…
NEGRO VET: Take it easy, soldier.
WHITE VET: What right has he got to talk to you that way?
DRIVER: I'll do more than talk. Go on, boy, don't make me tell you twice.
WHITE VET: Take your hands off him.
DRIVER: Listen, you damn Yankee…
WHITE VET: I said take your hands off.
  (*He throws the Driver back into his seat.*)
DRIVER: You asked for trouble, and, by God, you're going to get it.
  (*He picks up a club. Vet disarms him and sits down.*)
WHITE VET: Take it easy, Jackson. You'll live longer.
DRIVER: Let go of me. I'll show that uppity, black ape…
WHITE VET: Leave that man alone. He's a friend of mine.
DRIVER: A friend of yours?
WHITE VET: Sure. We both belong to the same lodge. The ancient and honorable Order of the Ruptured Duck.[44] He's an ex-service man, and so am I. And you're not going to push him around. Not while I'm here.

Not long after this the professor intercedes, stopping the argument before it escalates into actual violence. Yet encapsulated in this brief and incendiary scene is not only the violence of Columbia, Tennessee, but the discrimination taking place throughout the U.S. immediately following the war. Gordon Allport, a psychologist and social ethics professor who founded Harvard's Department of Social Relations during the 1940s, reported that racial and religious bigotry actually increases during wartime and immediately thereafter. According to Allport, "War and its aftermath multiply and augment our frustrations… There are the minor irritations of gas shortages, red tape of rationing, mounting taxes and higher prices. Both wage-earner and white collar workers are fearful for the future. Our worries give us the pinioned feeling which makes us want to attack something—something visible, near-lying and outlandish. Minority groups, being visible, near at hand, and a bit outlandish provide the outlet we need. We don't care particularly what we attack them for. If one excuse (The Jews all keep to themselves) is proved invalid, we seize another (They pry into Christian groups)."[45] Toward the end of *Skin Deep*, while consulting the psychologist character, Allport's views—as well as those of *Races of Mankind's* authors—are performed for the audience, illustrating how war accelerates the anxieties leading to bigotry and prejudice:

PSYCHOLOGIST: These prejudices are based on fear.
GEORGIA B: How do you mean?
PSYCHOLOGIST: Most people are afraid of something.
DRIVER: I'm afraid of losing my job.
NEGRO GIRL: I'm afraid of a penniless old age.
GEORGIA B: I'm afraid of sickness with no doctor.
WHITE VET: (*Enters*) I'm afraid of losing my money and all I have. But why? Why am I afraid? Whose fault is it?
ALL: It's your fault! It's your fault! It's your fault!
   (*Pointing at each other and overlapping*)
DRIVER: It's the Negroes' fault! (*Others echo him*)
NEGRO GIRL: It's the Jews' fault! (*Others echo her*)
GEORGIA B: It's the Catholics' fault! (*Others echo her*)
WHITE VET: It's the foreigners' fault! (*Others echo him*)

Ultimately it is Sergeant McGinnis who stops this argument, and by the end of the play it's decided that "our differences are only skin deep. Under the skin, we're all brothers." The overarching message of the play underscored the lived experiences of many returning veterans. Four years of research by sociologist Henry A. Singer convincingly argues that for men serving in the few existing interracial platoons during World War II, attitudes regarding race showed significant improvement following the war. Singer's findings corroborate SFA's intentions that "through creative and educational mediums it is possible to compete successfully with [those] insidious influences," such as the St. Sebastian Brigade of Charles Coughlin, the "gentile-only" American Order of Patriots, and the anti-Semitic Christian Veterans of America, naming only a few of the post–World War II native fascist groups.[46] Singer continues, "By each of us participating in the social action force in our communities and by making democracy work in the classrooms, the offices, the shops, the subways, the recreation halls, the taverns, the cafeterias, the clubs, and anywhere when the opportunity for good human relationships presents itself, further advances will be possible."[47] Unfortunately, *Skin Deep*'s call to social action and espousal that differences between people are culturally constructed came too late for the Ferguson brothers in Freeport, Long Island, as well as James Johnson and William Gordon in Columbia, Tennessee.

Despite continued violence against many cultural minorities, archival records indicate that *Skin Deep* was one of the most popular pieces in SFA's 1945–1946 season. *Skin Deep*'s popularity centers on its ability to guide an audience through a journey transcending geographical and temporal boundaries. The performance situates audience members in an interstitial passage in which they are able to actively transgress, if only for a brief period of time, the culturally and historically formed barriers of race, religion, and ethnicity. Spectators are called upon to make "hypothetical adjustments to [their] structure" in Brechtian terms because "characters on the stage are moved by social impulses...mak[ing] it harder for the spectator to identify himself with them."[48] Hailing (though not influenced by) Bertolt Brecht's theory in "A Short Organum for the Theatre," *Skin Deep* attempts to deal with its own time as if it were historical. In doing so, as Brecht states, "perhaps the circumstances under which [the spectator] acts will strike him as equally odd; and this is where the critical attitude begins."[49] Critically analyzing an event or experience while the experience is in progress is an area of study for contemporary cultural theorists as well. Homi Bhabha defines this process as "dislocation," building upon Walter Benjamin's theory that certain performances (Brecht's specifically) have the potential for "damming the stream of real life."[50] Though the damming lasts only the duration of a performance, it allows the audience to operate in a geographically and temporally limitless realm in which the hegemonic or normative order of cultural understanding is placed on hold. This allows necessary space (Bhabha's "temporal caesura" or historically transformative moment) for critical response to the political content of the play.[51]

Dislocation is defined as putting something out of place or upsetting the order and position of things—perhaps even uncomfortably or painfully—and this was SFA's intention during the performance of *Skin Deep*. When a body part (a shoulder, for example) is dislocated, the injured person encounters a very brief moment of cognitive clarity regarding their injury prior to the corporeal experience of pain. The injured person may make a full body recovery from a dislocation injury, but they never forget the pain and are generally perpetually cognizant (perhaps even haunted by) how the injury occurred. They are hypersensitized to, and often avoidant of, activities potentially resulting in reinjury. This is the mind/body impact of dislocation and this cognitive/corporeal impact is the ultimate desire of many social activist performance creators. It is in this liminal period of dislocation that progress or change can happen because supposedly fixed identifications ("I'm fine/Society is fine" rapidly and viscerally transforming into "I'm not fine/Society is not fine") are challenged and a new perception of life entertained "without an assumed or imposed hierarchy."[52] Brecht would acknowledge this period of dislocation as engaging in both the "pleasure of exploration...together with the terror of [their] unceasing transformation."[53] *Skin Deep* is not simply a counter-narrative that "evokes and erases" the "totalizing boundaries—both actual and conceptual" of essentialist racial identities in the United States; it is also disrupting and transforming the temporal, geographical, and historical understanding of how racial hegemony is formulated.⁵⁴ The audience is in a safe, albeit potentially uncomfortable, liminality in which they can collectively question and move beyond cultural methods of knowing. Jan Cohan-Cruz cogently argues in the introduction to *Engaging Performance: Theatre as Call and Response*, "Such performances provide the opportunity to see a little utopia, something that doesn't entirely exist in the world except as a possibility. Evoking collective aspirations, engaged performances are situated in semi-imaginary, semi-hyper-real realms, one foot in a utopian nowhere, the other in a very real striving toward somewhere, because the effort does not end when the lights go up."⁵⁵ *Skin Deep*'s power of dislocation allowed audiences the mind space to critically analyze battles against fascism abroad as extensions of the war on fascism at home; conceiving of the potential actions necessary for combating native fascism (e.g., racism). The authors of *Races of Mankind* realized that World War II transformed traditional perspectives on nationhood when they stated, "The war, for the first time, brought home to Americans the fact that the whole world has been made one neighborhood." SFA used *Skin Deep* to activate the message that racism at home proved detrimental to the U.S. position in this new global "neighborhood."

Additionally, the dislocating and therefore activating impact of *Skin Deep* was not limited to SFA audiences. Oakley C. Johnson, a guest professor of English during the 1946–1947 school year at at the all-black Talladega College in Alabama, was placed in charge of their theatre program.⁵⁶ Johnson contacted Abram Hill, founding member and director of the American Negro Theatre and vice chairman of SFA, for script recommendations. *Skin Deep* was recommended and Johnson states it was Talladega's "most popular production, staged seven times in a single year."⁵⁷ The piece was so popular the students took the play on tour, performing before both white and black audiences in Talladega, Montgomery, and Birmingham. In his reflection of the performances, Johnson writes, "Excitement, thrills, laughter—that's the recipe for entertainment. And *Skin Deep* gives them all, plus social content… I have often in my heart thanked the [unknown] authors of *Skin Deep* for a very skillful, effective, and socially valuable dramatic vehicle."⁵⁸ The Talladega students performed for audiences ranging from fifty to one thousand people, and in feedback questionnaires collected after the performances audiences commented that *Skin Deep* "would help break down barriers between white and black."⁵⁹ But what is most radical about this specific tour is that it was performed in the segregated South twenty years prior to the arrival of the Free Southern Theater and while segregationists such as Theodore Bilbo, Strom Thurmond, and John Rankin were still in office and lynching was a common occurrence. Additionally, the play was performed by an all-black and predominantly female cast.

The performances of Stage For Action intentionally pushed and stretched geographical and temporal bounds in order to reconfigure and transgress ideological boundaries concerning cultural identity during the 1940s. In doing so, they pushed the political buttons of many government officials in an increasingly conservative climate. SFA was affiliated with the Communist Party of the United States of America, and by the time the McCarran Act—legislation that scrutinized all Communist organizations by requiring them to register with the U.S. Attorney General—was instituted in 1950, all the SFA branches had dissolved under political pressure. Their brief existence does not weaken the intentionality of SFA's overarching mission, namely "assuming personal responsibility for maintaining democracy."[60] Although many members were blacklisted, and some lost their careers because of involvement with Stage For Action, their legacy is significant to theatre history. Through works such as *Skin Deep*, SFA demonstrated a unique ability to dislocate audiences from apathy during and following the war with regard to native fascism and to compel them into a stance of critical analysis and action.

Notes

1. I am not suggesting that the personal lives of U.S. civilians were not completely uprooted by the war effort, but instead addressing the prevailing lack of clarity on how the war abroad directly connected to political issues on U.S. soil.
2. Peter Royston, *Equity at 90: Our Lesson and Our Legacy*, "1940's: Hurry Up and Close That Big Show," accessed May 2007, http://www.actorsequity.org/AboutEquity/timeline/timeline_1940.html.
3. "Roosevelt Lauds Show Business," *Billboard* 55, no. 24 (June 1943): 3.
4. Susan Sontag, *Regarding the Pain of Others* (New York: Picador, 2003), 101.
5. Sam Zolotow, "Patricia Kirkland Gets a Lead Role," *New York Times*, March 27, 1944.
6. George Seldes, *Facts and Fascism* (New York: In Fact, Inc., 1947), 277.
7. Brooks Atkinson, "It Can't Happen: Not So Long as Sinclair Lewis and the Federal Theatre Fly a Warning Flag," *New York Times*, November 8, 1936.
8. Franklin Delano Roosevelt, *The American Presidency Project*, "Address at Chautauqua, NY," accessed April 2012, http://www.presidency.ucsb.edu/ws/index.php?pid=15097.
9. Antony Beever, *The Battle for Spain: The Spanish Civil War 1936–1939*, rev. ed. (New York: Penguin Books, 2006), 138.
10. Ibid., 240.
11. Ibid., 158.
12. Gunnar Myrdal, *An American Dilemma: The Negro Problem and American Democracy* (New York: Harper and Row, 1944), 1004.
13. The *Pittsburgh Courier* defined the Double V campaign during the war as "the drive for

14. Homi K. Bhabha, *The Location of Culture* (New York: Routledge, 1994), 4.
15. Zolotow, "Patricia Kirkland Gets a Lead Role."
16. Arnaud d'Usseau and James Gow, "Another Definition for Commercialism," *New York Times*, September 22, 1946.
17. "'Skin Deep' to Hit Race Discrimination," *New York Amsterdam News*, March 31, 1945; "Through Harlem," *Chicago Defender*, June 23, 1945.
18. Margaret Mayorga, ed., *The Best One-Act Plays of 1945* (New York: Dodd, Mead & Company, 1946), 139.
19. Ibid.
20. Joseph Lieberman, *Best Stage For Action Plays* (New York: privately published, c. 1955), 1.
21. For analysis of the *Races of Mankind* pamphlet and its impact, see John P. Jackson Jr., *Science for Segregation: Race, Law, and the Case against Brown v. Board of Education* (New York: New York University Press, 2005), 39.
22. Frederic D. Schwarz, "1947," accessed July 8, 2014, *American Heritage* 48, no. 4 (July 1997): 98. *Academic Search Premier*, EBSCOhost.
23. Jackson, *Science for Segregation*, 39.
24. It is unknown if alterations to *Skin Deep* in 1946 were approved by Polacheck.
25. "Laymen to Preach in City Churches," *New York Times*, October 20, 1945.
26. Michael C. Johande and John L. Puckett, *Leonard Covello and the Making of Benjamin Franklin High School* (Philadelphia: Temple University Press, 2006), 203.
27. Ibid., 2.
28. "Student 'Strikes' Flare into Riots in Harlem Schools," *New York Times*, September 29, 1945.
29. Ibid.
30. "Churchmen Urge End of Racial Prejudice," *New York Times*, February 25, 1943.
31. "Negro Councilman Warns Mayor of the Danger of Race Riots Here," *New York Times*, June 25, 1943.
32. Ibid.; "Harlem Is Orderly with Heavy Guard Ready for Trouble," *New York Times*, August 3, 1943.
33. "Harlem's Tragedy," *New York Times*, August 3, 1943.
34. "Warns of Race Tensions," *New York Times*, June 10, 1944.
35. "How State Senate Voted on the Anti-Racial Bill," *New York Times*, March 6, 1945; "Anti-Racial Bill Signed by Dewey," *New York Times*, March 13, 1945; "CIO Urges Albany Pass Job-Bias Bill," *New York Times*, February 8, 1945; "Anti-Bias Bill Is Passed, 109–32, By Assembly without Amendment," *New York Times*, March 1, 1945.
36. "Dewey Criticized on Anti-Bias Bill," *New York Times*, May 12, 1945.
37. "Jobs for Veterans in 'Alarming' State," *New York Times*, January 10, 1946.
38. "Race Hatred Cited as Principal Peril," *New York Times*, November 10, 1945.
39. Ibid.
40. [Charles Polacheck] for Stage For Action, *Skin Deep*, Schomburg Center for Research in Black Culture, Manuscripts, Archives and Rare Books Division, New York Public Library, 1.
41. Ibid., 16–17.
42. Carroll Van West, *The Tennessee Encyclopedia of History and Culture*, "Columbia Race

Riot, 1946," accessed January 2013, http://tennesseeencyclopedia.net/entry.php?rec=296#.UP84vS3N-t4.email.
43. Will Sarvis, "Leaders in the Court and Community: Z. Alexander Looby, Avon N. Williams, Jr., and the Legal Fight for Civil Rights in Tennessee, 1940–1970," *Journal of African American History* 88, no. 1 (Winter 2003): 50.
44. The Loyal Order of the Ruptured Duck refers to a military service honorable discharge. The lapel pin—which sports an eagle, not a duck—worn by honorably discharged servicemen allowed them to continue to wear their service uniform, despite being discharged from the military, because they were not yet able to afford civilian clothes. It is also a symbol of their service to the country.
45. Quoted in Henry A. Singer, "The Veteran and Race Relations," *Journal of Educational Sociology* 21, no. 7 (March 1948): 400.
46. Ibid., 408.
47. Ibid.
48. Bertolt Brecht, *Brecht on Theatre: The Development of an Aesthetic*, trans. and ed. John Willett (New York: Hill and Wang, 1992), 190–91.
49. Ibid., 190.
50. Bhabha, *The Location of Culture*, 253.
51. Ibid., 242.
52. Ibid., 4.
53. Brecht, *Brecht on Theatre*, 204–5.
54. Ibid., 149.
55. Jan Cohen-Cruz, *Engaging Performance: Theatre as Call and Response* (New York: Routledge, 2010), 16.
56. Oakley C. Johnson (1890–1976) is remembered as a social activist, teacher, and leader in U.S. radical scholarship who contributed to the *Daily Worker* and the *Monthly Review*. His papers are housed at Stony Brook University.
57. Oakley C. Johnson, "One Year in the Deep South: A Documentary of Seventeen Years Earlier," *Journal of Human Relations* 12, no. 1 (1964): 46.
58. Ibid., 46–47.
59. Ibid., 48.
60. "Jewish Women Will See Two One Act Plays," *Chicago Tribune*, December 8, 1946.

Binding and Unbinding Insurrection in Madagascar

Jean Luc Raharimanana's *47*

—HADDY KREIE

On March 29, 1947, in the eastern forests of Madagascar, a group of rebel soldiers staged "the world's bloodiest colonial repression."[1] In the insurrection against colonial French occupiers, between 90,000–100,000 Malagasy people on the island of Madagascar lost their lives as a result of fighting, torture, execution, starvation, or disease, including rebel soldiers and civilians. Only 550 French occupiers perished during the nearly two years of fighting.[2] This insurrection lives deep in the memories of the Malagasy even though young generations know little about it, and it has reemerged multiple times over the decades, shifting and transforming the narrative of Malagasy national identity, especially in the period since independence in 1961. Various political regimes have manipulated the narrative of the event, but very few official records exist outside of those produced by the colonial French regime during and shortly after the insurrection. In order to confront the forgotten history's multiplicity, and its fragmentary and forgotten nature, Malagasy playwright Jean Luc Raharimanana created *47*, a play that ultimately questions the purpose and validity of the acts of remembering that persist and/or remain.

In 2008, Thierry Bedard, a French theatre-maker, directed the original production of *47* at Albert Camus Cultural Center in Antananarivo, Madagascar. His production begins with a single Malagasy man standing on stage in the dark, with only enough light to illuminate his silhouette. In the first segment he situates himself as the storyteller, as a Malagasy man who questions his relationship to the memory of the insurrection, and who struggles to define his position as its descendant.[3] Speaking in French, he introduces his performance as "that quest for the memory that haunts [him]."[4] Throughout the performance he reveals that his memory comes from the communal consciousness of his nation; he did not experience the battles of 1947 directly, but he carries the unspoken transgenerational memories of his own father or grandfather. Notwithstanding (or perhaps because of) its unspoken nature, the memory of the insurrection haunts him. Significantly, the play closes with a Malagasy proverb that casts doubt on the entire process of remembering: "Words, they say, are like wrapping, that which binds also loosens."[5] In this proverb, the Malagasy storyteller asks the questions: What purpose does this memory serve? The events happened. "As for me, I remember nothing. Absolutely nothing… Only one date like a hot iron: March 29, 1947."[6] He is Malagasy. He is imprinted with the memory. But like many contemporary Malagasy of the younger generations, he remembers nothing, posing powerful questions regarding the position of memory in a post/colonial struggle for independent national subjectivity. However, the play itself practices remembering even while it faces the challenge that words will never fully recapture the memory. The memory itself lives in the bodies that died, and the families and friends who lost loved ones; it lives in altered family customs; and it lives in the bodies that remain, that carry the suffering, destruction, trauma, and shame of the insurrection.

In this essay I propose that the strategies of structuring and staging memory in and of Raharimanana's 2008 play intervene in the contemporary post/colonial[7] desire for independent national subjectivity. Through reading the text, I identify seven distinct though unmarked memorial fragments; the text is not divided into scenes. The published version of the text[8] also does not attribute the dialogue to particular characters; it exists as a continuous text. The text places the responsibility on the director to choose the number of people in the performance and the division of the storytelling. The 2008 performance materialized these fragments through the voices, bodies, and subjectivities of two actors—one Malagasy man and one French man—and the working manuscript from that performance clearly divides the text between them. Three of the seven fragments that I identify deliver bilingual accounts in Malagasy and French. The others primarily utilize French lightly peppered with Malagasy words or phrases. In addition to these textual fragments, the performance also incorporates three moments of movement that punctuate significant ideologies within the text itself. While the published volume of the piece contains a version in French and a version in Malagasy, one after the other, in this essay I look at the performance and the unpublished manuscript of the performance version of the text. I analyze the fragmentary structure of the play and the use of language to explore how the play deals with remembering and forgetting the 1947 insurrection, particularly as these elements differ from much of the performance discourse on war and trauma. According to Laura Edmondson, narratives of conclusion and teleological triumph often emerge in theatres of conflict and war, and "the 'epistemic murk' of terror-warfare [is replaced by] the linear sequence of serenity, suffering and terror, intervention, and restoration [and] is laboriously sustained despite the chaos and confusion that surround its production."[9] Edmondson's analysis of this need to streamline trauma into triumph provides an entry point for me in understanding the significance of Raharimanana's exploration. Rather than molding a narrative of triumph over colonial forces, Raharimanana's play dwells in the entanglement and the "epistemic murk" of personal and state produced narratives (both domestic and foreign) of the event that precede his own rendering. While he refuses to offer a happy ending, the play, nevertheless, tries to make sense of the event, its memory, and its erasure from history.

In this essay, weaving together the theatrical murk and the murk of history, I will provide an aesthetic analysis of the play alongside explorations of the cultural practices of remembering, a historical investigation of postindependence political rhetoric regarding the insurrection, and an analysis of the significance of remembering the event for contemporary Malagasy. Ultimately I wish to expose two primary tensions: the tension between the multiple locations of the event's memory that require new constructions of post/colonial relationships, and the tension between continuity and disruption in processes of intentional remembering and forgetting. The use and compilation of fragmentary memories and narratives and the multilingual structure and performance (I include movement here as a form of language, as well as the biracial blocking within the movement and in relation to the dialogue) highlight the multiple and simultaneous subject positions that intersect to create the memory of the 1947 insurrection that exists, perhaps latently, in the contemporary Malagasy imaginary. The multilingual mode of storytelling and the occasional "simultaneous translation" provide opportunities for witnessing Malagasy *and* French experiences of the event and their respective traumas of the battles that persist in contemporaneity. The original staging exploits the biracial casting to subvert the colonizer-colonized binary and embody the simultaneity and multiplicity that the structure of the piece introduces. The primarily presentational style (in the form of multilingual direct address) that integrates momentary fragments of movement without dialogue provides multiple approaches to remembering the event, exploiting simultaneous repetitions of memory to reroot the national imaginary in the materiality of everyday life. I ultimately argue that Raharimanana's strategic aesthetics of intentional forgetting cultivate an approach to post/colonial relations that relocates power within and outside of the colonizer-colonized binary.

Remembering Insurrection

Anticolonial tensions with France quickly escalated after World War II ended, as the Malagasy people awaited repatriation of the 10,000 Malagasy troops who fought for France, and as they awaited the recovery of the sluggish, war-drained economy.[10] International agreements made during the war had encouraged the Malagasy to believe that they would soon gain independence from France.[11] Toward the end of the war, France issued the Brazzaville Statement that granted the colonies, including Madagascar, political representation in the French government even though it did not grant them independence. Two political parties emerged as front-runners in Malagasy politics and claimed their right to representation in Paris.[12] First, The MDRM (Democratic Movement for Malagasy Renewal)—purportedly led primarily by the Merina (although its representation included strong leaders from other ethnic groups including Betsimisaraka)—gained rapid support from the Malagasy around the island who favored an independent Malagasy state.[13] The MDRM ran on a "clear program of decolonization and national revival" that inspired widespread anticolonial sentiments and a desire for independence.[14] Shortly thereafter, in defense against the MDRM's Malagasy nationalist ideology, the French encouraged the founding of an alternative party: PADESM (Party of the Disinherited of Madagascar), which ostensibly reached out to disenfranchised Malagasy—coastal peoples like the Betsimisaraka and descendants of slaves (anyone not of the ruling Merina class).[15] Because of historical tensions between ethnic and social classes—such as those that resulted from the Merina imperial conquest of the seventeenth and eighteenth centuries—the party line of PADESM supported French policies against the MDRM, which many members of PADESM perceived as an arm of the former imperial Merina. Like any multiparty political system, the multiple voices elicit varied perspectives of the tale, so this schism, in part, contributes to the multiple narratives that remember the rebellion of 1947, especially in terms of relationships between the contemporary Malagasy public and the government.

In Raharimanana's text, for example, one fragment describes two Malagasy university students who, hoping to speak to survivors of the rebellion, travel from the capital, located in the Merina region of the island, to a village in the eastern Betsimisaraka region where the bulk of the fighting occurred. When they arrived armed with pens and paper, however, the villagers perceived the two university students as an arm of the government, which had formerly collected names of the rebel soldiers and dissidents for punishment. When the narrator proclaims "But that was the Vazaha!" the villagers respond, "Vazaha or Malagasy, the government is still the government!"[16] The villager in this scene makes no distinction between the Colonial French Military, the former Merina imperial government, or the postcolonial government of the Republic of Madagascar. The university students, however, whose relationships to the various regimes differ from the villagers, make specific distinctions between the regimes. While Raharimanana resists marking the ethnicities of the university students or the prevailing government of the time, the invocation of the word "government," spoken in Malagasy within a French sentence ("*Vazaha ou Malgache, le Fanjakana reste le Fanjakana!*"), inheres a long history of French colonial *and* Merina imperial oppressive governments. The geographical dislocation between the students and the villagers also implies their ethnic differences.[17] As a result, the two parties—the university students and the villagers—carry different narratives of the insurrection and of the role of government through their daily lives: the university students (presumably members of the empowered Merina group), removed from the insurrection through time, geography, and privilege, can approach the event through the distance of research and relative power; while the villagers, living in fear of another repeat suppression, continue to experience memory as an always possible future. In this instance, the university students, seeking to recuperate a nearly lost history, represent a complex position of power. They are simultaneously oppressor and oppressed, distant from, yet descendant of, the horrific battles of 1947. These students wish to tell an untold story that perhaps only tangentially belongs to them. In her exploration into history and memory, Sandra Richards cautions: "Our capacity to imagine ourselves as surrogates standing in the place of long-gone ancestors is not without danger. We run the risk of displacing the past entirely, planting ourselves center on the stage of the past rather than seeking to negotiate our relationship to that past."[18] Two important questions regarding the relationship between the university students, the villagers, and history revolve around whether the event has temporally passed and how it continues to impact the daily lives of various groups of Malagasy. In Raharimanana's text, language plays an important role in confronting these multiple memories. While the play attempts to recuperate a geographically specific history as part of a national memory and identity, I argue that the multiple languages through which *47* speaks resist placing any group at the center. Instead, the constant temporal and subjective shifting and flexing emphasizes the practice of negotiating the event, its presence in contemporaneity, and the relationship of contemporaneity to it.

Weaving together Malagasy and French verbal languages through which narratives of the event have passed—the language of lived materiality written upon the bodies of the insurrection's descendants, and the language of their altered cultural customs—*47* challenges the languages through which the narrator's memory has formed. Significantly, the narrating figure, a Malagasy man, frames the performance in the French language. When he identifies himself in the opening monologue as "born in independence, wearing the words of impostors," he establishes a conflicted framework through which he articulates the multiple narratives of the memory: the framework of using an "impostors" language to convey the memory makes integral the mediation through which the narrator knows the history of his community.[19] In some ways it sets up the performance to speak back to the colonizer. Setting the French framework against other modes of delivery in the performance, however, the play protects some moments of remembering from the colonizer, and also speaks to third audiences—those both or never Malagasy n/or French. This interplay between the modes of delivery decenters the language of domination (French) within the Malagasy experience of colonialism even while the narrator utilizes French to frame the performance. Furthermore, by delivering some moments in French, some in Malagasy, and some in the language of movement, the play compartmentalizes modes of identity construction, allowing for a valid Malagasy experience of the events not always already inflicted with the French narrative and perspective. And finally, perhaps creating a fractured experience among the Malagasy, the text employs the Betsimisaraka dialect rather than Official Malagasy (Merina), even though the play was performed in Antananarivo, located geographically within the Merina region.[20] The Betsimisaraka dialect locates the memories culturally and geographically, acknowledging that not all areas of Madagascar experience colonialism or the insurrection in the same ways.

The multilingual structure illustrates the ways in which the French and Malagasy languages re-present the event and the memory differently. For example, in the above anecdote about the university students, the villagers perceive the students, with their pens and paper, as representatives of the government, who arrived from the central plateau. The geographic overlapping as well as the overlapping of "weaponry" makes it easy for the villagers to conflate Merina Malagasy with the French government. The student researcher narrates the event in French, and only a select few of the villager's words are spoken in Malagasy. In this way the play also conflates French language with urbanity, and dialect Malagasy with rural areas—another binary of factors that will inflict the way each of these characters interacts with the historical moment. But the play also simultaneously distinguishes a shared Malagasy experience from the French experience. The play invokes the Malagasy language in moments specifically designed to contrast the narratives that emerge in French: the moments that utilize Malagasy primarily focus on the visceral and material memories and open up a space of an embodied understanding of the events; for exposition and analysis, the play relies almost entirely on the French language; and the moments conveyed through movement speak to widely circulated narratives of colonial attitudes and circumstances but do not attempt to represent specific memories or characters represented in the script. However, the varied languages and their stories intersect, commingle, and sometimes conflict while simultaneously demonstrating the validity of discrete ways of knowing that also always already commingle: culturally specific ways of knowing through language, as well as an array of intersections and blurring of boundaries between the mind and the body. Together, these intersections provide moments to witness the history of the event (by those who did and did not live it) and to build new relationships between colonizer and colonized.

As I mentioned earlier, three (of the seven spoken or ten total) moments deliver memories in simultaneous translation from Malagasy to French, or vice versa, each of which indulges in bodily memories. For example, one fragment told in Malagasy recalls the bloody battles in the forest. The narrator recounts a story by an old man who lived through the battle and how the suffering and desperation drove him to retaliate in ways that still haunt him: "Terrible things that I did, shouldn't be done to human beings. I drove my short spear into the woman's neck. Her belly ripped open. Over here, over there, the fetus from her belly spilled onto the ground, nothing holding her together. But it wasn't a newborn baby there, but a fetus begging for life, full of blood, covered in its mother's fluid… I went home. I didn't fight any longer." The act of remembering the terrifying, palpable moments calls attention to the physical violence and the embodied trauma of the event: "Right here, in my throat here, the short spear that my father gave me, I sunk it good and deep here. Right here planted in my throat." The old man carries the pain of his suffering and of his retaliation, feeling the pain of his actions metaphorically stabbing into his throat as he speaks the words. The words serve as a mode of translating the physical and embodied memory of the event into a communicable language, but the violence of the language and repetition of bodily references prioritizes embodied memory in that moment.[21]

While the Malagasy figure relates this memory in Malagasy in performance, the French figure stands slightly behind and to one side of him, offering a simultaneous French translation of the man's story. While the playwright has scripted the translation, the slight differences in details mimics an unrehearsed simultaneous interpretation—a method of interpretation employed, for example, during the Truth and Reconciliation Commission (TRC) trials in South Africa following the end of apartheid. For French-speaking members of the audience, much like the listeners of the TRC trials, "the very first line of transmission was mediated and interpolated—not identical to itself. Interpretation was central to the...process. As one observer said, 'There would be no truth without the interpreters.' Yet the process of interpretation produced *particular kinds of truths.*"[22] For example, when the Malagasy figure describes the image of the dead mother and child that lay before him, he says: "Her belly ripped open. Over here, over there, the fetus from her belly spilled onto the ground, nothing holding her together" (*Kibonazy igny vaky triatra. Ankilany eo, tankilany teo, zazarano tankibony igny, tamin'ny tany teo, raraka tsy nisy nitana*). He describes the ripped-open belly of the woman and the dismemberment of the fetus strewn about over here, and over there. The French interpretation that follows simply says: "And by her side, near her, was her baby, having left her belly" (*Et tout à côté, près d'elle était son bébé, sorti de son ventre*).[23] Failing to capture the horror in its entirety, the tempered interpretation "thus conveys a reduced truth. It provides a *functional* rendering of content created within the constraints of an improvised setting."[24] Later in the same fragment, the Malagasy figure describes how, as he stood looking at the two bodies on the ground, he hears the gunfire of an enemy gun, and then flees. The French interpretation omits the gunfire entirely, creating vastly different implications regarding the rebel soldier's flight from the space. In the Malagasy version we might understand that an outside force drove him from the site of the mutilated woman, perhaps against his volition. But the French version limits the opportunity for such an interpretation, suggesting instead that the man merely abandoned the situation. While the suggestion I make here may or may not be an intended consequence of the Malagasy version, I wish to emphasize the point that the process of translation renders the events differently, for different audiences, perhaps with different pontentialities. However, significantly, Raharimanana *scripts these differences*, perpetuating the discontinuities, the miscommunications, the multiplicities of renderings, and the murk of history, and illustrating the varied perspectives that inevitably emerge.

Performed at the Albert Camus Cultural Center, an arm of the Alliance Française in Antananarivo, the capital of Madagascar, the anticipated audience for the original production likely included primarily French speakers, including French expatriates living in Madagascar and relatively wealthy, well-educated urban Malagasy. The film version of the performance scans the audience before they enter, revealing a mixture of Malagasy and white foreigners, composed primarily of young people, characteristic, at least in my experience, of most of the services provided by the ACCC.[25] The bilingual structure, as well as the choice to deliver only certain fragments bilingually seems cultivated specifically for this performance. While the three segments that employ Malagasy and its simultaneous translation emphasize the embodied memories of various figures, the play delivers other segments in French only, for a very different purpose. These segments of the play tend to transmit statistics, record keeping, and analyses, and also commentary on the chaos and mediation of historic memories in the contemporary imagination: "When the numbers now determine the words we use—drift, killing, suppression, massacre, genocide...what credit should be given to that kind of interpretation?"[26] Interestingly, only *in the language of French* does the play challenge the ability of language to fully represent the events. In response to the "scientific" language of French, the "nonscientific" language of Malagasy responds with visceral accounts of the terror that materialize it in ways that calculated words like "massacre" and "genocide" never can. In this way the play further dwells in the murk of the multiple processes of analysis through which contemporary audiences receive this history, and it speaks directly to the mixture of subjects in the audience at the ACCC. By isolating the different ways of coping with this particular history (statistical analysis, critical commentary, embodied memory) to the particularities of either French of Malagasy language, the performance emphasizes the multiple processes of coping. The actors embody multiple characters, but the bilingual format is not contained by the biracial casting. By containing certain processes within one language and other processes within another language, the performance marks them as distinct ways of knowing. Through the embodied performance of multiple characters by only two actors, however, the performance resists defining either French or Malagasy by only one way of knowing. In fact, the differences distinctly allow the staging to intervene by showing how the diverging perspectives *complement* one another. Rather, each performer hosts a multiplicity of epistemologies regarding history. Nevertheless, this use of language still proclaims that the Malagasy and the French experienced the events of 1947 very differently on both individual and national levels.

Jennifer Cole, a prominent ethnologist of Malagasy historical culture and of the 1947 insurrection in particular, identifies throughout the recent history of Madagascar several state-produced narratives of the events surrounding the insurrection that sustain the historical murk on a national level. According to Cole, the French, primarily, constructed and distributed the "MDRM Plot"—far and away the most dominant "official" narrative. In the days immediately following the first rebel attacks, and after the official cessation of the rebellion in 1948, the French and French sympathizers spread the word that Merina leaders of the MDRM had initiated, instigated, and led the attack that sacrificed thousands of Malagasy lives.[27] This narrative suggests that the Merina leaders of the MDRM willingly exploited the combat forces in the Betsimisaraka region (conveniently located near a major trade port with France) to expel the French occupiers and return power to the Merina Empire. The French occupiers successfully executed many of these Merina MDRM leaders before they had a chance to refute the story. In 1948, however, before his execution, Samuel Rakotondrabe, the alleged "general" of the rebellion, and in 1990, Jacques Rabemananjara, a Betsimisaraka writer and one of the founders of the MDRM, both accused the French of provoking the entire event and blaming it on the MDRM to destroy the nationalist movement for independence.[28] To this end, blaming members of the MDRM, in particular Merina members of the MDRM, allowed the French to exploit ethnic and social conflicts among the Malagasy, thus diverting attention from the suffering they themselves had imposed as a part of the colonial project. This also allowed the French to give power to the competing political party PADESM, known for sympathizing with French interests.[29]

During the First Republic of Madagascar, after independence in 1961, under the administration of Philibert Tsiranana, the Tsimihety president of Madagascar, many members of the MDRM came forward and denied having had any involvement in plotting the rebellion.[30] They defended the MDRM as having worked for independence *within* the political channels available—through representation in Paris and by lobbying for independence through legal charters and agreements—and claimed that members of smaller, more radical parties only loosely associated with MDRM, like independent veteran soldiers and rebel farm workers, devised the attacks. President Tsiranana belonged to a moderate political party in favor of autonomy from France but with strong French sympathies. During Tsiranana's rule, then, the nationalist inclinations of the narrative of the rebellion lessened. Rather, Tsiranana and his administration referred to the insurrection as a "senseless tragedy in which thousands of people had died."[31] In other words, he deemphasized the event as a marker of national pride and identity and played down its political implications as well as its consequences for the daily lives of the citizens—likely because of his strong ties to France and his desire to create a strong sense of unity by curbing ethnic tensions in the newly independent nation.

During a subsequent Socialist Second Republic under Betsimisaraka president Didier Ratsiraka (1975–1991, 1996–2002), the political rhetoric returned to a narrative of nationalist pride and anti-French sentiment, but Ratsiraka reevaluated who constituted the nation. In an attempt to distance Madagascar from French control and to distance himself from Merina rule, Ratsiraka focused his policies on three primary anticolonial movements in Madagascar, including the rebellion of 1947. During his presidency he promised pensions to the *anciens combatants* (veterans) who had been caught with "arms in their hands."[32] According to Cole:

> The effects of meting out state rewards in this way are threefold. First, during the state socialist phase of the Second Republic, this definition enabled Ratsiraka to distinguish between the MDRM, represented as an elite Merina faction of the population, and the "true" peasant nationalists. In turn, it suggested that the real martyrs were free of any association with a political party or partisan interests, thereby sidestepping the thorny question of what kind of national community those peasants might have imagined, if they did so at all. Finally, it emphasized that it was primarily coastal people who suffered and died, thereby recuperating the divisive colonial reading and making it possible for the nationalist narrative developed throughout the socialist period to also tell an ethnically partisan story.[33]

While the "nationalist" narrative of the MDRM plot glorified the Merina, Ratsiraka's narrative placed coastal peoples at the center of the national independence movement.

Finally, in the 1990s, the regionalist and ethnic narrative—begun through Ratsiraka's redefinition of the nation through his policies regarding the *anciens combatants* of 1947—took precedence as pro-federalist groups took the opportunity to use the exploitation of combat forces in Toamasina (the Betsimisaraka region) as an example of how regional groups should not be exploited for national gains.[34]

Raharimanana's play turns to a more contemporary national narrative of the event. One fragment refers to the French president making a trip to Madagascar in 2005 to repent of the events of "dark periods in our shared history."[35] In response, the contemporaneous president of Madagascar proclaims that he "did not understand much in history and prefers to look to the future, and wasn't he, after all, born in 1949, 2 years after the rebellion? An eternity!"[36] While the text avoids naming the president outright, the date would refer the spectator to the former president Marc Ravalomanana, who succeeded Betsimisaraka president Ratsiraka. Ravalomanana, a self-made business tycoon who cornered the dairy market in Madagascar and is also ethnically Merina. Given the history of the rhetoric of the insurrection, such an alleged statement within the performance carries layers of implications. To me, this line implies that a Merina president of Madagascar preferred to ignore the history of a politically minoritarian ethnic group while at the same time genuflecting to the French government, a necessary ally for economic development in contemporaneous Madagascar.

These various shifts in rhetorical use of the events of 1947 demonstrate the relatively limited concrete information available regarding the events. According to Allen: "The campaign transpired under a virtual blackout of news. All leftist sympathizers in the French community had been forceably [sic] repatriated, all nationalist leaders jailed for putative inculpation in the revolt. All rebel field chiefs were dead before the public could hear their story."[37] Thus, the historical accounting of the events relies almost entirely on reconstructed narratives of the various political regimes that exploited the event in a variety of ways to gain favor with the people, a factor that may well have contributed to the position that Madagascar should look to the future rather than history that occurred an "eternity" ago. Furthermore, after the Malagasy president's comments, the play cites a group of over forty political associations demanding that the French archives regarding the insurrection be opened to the public.[38] If the written, archived documentation has been sealed off from the public, the only "authoritative" narrative reaches them through the country's ruling government of the time. By calling attention to how "authoritative" narratives have been politicized, Raharimanana works to combat their authority. Authoritative or not, however, each of these narratives exists in the contemporary national imaginary alongside other kinds of narratives; each narrative continues to circulate and impact material life. Because of the ambivalent history of the event, political leaders have repeatedly dislocated its implications from its historical moment and variously resituated it throughout the history of an independent Madagascar. As a result, the processes of remembering the events of 1947 have created rhizomatic relationships between history and contemporaneity. Drawing on the multiplicitous narratives, Raharimanana exploits the selective fragmentary nature of the remembered event to "constitute a productive remembering that deploy[s] empathy but recognize[s] difference, disjuncture, and irrecoverable loss as a starting point for reconfiguring the present and imagining another future."[39] The discrete reemergences of the event disrupt teleological chronologies by illustrating the continuing and multiplicitous relevance of the event in contemporaneity. History is not merely relegated to the past. It also exposes biased or politicized memories that distort the reality of the historical moment and challenge the validity of remembering at all.

Rather than packaging a streamlined, triumphant narrative, *47* explores the chaos and confusion of history, war, and trauma. Raharimanana exploits the chaos of governmental narratives and extends that fragmentation beyond the government to illustrate the inadequacy of official national narratives in penetrating the public body. While various official narratives have penetrated different parts of the public body, the public body also creates its own narratives. The historic and contemporary public bodies create, utilize, and need particularized narratives and also rely on narratives created by other public bodies. Rather than limiting it to the rhetoric of the state, the play also relocates the narrative in the histories of multiple subject positions including: contemporary university students conducting research of the event's consequences, the rebels who fought in the battles, media coverage, and descendants of missing rebels who bear the burden of altered family customs. By dwelling in the simultaneity, multiplicity, and "epistemic murk" of remembering, the play demonstrates the productive effects of witnessing the various descendants' struggles in reconstituting an independent Malagasy national subjectivity. Through a collage of narratives drawn from individual accounts and historical and contemporary political rhetoric regarding the insurrection of 1947, *47* at once recounts the memories of the event and questions the function of remembering. When decades of state-produced narrative, rumors, objectification, statistics, "scientific language," and politics have repeatedly rearticulated the memory of the event, *47* interrogates the authority and purpose of the residual narratives; it questions both the authority of state-produced narratives and the validity of embodied memories of the rebels. When both the archived memory and embodied memory become sites of contestation in the struggle for the identity of the Self and the Other, the location of oppression becomes precarious. In *47*, the intersection of multiple memories, the multilingual retelling and biracial recasting of those memories, and their theatrical representations challenge the contemporary source of coloniality. The processes through which the nation and its subjects remember unsettles the location of oppression by breaking down the colonizer/colonized binary.

Forgetting Insurrection

While the above analysis of the multilinguality of the performance demonstrates and explores the multiplicities, discontinuities, and contradictions of remembering 1947, the collage structure and staging of the performance both filter and reinterpret the murk of memory by redefining multiple relationships between multiple subject positions. Through the extensive exploration of the falsifications and/or multiple truths of mediated acts of remembering, *47* ultimately proposes to "Forget. Forget everything."[40] In doing so, it reminds us that forgetting also plays an important role in incorporating such traumatic events into the national identity. According to Cole, forgetting plays a deliberately reconstructive role in Malagasy life.[41] The cultural practice called *fafy* demonstrates a practice of forgetting that contrasts with definitions of neglect or omission. Instead, the ritual forgetting cleanses or repurposes the event. For example, men who join the military and who have forcibly foregone certain cultural taboos participate in a ritual sacrifice intended to cleanse or "forget" the offenses that they encountered, and to restore the laws of their ancestors: "In short, through washing achieved in sacrifice, villagers reconstitute boundaries between themselves and the outside, as the traveler is 'washed' of experiences in the outside world and made to remember his or her place in an ancestrally conceived and constituted order… [Fafy] filters new practices and objects, they lose their former meanings and are interpreted, at least in the context of everyday life, in local terms…although the traces remain everywhere apparent."[42] The cleansing process allows the participants of fafy to choose the outcomes and impacts of the painful events they encounter. In another instance, Malagasy use fafy to "forget" cultural taboos that occur *within* the community. Many Malagasy ethnicities prohibit incestual marriage, for example. In the instance where an incestual marriage has occurred, the parties involved perform a ritual sacrifice to annul a marriage that breaks laws of incest, or to overrule laws of incest: "[The purification is] a dispensation from the impediment of kinship: a suspension of law against incest in a special case, which enables an exceptional authorization to override an established rule. This exemption allows the preferential marriages and implies the idea of a favor granted, of an exemption, permission to act against the law."[43] In other words, in this case fafy either "forgets" the crime and restores the honor of both parties, or cleanses the union in a fashion that does not contradict established social mores. Both cases of fafy make prominent the historical and contemporary circumstances that require discrete reactions or approaches to behaviors or events and multiple truths.

By alleviating the dichotomy and resisting a colonizer-colonized binary, the play complicates ideas of good and evil that would lend themselves to a triumphant narrative of war where the protagonists have heroically overcome the troubles of colonialism and insurrection. Rather, it dwells in the complexities and exposes the conflicts of incorporating the experience of war into the national identity. To aid in this process, the particularities of the nonlinear structure represent the nonchronological ways that the events still impact contemporary lives, suggesting not an end to but a continued struggle with the multiplicity of "truth" in the historic memory. So far, I have explored the way that the structure of collage in *47* utilizes culturally specific languages and language in translation to reconfigure memories of the insurrection, but the collage also demonstrates other forms of mediation including time, trauma, and juxtaposition against other narratives that each challenge the validity of memory. Rumors, politically motivated narratives, and exaggerated or tempered intergenerational stories that frame 1947 engender complicated "second-hand" experiences of the events. For example, fear, cultivated by state-produced narratives, stories from other fighters, and witnesses of the battles, contributed to rumors and other "distortions" of the insurrection, mediating retellings of the events and influencing expectations of how the narratives *should* look or sound. In order to cleanse the historical event and relocate its memory in contemporaneity in an efficacious way, Raharimanana dwells in these mediations as much or more than he does the state mediations.

In one segment the narrator divulges how supposed rumors embed themselves so easily into the public narrative that they *become* the narrative, camouflaging but not replacing the actual realities: "The colonized, their humanity denied, imagine all the possibilities of death, the maddening rumors of unspeakable atrocities are invented and reported. The unspeakable is put forth and accepted... The massacres could then proceed outside of the realm of truth, outside of memory."[44] For example, the play recounts the effects of a particular poison that impeded the rebels' pursuit. The fragment positions the poison as a French tactic to stave off the rebels. However, revealing the tactic just after a diatribe on the authority of rumors, the play seems to suggest that rumors and fear constructed this story; that perhaps foliage and not the French caused the wound that spread all over the body, oozing, and causing the skin to fall off.[45] Through this ambivalent reality the play demonstrates how strategic rumors might serve to squelch particular modes of resistance. However, the extremity of the rumors also allows other atrocities to escape unnoticed. The rumors actively reveal both the presence of heinous atrocities and the fact that the effects of those atrocities extend beyond the individuated moment of action. The interplay between statistical narratives and emotionally driven narratives threatens both the colonizer and the colonized. The ambivalence of the actuality of the events cultivates fear, but the rumors in return dramatize the horror, burgeoning through rhetoric a determination to fight back. The actual cause of the disease becomes irrelevant when the rhetoric of the disease becomes a tool used by both sides.

While the narrator seems to live in a place where his memory of the insurrection has come primarily through second- or thirdhand accounts, through retellings of retellings where multiple modes of communication have failed to effectively represent shifted and altered "truths" of the actual event—through myths, state rhetoric, political criticism, and rumors—firsthand accounts still occasionally make their way into the national imagination more than sixty years after the event. Nevertheless, the play also questions the validity of memories of the living rebels mediated by pain and trauma. In one fragment, the narrator proclaims: "When memory fails, pain is steep... If we are told that we remember the insurrection as an illusion, as a nightmare, we respond, 'Yes Sir.'"[46] The narrator here implies that positionality and/or power dictate the rebels' memories. Immediately afterward, the narrator recounts a rebel's encounter with a Vazaha woman whom he killed. He describes how he split her open, spilling her unborn, bloody baby on the ground. While the statement that qualifies the memory as a nightmare suggests that external forces alter the memory, its proximity and relation to the account of attacking a pregnant woman imply the potential fallacy of that memory. Perhaps the horrible image he describes is *imagined after the fact*, influenced by rumors and other rebel accounts. If even firsthand accounts offer distorted descriptions of the battle, what is the significance of remembering the "actual" events? On the other hand, what is the value of exploring the affective difference of the *experience* of those events? The staging of the performance in particular grapples with these questions as it begins to redefine the relationships which have been inflected by language and rhetoric.

In the performance of one bilingual segment of the play, the Malagasy figure stands center stage in a dim pool of light, facing the spectators, arms hanging straight at his sides. Just behind him and to the right, the French figure stands behind him with his hand on the Malagasy man's shoulder. The physical relationship between the Malagasy and French figures positions them in relationship to the story. The Frenchman as interpreter stands at a distance to the story, reacting to the story, experiencing the story secondhand.[47] As the first line of reconciliation for the disproportional pain and suffering felt by the Malagasy insurrectionists, he models the reaction to the initial telling. But the audience watches both tellings simultaneously, some accessing one version or the other, some accessing both versions, but all witnessing the relationship between the two: The Malagasy man confronts the experience directly, turned out fully to the audience, in direct address. The French man, behind and to one side, looking only at the Malagasy man, watches the story of suffering unfold. The Malagasy man delivers the story with passion and pain in his voice, while the French man interprets the lines in a rather neutral tone.

The disparity between the quavering voice of the Malagasy man and the calm interpretive voice of the French man in conjunction with the specific blocking layers the effect of the quavering voice, endowing it with emotion and affective power, and also with a sense of authority over the memory that the French figure does not appear to have. In this way the performance empowers the somatic experience even through verbal language, a strategic resistance to the "language of modernity" that the Malagasy man refers to in his opening monologue. The two figures, however, remain physically connected throughout this fragment. Their constant connection resists the implication that embodied knowledge belongs to the Malagasy while abstract analytical knowledge belongs to the French. Rather, linked together, the embodied and analytical flow between the two actors, shared, equal.

Instead of merely offering a reduced truth, the simultaneous translation allows the French figure to witness the atrocities suffered by the Malagasy. Cole argues in her analysis of the TRC, quoting Chairperson Desmond Tutu, that the interpreters act as a first line of reconciliation, as they undergo "the trauma of not just hearing or reading about the atrocities, but [they] have had to speak in the first person as a victim or perpetrator."[48] In the TRC: "Interpreters occupied a contradictory position with the commission. They were at once invisible and highly visible. They were 'to reproduce the speaker's account as reliably as possible' and in the first person, yet they were supposed to maintain neutrality and emotional distance, even when the witness's demeanor was intensely emotional. Emotional expressiveness was somehow not considered part of the witness's narrative truth."[49] The French figure resembles this description very closely in his own scripted act of interpretation. In translation, the neutrality of his interpretation mediates the story, reduces its visceral impacts, and limits its possibilities. However, the French figure also acts as a representative of the French perpetrators. While the act of interpretation conveys one message, the relationship between the two figures onstage conveys another, reconfiguring the power dynamic between the descendants of the colonizers and the colonized. While the French figure verbally transmits a limited, less impassioned version of the memory, his body language demonstrates support and compassion, and a kind of surrender, allowing, even through his interpretation, the power of the Malagasy delivery to convey the nuances of the memory, rather than competing for the glory of storytelling.

Through this reconfiguration power, the staging positions the French man as something other than the enemy, other than the oppressor. Positioned to the right and slightly behind, connected by the touch of a hand and with a steady gaze of intent and compassionate listening, the French figure offers a representation of the French that shares the need to tell the story of these atrocities, to reconcile the crimes on previous generations, to create and build new relationships of alliance that do not consist primarily of exploiting the Malagasy for capital gains. Far from absolving the French from the crimes committed against the Malagasy and the horrors of the insurrection of 1947, the staging intervenes in the strict colonizer-colonized binary by demonstrating the ongoing shifts in the relationship between the two figures that does not rely on power dynamics created during the colonial period. Instead it illustrates a horizontal rather than vertical relationship between the French and the Malagasy, and between the Malagasy state and the Malagasy people that reconstructs how the memories of all those involved influence the continually reproduced narratives.

For instance, the bilingual structure of the spoken text is not contained by the biracial dichotomy of the cast. The Malagasy figure in the play uses both Malagasy and French throughout, demonstrating yet another way that the bilingual structure allows the play to dislocate logical/analytical thinking and embodied thinking from a colonizer-colonized binary. Likewise, the French figure is not confined to the telling of the French version of the story. When read alongside an inferred conflation of Merina Imperial and French Colonial powers, the fluid characterization by the French figure inheres a responsibility for the story in groups outside of the Betsimisaraka that encompass all Malagasy and French. Through the linguistic and epistemological nuances, Raharimanana establishes multiple modes of accessing the memory. Having disassociated the bilingual structure from a strict colonizer-colonized binary, the play offers a wide range of perspectives on the events that constitute the narrative in the national imaginary including perspectives from elite Malagasy studying at universities, Malagasy and French politicians, Malagasy from rural parts of the island, the young and the elderly, the media, and the diaspora, thus relocating the construction of national identity in the experiences of a variety of subject positions rather than merely in the dictums of the state.

Finally, the staging of movement pieces in between the various dialogic mediations also multiplies the layers of the memories and contributes to the way that the insurrection means in the national imaginary. While the structure and modes of verbal mediation disrupt the chronological frameworks of memory and the colonizer-colonized power structures, the moments of movement unaccompanied by dialogue add additional layers of murk to the memory of the insurrection by creating intersections between specific events of 1947 and more widely held conceptions of colonialism and its structures of power. For example, in the opening monologue, as the Malagasy figure expounds upon the "inferiority" of oral or "primitive"[50] languages, jungle and ape sounds fade up into the soundscape and the performer drops into a crouched position to imitate an ape—gamboling about across the stage, rolling onto his back, rubbing his belly, and picking at something behind his ears.[51] The imitation lasts about one minute before the performer regains his composure and continues his diatribe about "oral" languages.[52] Bedard sets apart this and other pieces of movement from the dialogue as distinct representational fragments that supplement the collage of narratives written into the text. In contrast to the moments of direct address—which deliver exposition, information, transitions, statistics, personal accounts, and memories related specifically to the insurrection of 1947—the moments expressed through movement and music portray the embodiment of domination and subjugation attributed to the Malagasy people as a result of colonial practices beyond the insurrection. As implications of the more extensive colonial project, the commentary in these moments responds to the stories written into the text as ideologically complementary and compounding.

By representing the memories of widespread colonial impacts that extend beyond the insurrection of 1947 through physicalization rather than oration, the pieces of movement seek to circumvent the failure of verbal language to fully depict the impact of the rhetorical ideas and structures of space and power on the bodies and daily lives of individuals. This moment and other movement fragments unite the varied Malagasy ethnicities through shared colonial experience, despite interethnic tensions prior to, during, and after the colonial period. The movement pieces tend to illustrate the relegation of the Malagasy body to positions of inferiority, stupidity, and submission, in contrast to the more presentational moments, which at many points empower Malagasy voices. This contrast illustrates the continuous struggle to reconcile the mind/body dichotomy that often complicates the fight for subjectivity—one of the dominant causes of the epistemic murk that surrounds the memory of 1947 and with which the Malagasy must reconcile in the constitution of a national identity that remembers specific battles of insurrection as well as widespread acts of colonial violence. This staging, through a possible reunification across ethnic lines, reconstructs a shared experience and identity produced by colonialism which in some ways has contributed to deepening schisms among some ethic groups. Cole argues that the process of fafy in daily life reconstructs an ancestral narrative. In my reading of this play, the cleansing of the memory acknowledges the schisms between Malagasy and French and between the Merina and the Betsimisaraka, and reconstructs a post/colonial Malagasy national identity, particularly in terms of complexities, mulitplicities, simultaneities, and additives rather than by losses, negation, and/or absences.

Conclusion

By jumping back and forth in time and space, by alternating between the embodied memories and the rhetorical narratives, by juxtaposing the "scientific" language against the "oral traditions," by including the experience of those who stayed on the island and those who emigrated, the play composes a collage that articulates the various perspectives and their contributions to the collective

Malagasy memory of the event. The intersections of these fragments lead the play to its ultimate conclusion: "Finally, we say that the events actually happened, that spears whistled their whistles of death, that the bullets have devoured and been absorbed, and that the corpses danced their gruesome dance... As for me, I remember nothing... Absolutely nothing. Only one date like a hot iron. March 29, 1947."[53] The narrator begins and ends the play with "They say the events really happened,"[54] but he does not know them, he cannot remember them. By demonstrating the life and becoming the memory in contemporaneity, the collage dislocates the memory from the past. The events happened. However, if they live in the present, if they will live in the future, perhaps they can never be *remembered* as events in a historical moment but only continuously reconstructed as events that live in contemporaneity. By exploring these mediations, the play dwells on a subjectivity *in formation* rather than a chronologically "post" colonial identity; for each fragment has hardly a recognizable beginning or ending, in a sense functioning like a Deleuzian plateau, related to each and every fragment within the text, producing new meanings as it comes into contact with them, and continually changing as each next fragment emerges before its audience.[55]

The multilingual montage of 47 parallels the purification process seen in fafy, which simultaneously and intentionally remembers *and* forgets in order to reinscribe the blank page of memory and make sense of past events in the contemporary moment. The processes of mediation selectively remember and therefore selectively, and intentionally, "forget." Perhaps one chooses a translated memory to witness a distant event without reliving the physical pain. Perhaps one chooses remembering it as a series of rumors in order to maintain unlimited possibilities. Like fafy, this large scale forgetting does not "[erase] the colonial past. Rather, through the work of memory, [the Malagasy] have recast its meaning and reworked its signs and practices so that many of the events of the colonial past can also invoke an ancestral narrative."[56] The ways in which the collage records the various narratives into history, and the resulting slippage, recontextualize the narratives in the contemporary, daily, material lives of the Malagasy. The collage of memories that the narrator can neither remember nor forget unravels the painful historical events and rebinds them to a contemporary, bilingual audience.

In the same way that fafy purifies a painful past, the multilingual representation of conflicting memories establishes a multiplicitous and murky epistemology of the events that allows the Malagasy protagonist to choose the ways that history infiltrates his daily, material life. The intentional plurality also creates a framework that allows the audience to experience multiple parallel reorientations of an obscure yet ever-present narrative. It "forgets" the order of events, or origin of some of the memories, and even the "truth" of many of the narratives, but it remembers that the events happened, and that traces of those events plague the daily material lives of their descendants. In this way, "Words, they say, are like wrapping, that which binds also loosens."[57] That which binds, also *un*binds, and while it may dislocate events from their originary place and time, it also nourishes opportunities for harnessing traumatic pasts to combat contemporary social and ethical battles. Proverbs may find their way into unexpected contexts, but the intentional forgetting promoted in Raharimanana's *47* that unbinds them also binds thems again to new, complex, and collaborative purposes.

As the dialogue on forgetting suggests, the events can never *be* remembered; they are always already distorted by the moments that surround them and that impact and change the subjects who attempt to remember. In the struggle for a definition of Self and Other that contributes to an independent national identity, the simultaneity and multiplicity implicit in the "always already" act as post/colonial interventions to reconstitute the nation in horizontal, rhizomatic, and nonchronological terms.

Notes

1. Maurice Bloch, *Placing the Dead: Tombs, Ancestral Villages and Kinship Organization in Madagascar* (Berkeley, CA: Berkeley Square House, 1971), 29.
2. Douglas Little, "Cold War and Colonialism in Africa: The United States, France, and the Madagascar Revolt of 1947," accessed December 17, 2011, *Pacific Historical Review* 59, no. 4 (November 1990): 527–52, http://www.jstor.com, 527; Jennifer Cole, "Narratives and Moral Projects: Generational Memories of the Malagasy 1947 Rebellion," *Ethos* 31, no. 1 (March 2003): 95–126, accessed December 17, 2011, http://www.jstor.com, 104; Philip M. Allen, *Madagascar: Conflicts of Authority in the Great Island*, (Boulder, CO: Westview Press, 1995), 47.
3. *47*, video of live performance, written by Jean-Luc Raharimanana, directed by Thierry Bedard (Antananarivo, Madagascar: Zanalany, 2008).
4. Jean-Luc Raharimanana, *47*, working playscript, Albert Camus Cultural Center, Antananarivo, Madagascar, 2008, 2. All translations from French and Malagasy are my own. For ease of reading and length I provide only the translation unless absolutely necessary.
5. Ibid., 14. A Malagasy proverb.
6. Ibid.
7. Post/colonial is a configuration I encountered in the work of Chris Bongie, and which I explore in depth in my master's thesis at Florida State University, "Toward a Post/colonial National Identity in the Theatre of Madagascar: Jean-Luc Raharimanana's *47* and *The Prophet and The President*." In short, the configuration resists the colonizer-colonized

binary and the idea that colonialism has ended, and instead implies the simultaneity and multiplicity of subjects belonging to former colonies and their nonchronological colonial and postcolonial experiences.

8. See Jean Luc Raharimanana, *Madagascar 1947*, 2nd ed. (La Roque-d'Anthéron, France: Vents d'ailleurs, 2008).
9. Laura Edmondson, "Marketing Trauma and the Theatre of War in Northern Uganda," *Theatre Journal* 57 (2005): 452.
10. Allen, *Madagascar: Conflicts of Authority*, 46.
11. Little, "Cold War and Colonialism," 528–29.
12. Ibid., 534.
13. MDRM: *Mouvement Democratique de la Rénovation Malgache*. Ethnically speaking, there are eighteen primary tribes of Malagasy around the island, each with a unique dialect and culture, but for the most part the eighteen tribes are able to communicate with one another. The official languages of Madagascar are *Malagasy Official*, which primarily consists of the *Merina* dialect, located in the high plateau region of Madagascar that surrounds the capital, Antananarivo; and French, which has been the primary language of the education system for much of the period after decolonization. The Merina occupy the central high plateau surrounding Antananarivo. Occupying and attempting to unify nearly two-thirds of the island, they became the primary representatives of the Malagasy in negotiations with European settlers, establishing the first permanent relations in the 1810s. The Betsimisaraka, an ethnic tribe in Madagascar, inhabit the region of Toamasina, where the bulk of the fighting of the 1947 insurrection occurred. Tomatave, the capital of the Toamasina region, was a major port for the French occupiers.
14. Allen, *Madagascar: Conflicts of Authority*, 45.
15. PADESM *Parti des Déshérités de Madagascar*. Many Malagasy societies had slaves prior to the arrival of the Europeans. The Merina empire used a significant amount of slave labor in the nineteenth century. Slaves and descendants of slaves, even today, are believed to be without ancestors, as the process of enslavement wiped clear their ancestral heritage. Allen, *Madagascar: Conflicts of Authority*, 57. According to Gillian Feeley-Harnik, "They were slaves precisely because, having been taken far away, they were 'lost, not knowing the land where their kin are' (*very, tsy mahay tany misy havana*.)" Feeley-Harnik, *A Green Estate: Restoring Independence in Madagascar* (Washington, DC: Smithsonian Institution Press, 1991); Jennifer Cole, "Narratives and Moral Projects," 105.
16. Raharimanana, *47*, 5. The definition of Vazaha (va za') is: White people or foreigners, usually European or American. Often carries derogatory connotations; "*Vazaha ou Malgache, le Fanjakana reste le Fanjakana!*"
17. Traditionally, many Malagasy ethnic groups practice a form of ancestral worship whereby descendants must tend to the land and tombs of the ancestors. This loyalty to location has maintained relatively marked ethnic boundaries throughout the island.
18. Sandra L. Richards, "Who Is This Ancestor? Performing Memory in Ghana's Slave Castle-Dungeons (A Multimedia Performance Meditation)," in *The SAGE Handbook of Performance Studies*, ed. D. Soyini Madison and Judith Hamera (Thousand Oaks, CA: Sage Publications, 2006), 491.
19. Raharimanana, *47*, 2.
20. While Merina and Betsimisaraka are two separate dialects of Malagasy, the geographical proximity of the two ethnicities as well as their relatively large sizes ensures that most

people who would have access to seeing this play would have not problem understanding the Betsimisaraka dialect. Even an outsider such as myself, trained in Malagasy Official and the Southeastern dialect of Antanala, was able to comprehend the Betsimisaraka dialect in this piece. Despite the fact that it would be comprehensible, the soundscape marks it specifically as not official, and as specific to a certain region of the country.

21. Raharimanana, *47*, 9–10; 10.
22. Catherine M. Cole, "Witnessing and Interpreting Testimony: Live, Present, Public, and Speaking in Many Tongues," *Performing South Africa's Truth Commission: Stages of Transition* (Bloomington: Indiana University Press, 2010), 68 (emphasis added).
23. Raharimanana, *47*, 9.
24. Cole, "Witnessing and Interpreting Testimony," 68 (emphasis added).
25. Raharimanana, *47*, video of live performance.
26. Raharimanana, *47*, 7.
27. Cole, "Witnessing and Interpreting Testimony," 104–5.
28. Allen, *Madagascar: Conflicts of Authority*, 46; and Philip M. Allen and Maureen Covell, *Historical Dictionary of Madagascar* (Lanham, MD: Scarecrow Press, 2005), xxxiii.
29. Cole, *Narratives and Moral Projects*, 105.
30. The *Tsimihety* are another of the eighteen major ethnic groups in Madagascar, residing primarily in North/Northeaster regions of Madagascar. During the process of decolonization, Philibert Tsiranana, a member of the PSD (Democratic Socialist Party), became the first president of the independent Republic of Madagascar. He served from 1959 to 1972.
31. Cole, *Narratives and Moral Projects*, 107.
32. Ibid., 108.
33. Ibid.
34. Ibid., 108–9.
35. Raharimanana, *47*, 6.
36. Ibid., 6.
37. Allen, *Madagascar: Conflicts of Authority*, 47.
38. Raharimanana, *47*, 6.
39. Richards, "Who Is This Ancestor," 491.
40. Raharimanana, *47*, 2.
41. Jennifer Cole, "The Work of Memory in Madagascar," *American Ethnologist* 25 (1998): 610–33, accessed December 17, 2011, http://www.jstor.com, 626.
42. Ibid., 623.
43. Robert Jaovelo-Dzao, *Rites d'invocation et de possession chez les Sakalava du Nord de Madagascar* (Paris: Karthala Editions,[1996]), 140.
44. Raharimanana, *47*, 11–12.
45. Ibid., 12.
46. Ibid., 8.
47. Raharimanana, *47*, video of live performance.
48. Cole, "Witnessing and Interpreting Testimony," 75.
49. Ibid., 74.
50. Raharimanana, *47*, 1.
51. Ibid.
52. Ibid., 2.

53. Ibid., 14.
54. Ibid., 1.
55. Gilles Deleuze and Félix Guattari, "Introduction: Rhizome," in *A Thousand Plateaus: Capitalism and Schizophrenia*, *The Norton Anthology of Theory and Criticism*, 2nd ed., Vincent B. Leitch, general editor (New York: W. W. Norton, 2010), 1459.
56. Cole, "The Work of Memory," 628.
57. Raharimanana, *47*, 14.

Beyond Political Propaganda

Performing Anticommunist Nostalgia in 1950s' Taiwan

—LI-WEN (JOY) WANG

The 1950s are known as the first decade of the anticommunist era in Taiwan. In order to fight against the Chinese communists, the Kuomintang government (KMT), which was then the ruling political party in Taiwan, proposed its anticommunist ideology that aimed at the elimination of the Chinese Communist power.[1] The Chinese Civil War, which lasted from 1927 to 1949, broke China into two parts. The Republic of China (ROC) held sway over Taiwan, and the People's Republic of China (PRC) controlled mainland China. After the split, anticommunist sentiment permeated dramatic works to the extent that a new genre of plays emerged that served as political propaganda for the KMT. Since anticommunist ideology was the central theme of that genre, the restoration of the lost motherland became one preferred motif used by playwrights. The constant calling of the motherland stirred up strong nostalgic sentiment toward the lost homeland. Although anticommunist plays are often criticized nowadays for their imposition of political ideology, this theatrical genre served a significant purpose in the 1950s: for those who were forced into exile, anticommunist plays not only fed their longings for the lost homeland but also provided a channel for them to let off their hatred against the Chinese Communists. In this essay, I discuss the concept of anticommunist nostalgia, which I define as a distinctive sentiment generated by the complicated interaction among the anticommunist ideology proposed by the government, the personal nostalgia the audience experienced, and a theatricalized nostalgia in anticommunist plays. I argue that the anticommunist nostalgia communicated through performance fed the emotional needs of the audience in that era. I investigate nostalgia in a prize-winning anticommunist play *The Romance of Daba Mountain (Dabashan zhi lian)*, a representative and well-known theatrical piece of its time; and I examine the correlation between anticommunism and nostalgic sentiment. I also explore how the performativity of anticommunist nostalgia contributed to the consolidation of nationalism in Taiwan in the 1950s.

The complicated sociopolitical background of Taiwan had its crucial influence upon the formation of the prevailing nostalgic sentiment for mainland China in the 1950s. Taiwan is a small island located about 100 miles from the southeastern Chinese mainland. Its original inhabitants were Malayo-Polynesian. Starting in the eighteenth century, large-scaled emigration from southeastern China began. These immigrants became the majority of the island population by the nineteenth century.[2] In 1886, Taiwan officially became a province of China, which was then under the sovereignty of the Qing dynasty. Eight years later, the Qing dynasty forfeited its control of the island to Japan in the First Sino-Japanese War (1894–1895). From then on, people in Taiwan underwent fifty years of Japanese colonization (1895–1945). Meanwhile, in mainland China, the Qing dynasty was overthrown and replaced by the newly established ROC in 1912. With the defeat of Japan in World War II, the ROC—led by Chiang Kai-shek—won back the sovereignty of Taiwan, placing it under the rule of the KMT. Government officials were first welcomed by the local residents because the KMT government had liberated Taiwan from the Japanese colonizer. However, confrontation between civilians and the authority quickly mounted due to language and cultural differences, and finally reached its climax by the end of February 1947.

On February 27, a widow selling illegal cigarettes was physically attacked by a few government officials. The widow was badly injured, and in the chaos, the officers killed another civilian by accident. The furious public started huge riots that lasted for days, during which the KMT government suppressed civilian protests with brutal violence. The event was later referred to as the 228 Incident (or February 28th Incident), a scar left by clashes between the KMT government and Taiwan local residents. Unfortunately, Chiang Kai-shek did not have the time or energy to deal with the growing tension on the island after the 228 Incident: he was actively engaged in his battle against the Chinese Communist Party (CCP) on the mainland. Eventually, Chiang Kai-shek led the main body of the KMT government into retreat in Taiwan, an act that symbolized the moving of a whole nation from the vast mainland China to the small island. On December 7, 1949, the KMT government officially announced its relocation. The resettlement of the government brought more than a million refugees, government personnel, and military staff.[3] These people, who came from different social and geographic locations but shared a common identity as "outsiders" on the island, were referred to as "mainlanders." In contrast with the mainlanders, the early immigrants from southeastern China and their descendants were called "islanders."[4] Thus, together with the native aboriginals, islanders and mainlanders have constituted the major population since the 1950s.

Taiwan after 1949: From Refuge to Nation

Although both groups were immigrants from mainland China, the distinction between mainlanders and islanders grew clearer given their different historical backgrounds. The mainlanders saw themselves as forced into exile, and the China they had lost was regarded as their real homeland: Taiwan was only a temporary shelter where they mapped out the plans for restoration. The islanders, in contrast, did not have such strong psychological ties to mainland China; they had not only lived in Taiwan for generations but also went through half a century of Japanese colonization. The distinction between these two groups was further deepened by the KMT government's continuing sovereignty over Taiwan. In the process of relocation, most of the major governmental officials came along with Chiang Kai-shek to Taiwan and held positions in a now downsized government. Only a few government positions were reserved for the islanders. As a result, mainlanders became the ruling class in Taiwan society even though they were the minority population.

The newly reestablished KMT government had two major challenges: externally, it had to survive the threat of the CCP, which had established the PRC in mainland China in 1949; internally, it had to find some way to create a general atmosphere of "family" to persuade the diverse population that everyone on the island was on the same side. Considering the unbalanced proportion of mainlanders and islanders relative to the power structure and society, their different historical backgrounds, and their different attitudes toward Taiwan, one cannot help but wonder how was it possible for these two groups to rebuild a nation together. How could the islanders recognize the sovereignty of the KMT government hitherto unknown to them before 1945? What factor caused the islanders to unify with the mainlanders in the face of external threats from the PRC, considering the islanders had experienced the brutal 228 Incident two years earlier?

Benedict Anderson defines nation as "an imagined political community," a definition I find fascinating when applied to the political circumstances of Taiwan. According to Anderson, a nation is imagined as "limited," "sovereign," and as a "community."[5] Geographically speaking, before the relocation, the territory of the Republic of China included both mainland China and Taiwan, yet after the retreat, with the resettlement of the whole government, the ROC was not only symbolically but also substantially "moved" to Taiwan. The moving of the nation thus brought up an interesting question: if a nation is an imagined community, can it be "moved" from one place to another? Before the retreat, the Republic of China had its vast land and its ancestral history that could be traced back five thousand years. Yet, after the split of 1949, the Republic of China came into existence in two ways—one political and one psychological—and each way redefined the nation. In its political reality, the territory of the Republic of China was "condensed" and limited to only a small part of its previous territory: Taiwan and several tiny archipelagoes nearby. Most of its civilians were early Chinese immigrants and refugees who came together with the government. In other words, the Republic of China still existed as a nation, only that its capital moved from Nanjing, China, to Taipei, Taiwan, and that its territory was much smaller than before.

On the psychological level, however, it was believed that the territory of the Republic of China went beyond these small islands. As shown and taught in the geography textbooks edited and published by the KMT government, the vast mainland—including Mongolia—was still legally part of the Republic of China's territory, and those who fell behind the bamboo curtain were still referred to as "our country fellowmen." This perspective saw the exile of KMT and the loss of mainland as a temporary matter. In other words, there seemed to be an *imagined* version of the imagined community: in that version, the Republic of China still owned the sovereignty over the mainland, which ironically highlighted the incompleteness of the nation and the incompetence of the KMT government.

Political theorist Ernest Renan considers "spiritual principle" to be the crucial factor that ties the members of a nation together. He writes, "A nation is a soul, a spiritual principle. Two things, which in truth are but one, constitute this soul or spiritual principle. One lies in the past, one in the present. One is the possession in common of a rich legacy of memories; the other is present-day consent, the desire to live together, the will to perpetuate the value of the heritage that one has received in an undivided form... The nation...is the culmination of a long past of endeavours, sacrifice, and devotion."[6] Carrying on the name of the Republic of China, the KMT government regarded itself as the legitimate Chinese regime. Therefore, it was not only the successor of authorized Chinese history, but also the heir of a profound Chinese cultural legacy. Such a mindset was evident in the naming of some cultural institutions established after the 1949 retreat. In the titles of these institutions, the word "Chinese" suggested their legitimacy of inheriting the spirit of China. For example, in March

1950, the KMT government established the Committee of Chinese Cultural Awards (*Zhonghua wen hua jiang jin wei yuan hui*) to promote the creation of anticommunist artworks.[7] Two months later, another cultural organization, the Chinese Literature and Art Association (*Zhongguo wen yi xie hui*), was set up and later became an influential cultural institution of that era. These two cultural organizations worked hand-in-hand to guide the direction of cultural development in Taiwan in the 1950s: the Chinese Literature and Art Association published a monthly journal, *Wen yi chuang zuo* ("The Creation of Art and Literature") from 1951 to 1956, the mission of which was to publish anticommunist artworks, and the Committee of Chinese Cultural Awards provided the funds for the journal and generous rewards for those who engaged in the creation of anticommunist artworks. In the names of these two cultural institutions, the word "Chinese" proclaimed the rightfulness of carrying on the national soul.

Indeed, through the widespread usage of the word "Chinese" in the naming of various official organizations (the above arts associations are just two examples), the repeated emphasis of the political legitimacy of the ROC, and the denial of the establishment of the PRC, the KMT government created a political/social/cultural milieu to convince people in Taiwan that they were the rightful heirs of the Chinese spirit. As Renan points out, the "essential conditions for being a people" is "to have common glories in the past and to have a common will in the present; to have performed great deeds together, to wish to perform still more."[8] Assuming or imagining all people in Taiwan shared the common glorious history from the past, the KMT government saw itself leading the people of the Republic of China to survive together in the present and so to have the chance to restore the lost homeland in the future.

Nostalgia and the Lost/New China

In *On Dramaturgy*, Li Mangui describes the anticommunist era as a period when "people's life, mind, emotion, and desire are all attached to the vision of returning to China."[9] Considered as a lost motherland, mainland China became, for the ROC, the object of nostalgic desire. The constant calling of the motherland in literature, radio, and newspapers marked one of the features of the anticommunist era. Yet the nature of such nostalgic sentiment should be questioned: did the desired homeland still exist after CCP/PRC's takeover? Did Red China, now a communist country, mean the same as the home left behind to the exiles? If so, did such nostalgia hinge upon the materiality of the land itself? If not, what did the nostalgia attach to?

In classical studies, nostalgia is associated with homesickness and melancholy. Deriving from two Greek roots—"*nostos*," which refers to "return to one's native land," and "*algos*," which means "pain, suffering, or grief"—nostalgia might be understood as an almost physically palpable homesickness. By the nineteenth century, the definition of nostalgia was broadened and could be used to describe "a general condition of estrangement, a state of ontological homelessness that became one of the period's key metaphors for the condition of modernity."[10] In other words, the concept of nostalgia is not necessarily tied to the physical loss of a homeland, but rather is more about the misplacement of a subject and the constant feeling of lack of belonging. Describing nostalgia as a "global epidemic," Svetlana Boym further names two kinds of nostalgia—restorative nostalgia and reflective nostalgia: "Restorative nostalgia stresses *nostos* and attempts a transhistorical reconstruction of the lost home. Reflective nostalgia thrives in *algia*, the longing itself, and delays the homecoming—wistfully, ironically, desperately. Restorative nostalgia does not think of itself as nostalgia, but rather as truth and tradition. Reflective nostalgia dwells on the ambivalences of human longing and belonging and does not shy away from the contradictions of modernity. Restorative nostalgia protects the absolute truth, while reflective nostalgia calls it into doubt."[11] In Taiwan of the 1950s, the nostalgic sentiment that prevailed in the cultural industry revealed a strong desire to reestablish the lost homeland. Such desire of homeland restoration was also made blatant in some popular political slogans.

One example is the political slogan that was proposed by Chiang Kai-shek in 1950: "First year is for preparation; second year is to fight back; third year is for wiping out the enemies; fifth year is destined to succeed." It is familiar to everyone who lived through the anticommunist era in Taiwan. In that slogan, China is presented as the desired object, with a five-year plan to regain it, while Taiwan is treated as a mere base for preparation of restoration. In fact, the general discourse of nostalgia in the anticommunist era followed this logic: the lost China was always better than the present Taiwan. In *On Longing*, Susan Stewart identifies the paradox of nostalgia. Unlike the general understanding of nostalgia, which sees the lost idyllic past, the good old days, as the object of longing, Stewart argues that the center of the desired object of nostalgia is in fact void: "Nostalgia is a sadness without an object, a sadness which creates a longing that of necessity is inauthentic because it does not take part in lived experience. Rather, it remains behind and before that experience. Nostalgia, like any form of narrative, is always ideological: the past it seeks has never existed except as narrative, and hence, always absent, that past continually threatens to reproduce itself as a felt lack."[12] Within the framework of nostalgia discourse of the 1950s, the desired object—the so-called homeland China—had never existed, for it was not considered as the eventual home of the exiled Chinese people until it was no longer their home; that is, the past "never existed except as narrative." As Boym writes, "Nostalgia…is a longing for a home that no longer exists or has never existed"; what was desired was the phantom of China.[13] In other words, the homeland China desired by the exiles was more an imagined place than an actual location: it existed only in the fantasy of the nostalgic mind.

When talking about restorative nostalgia, Boym identifies its two narrative plots: the restoration of origins and the conspiracy theory.[14] According to Boym, the conspiracy theory presumes a set of absolute oppositional value: good and evil. It imagines that "we" (the conspiracy theorists) project our dislike on our enemies, who serve as the scapegoat for our misfortune in the modern world. "We" believe that "they" conspire against "our" homecoming and therefore "we" have to conspire against "them" in order to restore "our" imagined community. For the conspiracy theorists, the idea of home is always under siege and needs to be protected. By identifying the subversive kinship of others, conspiracy theorists solidify their imagined community not based upon affection but upon exclusion.[15] The narrative of restorative nostalgia tends to make a clear-cut distinction between "our" people and the enemies. Such differentiation not only highlights the sameness shared by our people but also spotlights how different the foes are from us. In the 1950s, inspired by the anticommunist sentiment and demanded by the government, theatre joined the cultural war against the PRC and a great number of anticommunist plays were produced. In anticommunist plays, one can find strong contrast between the portrayal of "us" and "them." By performing anticommunist/restorative nostalgia, the text and performance of this theatrical genre engendered nationalism. Although evidence shows that anticommunist theatrical activities were very popular in the 1950s, only a few visual records are left for the studies of this theatrical genre: considering the poor economic condition in the 1950s, there were limited resources for recording theatrical performance. While it is difficult to examine the performativity of anticommunist nostalgia through analyzing theatrical performances during that time, the play texts provide some clues.

Wishes of Homeland Restoration in *The Romance of Daba Mountain*

The Romance of Daba Mountain won the prize in the contest for drama held by the Committee of Chinese Cultural Awards in 1951. It is an anticommunist play written by the mainlander playwright Guo Sifen. The play is set in 1949, when the Chinese Communist Party was about to take over China. The backdrop of the play is a small village near Daba Mountain in the Sichuan province.[16] Yang Daming, an adopted son of old lady Yang, comes back to his home village after five years of fighting the Chinese Communists with the KMT government in the civil war. His return has caught the attention of the township mayor, Li Mingde, and his assistant, Li Erhu, both of whom are communist-friendly. Li Mingde's daughter, Li Menglan, used to be Daming's sweetheart before he left the village five years ago. However, when he pays his visit to the girl, the two have a huge fight because Daming tells her to marry someone else since her father holds strong hostility against him. As the story goes on, a time-buried family secret is revealed: Daming's father was killed by his brother, Li Mingde, twenty years ago, when Daming's home was burned to the ground in chaos and only Daming and his twin brother, Li Erhu, were saved from the fire. With the revelation of the family secret, Daming and Menglan finally realize they are in fact cousins. Daming starts to organize the villagers after the CCP takes over the village. In a riot against the CCP, Li Mingde is shot to death by a CCP commissar, who later fabricates that it was Daming who took the mayor's life. Daming uncovers the commissar's scheme in front of Menglan. To avenge her father, Menglan decides to work with Daming and fight against the Chinese Communists together with the villagers. The play ends with Daming's exciting statement: "This is just a beginning, we will continuously fight together with all of the armed anticommunist comrades till the restoration of entire China!"[17]

In the play, the unbreakable connection between an individual and his birthplace is repeatedly presented surrounding the protagonist Yang Daming, who experiences and seeks a homecoming. When the curtains rise, the audience immediately learns the news of Daming's return. A few days after his homecoming, Daming tells his sister Yang how much the word "home" means to him:

DAMING: When I traveled, I was much distressed. I thought everyone has a home or somewhere he belongs to. But I don't.
SISTER YANG: Why not? Don't you belong here?
DAMING: It's true. Although I have been roaming from one place to another for five years, I can never forget people here, especially mom (old lady Yang) and you. How much you both have been kind to me.
SISTER YANG: Brother, don't you ever say that.
DAMING: You don't understand, sister. It is true: I don't know where I came from. I don't even know who my parents are. I grew up on this land, but I cannot find my roots here.[18]

In this passage, a strong tie between an individual and his birthplace is presented. Since Daming does not know where he was born, for him the concept of homeland is in fact constructed upon an imagined place. The imagined homeland has its significance for Daming and cannot be replaced by any other place: being an orphan, Daming is sensitive enough to know the difference between "home" and "hometown." For Daming, while the former refers to the place of one's origin, the latter means the place where one settles down and grows up. Daming's different definitions of home and hometown parallel the definitions of China and Taiwan in the political rhetoric of the 1950s: while China was seen as the root of individual origin (home), Taiwan was taken as the temporary refuge (hometown). Considering the sociopolitical situation, Daming's search for an eventual homecoming tells the story of more than one million people, who came to Taiwan in exile but longed to return to (or suffered nostalgically for) the lost motherland. In this light, Daming serves as a theatrical metaphor of the mainlanders who came to Taiwan in 1949. In a conversation, Daming tells Menglan about his travel and his search for the hometown:

DAMING: Menglan, you wouldn't understand how an orphan feels. A vagrant orphan who has entrusted his wondering soul upon a lofty hope, yet what he gets in return is an eternal silence... Leaving Beijing, I pondered, and I started to think of the loveliness of one's hometown. As a poet writes, "Only the mountains in hometown are high, only the water in hometown is clear. Only the moon in hometown is bright, only the people in hometown are nice." So, here I am. Dragging my exhausted body and soul, I came back.[19]

If Daming can be read as epitomizing the mainlanders, it is interesting to see how this passage embodies exiles in the 1950s. Set in the framework of Chinese Civil War, Daming's experience as a KMT follower, who travels along with the army and fights against the CCP for several years, recalls the collective memories of the exiled mainlanders. Before the KMT retreated to Taiwan, the capital had been moved all the way from Nanjing, to Guangzhou, Chongqing, and Chengdu as it was defeated by the CCP. When the government and the army finally came to Taiwan in 1949, they were both physically and mentally exhausted. Parting from their motherland, the mainlanders shared some psychological ties to the lost mainland. Just like Daming, who thinks Menglan would never understand his feelings, for she never suffers from the lack of home, the mainlanders found that the islanders cannot understand their yearning for the lost motherland.

Since *The Romance of Daba Mountain* centers on the eventual homecoming of Daming, who represents mainlanders in Taiwan, how can the islanders locate themselves in the play? Provided the differences between Daming and Menglan, is it possible that the play tries to deepen the community gap between the mainlanders and the islanders? Although Daming and Menglan have a huge fight over some misunderstanding, they eventually reconcile and become allies in the fight against their common enemy: the Chinese Communists. In act 4, there is a moving scene that portrays the reconciliation between the two. When Daming appears in front of Menglan, who mistakenly thinks Daming murdered her father, the girl pulls out a gun and points at Daming.

> (*Holding the gun, Menglan is so nervous that her hands keep shaking.*)
> DAMING: Calm down, Miss. I am standing right in front of you.
> MENGLAN: Do you think I am afraid to take your life?
> DAMING: Do it if you will! (*He keeps walking to her, till the gun touches his chest.*) You won't miss the aim then!
> (*Menglan stares at Daming. Her hands are shaking. Silence.*)
> DAMING (*taking over her gun*): No bullets? Please use my revolver! (*He takes out his gun and gives it to her.*)
> (*Instead of taking the gun, Menglan falls into his arms.*)[20]

In this excerpt, the confrontation between Daming and Menglan ends up in reconciliation that further establishes emotional bonding between the two. This suggests that the ongoing tension between mainlanders and islanders would end up in happy reconciliation as well. With Menglan throwing herself into the arms of Daming, who is then fighting bravely against the Chinese Communists, the play suggests the islanders forgive and forget the misunderstandings that resulted in confrontations and work together with the mainlanders to fight against the common enemy for a better future. After all, as the play reveals in the end, Daming and Menglan are in fact family. Connected by flesh and blood, families should not turn against each other, and so it is with the mainlanders and the islanders: since the latter are early immigrants from China, the two groups share the same ancestral roots, and therefore should treat each other as friends and fellowmen, not enemies.

Within the sociopolitical context of the 1950s Taiwan, when the play *The Romance of Daba Mountain* was performed on stage, Daming's nostalgia for his home and his profound attachment to the land reminded the audience of the lost China. The nostalgic sentiment for the lost motherland is incited every time when Daming laments his lack of home. Writing about nostalgia, Bryan Turner points out that one of the four elements of the nostalgic paradigm is "a sense of the absence or loss of personal wholeness and moral certainty."[21] Daming's constant search for home reveals an awareness of his incompleteness. His journey comes to its climax when he comes to the front door of the burned house. Accompanied by his friends Zhang Minghui and Wang Guodong, Daming walks around the burned house, waiting for the gathering villagers.

DAMING: I seem to have a special impression on this place. I often dreamed about this place when I was traveling. It is such attachment to this place that drove me back. I came here alone many times ever since I came back.
WANG: Do you mean this burnt house?
DAMING: Yes. I often walk around it, as if I am looking for something I have lost. I don't even know what the connection between me and the house is.[22]

With the family story revealed previously by old lady Yang, the audience recognizes the burned house is in fact what Daming has been looking for: his origin, his home. The connection between an individual and his homeland is once again put under the spotlight and arouses the audience's nostalgic sentiment for one's motherland. If the burned house can be taken as the metaphor of the lost China, which is often described as been trampled and burned by the Chinese Communists in the 1950s political rhetoric, then Daming's homecoming lights up the hope of restoring the lost homeland in the coming future.

With direct speeches condemning the cruelty of the Chinese Communist Party, *The Romance of Daba Mountain*, and plays like it, constructs a nation for the ROC by drawing a line between "we" (all people in Taiwan) and "they" (the Chinese Communists/PRC). In the play, the villagers gather at the burned house to join Daming's anticommunist revolution. When the crowds come, Daming makes a speech that points out the inhumanity of the CCP:

> Ever since the communist bandits took over our hometown, everyone has experienced the struggling and enforced levies every month. However, it is just the beginning. Our food has been transported to somewhere else. What are we going to eat next year? Our young men have been sent to the army, who is going to plant the crops? Who can feed our parents and wife? Are we going to survive all this?
> …
> The communist bandits do not want us to live the way we choose to live. They want to tear our family apart, destroy our traditional values, and enslave the people. They want everyone to become their slaves. You cannot enjoy a peaceful life unless you work for them.[23]

When performed on stage, the speech is addressed to two different groups: the characters on stage and the audience in theatre. By making an appeal directly to the villagers on stage, the play skillfully reveals the ugliness of the communists to the audience. The same technique of such direct speech is used once again at the end of the play, when Daming asks everyone to arm himself and fight against the communists. His patriotic notion of fighting together continuously in order to restore China is followed by a song that celebrates the beauty of one's homeland:

> Daba Mountain, it covers ten thousand miles!
> The mountains are so high,
> The rivers are so long,
> And the people are so nice!
> The flowers are so sweet!
> Oh, the flowers are so sweet!
> It is the place where we grow up.
> It is the place where our ancestors rest in peace,
> It is the place where our aging parents live.
> It is a sacred place.
> How can we let it fall into the dark side?
> …
> We'll never yield!
> We'll never go into exile![24]

Fully immersed in the melody and lyrics of the song, the audience is again reminded of the beauty of the lost homeland and of the evilness of the enemies. *The Romance of Daba Mountain*, like the song at the end, provides a more optimistic vision of the coming future to the audience.

The nostalgic sentiment of *The Romance of Daba Mountain* grows from the love and longing for the lost homeland. The homeland China is there, waiting for its restoration. Daming, who spent years in search of his origin and his eventual home, surprisingly finds that the burned house he used to visit in the hometown is in fact the place he has long searched for. The discovery makes the village where he grows up becomes his actual home, and what he has recovered is his history that contributes to the idea of "home." Perhaps the metaphor of this play—Daming's discovery of "home" as it relates to the ROC's nostalgia for "China"—is a prediction of the Taiwan-China situation nowadays: unable to fight back, the ROC has relocated to Taiwan. The original temporary refuge has become the mainlanders' eternal home, a situation foreshadowed in the play written in 1951.

Conclusion

As the Republic of China cheerfully celebrated its 100-year anniversary in 2011, its national history is again under examination. Standing as a representative anticommunist play of the 1950s in Taiwan, *The Romance of Daba Mountain* tells the national story of both that chaotic postwar era as well as the story of more than a million exiled mainlanders. On the one hand, the anticommunist nostalgia in the play fed the emotional needs of the audience: by visualizing the depravity of the Chinese Communists, the play galvanized public hatred toward the enemy; and by presenting stories about the fallen China, the play aroused the audience's nostalgic sentiment for the lost homeland, a sentiment that contributed to nation building and helped identify and fortify the ROC's imagined community. On the other hand, as the work of a theatrical genre, the anticommunist play also demonstrated the KMT government's interference in the cultural industry.

While many scholars nowadays condemn the KMT government for its imposition of anticommunist ideology on theatre half a century ago, one cannot deny the contribution of anticommunist plays: first of all, as a theatrical genre, anticommunist plays helped the theatre in Taiwan live through the difficult era of 1950s. In order to promote the government's political ideology, the annual anticommunist plays competition held by the Committee of Chinese Cultural Awards stimulated the creation of theatrical works. The tempting rewards provided by the government inspired many people, some of whom were not even writers, to start their career as playwrights. According to Li Mangui's estimation, within the first two decades after the relocation, more than three thousand plays had been written, among which at least one thousand were produced.[25] Theatre owed its survival, or even its prosperity, through this difficult era to the KMT government's support. Second, considering the lack of resources after the retreat and the enforcement of Martial Law (1949–1987), the frequent performances of anticommunist plays provided the public with opportunities to assemble legally and the satisfaction of watching theatre with friends and families. Resembling melodrama in their highly sensational plots and much exaggerated characters, anticommunist plays are very entertaining to watch. For example, Daming's hidden family story in *The Romance of Daba Mountain* gives suspense to the politically oriented play. Watching the performance, the audience had a great time exploring the family secrets, guessing what will happen between Daming and Menglan and condemning the villains. By the end of the play, the death of the evil Communists on stage also provided the audience with emotional satisfaction, knowing that the villains will be punished, justice will be asserted, the restoration of China is near, and the longing for the lost homeland will soon be satisfied. As a public entertainment, a wish fulfillment, or restorative nostalgia, anticommunist plays met the audience's emotional, psychological, and political needs.

Moreover, anticommunist plays helped somewhat to ease the inner confrontations between mainlanders and islanders by shifting the object of hostility from a close friend to the distant enemy. The ugly images of the Chinese Communists presented in *The Romance of Daba Mountain* helped the audience, some of whom had little context for the CCP, to identify and personify their common enemy. In that chaotic era, the same goal of fighting against the Chinese Communists helped the government maintain its social stability. Finally, the nostalgic sentiment that flowed in anticommunist plays aroused the audience's desire for the lost homeland, a desire for the lost completeness of the Republic of China before its split. Such desire helped to strengthen the will of restoring the lost China. As Boym says, nostalgia functions as "a defense mechanism in a time of accelerated rhythms of life and historical upheavals."[26] It is the anticommunist nostalgia in this theatrical genre that brought up the audience's love for the country, blurred the inner conflicts, and further focused on the resistance against the external enemies. With the constant longing for the desired past, the sentiment of anticommunist nostalgia led people of the Republic of China to move forward and survive through the tumultuous 1950s.

Notes

1. The Kuomintang (KMT, or Guomindang) government is also known as the Chinese Nationalist Party. KMT had been the ruling political party of the Republic of China from the establishment of the nation (1912) until 2000, when the Democratic Progressive Party (Minjindang, also known as DPP), the major oppositional party in Taiwan, won the presidential election.
2. These immigrants mainly came from Guangdong and Fujian Provinces. With the growing domestic hardship in mainland China and the possible business opportunities on the island, the population of the Chinese immigrants kept increasing. According to Nancy Guy, the population of the immigrants had reached around three million by the late 1890s. See John Copper, *Taiwan: Nation-State or Province?* (Boulder, CO: Westview Press, 1990), 8; Nancy Guy, "Governing the State: Peking Opera and Political Authority in Taiwan," *Ethnomusicology* 43, no. 3 (1999): 509. In her *Operatic China*, Daphne Lei mentions that the Taiping Rebellion (1851–1864) was also a possible reason that led to the immigration wave in the nineteenth century. See Daphne Lei, *Operatic China* (New York: Palgrave Macmillan, 2006), 26.
3. Scholars could not agree upon the number of mainlander refugees, but it is estimated

that the number could reach as high as 1.2 million. According to the Census Bureau, from 1945 to 1956, around 640,000 of mainlanders moved to Taiwan, but the number did not include military staff. The bureau also indicates that in 1956 the population of the mainlanders was around 930,000 while the islanders numbered nearly 8.38 million. Also, in her article, Nancy Guy states that the amount of refugees, governmental officials, and military staff might reach around 2 million. See Census Bureau of Taiwan Province, *Census Report on The Republic of China* (Taipei: Census Bureau of Taiwan Province, 1956), 1–2, 719–22; Guy, "Governing the State," 510.
4. Guy, "Governing the State," 510.
5. Benedict Anderson, introduction to *Imagined Community* (London: Verso, 1983), 6–7.
6. Ernest Renan, "What Is a Nation," *Nation and Narration*, ed. Homi K. Bhabha (London: Routledge, 1990), 19.
7. Generally speaking, the English translation of the word "Chinese" has several meanings: it may refer to the Chinese ethnicity and the Chinese language. Linguistically, it is also the adjective and possessive term of the word China, *Zhongguo*. In the case of the Committee of Chinese Cultural Awards, the word "Chinese" has a broader meaning: it is the translation of the term *Zhonghua*, a term that derives its roots from both *Zhongguo*, China the country, and *Huaxia*, the major ethnic group of the Chinese people. The usage of the term *Zhonghua* in the Chinese title of the cultural organization suggested its ambition of inheriting what was considered as the Chinese substance.
8. Renan, "What Is a Nation," 19.
9. Li Mangui, *On Dramaturgy* 編劇概論 (Taipei: Kangle, 1954), 73.
10. Eugene B. Daniels, "Nostalgia and Hidden Meaning," *American Image* 42 (1985): 371; Johannes Hofer, "Medical Dissertation on Nostalgia by Johannes Hofer, 1688," *Bulletin of the History of Medicine* 2 (1934): 376–91; Susan L. Hotak and William J. Havlena, "Nostalgia: An Exploratory Study of Themes and Emotions in the Nostalgic Experience," *Advances in Consumer Research* 19 (1992): 380; John Frow, "Tourism and the Semiotic of Nostalgia," October 57 (1991): 135. Also, Boym provides an alternative way to look at the word "nostalgia." She divides the word into "*nostos*" and "*algia*," while the former refers to "the return home," the latter to "longing." See Svetlana Boym, *The Future of Nostalgia* (New York: Basic Books, 2001), xv–xvi.
11. Boym, *The Future of Nostalgia*, xviii.
12. Susan Stewart, *On Longing: Narratives of the Miniature, the Gigantic, the Souvenir, the Collection* (Baltimore: Johns Hopkins University Press, 1984), 23.
13. Boym, *The Future of Nostalgia*, xiii.
14. In her book, Daphne Lei uses Boym's theory of nostalgia to analyze cultural policies and productions of traditional Chinese opera after the 1949 retreat. While Lei applies the conspiracy theory, one of the narrative plots of restorative nostalgia, to examine the Cultural Restoration movement, which started in 1966 to counter the Cultural Revolution (1966–1976) in China, I am using conspiracy theory to explore the oppositional images of the pro-KMT people and the communists in anticommunist plays. See Daphne Lei, *Alternative Chinese Opera in the Age of Globalization: Performing Zero* (New York: Palgrave Macmillan, 2011), 15–18, 29–32.
15. Boym, *The Future of Nostalgia*, 43.
16. While the village in the play might be fictional, Daba Mountain is factual. The usage of a real geographic location of mainland China is a dramaturgical measure often seen in

anticommunist plays. By mentioning the familiar geographic names and visualizing the landscape of the lost China on stage, these plays could easily arouse the audience's longing for the motherland.

17. Guo Sifen, *The Romance of Daba Mountain* 大巴山之戀, *Collections of Chinese Drama* 中華戲劇集, ed. Li Mangui and Liu Shuofu (Taipei: Chinese Dramatic Art Center, 1971), 7:404.
18. Ibid., 324–25. In this essay, all quotations from *The Romance of Daba Mountain* are my translations from Mandarin Chinese.
19. Ibid., 328–29.
20. Ibid., 381–82.
21. The other three elements are "a sense of historical decline and loss, involving a departure from some golden age of 'homefulness'"; "a sense of the loss of individual freedom and autonomy with the disappearance of genuine social relationships"; and "the idea of a loss of simplicity, personal authenticity and emotional spontaneity." See Bryan S. Turner, "A Note on Nostalgia," *Theory, Culture and Society* 4 (1987): 150–51.
22. Guo Sifen, *The Romance of Daba Mountain*, 352–53.
23. Ibid., 357–58.
24. Ibid., 405.
25. Li Mangui, foreword to *Collections of Chinese Drama* (Taipei: Center of Chinese Theater and Arts, 1970), 1:2.
26. Boym, *The Future of Nostalgia*, xiv.

Marilyn Monroe

Soldier in Greasepaint

—KRISTI GOOD

A favorite story from my childhood was told by my great-uncle Jack Forsha, who served in the Korean War in the same unit with his identical twin brother, Jim. At family gatherings, Jack would pass around the photos he had taken of Marilyn Monroe during her post-war Korean USO show in February 1954, as well as the book he had purchased when he realized it showed a picture of Marilyn onstage with him and Jim just a few rows away in the audience. As a graduate student learning about performance theory and cognitive science, I began to wonder about his personal experience with this cultural icon.

Jack remembers sitting and chatting with Jim and several other servicemen when Monroe arrived at K-47 base in Chunchon, Korea, with her military escort. Jack and Jim had been stationed at K-47 with approximately one thousand other airmen since May 1953, just two months before the cease-fire agreement. Talk of a cease-fire had been going on for two years, but it was not until July 27, 1953, that the United Nations Command, the Democratic People's Republic of Korea, and the Chinese People's Volunteers signed the official Armistice Agreement. The war is widely considered to have concluded with the signing of the Armistice Agreement, and actions such as the establishment of the Demilitarized Zone and the exchange of prisoners of war and deceased soldiers occurred following the cease-fire without an official peace treaty. In order to keep the men occupied after the cease-fire had been arranged, K-47 base organized the men into sports teams that would compete with other bases in tournaments. Jack admitted, with a chuckle, that he spent most of his time in Korea playing baseball and basketball. When they heard the news of the upcoming USO show, Jack said, "We were buffaloed-over that Marilyn was coming. I didn't know what to expect. I had never met a celebrity."[1]

Sitting with Jack and Jim were Gerald Kasper and his identical twin brother, Robert; the Forshas and the Kaspers were two of four pairs of twins at the base. Jack recalls that when Monroe arrived, the escort was not allowing her to sign autographs because she was scheduled to attend an officers' dinner. Monroe stopped to talk to the twins, however, because Gerald had recently broken his leg after falling out of a truck. Monroe chatted with the men for a moment or two, learning their names and signing Gerald's cast. Jack remembers at dinner that night that Monroe "table-hopped" to spend time with the men, rather than sitting at the head table reserved for officers.

At the official USO Camp Show performance, Jack and Jim were approximately five rows away from the stage—an impressive feat, given the number of military personnel in attendance. Monroe came to the edge of the stage after performing her songs to shake hands and sign autographs. After a few moments, she began to walk offstage, but turned back when she noticed that Jack had just taken a picture of her from the fifth row. She said, "Did you get that, Jack?" and he replied, "No!" (see fig. 1). She returned to the edge of the stage and motioned for him to approach. He moved to the first row and she posed for him before leaving the stage (see fig. 2).[2]

Figure 1. Marilyn Monroe asks, "Did you get that, Jack?" USO Show, Korea, 1954. Photo by Jack Forsha.

Figure 2. Marilyn Monroe poses at the USO Show, Korea, 1954. Photo by Jack Forsha.

Many of us have stories about encounters with a celebrity, and in a time when social media and fan conventions like Comic-Con can bring us into close proximity and interaction with our favorite stars, it is unusual to find someone who has not shared a moment with a famous icon. The experiences of the U.S. soldiers in Korea, however, seem to indicate moments that are much more intimate and meaningful than what we come into contact with today. The project initiated by the United Services Organization that made these experiences possible is a very important factor in investigating the nature of these celebrity interactions. Was the USO simply trying to give the soldiers a bit of fun, a brush with a celebrity, or was there a more complex agenda behind the USO Camp Shows that culminated in unique encounters, such as those experienced by the Forshas?

Monroe's status as a Hollywood star in 1954 is undeniable, but the nature of her celebrity in general is a mysterious concept. Many biographers have attempted to capture the qualities of Monroe's life that made her so famous. Joseph Roach deftly tackles the elusive nature of celebrity in his 2007 book *It*, which serves here as a tool to explore the effect of Monroe's celebrity on the public, rather than on her life story. The project of the USO and the experiences of the U.S. soldiers in Korea are important parts of this research. To understand those experiences, the final section of my essay deals with cognitive science theories of audience engagement. I employ cognitive science to examine the relationship between audience and performer in light of the unusual circumstances of Monroe's live performance for the U.S. troops, specifically her oscillation between celebrity and ordinary volunteer; she was not only performing live for the first time in her life, but she was also interacting with the servicemen away from the stage. By investigating Monroe's role as a USO performer in 1954 Korea through the use of Roach's theory of celebrity and cognitive theories on audience engagement, I examine the relationship between spectator and performance within a wartime context in a new light. Moreover, I argue that the USO created "scripted" performances in order to encourage feelings of nationalism within the troops in Korea during the winter of 1954.

The academic pursuit of making sense of the life of Marilyn Monroe is a daunting one. There are countless biographies and tell-all books that claim to have singular ownership of the true story of Monroe's life, psyche, and career. Any given anecdote about her life could exist in three distinctly disparate forms in as many books. In the end, this study is not *about* Monroe. It is, rather, about the *effect* of Monroe and how cognitive science can help us to speak with more scientific validity about that effect. The application of cognitive science to performance studies is a comparatively recent practice. The traditional practice of employing theory in an academic analysis may result in holes and questions, but cognitive science can often help fill in the gaps. The word "theory" connotes a generally accepted hypothesis that can continue to be tested by predicting future outcomes. The information we have about the human mind grows by leaps and bounds every day due to the rigorous and methodical exploration carried out by scientists around the globe. The information that cognitive studies yields has been systematically observed, tested, and measured so that it moves farther and farther from theory and closer to fact. By implementing both theory and scientific fact in this essay, I hope to close some of the gaps that my questions leave about the reception of Marilyn Monroe during her tour in Korea, specifically regarding how the USO succeeded in creating a "scripted" performance to promote a nationalistic agenda and what the experience of interacting with a celebrity under these conditions meant to the servicemen.

In 1954, Marilyn Monroe was exploding onto the Hollywood scene. She was quickly becoming a popular cultural icon and made headlines, once again, by marrying baseball star Joe DiMaggio. Yet she was unknown as a stage performer. Even though she would study with the Strasbergs at the Actors Studio in New York, she used her actor training in the movies and not in the theatre. The USO tour was an impromptu arrangement made while on her honeymoon in Japan. According to biographer Donald Spoto, the couple's arrival in Tokyo produced excitement in the news and prompted General John E. Hall to contact Monroe the next day with a request to perform for the troops, provided that proper government clearances and USO documents could be furnished.[3] Fred Lawrence Guiles writes that when DiMaggio objected, Monroe responded, "But it's the least anyone can do."[4] Within two weeks, the necessary documents were in hand, and Monroe was on her way to Korea for her first live performance.

How was Monroe received at this live USO show? What were the experiences of soldiers like Jack and Jim Forsha who came into contact with her? What did it really mean for a serviceman to watch a glamorous movie star like Marilyn Monroe perform live onstage and then have the opportunity simply to chat with or be served dinner by this same celebrity? The USO made these personal experiences possible, and after seventy years of providing Camp Shows and other amenities for our servicemen and women around the globe, that success raises some questions. What techniques were the USO using to create a celebrity encounter that was more than just a brush with fame? And to what end?

Roach's book *It* takes a theoretical look at the nature of celebrity and helps to explain encounters such as the one the Forsha brothers had with Monroe in Korea. As he writes, "'It' is the power of apparently effortless embodiment of contradictory qualities simultaneously: strength *and* vulnerability, innocence *and* experience, and singularity *and* typicality among them."[5] These are the qualities that most biographies of Monroe attempt to uncover, with varying results. More important than pinning down the particular qualities of "It" that Marilyn possessed is the examination of the effects of those qualities on her audience.

Roach outlines three particular aspects of the effect of "It." These are conditions that exist outside of the personal qualities that a person with "It" exhibits. Public intimacy is the first of these conditions, and it refers to the illusion of availability. This occurs when celebrities are constructed as products of the media; their appearance on magazine covers, the movie screen, the Internet, and newspapers produces a false sense of intimacy with spectators.[6] Images of Monroe are ever-present today, but in the years leading up to 1954 she was just reaching her peak as a Hollywood celebrity. She began playing small roles in 1948, and by the end of 1953 she had over twenty films to her credit. While many of her early onscreen roles consisted of walk-on parts with one or two lines, the later films leading up to 1953 would prove to be milestones in her career: *Monkey Business*, *Niagara*, *Gentlemen Prefer Blondes*, and *How to Marry a Millionaire*.[7] The public saw Monroe regularly in the magazines, especially as her screen time increased in her movies. She appeared on the covers and interior pages of *Look*, *Cosmopolitan*, *Esquire*, and *Time*, as well as numerous others publications.

She was featured on the cover of *Life* for the first time in April 1952. She would occupy this coveted space six more times between then and her death in 1962.[8]

Closely tied with the idea of public intimacy is Roach's second condition of synthetic experience. Synthetic experience, he writes, must "answer the human need, regulated by both curiosity and fear, to experience life vicariously as well as directly."[9] This condition, then, relies on the consumption of those products that enhance public intimacy. Fans purchase movie tickets, read magazines and interviews, and bedeck their computer desktops with images in order to feel closer to and understand more about a celebrity. Synthetic experience feeds into and intensifies the illusion of availability that public intimacy provides. For the general public in the 1950s, two events in particular drove these conditions of synthetic experience to a new level for Monroe's celebrity status: the nude calendar photos of 1949 and the first issue of *Playboy* magazine in December 1953.

In May 1949, Monroe sat for a collection of nude photographs in the studio of Tom Kelley that were to be used in a calendar. There are various stories regarding Monroe's hesitation to sit for the photographs and her eventual capitulation: her car had been repossessed, she was late with the rent, she wasn't eating enough.[10] Regardless of the specific reason, the assumption is that she submitted out of poverty. Monroe was still relatively unknown as an actress at the time, so the intention was not for a celebrity nude photo. In fact, she had not yet developed her signature style. The photo, entitled "Golden Dreams," of the naked woman sprawled across red velvet, shows golden-auburn, shoulder-length hair—not the bleached-blonde short hairdo associated with the iconic Marilyn Monroe. Marilyn's notability in the movie industry was only beginning to take off when the calendar appeared three years later in 1952, and people recognized her in the nude photos immediately.

One year later, in December 1953, Hugh Hefner released the first issue of *Playboy* magazine with the photos Kelley had taken of Monroe in 1949. Kelley had paid Monroe fifty dollars for the nude photography session, but the photos did not belong to him or to her. Hefner purchased the negatives of the photographs from the company who produced the calendar and printed them without Monroe's permission.[11] The nude calendar was now an item of secondary importance, being only tacitly understood as a synthetic experience of Monroe, since it did not bear her name and was not specifically marketed as a Marilyn Monroe "product." The same photo in *Playboy,* however, was explicitly tied to Monroe, and its intensity in terms of public intimacy skyrocketed when Hefner made it readily available for consumption on every newsstand across the country.

Roach concludes his trio of conditions with the It-Effect, or the "deifying reception" of these synthetic experiences.[12] The particular It-Effect under examination here is Monroe's live performance for the USO in Korea. As previously noted, while Monroe was a singer and dancer, one did not buy tickets to see her at a theatre; she was a product of the silver screen and the magazine cover (*and* centerfold), always appearing in a mediatized form. This synthetic construction heightens the impact of her live appearance on the USO stage and her personal interactions with servicemen away from the stage because the illusion of availability was intensified through the rarity of her physical presence. Roach identifies the It-Effect with a certain quality called effervescence, writing that "the very thought of the proximity of It has triggered the exhilaration of the ensemble," and likening it to the "crush at a rock concert or other celebrity gala."[13] The feeling of effervescence—the exhilaration and excitement of the crowd—would have begun when it was clear that Monroe would be visiting the bases in Korea and increased when she arrived in person. The crowds began to gather before her arrival and became even more unruly at the sight of her.

Monroe's live appearance incited riots at many of the ten locations she visited on her four-day tour, a testament to Roach's idea of the It-Effect. Various film clips and footage from the tour show hundreds upon thousands of men in uniform packed against one another wherever Monroe appears: descending from helicopters, riding in jeeps, walking through camps, and—undoubtedly—while on stage. A brief clip from British Pathé's website shows a military police officer admonishing and gesturing to a crowd of men who seem to have pushed too close to the stage, with thousands of other men swarming behind them.[14] Other footage shows Marilyn and her escort in the middle of a crowd of soldiers with cameras. As Marilyn attempts to make her way to a nearby helicopter, the mass cannot disperse, because the men are packed in around her so tightly that she is barely able to squeeze through.[15]

Hanson Baldwin was the Pulitzer Prize-winning military editor for the *New York Times*. He openly complained in the *Times* about the uproar caused by Monroe's visit to the troops in Korea, criticizing Army Secretary Robert Stevens and Chief of Staff General James Ridgway for it. Baldwin wrote in 1954: "Correct the weakness in service morale epitomized by the visit of Miss Monroe to Korea. On two occasions during the visit of the motion picture actress, troops rioted wildly and behaved like bobby-soxers in Time Square, not like soldiers proud of their uniform."[16] These incidents appear to originate solely from the effervescence felt in conjunction with the presence of a celebrity—the It-Effect—rather than any of Monroe's particular actions. Actress Terry Moore caused a stir when she performed in Korea with Bob Hope in 1953, wearing only an ermine-fur bathing suit.[17] Unlike Monroe—whose mere appearance in baggy army fatigues was the catalyst for unruly behavior—Moore created a scene because of her racy attire. This was not appropriate according to USO standards, as the USO standard of decorum sought to prevent disruptions at any cost.

The USO had been disbanded after World War II with the notion that, since the war was over, the purpose of the organization had been fulfilled. With the rise of the conflict in Korea, the USO re-formed to continue their original mission: "to bolster and maintain the morale of America's servicemen and women."[18] Regardless of the changing decades, the emotional needs of men in combat had not changed. The Camp Shows in World War II had been a major method of boosting morale, and the expectations for the USO Camp Shows were high. The National Association of Broadcasters extended its code of ethics to the shows, and the former national chairman of the Code Committee of the National Association of Broadcasters, Earl J. Glade, commented on this code in 1943. "An audience of four thousand or more males wants hearty, punchy, he-man entertainment, but that doesn't mean that it must be dirty or nasty… Most boys coming into camps now are teen-aged. They are nervous, impressionable, lonely, and (sometimes even hospitalized) for nothing more serious than nostalgia. They are easily shocked and react badly to any sordidness in their entertainment."[19] In a letter home by an unidentified female USO performer, the sentiments are echoed on a more personal level: "Don't ever underestimate [the GI] by thinking all he wants is a leg show and dirty cracks. He talks and listens to 'men talk' day in and day out. Every woman back home wears a halo now and those who represent her had better keep theirs on too."[20] And in a pamphlet published by USO Camp Shows during World War II, seasoned performers offered advice to new "troupers" on their first circuit. "The most important baggage is your stage wardrobe. A GI doesn't want to see you in slacks, and he's not interested in your uniform. He wants to see you look like the girls back home on an important Saturday night date. Remember that, and take your best clothes with you."[21] These two statements suggest that the USO was advocating a particular image of women. The first paints a picture of a wholesome, nonsexualized woman, a saintly ideal, perhaps a mother or sister figure. The second points specifically to the idea of the sweetheart, a woman who is more alluring in her date dress than a mother or sister, but still not painted in a sexually inappropriate way.

The standards of the Camp Shows and the USO's expectations of decorum were not any different in the Korean War. In a collection of her essays—in an entry called "Korean Serenade"—Marilyn Monroe recounts moments of her whirlwind tour of Korea. She remembers singing "Do It Again" for wounded soldiers in a hospital. The officer in charge of her tour said she had to sing a "classy" song instead. "But 'Do It Again' is a classy song," she said. "It's a George Gershwin song." He agreed to the performance, but only after she suggested changing the words to "Kiss Me Again." At her first stage performance for the troops, Monroe had second thoughts about another of her songs, "Diamonds Are a Girl's Best Friend." She wrote, "It seemed like the wrong thing to say to soldiers in Korea, earning only soldiers' pay. Then I remembered the dance I did after the song. It was a cute dance. I knew they would like it."[22] While Monroe traveled from base to base in military-issued clothing, she wore her best "Saturday Night Date" outfit on stage. It appears as though she consoled herself with the idea that any message that could be misconstrued on stage as a political statement would be forgiven if she presented a more alluring and carefree image.[23]

For all the care the USO took in providing quality, clean entertainment, they won the admiration of countless servicemen and women. What was it about these performances that had such an impact on the troops? The cognitive science used in Bruce McConachie's book *Engaging Audiences: A Cognitive Approach to Spectating in the Theatre* is an effective tool for determining what could have been happening in the brains of the U.S. servicemen when they came into contact with USO performances in general and Marilyn Monroe in particular. By examining the scientific workings behind these human reactions, we can better understand how the USO was able to reinvigorate the weary soldiers and urge them to continue their duty with a renewed sense of nationalism. McConachie specifically points to human memory as one aspect of human cognition, among others, that enables audience engagement.[24]

In his book *The Haunted Stage*, Marvin Carlson writes, "We are able to 'read' new works…only because we recognize within them elements that have been recycled from other structures of experience that we have experienced earlier."[25] Carlson's explanation is a theoretical version of the cognitive science behind memory. While there are differing theories of memory in the world of neuroscience, some are more viable than others. The metaphor of memory as a dropbox or computer storage has been popular for many years, but McConachie rightly assesses that this metaphor can lead to many problems concerning ideas of precoding and recall. He prefers Gerald Edelman's idea of "constructive recategorization."[26] In constructive recategorization, a person matches a current contextual signal with a prior signal that has already been encoded in the brain. "A person is able to remember such things because those previous actions prompted the brain to make alterations so that a similar signal at a later time would engage a similar response. As the brain continues to remake itself in response to experience, it reallocates different neuronal groups and synapses among the several billions of neurons available."[27]

If we see a chair or a dog or a familiar person in front of us, we do not search our brains in order to match the image that we see to an image that we have "stored." Instead, through constructive recategorization, the chair or dog or familiar person we encounter sets off a neuronal firing pattern that triggers the last encounter with a similar object. So, if we see a chair made out of metal and our previous experience has always been with chairs made out of wood, we can still recognize it as a chair because of the similarity between the two neuronal firing patterns. The original signal for the wooden chair will be reencoded when we encounter the chair made out of metal. The next time we come upon a chair made out of unusual material such as hockey sticks or cardboard or beer cans, the same process will occur again.

This process of recategorization can also be illustrated in the accompanying photograph from Julia M. H. Carson's book *Home Away from Home: The Story of the USO*. The photograph shows a dock in front of a towering boat fully laden with servicemen (see fig. 3).[28] The grainy photo is a testament to what the USO was trying to accomplish. The female singer stands on a small "stage" represented by a wooden skid, a crudely constructed platform only six inches off the ground. In fact, it does not even seem constructed at all. Several smaller sections of skid appear haphazardly stacked in the foreground of the photograph, which give the impression that the performers chose the skid with the largest surface area. If the singer were simply standing on the ground with a microphone, there would be fewer associations for the spectatorial brains to make.

Figure 3. USO Camp Show. From Julia M. H. Carson's *Home Away from Home: The Story of the USO*.

The skid itself is the important factor in arousing the neuronal firing patterns in the audience: a skid is a raised surface, a raised surface is a platform, a platform is like a stage, this skid is like the stages back home in Anywhere, U.S.A. Cognitive scientists point out that we are not conscious of this process; it happens quickly and involuntarily. The contextual signal of the crude "stage" prompts the brains of the servicemen present to engage with the previously encoded signal of any stage they may have encountered in their civilian life—since it is unlikely they would have attended local theaters or performances while deployed—whether at the fairgrounds, a musical concert, theatrical production, or public-speaking event. This is not the only kind of temporary stage that the USO created, and, in fact, the word "stage" took on an entirely new meaning, as car hoods and truck beds were also frequently used for performers in remote military outposts.[29] The effort of creating a makeshift stage, no matter how simple, was the USO's way of creating a structure that immediately and intuitively aroused a memory of stages and performances back home.

This illustration segues into McConachie's assertion that "all theatres come to spectators freighted with a history and culture that will partly control how spectators look at performers."[30] The memory of home sparked by a crude makeshift theatre and the standards of the USO controlled how the men in Korea looked at Marilyn Monroe. The USO did its best to re-create the idea of home to boost the spirits of the soldiers: All-American music, All-American movies, All-American performers, All-American humor. Lieutenant James F. Orlay of the Second U.S. Infantry Division in Korea wrote a letter to the editor of *Life* magazine in response to Hanson Baldwin's aforementioned critique of the servicemen's behavior: "Since the sudden switch from fighting to training and never-ending inspections in the cold Manchurian winds, our morale has ebbed. Miss Monroe's visit was the World Series, the Fourth of July and the Mardi Gras rolled in one. Not many of the famous have come over to see us. It took The Blonde, who looked so fresh, healthy and American, to raise our spirits and make us feel like men again. God bless her."[31] Orlay perfectly describes the ideal image of a USO woman: an All-American 4th of July with a dash of Mardi Gras.

Most importantly, as seen from the advice given by World War II USO "troupers," the USO promoted the image of the Girl Back Home. Jack Forsha responded emphatically to a question about the 1953 *Playboy* that featured Monroe's 1949 nude calendar photos, immediately recalling the red velvet background. He said one of his friends at the base had the magazine, but when the airman asked Monroe to autograph it, her escort refused to allow it.[32] One might argue, via Roach, that the airman was attempting to increase the illusion of availability and his own synthetic experience by adding Monroe's autograph to the nude photo. The photo would not only be connected with her name—unlike the calendar itself—but also be officially approved by Monroe "signing off" on it. The attempt, of course, was foiled by the standard of decorum enforced by the USO. The organization marketed Monroe not as a sexpot movie star, but as a distinguished representative of the All-American Girl Back Home.

Along with memory, McConachie includes conceptual blending as another cognitive process involved in spectating.[33] For spectators in the theatre to conceptually blend the identities of an actor with a character, they merge any pre-existing ideas they may already have about the actor onstage with any ideas they are experiencing through the representation of a character, which results in a conceptual blend of the figure the spectators are witnessing onstage. The blending of these two separate identities into one can be described as an almost imperceptible and continual oscillation between actor and character that produces a melded, yet continually fluctuating, actor/character identity. The final conceptual blend is contingent upon how much of the actor and how much of the character any given audience member fuses together.[34] This is, like the reconstructive categorization of memory, an immediate and unconscious function of the brain. The process of conceptual blending when watching actors in a play is identical to the process of conceptual blending while watching Monroe's performance in Korea, but the concepts being blended are not "actor" and "character." The conceptual blend for many spectators at the USO show in Korea was the complex metaphor so graciously supplied by Lieutenant Orlay: Marilyn Monroe merged with the concept of the All-American Girl Back Home.

It is important to specify that there is no guarantee that any two people will conceptually blend in the same way. Every audience member has his or her own experiences from which he or she draws. Therefore, there is no empirical evidence that can prove that all the members of the audience during Monroe's USO tour were experiencing the same blend or constructing the same metaphor as Lieutenant Orlay. However, we can suppose that the circumstances surrounding Monroe's USO tour did indeed lead to similar experiences for many of the men in the audience.

There are various accounts of the impact the USO Camp Shows had on the morale of servicemen in Korea. In particular, historian Paul Edwards notes that for many of the servicemen, a USO Camp Show offered the GIs what was probably their first view of an American woman since they had come to Korea and, in addition, "The show was a touch of home, a moment of joy away from the routine."[35] Korea War veteran Scott L. Defebaugh confirms this view, saying, "For two hours, the men could forget they were soldiers at war."[36] Even a decade or more after the inception of the USO, their goals had not changed, because the human experience of wartime circumstances were similar, even if the historical contexts were different: USO shows during the Korean War strove—as they did in World War II—to provide the comfort of home in a foreign place. To prevent the shock that many members of the armed forces faced in those trying circumstances, the USO provided a familiar and comforting respite from the physical and emotional exhaustion of wartime service. These men were homesick, and the USO did a tremendous job of providing as many comforts of home as they could, while also strategically reinforcing a strong sense of nationalism that would enable a soldier to return to battle despite the hardship. By the end of the war, the USO had 294 centers in operation in the United States and abroad, staffed with over 113,000 volunteers.[37]

The USO standard regarding the modesty and wholesomeness of Camp Show performances was one way of achieving that comfort. It is fairly safe to assume that the majority of the audience at a USO Camp Show felt a deep connection with America. When Terry Moore appeared onstage in her ermine-fur bathing suit, the overwhelming reaction from journalists in America was that she should be sent home, because they felt the bathing suit was indecent and below the standards of the USO. Edwards writes, "GIs argued that she should stay, saying that if she had to go home they would go with her. She stayed."[38] USO Camp Show performers meant a great deal to the wartime audiences and were even graced with the affectionate nickname "soldiers in greasepaint." The servicemen clearly felt a personal connection to Moore and many of the USO Camp Show performers. Marilyn Monroe was no exception.

The nature of these special connections that many servicemen felt with celebrities is multiple and varied. Amy Cook's work on conceptual blending leads this discussion to the impact of the blend that the USO aided in creating for the Camp Show audiences. Because any given blend can be different from person to person, the implication is that the possibilities of types of blend are countless. In addition, Cook suggests that "the network of spaces prompted in a given situation is more powerful as a process in flux, a series of variables, than simply a final blend."[39] McConachie explains that the actor/character blend is continually oscillating, and Cook supports this by pointing out that the process itself is the most powerful aspect of the blend. We know that at least one serviceman in Korea was blending the concept of "Monroe" with the concept of "Celebrity," as evidenced by Forsha's friend who attempted to get an autograph for his copy of *Playboy*, but the USO was working overtime to introduce variables into the blending process that would ensure the servicemen were not solely imagining Monroe as the *Playboy* centerfold.

The rigorous USO standards encouraged a blend that would include not only "Monroe as Celebrity," but also "Monroe as All-American Girl Back Home" by implementing numerous tactics, the rejection of the *Playboy* magazine and the questioning of song lyrics being only two of them. One film clip shows Monroe's bedside visit to GIs in hospital, when she leans down to hug a man in his bed for a photo op. The young man smiles with his arm around her and chastely kisses her on the cheek.[40] A photo from the book in which Jack Forsha found his own photograph shows Monroe wearing a 2nd Infantry Division "Honorary Member" patch safety-pinned to her sleeve as she dishes out hot food in a mess hall. In the photo below that one, a serviceman holds a piece of cake in his hand as Monroe unabashedly takes a large bite.[41] As Forsha remembers, Monroe table-hopped and chatted with the servicemen instead of being sequestered at the officers' table. These simple services, enacted by Monroe, suggested not celebrity but that carefully balanced mix of mother, sister, and sweetheart, reminding the men of the actions of their loved-ones back home. In fact, another film clip shows Monroe waving from a doorway where a large heart-shaped sign, complete with Cupid's arrow, shows the name "Marilyn" in script with the subtitle "Sweetheart of the Bayonet Division." Below that is a small rectangular sign with the name of Monroe's companion, "Mrs. O'Doul," printed in plain block letters.[42]

Some GIs no doubt filled their mental space labeled "Monroe as Celebrity" with blonde hair, the *Playboy* centerfold, Hollywood, "Diamonds Are a Girl's Best Friend," and many other associations. Yet the space labeled "All-American Girl Back Home" would contain fond memories of sweethearts, sisters, mothers, home-cooked meals, and any number of personal memories of life as a civilian. As the cease-fire suggested an end to service in Korea, the men were looking forward to returning home. As Cook argues, the emergent structure of the blend is rife with other networks of ideas,[43] evocative associations that suggested that Monroe was more than just a movie star on a makeshift stage. She was America. She was home.

Roach states that the It-Effect intensifies the need for increased intimacy with the unattainable object.[44] The effervescence felt when seeing a celebrity in person fuels the need for more interaction. Conversing at length outside the stage door with a favorite celebrity or finding yourself at a banquet table next to a political role model are occurrences that could have a myriad of effects. You have your photograph taken with a famous actor or you continually tell the story of "When I Met So-and-So." In the quest for more experiences of the It-Effect— and consequently, more meaningful encounters, such as personal interactions and celebrity-approved mementos—people strive to increase the proximity to and understanding of the celebrity. This need to become "closer"—physically, psychologically, emotionally—is, in effect, a desire to unlock and understand the nature of It as it is embodied by a particular individual. The greater the intimacy of these real-life encounters, however, the greater the need for continued and more deeply intimate encounters. If one is not able to come closer to understanding It, then he or she must continue to seek more synthetic experiences and more chances to experience the It-Effect in the presence of the celebrity.

The same goes for the servicemen's varied experiences with Marilyn Monroe, from watching her USO performance from fifty rows back or having her autograph a leg cast. Due to the efforts of the USO to create a nostalgic sense for the All-American Girl Back Home, I believe they succeeded in maintaining the unattainable nature of intimacy with Monroe by discouraging the "Monroe as Celebrity" blend. While many servicemen may have experienced the "Monroe as Celebrity" blend, the USO went to great lengths to ensure that reminders of "Monroe as All-American Girl Back Home" entered into the blending process more frequently and forcefully. The USO created these intimate encounters with a remarkable icon, all the time promoting a conceptual blend that made the servicemen think of the girls back home. This It-Effect—which combined the excitement of a celebrity and the tenderness of a loved one back home—provided a very high level of intimacy for servicemen, albeit one that focused more on their loved ones than the celebrity in front of them. The intimacy with Monroe was overshadowed by the recollection of home, and even though the encounter with Monroe possessed a special level of intimacy, it did not lead to any privileged information about her that would promote actual intimacy. Though Jack Forsha's stories and photographs are not the only surviving memories of Monroe's USO tour, these mementos have not brought any of their keepers to a deeper understanding of who Marilyn Monroe was. They can only serve as detailed and poignant reminders of an encounter with the It-Effect that will continue to fascinate the world as we attempt more and more furiously to capture and contemplate It.

Notes

1. Jack Forsha, in discussion with the author, November 25, 2010, Lancaster, PA.
2. Ibid.
3. Donald Spoto, *Marilyn Monroe: The Biography* (New York: Cooper Square Press, 1993), 263–64.

4. Fred Lawrence Guiles, *Norma Jean: The Life of Marilyn Monroe* (New York: McGraw-Hill, 1969), 149.
5. Joseph Roach, *It* (Ann Arbor: University of Michigan Press, 2007), 8 (emphasis in original).
6. Ibid., 3.
7. Fred Lawrence Guiles, *Legend: The Life and Death of Marilyn Monroe* (New York: Stein and Day, 1984), 449–66.
8. "Marilyn Monroe: The *LIFE* Covers, 1952–1962," http://life.time.com/icons/marilyn-monroe-life-magazine-covers-photos/#1, Accessed August 4, 2014.
9. Roach, *It*, 28.
10. Spoto, *Marilyn Monroe: The Biography*, 151–52.
11. Churchwell, *Many Lives*, 37.
12. Roach, *It*, 44.
13. Ibid., 18.
14. "Marilyn Monroe in Korea 1954," http://www.britishpathe.com/video/marilyn-monroe-in-korea/query/monroe, accessed August 3, 2014. Footage of MP and troops appears at 00:26 and 00:35.
15. "Marilyn Monroe—Footage with the Troops in Korea 1954," http://www.youtube.com/watch?v=u7zxdB_AneM, accessed August 3, 2014. Footage of crowd begins at 4:36.
16. Guiles, *Legend*, 240.
17. Paul M. Edwards, *The Korean War* (Westport, CT: Greenwood Press, 2006), 123.
18. Maxene Andrews, *Over Here, Over There: The Andrews Sisters and the USO Stars in World War II* (New York: Zebra Books, 1993), 30.
19. Ibid., 129–30.
20. Ibid., 129.
21. Ibid., 229–30.
22. Marilyn Monroe, *My Story* (New York: Stein and Day, 1974), 142–43.
23. My research has not uncovered any published scholarship regarding gender representation in the USO Camp Shows, although an unpublished thesis by Samantha Joy Pearlman at Wesleyan University in 2011 treats the subject quite competently (Pearlman, "'Something for the Boys': An Analysis of the Women of the USO Camp Shows, Inc. and their Performed Gender," available at http://wesscholar.wesleyan.edu/cgi/viewcontent.cgi?article=1656&context=etd_hon_theses, accessed August 3, 2014). Gender representations of the women who served as USO hostesses are quite fully examined by Margaret Winchell in her book *Good Girls, Good Food, Good Fun: The Story of USO Hostesses During World War II* (Chapel Hill: University of North Carolina Press, 2008).
24. Bruce McConachie, *Engaging Audiences: A Cognitive Approach to Spectating in the Theatre* (New York: Palgrave Macmillan, 2008), 63.
25. Marvin Carlson, *The Haunted Stage: The Theatre as Memory Machine* (Ann Arbor: University of Michigan Press, 2001), 4.
26. McConachie, *Engaging Audiences*, 33. "Constructive recategorization" from Gerald M. Edelman and Giulio Tononi, *A Universe of Consciousness: How Matter Becomes Imagination* (New York: Basic Books, 2000).
27. Ibid.
28. Julia Carson, *Home Away from Home: The Story of the USO* (New York: Harper & Brothers, 1946). Found in unnumbered photo insert, bottom photo on page 15 of the insert.

29. "Air Force Now," http://www.youtube.com/watch?v=2UGWldXzKjM, accessed August 3, 2014. Quote appears at 8:00.
30. McConachie, *Engaging Audiences*, 134.
31. James F. Orlay, "Letters to the Editor" *Life*, March 22, 1954, 20.
32. Forsha, discussion with the author.
33. McConachie, *Engaging Audiences*, 63.
34. Ibid., 41–44.
35. Edwards, *The Korean War*, 151.
36. Scott L. Defebaugh, "Something to Enjoy," in Linda Granfield, *I Remember Korea: Veterans Tell Their Stories of the Korean War, 1950–1953* (New York: Clarion Books, 2003), 53.
37. Edwards, *The Korean War*, 123.
38. Ibid., 123–24.
39. Amy Cook, *Shakespearean Neuroplay: Reinvigorating the Study of Dramatic Texts and Performance through Cognitive Science* (New York: Palgrave MacMillan, 2010), 91.
40. "Marilyn Monroe—The Korea film RARE!" http://www.youtube.com/watch?v=HtZV9_hfpBI, accessed August 3, 2014. Footage appears at 2:42.
41. Marie Clayton, *Marilyn Monroe: The Unseen Archives* (Bath: Parragon Publishing, 2005), 123.
42. "Marilyn Monroe—The Korea film RARE!" Footage appears at 6:34. Mrs. Jean O'Doul and her husband, baseball player Frank "Lefty" O'Doul, had accompanied Monroe and DiMaggio to Japan.
43. Cook, *Shakespearean Neuroplay*, 12–13.
44. Roach, *It*, 44.

Birnam Wood

Scotland, Nationalism, and Theatres of War

—ARIEL WATSON

The National Theatre will also look beyond Scotland for inspiration, and stimulate interest in Scottish culture from other countries and cultures. The work will reflect the diversity of Scotland's culture… National Theatre of Scotland will not have a theatre building of its own. It will present work in the existing network of theatres and venues, or exciting venues annexed for the occasion… Work will also be toured abroad when appropriate.
NATIONAL THEATRE OF SCOTLAND NEWSLETTER, NOVEMBER 2003

Third Apparition
Macbeth shall never vanquished be until
Great Birnam Wood to high Dunsinane Hill
Shall come against him.

Macbeth
That will never be.
Who can impress the forest, bid the tree
Unfix his earthbound root? Sweet bodements, good!
Rebellious dead, rise never till the wood
Of Birnam rise…
WILLIAM SHAKESPEARE

As the tenth anniversary of the founding manifesto of its National Theatre approaches, Scotland finds itself at a crossroads of both theatrical and political nationalism. In the years preceding the 2014 referendum on Scottish independence, two of the leading voices of the young National Theatre of Scotland (or NTS)—Artistic Director Vicky Featherstone and Associate Director for New

Work John Tiffany—left the organization. Both have been involved with the NTS since its founding: Featherstone was responsible for commissioning the company's first major local and global success, Gregory Burke's war drama *Black Watch*, and Tiffany for its development and direction. The shift to the company's second generation of visionary administrators, accompanied by a move to new operational offices, seems an opportunity for reflection, evaluation, and shift in a company that was already in a state of constant (self-)scrutiny.

The development of the NTS has an almost microcosmic relation to Scotland's status as a devolved nation, and potentially a political state: indeed, in the summer of 2007 Scotland's First Minister, the Scottish Nationalist Alex Salmond, arranged for a special performance of *Black Watch* to mark the opening of the Scottish Parliament. This sympathetic resonance with the Scottish independence movement, which coincided exactly and paradoxically with the play's first international tour under the aegis of the British Council, speaks to *Black Watch*'s ability to stand in for this moment of decisive split and self-contradiction in both the realms of theatrical and political nationalism. By examining the dissolution of the Scottish Black Watch regiment in the contemporary moment of British and American war in Iraq and Afghanistan, the play uses military occupation as a premise for reflecting on the conflicting experience, both political and psychological, of a nation within a nation-state. This symbolic move would find an echo in the company's later war play, David Greig's *Dunsinane*. In representing, semifictionally, the futile attempt of a documentary playwright to capture the warfront experience of the soldiers, newly returned to Scotland, *Black Watch* uses creative conflict as a premise for debating the issues of home and estrangement; corps and exclusion; loss corporeal, linguistic, and narrative that would come to define the NTS's repertoire of original work as a theatre. War—international conflict—stands in allegorically for the intranational conflict and the particular national struggle that defines Scottishness, as does the creative and linguistic battle for expression, articulation, and representation. This creative conflict surrounding the documentarian's research—a conflict between experience and representation, aesthetics and the inexpressible—crucially stages the anxiety surrounding the NTS's developing praxis (which closely resembles that of the naive fictional playwright) and purpose. How can a national theatre hope to represent the truth of a diverse and conflicted national experience? What does it mean to hold a mirror up to nation?

The foundation and practice of the National Theatre is the site, instigation, and validation of the utopian project of national definition. As Loren Kruger puts it, dramas of theatrical nationhood "share with the critical and legislative texts the task of representing not merely the question of national identity but also the anxiety and aspirations invested in the articulation and resolution of that question."[1] If, as David McCrone, Angela Morris, and Richard Kiely argue, Scotland's historical status as a stateless nation means that "over the last 300 years its population has been very aware of the difference between its cultural and political identities," then this is truly a crossroads: a moment in which the schism is transcended, and the dual byways of cultural and political nationalism converge for a time.[2]

Thus, as the intricacies of political devolution continue to unfurl in Scotland, the debate about national identity takes as its battlefield matters of cultural nationalism. On December 16, 2012, the *Scotsman* reported that the novelist Alasdair Gray, in the yet-to-be-published volume *Unstated: Writers on Scottish Independence*, drew a castigating distinction between cultural "invaders" he called "colonists" and those he termed "settlers," and that among the colonists he had named Vicky Featherstone, who hailed originally from England and was about to return there.[3] Settlers, Gray asserts in the article, stand to enrich their adopted land through their long-term investment in its future, and are marked by an assimilative respect for the traditions of its past.[4] Colonists, by contrast, are marked by their disengagement from the site—cultural and social—in which they live and work, and by their lack of interest in fostering organic local structures of creation and production. They are marked by their transience and their rootlessness, their disconnection to time and space: "Vicky Featherstone," Gray says mildly in the passage that sparked the controversy, "may be leaving in 2013 for work nearer London. That is my only reason for thinking her a colonist."[5] At issue, as we will see, is not simply the crucial question of whether Scottishness is to be defined along purely ethnic lines, but more pressingly the idea of *home*, and by extension of *homelessness*, that has proven so central to the discourse surrounding the Scottish national theatre. Scotland is in a state of institutional and cultural siege, this rhetoric asserts, from arts administrators with no local foundations or expertise, who seek only to build their *curriculum vitae* and not a sense of Scottish cultural identity. Professionalism and ambition are the values that disguise a perilous deracination, in Gray's argument. As for Macbeth at Dunsinane, there is a peril in underestimating rootless foes, particularly when they come in the camouflage of nationalism, obscuring the trees amidst the political forest.

A furor erupted in the Scottish and English press, with authors and theatre practitioners rallying to Gray's side in a call for a greater focus on the development and employment of Scottish talent, and others swiftly defending the Featherstone-era National Theatre's emphasis on fostering contemporary Scottish writing and acting, her open-mindedness in considering collaborations and spatial models for production, and the company's success as a cultural ambassador for diverse and recognizable ideas of Scottishness. From the perspective of theatre scholarship, one of the most remarkable facets of this controversy is the way in which it maps anxieties surrounding cultural and political *settlement* and *occupation* onto the theatre as an art form both intrinsically local and fundamentally mobile. In the pages that follow, I trace the anxieties of this temporal crossroads of political and cultural devolution through the thematic nexus of the NTS's war plays. These plays form, via institutional structures of touring and collaboration and formal structures of allusion and allegory, a crucial part of the import/export networks that define and constitute Scottish national identity for both local and global audiences.

The NTS's emphasis on touring is intimately tied to its larger philosophical attitude toward the concepts of place and home. In its short production history, the National Theatre of Scotland has been acclaimed for its radical decentering, even explosion, of the standing model of theatrical nationalism and national theatre. In an age of rapidly diminishing government support of the arts, this model has boasted a prudent efficiency as well as a political idealism: in the absence of a single (undoubtedly cosmopolitan) performance venue, the bulk of funding that would be dedicated to the expense of real estate can instead be channeled into a variety of collaborative funding relationships, development projects at various stages, and touring endeavors. From the earliest discussions in 1998 about the possibility of a National Theatre in Scotland[6]—hot on the heels of the referendum that established a devolved Scottish parliament—to its institutional establishment in 2003, the self-conception of the NTS was built on a radical notion of both *place* and *displacement*, a decentralized model of nation and nationalism that leaves no doubt about the politics of the formal. Structural and aesthetic fragmentation become tropes for a devolved and diverse Scotland: individualistic, autonomous, yet collaborative. The NTS pointedly eschews anchoring itself in a fixed location, as its counterpart in London did on the South Bank,[7] and departs from the common and magnetic rhetoric of theatre buildings as community centers and creative hubs—in brief, as forces of unification in a diverse, atomized, and often conflicting world.[8]

Thus it's hardly unexpected that, rather than staging the resolution of dissonances in its chosen and commissioned performances, the NTS would find itself turning to this conflicting world as a source of inspiration, both formally and thematically. *Black Watch* (2006) takes up the Scottish involvement in global conflicts over the course of several centuries, using the contemporary war in Iraq as an aperture. In 2011, the NTS returned to the quintessential war drama, the proverbial "Scottish Play," for the third of what is now four changes it has rung on *Macbeth*: David Greig's *Dunsinane*. Greig's play attempts to reboot Shakespeare's martial tragedy as a lens through which to view both the English presence in Scotland and the British military presence in Iraq and Afghanistan. Putting these two productions in dialogue, with their common tropes of mercenarism, occupation, and Scottish nationalism, produces a keen sense of how theatre functions as a working metaphor for nation in the Scottish context, and how war operates as a working metaphor for both. More than this, by examining the crucial issue of the varying spectatorship for the two plays (which toured more or less widely), the value of the way in which war dramas signify (connecting a variety of different experiences of battle, alienation, violence, esprit de corps, patriotism, and mercenarism) becomes evident. War, as a theatrical theme, provides the National Theatre with the opportunity to engage in its fundamental project of connection through constellation: by signifying both wars present and past, it bridges divides geographically, historically, and culturally distant. What emerges from these two plays is a portrayal of *nation as conflict* that is profoundly dialogical, humane, and ambivalent. Like Birnam Wood, its subversions rest in the mobility of its significations, and the diverse ironies of its receptions.

National Theatre of Scotland: Devolution as Theatrical Practice

The continuous concern of the NTS has been to bridge the cavernous political and ethical divides that haunt a national theatre, which is inevitably charged, in Kruger's formulation of "theatrical nationhood," with "constituting or even standing in for an absent or imperfect national identity."[9] This is the chicken-or-egg problem of the constitution of nationhood *through* a national theatre that has been itself called into being through revolution or devolution: "If the poets were allied in aim," said Schiller of Romantic nationalism, "there would be a national stage, and we should become a nation."[10] Featherstone's own vision for the role of the NTS reflects this ambivalent causality: "It's only once in the history of any country that you get to create a national theatre. It's only once that you have an opportunity to create something that places theatre at the heart of a nation, that can reflect a people back to themselves."[11] Roger Savage, writing about the hypothetical mandate of a Scottish "notional national" less than a decade before the founding of the NTS, observes in its predecessors an array of ideological demands and possibilities: national theatre as the preservation of a cultural corpus (the Royal Shakespeare Company or the Japanese

National Theatre) or its creation (Ireland's Abbey Theatre), as the means of linguistic unification (Poland and Finland), as a revolutionary statement (Senegal and Bulgaria) or an authoritarian tool (France's Comédie Française).[12] There's much at stake in determining the locus and inflection of the nation in a National Theatre, Savage argues: is it to be national, nationalist, or nationalized?[13] How is it to avoid the centrism of its early modern antecedents, the ethnic exclusivity and idealism of its nineteenth-century forebears, the replication of imperial patterns that emerged in many mid-twentieth-century revolutionary and postcolonial theatres, the narrow cosmopolitanism of the Royal National Theatre in London, and the ubiquitous commodification of nation in the age of New Labour's Cool Britannia?

The bridging of these competing claims on the Scottish National Theatre involves not simply the need to weigh the demands of its urban and rural constituents (both artists and audiences) against the value of representing Scotland in the U.K. and abroad, or the desire to counterbalance the preservation of a Scottish canon with the production of new and counter-canons. Most importantly it involves pairing the carving out of a national(ist) identity that is distinct and celebratory with the necessity of acknowledging the capaciousness and diversity of the nation by interrogating these very hegemonic and celebratory mythologies. The priorities laid out in the founding documents of the company thus include spatial and geographical mobility (or, more nearly, independence),[14] range and variety in the texts and projects chosen for development, accessibility to a wide variety of audiences and creators both within and outside Scotland, and a fundamental emphasis on collaboration. This last established the company as both an importer and exporter of cultural capital, to echo the Blairite neoliberal rhetoric that Jen Harvie unpacks so effectively in *Staging the UK*: "Like Britain, Scotland and the other small nations have been encouraged to adopt the language of the 'creative industries' and to rebrand themselves in the image of 'New Britain,' especially in an international context."[15] This would allow the NTS, in subsequent years, to partner with other companies nationally and internationally, to commission new work along a variety of different structures and calendars, and to bring productions with Scottish resonance to the country from outside. The NTS, in Zoltán Imre's terms, is taking a project (the national theatre) that imposes centralized ideas of nation and culture "from above" and formulating it (as a public theatre) "from below" and disparately.[16]

The first year of the NTS's existence as an active producer of theatre (2006) saw a performance that would be emblematic of the company's modus operandi without representing any sort of dogmatic precedent. This was the inaugural production, *Home*, which interrogated the ideas of nation and belonging with ten linked performances in found (often liminal) spaces across Scotland, each of which had been developed autonomously, but existed in dialogue with the others. Each locality had access to a radically different theatrical interpretation of the idea of "home": the whole formed a pattern, but this pattern was almost impossible to experience except through an act of collaborative spectatorship, entering into discussion about the different subjective experiences across geographical distances. This collaborative spectatorship, necessary to any hope of completist access to the whole, demands an empathy—an ability to place oneself in another's experiential perspective—that is imbricated with an acknowledgment of difference and incompleteness. This is devolution expressed as theatrical practice: it posits home(land) and theatre as a site for collaboration as constellation, rather than for unification.

The rich irony of *Home* is that it underscored the company's embrace of belonging as synonymous with its refusal of rootedness. The founding mythology of the NTS describes the newly hired Featherstone working in an empty, unfurnished office space with nothing but her cellular phone. The theatre's aesthetic of transience—it is described enthusiastically as a "theatre without walls and without a permanent company" by administrators and journalists alike[17]—is transformed in public discourse into an insistent refrain about homelessness, the marginal, and state subsidy: "Housing scheme is home to national theatre," exclaimed the 2003 *Scotsman* headlines that greeted the company's administrative advent; "Scotland's new national theatre will be based in a peripheral Glasgow housing estate once blighted by drugs and violence."[18] "The homeless home of Scottish theatre," a *Guardian* article dubbed the NTS in 2007,[19] and by the following year the newspaper's headlines declared it "the homeless, skeleton-staffed National Theatre of Scotland."[20] More recently the administrative shifts in leadership and space have led to a speculative shift in the discourse: "National Theatre of Scotland finds permanent home," declares a January 2013 article. "The National Theatre of Scotland has made a virtue of its nomadic existence, winning praise for its ability to cover the length and breadth of country since its formation in 2006. Now it looks set to lay down some roots."[21] The fact that these "roots" will not include a performance space, and that the company will inhabit its "home" as renters, emerges as an afterthought in these narratives, which take on the tone of a conservative domestic comedy of initial oat-sowing and ultimate marital bliss.

"What they've got going there is too good to be nomadic forever," said Nicholas Hytner, who admired *Black Watch* tremendously but failed to convince the NTS that the Royal National Theatre would be an appropriate venue in which to stage its London run. "That's not how the theatre's ever been."[22] The essentialism of this statement reveals much about the difference in outlook between London's nationalist theatre project and the NTS, despite mutual admiration. For Featherstone and her collaborators, "that's not how the theatre's ever been" is a gauntlet rather than a piece of weary fatalism. Hytner places the spatial issue of a centralized national theatre in clear terms of power and control: "The NTS has to construct its programme around the availability of the buildings... That's why it should have a base: it should be in control of its own destiny." From the perspective of the NTS, however, it is the expense and spatial signification of a "base" that is a limit on freedom and autonomy: "Nick Hytner's job is to prove that his building can be a national theatre," responded Featherstone. "My job has to be to prove that a national theatre doesn't have to have a building. I think we can probably prove both things."[23] In rejecting a fixed theatrical site or home for the company, and refusing to be confined to Edinburgh and Glasgow in its performances, the NTS made a bold claim not just to a devolved model of power in opposition to Westminster and the South Bank, but also to a model that is diffuse, peripatetic, and peripheral.

Black Watch: Mercenarism, Palimpsest, and the Rebellious Dead

> The army does not recruit well in London or any other big city. Metropolitanism and multiculturalism are not the things that are welded into a cohesive fighting force. Fighting units tend to be more at home with homogeneity. Not that there aren't other nationalities in the Black Watch. There are Fijians and Zimbabweans, even a few Glaswegians. However, the central core of the regiment has always been the heartland of Perthshire, Fife, Dundee, and Angus. It both represents and reflects those communities. The Black Watch is a tribe.
> GREGORY BURKE, AUTHOR'S NOTE, *BLACK WATCH*, FEBRUARY 2007

Within a year of the qualified success of *Home*, the NTS had staged the production that has come, in many ways, to define its work on the international stage: *Black Watch*, the fictional account of a verbatim playwright who attempts to document the amalgamation (and thus dissolution) of the storied Scottish Black Watch regiment. If *Home* used a distinctly located, spatially and temporally unique constellation of events to interrogate the idea of belonging and its relation to myths and narratives of Scottishness, *Black Watch*, in a spare production well suited to export and touring,[24] moves these questions from the domestic to the imperial front, forcing us to contemplate the full implications of the theatre(s) of war. Where *Home* served as the perfectly attuned emblem of how theatre could provide a formal model for the democratic, diverse, and dispersed nation that was just coming into being, *Black Watch* raises the question of what appeal a military narrative, with its mythologies and structures of homogeneity (as playwright Gregory Burke himself recognizes), can have for a theatrical community invested in heteroglossia, fragmentation, and constellation. In part it is a matter of sympathies of spectacle: "When I began," Burke notes, "I didn't realize quite how much of a theatrical business the army is. Why it hadn't occurred to me before, I don't know. After all, many people's sole experience of the Edinburgh Festival takes place at the Military Tattoo."[25] Indeed, the original production was staged in the Drill Hall underneath Edinburgh Castle: "I knew," writes director John Tiffany, "that I wanted to perform the piece in a space in which we could create our own version of the Tattoo, with seating banks down either side of an esplanade. This we found in Edinburgh, in an old drill hall near the Castle that was being used as a car park by the university,"[26] a resonant shift of spatial priorities. Subsequent stagings on the tour have endeavored, wherever possible, to preserve that sense of the open parade ground on which the pageantry of nation performs. Indeed, the facility with which *Black Watch* tours is a testament to the unifying power of war narratives: as tales of violence, isolation, loss, heroism, and sacrifice they are remarkably portable across cultural and political boundaries. Given how remarkably specific their circumstances are, wars echo historically, and the successful marketing of *Black Watch* to veterans' communities in the various nations it visits testifies to the way in which war narratives and touring shows are constructed as sites of universal reception and communion. As we shall see, however, the NTS's production of *Black Watch* did not function transcendently, overriding differences of cultural and political context, but rather shifted, like a shibboleth, to the conditions of reception across its tour of the Commonwealth and the United States, functioning, in Ric Knowles's formulation, "as guerrillas rather than as free-floating signifiers open to appropriation or commodification by contexts and interests over which they have no control."[27]

What *Black Watch* is really interested in is not replicating the processes of militaristic unification and exhortation, although the actors reportedly enjoyed their success in marshaling their bodies and minds to the performance of marching so much that at least one considered joining the army as an alternative career, should acting prove too unstable.[28] Instead, what *Black Watch* provides to the fledging National Theatre of Scotland is the opportunity to view "home" or "nation" through the lens of international deployment and mercenarism: a Scottish national identity that is in the service of British aims, which themselves are subject to American foreign policy. More than this, *Black Watch*'s interest in the most current of current events—an active war, the contemporaneous dissolution of the Black Watch and its distinctively theatrical culture of song, uniform, narrative, and genealogical tradition—becomes, in the hands of Burke and Tiffany, a palimpsestic examination of the whole history of the Black Watch, and of Scottish service in British theatres of war.

Throughout the play, the NTS stages fluid and (meta)theatrical movements through history, as when the distinctive uniform of the Black Watch soldier develops over the centuries, with actors rapidly stripping and costuming one of their own as he delivers an account of the history of the regiment. Or when the audience bears witness to an aristocratic exhortation of potential Black Watch members, as the soldiers in Iraq recall Lord Elgin's attempts to lure their First World War homologues into enlisting with the ritual display of Robert the Bruce's sword and a rousing comparison of Scotland's current need to the ancient "fight for freedom from the tyranny of a foreign power."[29] Elgin's audience is unmoved—they ultimately enlist out of sheer despair over the impoverished reality of their alternatives in the pits—and the audience is encouraged to join their skepticism about grand historical narratives. The result of this palimpsestic parade of regimental mythos can be both oddly stirring for the NTS's various audiences (this panhistorical pageantry is nothing if not effective spectacle) and cynically defamiliarizing. What emerges is a typology along medieval theatrical lines: behind the events of the current day, there drift the ghosts of the world wars, of Robert the Bruce, of Culloden. The significances of disparate histories speak across this palimpsest. This ghosting works not only temporally, however, but also across the historical distance of geography and politics: in examining the Scottish role in the occupation of Iraq, we find a metaphor for the peculiarly internal colonialism of Scotland's situation: absorbed, Othered, occupied, and hired out as mercenaries. "We started before Culloden," says a soldier as he's dressed and undressed in the shifting costumes of historical flux. "We dinnay really ken when. 1715, or maybe 1725. When Scotland was an independent nation we were fucking mercenaries tay half fuckin Europe. But it was 1739 when we really threw our lot in way the British. [*Beat.*] Some people thought we chose this dark tartan tay reflect our black betraying hearts. Bollocks. Fuck all that Cullodenshite. The Highlands were fucked. [*Beat.*] And they let us keep our weapons. Our kilts and our bagpipes. And they told us that we'd never have tay serve abroad. (*Laughs.*) But that's the fucking army for you."[30] Mercenarism draws the soldiers into the violence of war and of imperial complicity, not merely through the promise of remuneration, but through the fetishizing of heritage objects: the tartan, the kilt, the bagpipes, the weapon. National identity, when filtered through the palimpsestic historical layers of war, emerges not as a mode of resistant distinction, but of hegemonic absorption. The challenge for the NTS is to operate within modes and signs of national identity without falling fully into the complicity of unquestioning unity.

Dunsinane: Language as Shibboleth and Forest

Four years later, in 2011, the NTS picked up this thematic thread of war, occupation, and mercenarism when it collaborated with the Royal Shakespeare Company to bring its production of David Greig's *Dunsinane* to locations throughout England and Scotland.[31] Such are the common concerns of *Dunsinane* and *Black Watch* with the subtleties of tribalism and war, the psychology of an occupying force, and the ethics of mercenarism that their differences become all the more telling. *Black Watch* presents a tale of Scottish soldiers, drafted into foreign conflicts under foreign flags as part of a long history of colonial mercenarism, and it asks its audiences to read through these current events in a distant place to the domestic scene (past, present, and future) of Scotland's emergence from English oversight. The occupation of Iraq by Scottish troops becomes a troubling trope for the occupation and cooptation of Scotland throughout history. In *Dunsinane*, the plot comcerns the aftermath of *Macbeth*: a tyrant has been overthrown by Scottish leaders and their English mercenaries. Now the English troops must stay indefinitely, to secure the northern border and prevent their neighbors from falling into a long, disruptive civil war. But they seem ill-equipped to understand the complexity of Scottish politics, or the length and intricacy of the history that affects every current negotiation. In both cases, war narratives provide the play with the opportunity to connect with the geographically, temporally, and culturally distant, and to view history typologically, as a clamor of competing and echoing significances. Where *Black Watch* provides the temporal present and asks its audiences in Scotland, England, the United States, Ireland, and the Commonwealth to view the spatially distant both literally and metaphorically, *Dunsinane* provides the Scottish setting but implicitly asks its audience to see the long-ago clan conflicts as a prototype for current wars. The "tribalism" so often marked as Scottish in both plays elides the difference between Scottish history and the narratives of incomprehension that characterized British and American accounts of the long withdrawal from Iraq and Afghanistan.

There is a further irony in the fact that *Dunsinane* is only qualifiedly structured around a Scottish point of view. The protagonist is the English mercenary

Siward, who is in Scotland fighting for Malcolm and Macduff in order to protect English interests in the internecine struggles of its northern neighbor. The play unfolds in both unglossed, unsubtitled English and Gaelic, and audiences who are not proficient in both languages have a necessarily fragmentary and alienated experience of the events they witness.[32] Gruach, the Scottish queen who survives the death of her tyrannical husband (Shakespeare's Macbeth), mocks Siward's language:

SIWARD: I don't like to be in the presence of people talking secretly.
GRUACH: You could learn our language.
SIWARD: Your language is hard to learn.
GRUACH: We like it that way.
SIWARD: Why?
GRUACH: Your English is a woodworker's tool.
   Siward.
   Hello, goodbye, that tree is green.
   Simple matters.
   A soldier's language sent out to capture the world in words.
   Always trying to describe.
   Throw words at the tree and eventually you'll force me to see the tree just as you see it.
   We long since gave up believing in descriptions.
   Our language is the forest.[33]

Heteroglossia becomes not simply a subversive act, a resistance to the invasions of language, but also an assertion of an aesthetics of suggestion, nuance, ambiguity. A triumph of the figurative over the literal; a defense of the incomplete and ungraspable. Language is the Birnam Wood of Siward's downfall; the topography he cannot interpret, shifting and oblique. It is Gruach who can impress the forest, bid the tree unfix his earthbound root.

When Siward asks Gruach, who has become his lover, to teach him the language that resists being learned, she plays a joke on him with profound political resonances:

GRUACH: [Maybe you already speak our language. Do you?]
SIWARD: What did you say?
GRUACH: I asked if you understood what I was saying.
SIWARD: How do you say 'yes'?
GRUACH: [No.]
SIWARD: [No.]
GRUACH: Yes.

SIWARD: Ask me again.
GRUACH: [Maybe you already speak our language. Do you?]
SIWARD: [No.]
   Gruach's women laugh. [...]
SIWARD: Look at you smiling. You smiling and your women laughing at me.
   Which of us is really the conqueror here and which of us is the conquered?[34]

Language is a shibboleth here, and non-Gaelic-speaking spectators are as bound to bungle the watchword as Siward. The joke's on him and the Anglophone audience, and it is a laughter that separates and fragments and is totally impenetrable without the linguistic key. In fact, this cultural illiteracy is representative of his entire experience in Scotland: in the scene that follows, he is spectator to an elaborate diplomatic spectacle based on multiple, palimpsestic significations. Two members of feuding clans embrace each other, laughing comfortably. Being a literal-minded spectator to Scottish politics, Siward believes this indicates mutual trust. No, Macduff tells him, "If they trusted each other, they wouldn't need to demonstrate it." But if everyone knows this, Siward asks, why bother to pretend? "It's a demonstration for your benefit, not mine," Macduff tells him, not entirely comfortingly.

MACDUFF: Now look there—this is Macneill. He's come from the islands... They sent Macneill as a messenger in fact because everyone knows that the Coll–Macleod's brother—is staying with his wife's family nearby in Stirling. It's Coll who should be here but Macleod's sent Macneill. It's a snub.
SIWARD: A snub to whom?
MACDUFF: You. The Isles are demonstrating their primary allegiance is to Norway, not to England. They want you to know how unimportant you are. That's their message.
SIWARD: But I didn't—I don't understand the message.
MACDUFF: It's not important that the message arrives, what matters is that it has been sent.[35]

So the message intended for Siward is actually a performance of his ignorance, a performance he engages in without even being aware of it. The snub is intended for him, just like the false jollity, but it is only legible to those who understand the codes of behavior and can read them across multiple levels. Culture itself, not simply the spoken word, is a shibboleth, a language that speaks differently to different audiences, palimpsestically and simultaneously. This is the central theme of *Dunsinane*, but it is nowhere more evident than in the shifting meanings of these two plays as they tour, multiply signifying to disparate audiences with different investments in the Scottish national project.

"'Till Birnam Wood Do Come to Dunsinane": Mobility and Nation

The anxieties about the porousness of national borders and the perilous mobility of Scottish talent that is so evident in Alasdair Gray's model of settlers and colonists is triggered and subverted by the community of artists that makes up the leadership of the NTS. Vicky Featherstone is English and came to Scotland for work. She brought with her a mentality of creative mobility from her previous job with the touring company Paines Plough, which calls itself "the UK's National Theatre of New Plays." John Tiffany is also English and was drawn to Scotland by his education, studying at Glasgow University and making the country his home thereafter. Gregory Burke and David Greig are Scottish-born and raised in Gibraltar and Nigeria, respectively. All of them work across British and, increasingly, international boundaries. Scotland is, indeed, a European nation, as well as an international one. Its artists reflect hybrid experiences of identity in their art, and indeed the process of touring these plays provides an opportunity for the National Theatre to reflect on its own structures of transit and exchange, as well as the multiple performances of nationhood that are required and interpellated by shifting audiences in Scotland's cities, its rural communities, its British tours, and its travels around the Anglophone world. The NTS has emphasized touring and international collaboration from the outset, and in these plays we see not simply an active pursuit of the question "Who is the audience for a national theatre?" but also a thematic reflection on the mobility of human populations and their cultural products in art and war, a mobility that destabilizes ideas of nation at every turn.

Touring thus becomes an essential part of the NTS's structural mandate of homelessness: it is homelessness reconceived as migration and diplomacy. The process of touring expresses the politics of the organization in multivalent ways. Domestic tours are a core element of the aesthetic and politics of diffusion through which the NTS defines Scottishness in opposition to British and English cosmopolitan centrality. Touring is a performative iteration that creates nation; it is the expression of "the idea of representing nation in the theatre, of summoning a representative audience that will in turn recognize itself as nation on stage."[36] Thus the tours both display ("represent") conceptions of the Scottish nation for debate and legitimation and create the "representative" social gatherings that form and legitimize that nation, performing nation in all senses of the term. They perform nationhood externally as well as internally, sometimes even before the tour has wandered far from the geographical boundaries of the nation. *Black Watch*, for instance, premiered both domestically and centrally in

Edinburgh, the longstanding cultural and political capital of Scotland. It was presented, however, as part of the Edinburgh Festival, which was founded as a project of utopian internationalism, with a mandate to bring artists and audiences together in Scotland from all over the world. Where *Home* was an intentionally diffuse, local performance of belonging to initiate the National Theatre project as a cultural institution of and for the people of Scotland, *Black Watch* was thus a play about Scottish interventions on the global stage that performed Scottishness for both an internal and external audience with bravura simultaneity.

Both *Black Watch* and *Dunsinane* toured throughout the United Kingdom, and it is easy to see this cultural collaboration and circulation as undermining the nationalist project of the NTS by affirming the interconnectedness of British culture. In fact, both plays, in performing Scottishness to British audiences outside Scotland, cannily destabilize myths of unity that position England as the standard of Britishness while also refusing to characterize Scots as victims of English colonialism. Through the trope of mercenarism, which carries within it histories of cooptation and exploitation, but also of powerful and complicit mobility, *Black Watch* underscores the extent to which Scots are both agents and hegemonic subjects within British colonialism and American imperialism. "Scotland pretends to have no part of exploitation," Burke has argued in interviews, "yet per-head they produce more soldiers than any other part of the UK. Scotland is not just a victim of conquest. Scotland has been part of the brutal suppression of freedom."[37] Thus the ambivalent mobility of mercenarism symbolized by the Black Watch (symbols of national pride and imperial power) becomes a type for the tour of the *Black Watch* theatrical corps, moving fluidly throughout Britain and in fact the world under funding from the Scottish government and the British Council.

International touring has been a part of the NTS's mandate since their original manifesto, an emphasis that places *Black Watch* in particular (since it toured more broadly to Canada, the United States, New Zealand, and Australia) in a historical context of cultural diplomacy and commodification. In contrast to academic critiques of the circulation and imposition of power through structures of national theatre and nationalist exportations of art by Kruger, Holdsworth, Knowles, Harvie, and others, the British Council has set forth a utopian theory of how *Black Watch* functions as public diplomacy, in the form of a public policy analysis by Nicholas J. Cull. Plays like *Black Watch*, even as and often because they function subversively, operate as (1) a "prestige gift" intended to build reciprocity between nations, (2) "cultural information" used to "counter stereotypes of the sponsoring country and develop understanding of life as it is really lived," (3) a context for "dialogue" that is enhanced by the touring of controversial pieces, and (4) a means of "capacity building" through which governments expand and express liberal conceptions of the value of the arts to a global "democratic public sphere."[38] Indeed, the internal ambivalences of the play about militarism, British and American influence on global politics, masculinity, and Scottish complicity only enhance its value as cultural diplomacy according to Cull, since "a self-confident state will even share works which are explicitly critical of its life" and "by sharing such work internationally the British Council is acting as a credible conduit for British culture. It is helping to build a reputation for itself and for Britain as honest and trustworthy."[39] Note, however, that Cull, viewing this production through the lens and under the sponsorship of the British Council's encouragement of scholarly dialogue between culture and politics, speaks of this tour as an official state-sponsored process of *British* cultural diplomacy. This certainly reflects the rationale for the British Council's funding of a tour that interrogates the wars in Iraq and, by extension, Afghanistan to regions that share a linguistic identity, a colonial history, and coalition priorities with the United Kingdom. It fails, however, to take into account the nation-sponsored process of cultural diplomacy embedded within the British state project. In staging and funding this tour, the Scottish Government and the National Theatre of Scotland ask the play to signify multiply, testifying in seemingly paradoxical ways both to the participation of Scotland in the British national identity and in international coalitions, and to its autonomous identity as a nation. In this latter capacity, the tour serves a very different role as cultural diplomacy: establishing Scotland and its National Theatre on the international stage as an autonomous and definable national body, distinct from a Britishness that defaults to Englishness.

As such, it partakes in a long tradition of exportation of a Scottish cultural brand. The nations visited by the *Black Watch* tour are, through no accident of history, not simply the former colonies of Britain that remain tied together by Commonwealth structures, a common language, and military concerns, but also major sites in the Scottish diaspora. The touring actors speak frequently to spectators and interviewers about the strong ties between ethnic Scots they encounter on their tours and the performance of Scottishness in which they are engaged. In this sense, the nation that is performed and interpellated by these tours is not simply geographical or political but also diasporic. It is also, by necessity, a fleeting and nostalgic chimera of nationhood, and one imbricated in the commercial and ideological processes of the heritage industry. The exportation of Scottishness as brand, as McCrone, Morris, and Kiely have argued, is a phenomenon that finds its roots in Sir Walter Scott's formulation of history as schismatically and romantically separate from the present day.[40] "This new past," in the words of David Lowenthal, "gradually came to be cherished as a heritage that validated and exalted the present."[41] This heritage, manufactured for internal consumption as a means of establishing national singularity, and exported as commodity to the nostalgia of diasporic communities and the sentiment of foreign publics, is a fictionalization of the continuity of Scottish history that encompasses the present day. In a swirl of tartan and shortbread, of Burns and Scott, of mythic narratives of Culloden and sovereignty, "we might even argue that Scotland suffers from too much heritage rather than too little… It has become an *idée fixe* of many Scottish intellectuals that Scotland suffers from a deformation of its culture; that it has sold out its political birthright for a mess of cultural pottage… It is argued that instead of a rounded thought-world in which culture and politics work together in gear, the prevalent images of Scotland are adrift from their political moorings."[42] The performance of nation that the NTS's tours are engaged in cannot be completely disentangled from the heritage industry. The tour of David Greig's verse drama *The Strange Undoing of Prudencia Hart*, for instance, which takes place in the found spaces of bars and pubs, was sponsored by the National Theatre of Scotland and Benromach Speyside Single Malt Scotch Whiskey, samples of which were offered as spectators took their seats. In an odd and compelling moment of cultural and commercial communion, each spectator imbibes a bit of Scotland while making conversation with a cast member whose opening gambit is "So…have you ever *been* to Scotland?" The nation is inseparable from its products, and heritage nostalgia is its ur-product.

Dunsinane and *Black Watch* are remarkable for the ways they both engage with and undermine Scotland-as-heritage. In *Macbeth* and the Black Watch regiment we have two iconic and complex sentimentalizations of Scottish heritage, steeped in ritual blood and draped in tartan. Both are compelling narratives that emerge from an imperial portrait of Scotland as a subject nation whose strength has been yoked and whose warrior ethos has been redirected to "orderly" ends. At the heart of Scottish heritage is often an imperial subtext that renders it surprisingly and powerfully treacherous in cultural representation: "Even those central icons of the British imperial past, the Highland regiments, have their vociferous defenders in the Scottish National Party. All is not what it seems. The heritage icons are malleable. They take on radical as well as conservative meanings."[43] It stands testament to the productive ambivalence of these productions that these evocations are sketched in all their nostalgic power, but also scoffingly undercut.

The international range of the *Black Watch* tour exists in fascinating contrast to the alternative mobility of *Dunsinane*, a play not about the Scottish presence in global politics, but about the historical English presence in Scotland. The shift in migratory focus and direction is echoed by the different structures of production that produced it and *Black Watch*. In *Black Watch*, the NTS saw a major success in their unconventional commissioning process: "We have about ten assignments a year," Featherstone writes, "where we ask playwrights and artists to follow something—anything from huge stories to fleeting moments—not needing to know where they will end." Artists are thus "embedded" (to use military diction) in current events, without the need to force historical and political narratives to unfold in compliance with the structures of institutional time. This was a production generated fully through the unique processes of the new NTS, processes that it critiques and parodies in the character of the naive documentarian. In *Dunsinane*, however, although the artist in question was Scottish and had worked extensively with the NTS as company dramaturg, and although much of the workshopping took place in Scotland, the production itself was an English one, spearheaded by no less canonical an institution than the Royal Shakespeare Company. Greig was engaged in reclaiming the most famous of Scottish narratives for Scotland—"I also had a cheeky desire," he said in a press release about the play, "to respond to the fact that the most famous Scottish play was written by the most famous English writer. I wanted to look at the story from a Scottish point of view"[44]—but he was doing so through English structures of funding and production.

The NTS's role here ran parallel to Greig's: their goal was to reappropriate a relevant production for the Scottish audience, a reclamation that involves a significant shift in the meaning of the play itself. For an English audience, viewing the play under the rubric of the Royal Shakespeare Company in their London or Stratford spaces, *Dunsinane* is an extension of British heritage, as exemplified by Shakespeare, that most marketable of English national symbols. From this perspective, it is a play about the incomprehensibility of tribal politics in the face of English rationalism. For the Scottish audience, it is a play about the arrogance of the colonist's excessive cultural literalism and the nuance of linguistic fluency as a symbol of culture.

In the structures of process, the play represents a rich reversal of colonial flows of production and commodity. In this case, the English audience (in the form of the Royal Shakespeare Company) has sent a classic English work to a Scottish playwright for transformation, and then consumes it as a commodity after its sea-change into something rich and strange. When the NTS picked up the production for importation and Scottish consumption, however, they co-opted the work of a Scottish playwright whose work has been transformed by the English theatrical industry. The process replicates the unsettling flow of commodities in the colonial model, is complicit with that model, and transforms it. For both audiences, however, the allegorical structure of the play multiplies its signification: the English mercenary force under Siward is a type for the *British* occupiers of Iraq and Afghanistan, and the narrative of war and colonization offers national identifications to both Scottish and English audiences that are neither easy nor self-congratulating.

Esprit de Corps and Theatres of War

The question that has haunted the preceding pages is a martial one: what is the particular appeal, anxious or nostalgic, of war plays to a nation and a National Theatre in a period of rapid flux and mobilization? "For the Black Watch," Cull concludes in his study of the diplomatic role of the NTS's first international hit, "the war in Iraq marked the end of an era of soldiering. For Scotland the international exhibition of the National Theatre of Scotland's *Black Watch* is part of the beginning of a new era of artistic self-representation."[45] How is the military corps transformed (through bodily mimesis and symbolic representation) into the theatrical corps, the national corpus, the body politic?

War plays are about the mobility of human populations and identities; they are about countries in flux and in conflict, strangers in a strange land reflecting on the *Verfremdungseffekt* of performing nation outside its boundaries. They are about occupiers and the occupied, and the ambivalences of identity in between. These are all issues that are integral to the NTS's conception of its role in Scotland, the United Kingdom, and the global byways of artistic circulation.

But these are also collaborative dramas of more than usual mobility. There is a claim to a transhistorical mythopoetics of war evident in these plays and their international reception. The success of these plays, according to the rhetoric of their reception, is the result of the universality of war. When war is critiqued as a state that transcends history, nation, and temporality, it runs the risk of becoming a critique without possibility of change, a critique whose true purpose is the construction of a transnational solidarity of suffering and sacrifice.

These plays are marked by their humane ambivalence about the warrior ethos, a sympathy (if not a lionization) that underscores its centrality to Scottishness. This palimpsestic mapping of the warrior ethos onto nation, class, and gender is at the heart of Aleks Sierz's critique of *Black Watch*: "By excluding the families of the men, especially their wives, it also presented war as a delirious festival of masculinity. And because it felt like a triumph for Scottish manhood, Scottish theatre and Scottish national pride, few were brave enough to raise an eyebrow about its implicitly militarist ideology."[46] Such was the ambivalence of its representation of militarism that few critics could agree on the nature of the play's implicit ideology. Certainly the playwright and director had embarked on the project in a spirit of confirmed pacifism: although the actors reported feeling that the intensive process of drilling had truly transformed them into a corps, "Tiffany was especially keen to develop the project as a subversion of Scottish military pageantry. He had a personal distaste for the annual spectacle of the Edinburgh Tattoo and the parading of soldiers as though to disguise their real identity as killing machines."[47] If Sierz's reading of the play underestimates its critique of complicit mercenarism, Cull certainly reads the play's militarism as less seductive than it was in my experience of the play: "Part of the play's achievement is to document the mindset without reproducing the effect. The camaraderie here is unenviable. It appears like a perverse analogue of class consciousness... Their regimental spirit, in Burke's hands, seems like an embezzlement of the resource of class solidarity."[48] The play does not, in my experience, entirely avoid reproducing the effect of esprit de corps, although it manages to ennoble fraternal loyalty and unity without glorifying war, which is largely portrayed as dull, exploitative, and tawdry in its everyday minutiae. The formation of a community of viewership in response to the spectacle of the performed community of militaristic service, however, is an effect that coexists with the play's critique of the macropolitical structures of war. Is the play also engaging in a theatrical embezzlement of esprit de corps for nationalist ends?

The answer to this problem comes at least in part in an examination of what Kruger calls the tendency of theatrical nationalism to resolve into "national monuments," standing ossified as testimony to a hegemonic portrait of national unity.[49] The military corps (and corpses) become, through the close relationship with the theatrical company, the body politic. Monuments certainly have the capacity to render history with a false sense of closure: history as heritage, nostalgic, distant, and commodified. They can stand mute, as fixed testimony to the past or to power, serving to contain and preserve a memory or ideology that can't bear constant scrutiny, constant reenactment. But monuments have a double valence: they can also serve a *memorial* function, as site for debate, disagreement, rehearsal, and re-membering. As such, monuments—National Theatres among them—are the sites of continual interrogations of history and politics, continually mobile processes of community formation and reformation.

ARIEL WATSON

Notes

1. Loren Kruger, *The National Stage: Theatre and Cultural Legitimation in England, France, and America* (Chicago: University of Chicago Press, 1992), 28.
2. David McCrone, Angela Morris, and Richard Kiely, *Scotland—the Brand* (Edinburgh: Edinburgh University Press, 1995), 4.
3. Tom Peterkin, "Alasdair Gray Attacks English for 'Colonising' Arts," *The Scotsman*, December 16, 2012.
4. Here Grey invokes the fraught example of W. B. Yeats and Lady Gregory, seeing in their foundation of an Irish national theatre a model for settler nationalism, and glossing over the extreme controversies of legitimacy that characterized the first decades of the Abbey Theatre's existence, in various forms. Alasdair Gray, "Settlers and Colonists," http://www.word-power.co.uk, accessed December 20, 2012.
5. Featherstone, who has since taken up the artistic directorship of the Royal Court Theatre in London, herself has said that one of the reasons for her move back to England is the skepticism surrounding internal hiring in Scottish arts administration: "In practice, I don't think Scotland has seen much of that kind of sideways movement in top arts jobs. In terms of the Scottish scene in general, I think boards are often not very confident about appointing people whose main experience is in Scotland. In fact, I often ask myself why so many boards in Scotland seem to assume that a person from England knows better, even though I'm from England myself." Joyce Macmillan, "Interview: Vicky Featherstone on Theatre in Scotland," *The Scotsman*, December 18, 2012.
6. A debate that was itself staged as a democratic discussion between representatives from a wide variety of Scottish theatre professions.
7. The NTS implicitly rejects the centrist, cosmopolitan, and monumental nature of its nearest models, the Abbey Theatre in Dublin and the Royal National Theatre in London. These two great examples, respectively, of the modernist and postwar national theatre movements, are deeply invested in rhetorics (political and architectural) of unification. Interestingly, the new National Theatre of Wales, founded in 2009, has followed the devolved, "homeless" model of the NTS, as well as its emphasis on international scope.
8. Indeed, the emphatic rejection of a centralized model of the national theatre marks the extent to which the NTS conceives of itself through oppositional practice, defining itself (and by extension Scotland) *against* English and British models of cosmopolitan and imperial power and nationhood. Thus the decentered, the peripheral, and the dispersed become integral parts of how the NTS conceives of creative processes, theatrical space, and nation itself. For discussion of the semiotics of spatial signification to the intersection of nation and theatre, see the treatment of center and periphery in Marvin Carlson's *Places of Performances: The Semiotics of Theatre Architecture* (Ithaca, NY: Cornell University Press, 1989), 73–97, and in Loren Kruger's *The National Stage* (12–13).
9. Kruger, *The National Stage*, 3.
10. Friedrich Schiller, "The Stage as Moral Institution," in *Essays Aesthetical and Philosophical, vol. 8* (London: G. Bell and Sons, 1884), 338.
11. Vicky Featherstone, "Rocky Road," *The Guardian*, February 27, 2008. Of course, this sense of historical singularity elides the long history of attempts, false starts, and temporally limited successes surrounding the idea of Scottish national theatre, which Roger Savage and others have documented. It also obscures that fact that just as ideologies of

nationhood are in a continual state of flux, so too the national theatre is not a foundational moment, but rather a process of reinvention and reflection. In other words, a performance of nation.

12. Roger Savage, "A Scottish National Theatre?," in *Scottish Theatre since the Seventies*, ed. Randall Stevenson and Gavin Wallace (Edinburgh: Edinburgh University Press, 1996), 23–24. Much interesting work has been done on what Ric Knowles has called the "materialist semiotics" of these localized national theatres, not least in Kruger's work; Nadine Holdsworth's pithy *Theatre & Nation* (London: Palgrave Macmillan, 2010), which places the NTS against the backdrop of a postfascist distrust of nationalism and the mid-century resurgence of postcolonial national theatres, as well as in the context of other devolved models in Australia and Finland; and S. E. Wilmer, ed., *National Theatres in a Changing Europe* (London: Palgrave Macmillan, 2008).

13. Savage, "A Scottish National Theatre?," 24–25.

14. This mobility has also allowed the NTS, as Robert Leach has shown, to contribute substantially to the theatrical infrastructure throughout Scotland, both with touring and local production in mind. Robert Leach, "The Short, Astonishing History of the National Theatre of Scotland," *New Theatre Quarterly (NTQ)* 23, no. 2 (2007): 171–83.

15. Jen Harvie, *Staging the UK* (Manchester: Manchester University Press, 2005), 31. Harvie writes idealistically of the NTS in the very moment of its conception, hoping that as "envisioned [it] will not devour all available public theatre funding, starving existing theatres and theatre work as other National institutions do," with particular reference to the longstanding Arts Council policy of supporting "few, but roses," as well as to the financial scandal involving the escalating cost of the new Scottish parliament building (32, 18). In fact, the NTS's emphasis on collaboration explicitly aims to forestall this possibility.

16. Zoltán Imre, "Staging the Nation," *NTQ* 24, no. 1 (2008): 76.

17. Joyce Macmillan, "Interview: Vicky Featherstone on Theatre in Scotland," *The Scotsman*, December 18, 2012.

18. "Housing Scheme is Home to National Theatre," *The Scotsman*, September 26, 2003.

19. Lyn Gardner, "The Homeless Home of Scottish Theatre," *The Guardian Theatre Blog*, January 25, 2007.

20. Vicky Featherstone, "Rocky Road," *The Guardian*, February 27, 2008.

21. Matt Trueman, "National Theatre of Scotland Finds Permanent Home," *The Guardian*, January 14, 2013.

22. Lyn Gardner, "The Homeless Home of Scottish Theatre," *The Guardian Theatre Blog*, January 25, 2007.

23. Ibid.

24. *Black Watch* was originally performed in the semiotically rich environment of the University of Edinburgh Drill Hall as part of the Edinburgh Fringe Festival—a fascinating juxtaposition of the resonantly local nationalism of place and the transnationalism of festival infrastructure that Ric Knowles calls its "placelessness." Ric Knowles, *Reading the Material Theatre* (Cambridge: Cambridge University Press, 2004), 90. This false transcendence of the material contexts of reception and production that is placelessness is not, of course, the same as the liberatory "homelessness" that enables the NTS to move fluidly through the shifting significations of touring locations, the production meaning differently in every venue. In 2007, 2008, and 2011, *Black Watch* went on to tour widely in Scotland, as well as to Toronto, Sydney, Perth, Wellington, London, Canterbury, Belfast,

Dublin, New York, Los Angeles, Chicago, the Universities of North Carolina and Texas, and the Virginia Arts Festival. These tours represent a fascinating schism in the representation of nationhood, between representations of the Iraq War to complicit and conflicted audiences in London and the United States and interrogations of the coercions and complications of "British" identity to audiences in Ireland, Northern Ireland, and the Anglophone Commonwealth.

25. Gregory Burke, *Black Watch* (London: Faber and Faber, 2007), viii.
26. Ibid., xii.
27. Knowles, *Reading the Material Theatre*, 91. Knowles's materialist semiotics are particularly useful in reminding us that the "political unconscious" that "speak[s] through" plays like *Black Watch* and *Dunsinane* depends as much on the conditions of individual performances, their contexts of reception, and of production, as on their "manifest content" (10).
28. Burke, *Black Watch*, vii.
29. Ibid., 25–26.
30. Ibid., 30–31.
31. The Royal Shakespeare Company's production of *Dunsinane* opened at the Hampstead Theatre in London, in the cosmopolitan center of empire rather than the mythical omphalos that the RSC has establish out of town at Stratford-upon-Avon. The play itself, however, defies both the centrality of Bardolatry and of cosmopolitanism, discarding huge portions of Shakespeare's enshrined narrative and relegating London and the English court to the forgotten margins of Scottish politics. After the collaboration with the National Theatre of Scotland was established, the production toured Edinburgh, Glasgow, and Stratford in 2011, and undertook a wider tour of English and Scottish cities including Inverness, Aberdeen, Oxford, Birmingham, and Bath in 2013.
32. This is a pointedly theatrical effect: readers of the published text encounter only English versions of the lines, with the translated sections from Gaelic set apart with brackets. The assumption is that the readership of the play will be Anglophone, and that they must have "complete" access to the language of the play.
33. David Greig, *Dunsinane* (London: Faber and Faber, 2010), 76.
34. Ibid., 76–77.
35. Ibid., 79.
36. Kruger, *The National Stage*, 3.
37. Nicholas J Cull, "The National Theatre of Scotland's *Black Watch*: Theatre as Cultural Diplomacy" (British Council and USC Center on Public Diplomacy, 2007), 10, http://uscpublicdiplomacy.org/sites/uscpublicdiplomacy.org/files/legacy/media/Black_Watch_Publication_010808.pdf, accessed July 28, 2014.
38. Ibid., 13–17.
39. Ibid., 14, 15.
40. McCrone, Morris, and Kiely, *Scotland—the Brand*, 4.
41. David Lowenthal, *The Past Is a Foreign Country* (Cambridge: Cambridge University Press, 1985), xvi.
42. McCrone, Morris, and Kiely, *Scotland—the Brand*, 5.
43. Ibid., 5.
44. "Dunsinane Receives Scottish Premiere," March 31, 2011, National Theatre of Scotland Press Release.

45. Cull, "Theatre as Cultural Diplomacy," 21.
46. Aleks Sierz, *Rewriting the Nation: British Theatre Today* (London: Methuen, 2011), 203.
47. Cull, "Theatre as Cultural Diplomacy," 4.
48. Ibid., 8.
49. Here Kruger cautions us against viewing these "national monuments" as truly stable: "Bearing in mind that the national ground on which these monuments stand is itself shifting, we ought to take account of the fluidity of the discourses delineating the nation." Kruger, *The National Theatre*, 26.

BOOK REVIEWS

"Uncle Tom's Cabin" on the American Stage and Screen. By John W. Frick. New York: Palgrave Macmillan, 2012. xvii + 308 pp. $95.00 cloth.

Sales of Harriet Beecher Stowe's *Uncle Tom's Cabin; or, Life among the Lowly* (serialized 1851; published as a novel 1852) were eclipsed in the nineteenth century only by sales of the Bible. The phenomenal social no less than financial success of Stowe's novel has subjected it to more scholarly scrutiny than the dramatizations of it, even though more people encountered and were influenced by *Uncle Tom's Cabin* as a play or film than ever read it.

"Uncle Tom's Cabin" on the American Stage and Screen is the first book-length updating of the novel's stage and screen history since Harry Birdoff's 1947 *The World's Greatest Hit*, extended and supported here by recent research and John W. Frick's own rigorous scholarship. Taken together with Heather Nathans's *Slavery and Sentiment on the American Stage, 1787–1861* (Cambridge 2009), scholars can now consider the range and impact of antislavery dramas during the postcolonial and antebellum eras and can trace the history of its most famous exemplar, *Uncle Tom's Cabin*, down even to our own times.

Frick, who established his bona fides as an expert in reform drama with *Theatre, Culture, and Temperance Reform in Nineteenth-Century America* (Cambridge 2003), is well equipped to undertake a cultural and social history of dramatizations of Stowe's novel from 1851 to modern stage and screen versions, and to resituate *Uncle Tom's Cabin* in its stage history (xii–xiii). Frick's book devotes a chapter to each of the following topics: the novel; the Aiken/Howard dramatization of it; the Conway/Kimball/Barnum dramatization (known as "the [Missouri] Compromise version"); spin-offs of the play from 1865 to 1900, including the development of "Tom Shows" (the general term used for stage adaptations of *Uncle Tom's Cabin*); a typical "Tom Show" in the twentieth century and professional revivals of *Uncle Tom's Cabin* on and off Broadway; and filmed versions between 1903 and 1965, plus an adaptation for television in 1987. The six chapters conclude in a brief epilogue, aptly titled "The Story that Won't Stay Dead," which carries us into the twenty-first century and the most recent, but likely not the last, professional production (in 2010) of *Uncle Tom's Cabin*. Generous notes accompany the text, and there is a substantial bibliography, including (teachers beware—potential plagiarism) the address of an *Uncle Tom's Cabin* website (xiv).

The first three chapters of *"Uncle Tom's Cabin" on the American Stage and Screen* offer few surprises to students of theatre in the antebellum era, though Frick's treatment of the Aiken and Conway plays and early productions of and research concerning them is thorough. Chapters 4 through 6, however, restore the "Tom Show" to its rightful place as a historical phenomenon and illustrate both the dramatic variants of *Uncle Tom's Cabin* and their power after the Civil War (an estimated four to five hundred "Tom" companies were on tour throughout the United States in 1900).

The great benefit of a book like *"Uncle Tom's Cabin" on the American Stage and Screen* is to demonstrate in detail why dramatizations of *Uncle Tom's Cabin* continued to draw audiences long after slavery had been abolished in America. Economically, *Uncle Tom's Cabin* was an established brand that promised heart-wrenching emotion, thrilling action, and spectacular situations. Theatrically, Stowe's material was flexible enough that whatever was popular elsewhere in the theatre could be accommodated by Tom Shows, including dog acts, horse chases, spectacular scenes and devices, jubilee singers, musical acts, minstrel players and formats, double character productions (two Toms, two Topsys, two Legrees), and "mammoth" Tom Shows with the traveling weight of a circus. Dramatically, Stowe's novel offered enough material to serve adaptations that erased George Harris as well as versions that made him the play's hero, dramas that focused on Eliza rather than Tom, dramas tailored to black actors playing Uncle Tom and the slaves, and versions that eliminated Aiken's and Conway's additions and restored Stowe's characters. Sociopolitically, dramatizations both supported Stowe's novel and turned it on its head, as in the 1852 "compromise *Uncle Tom*," which Stowe is alleged to have left mid-performance (96), and postbellum southern productions that shifted Stowe's narrative from the poor slave to the poor slave owner (116–17).

If the strength of *"Uncle Tom's Cabin" on the American Stage and Screen* is its concentration and presentation of content, form is its weakness. The text is peppered with subheadings that jump-cut from topic to topic rather than connecting ideas through seamless prose, a problem that besets the overall writing of this book. There are typos, including the risible "viscous slave-hunting dogs" (172). More serious affronts to linguistic sensibilities include "less" substituted for "fewer" (162) and "like" for "as" (193), and jargon that intrudes into a series devoted to jargon-free scholarship, for example, "its omission (or 'diluation' to be more precise) (59)," or "the salvific agency of Tom" (62). Run-on sentences beginning with 'and' or 'or' are numerous, and the text is peppered with semicolons to splice these sentences together. Throughout, *sic* appears as *sic!* (evoking a startle reflex in this reader), and is at least once invoked incorrectly (212) when it flags "manoeuvre," an acceptable variant spelling of the more common "maneuver." Surely, we will all fail as our own editors. For this reason, competent and dedicated copyeditors must hold our feet to the fire. To that failing on the part of the press can be added the creation of a cover that suffuses Uncle Tom and the old plantation in pastel shades of pink and green against magenta boards, a presentation that gives Frick's scholarly work the appearance of a high school textbook.

Warts and all, however, it would be hard to overstate the importance of *Uncle Tom's Cabin*, in all its forms, to the history of theatre and culture in the United States. We can appreciate that importance because John Frick's *"Uncle Tom's Cabin" on the American Stage and Screen* reveals the social contexts of performances that have, among other things, transformed Stowe's nineteenth-century noble Christian martyr into a twentieth-century race traitor. Frick's diligent attention to the contents of playtexts, variety shows, and screenplays of *Uncle Tom's Cabin* allows us to follow the tension between slavery and attempts to whitewash it as "that peculiar institution" (65), and to feel the treachery of transforming Stowe's morally corrupt slaveholders into "kindly, considerate" Southerners (215). Yet, even as *Uncle Tom's Cabin* has reflected our national discussions of race, *"Uncle Tom's Cabin" on the American Stage and Screen* makes clear that it is forever "a part of our national heritage and common culture" (228).

—ROSEMARIE K. BANK
Kent State University

Spectacles of Reform: Theater and Activism in Nineteenth-Century America. By Amy E. Hughes. Ann Arbor: University of Michigan Press, 2012. vii + 248 pp. $75 cloth.

Spectacles of Reform: Theater and Activism in Nineteenth-Century America by Amy Hughes takes the reader through three particular and significant spectacles. According to Hughes, melodrama exemplifies "decadence, extremity, and excess," which together serve to pull in audiences (1). Building on the work of theatre historians and theorists such as Joseph Roach and Marvin Carlson, Hughes investigates spectacle as a "unique system of communication, employed in myriad contexts, that rehearses and sustains conceptions of race, gender, and class in extremely powerful ways" (4). Thus, while theatre for social change is often framed as a twentieth-century invention, *Spectacles of Reform* demonstrates how theatre has been used for reform since at least the nineteenth century.

Hughes acknowledges that the intersection of spectacle and reform is a peculiar one but suggests that this intersection allows for the combination of "excess and normalcy that, arguably, continue(s) to obsess and regulate individuals today" (5). The book focuses on three scenes in nineteenth-century melodramas: the episode of delirium tremens in W. H. Smith's *The Drunkard* (1844), Eliza crossing the icy Ohio River in stage adaptations of Harriet Beecher Stowe's novel *Uncle Tom's Cabin* (1852), and the railroad rescue in Augustin Daly's play *Under the Gaslight* (1867). While acknowledging that there are many important examples of spectacle, not only in nineteenth-century melodrama but also throughout theatre history, Hughes limits her discussion to these case studies and the respective social dilemmas (temperance, abolition, and suffrage) that each scene dramatizes.

The first chapter, "The Body/as/in/at the Spectacle," utilizes Stanton B. Garner's theory of the *spectacular instant*, a heightened and visceral moment in performance for the spectator by embodying the display on stage. After laying this critical foundation, Hughes then examines "performances of excess, whether *as* the spectacle (extraordinary bodies in freak shows), *in* the spectacle (actors in sensation scenes), or *at* the spectacle (people who witness performance)" (14). By analyzing the actual bodies of the performer and spectator through unique gesture and movement, Hughes calls attention to the human dynamics of spectacle. Therefore, this section emphasizes the importance and utility of the body as a means of both spectacle and reform.

The second chapter, "The *Delirium Tremens*: Spectacular Insanity in *The Drunkard*," examines temperance through abstention (and withdrawal) from alcohol. Hughes outlines the historiography of temperance via medical research and, as an example, discusses the work of John B. Gough, a former alcoholic turned lecturer from 1840s New England. Gough's lecturers became spectacles through his humor, charisma, and display of delirium tremens. Gough was performing in Boston at the same time as the initial run of *The Drunkard*, which he attended. Edward Middleton, the title character in *The Drunkard*, became, next to Gough himself, the best-known embodiment of delirium tremens. Smith's play, argues Hughes, closely ties delirium tremens, insanity, and normality together as a spectacle in life.

Chapter 3, "The Fugitive Slave: Eliza's Flight in *Uncle Tom's Cabin*," explores the imagery and reality of escape from slavery. The iconography of Eliza's flight is highly recognizable, so much so that the image of Eliza on the ice serves as the cover image for the book. Both in the broader discourse of slavery and in *Uncle Tom's Cabin* in particular, the river represented freedom, hope, and danger. Spectacle operates as "both method and matter in Eliza's escapade," writes Hughes, as the escape represents a transformation from property to person (86). This transformation, and the image of it, is relevant and significant in attempting to communicate the experiences and stories of slaves.

The fourth chapter, "The Railroad Rescue: Suffrage and Citizenship in *Under the Gaslight*," investigates what Hughes cites as one of the most famous spectacles in American melodrama. In *Under the Gaslight*, Laura Courtland uses an axe to break out of a locked shed in time to save Snorkey, a Civil War veteran, who is tied to the railroad tracks as a train approaches. This was not the first use of this kind of railroad sensation, but it initiated its popularity in the United States. The incongruity (to period audiences) of Courtland, or any woman, wielding an axe creates a space for commentary on the role of women in society as well as exemplifying the potential spectacle creates for communicating subtle yet profound ideas to audiences. The axe was and continued to be a representation of the "ingenuity, creativity, and fortitude of those populating the continent" (145). By placing the axe in the hands of a woman, the scene incorporated nationalism and reinforced women's patriotism and strength. Courtland's use of the axe in Daly's play, Hughes argues, represents the continual push toward women's rights and gender equality.

In the final chapter, "Afterword: Our Sensations, Our Heroes, Our Freaks," Hughes emphasizes how hot topics such as temperance, abolition, and women's rights were effectively utilized by playwrights and theatre managers in an attempt to engage and communicate morality to American audiences in pivotal historical moments. Theatre is thus shown to be able to enact social reformation through spectacle.

Spectacle, as Hughes notes, is an enduring element of theatre going back to Aristotle's *Poetics* and his six parts of tragedy. While Aristotle lists spectacle last, Hughes argues that it is a necessary and useful communication strategy. In Hughes's own words, *Spectacles of Reform* is a study on "the perpetual power, appeal, and political immanence of the sensation scene in American culture"

(154); it succeeds as a significant contribution to the scholarship on theatre for social change.

—AMANDA BOYLE
University of Kansas

Dramatic Revisions of Myths, Fairy Tales and Legends: Essays on Recent Plays. Edited by Verna A. Foster. Jefferson, NC: McFarland and Company, 2012. viii + 250 pp. $40.00 paper.

This collection is an ambitious attempt to bring together a group of essays that represent several disparate approaches to the study of dramatic adaptation. The use of "Dramatic Revisions" is accurate, as the essays are squarely focused on the dramatic material and how it is conveyed in different versions. There are many plot summaries here, as the old and revised narratives are literally retold so that we as audience understand the similarities and differences. The value of this breadth eventually becomes apparent, as the collection provides an opportunity to see a number of approaches to analyzing drama and its relationships to myth, fairy tales, and legends. While some of the approaches are stronger and more convincing than others, the collection provides new ideas and possibilities through several compelling overlaps and surprisingly connected analyses.

Foster's introduction sets out definitions of myth, fairy tale, and legend and argues that the continued resonances of the stories make them the basic cultural material from which new revisions of those stories are made. Miriam Chirico furthers this perspective in the first chapter, defining "mythic revision" as "the act of creatively re-writing a myth in order to move closer to the myth's essential meaning" (16). Using Claude Lévi-Strauss's metaphor of "the room," she explicates the adaptation of myth as looking through various windows and mirrors into a room in which the myth resides; through this framework, dramatic adaptation gives us more glimpses of the myth inside the room, and thus more perspectives on its "essential meaning." Chirico also provides a summary of different approaches to analyzing adaptation (thematic, comparative, and structuralist) and proposes an extended structuralist methodology that would also include "dramaturgical adoption" (20) as a gesture to the significance of the performative in dramatic adaptations. The rest of Chirico's chapter, and of the anthology, offers some illuminating readings of dramatic adaptations while only occasionally hinting at their effect as theatrical productions. Unfortunately, as many of the essays remain mostly thematic and/or comparative, they often rely upon overarching statements that compare the ancient Athenian dramas and context to the contemporary ones with some variation of Karelisa Hartigan's observation that "tragedy today is not defined by the universal but by the individual" (47).

Elizabeth Scharffenberger's chapter analyzing Ellen McLaughlin's *Helen* and Saviana Stanescu and Richard Schechner's *YokastaS* is the strongest essay in the book, connecting myth with theatrical practice by examining the way these pieces function for their contemporary audiences. Scharffenberger addresses the "unmaking" of the narrative of the McLaughlin *Helen*, with its frustrating refusal to get rid of one of the Helens. She productively compares this to the multiple Yokastas that exist concurrently and in conflict in Stanescu and Schechner's piece, which attempts to "set the record straight" (52) by taking the narrative out of the hands of men, giving the character of Yokasta agency and psychological depth beyond the shallower archetypes of Sophocles and Seneca (and Freud).

Kevin Wetmore's chapter on Tarell Alvin McCraney's *The Brother/Sister Plays* demonstrates how the playwright revises Yoruba myths and their American adaptations to create space for a new myth, one that is inclusive of homosexuality. As Wetmore argues, this occurs through the use of Eshu, a trickster god who is able to transform and create, just as McCraney himself does. For an audience that does not know the Yoruba myths, McCraney's revisions exist as new myths, with as much legitimacy as other myths. This use of the trickster is also emphasized in Christy Stanlake's analysis of Tomson Highway's *Dry Lips Oughta Move to Kapuskasing* and Amelia Howe Kritzer's discussion of Caryl Churchill's *The Skriker*. In each case the trickster character guides the story and transforms the myths to suit the ideological tendencies of the more contemporary time and place: for Highway to subvert the patriarchal Christian and Native American myths that allow for male violence in Native culture, and for Churchill to demonstrate the insidious power dynamics of Thatcherian England and the ways they stifled normal growth and development. Myth here is revised to be both highly contemporary but also, as Kritzer states, "beyond its immediate historical moment" (122).

The most useful chapters in thinking about approaches to analyzing revision are those that investigate works through a materialist and historiographical framework, focusing on what Herb Wylie, quoted in Laura Snyder's chapter on Sharon Pollock's play *Blood Relations*, calls "a view of history as the product of story-making" (216). Through this lens, Lizzie Borden's history depends upon the act of storytelling for its efficacy, and thus the myth changes according to the way the story is told. Anthony Ellis's chapter illuminates the metanarrative layers of storytelling in Martin McDonagh's *The Pillowman* and how they traffic not only in myths about art and writers but also in the use of myth and fairy tale to relate messages that will only be available to certain readers or audiences, and are in fact meant to be understood differently by those different audiences. So Katurian's one published story, a revision of the Pied Piper narrative, might have been read by those who published it as a subversive piece of political critique, while presumably the authorities would not understand, or at least not be able to prove, any kind of political protest or incitement.

The issue of audience knowledge of a given work's source material is repeated through this collection. However, most of the essays maintain a literary stance toward the issue of adaptation, relegating spectator interpretation to the margins, if it is mentioned at all. The efficacy of these revisions of myth, folklore, and legend in drama depends, ultimately, on their audiences, and in reading the collection in its entirety I came to wonder about the idea that any of these myths have even a fragmentary "essential meaning" beyond the fact of their continual revision. The range of approaches in this collection clearly shows that each approach is individually unable to bring together the vast types and reasons for revising this material; however, several of them help expand our understandings as we continue to revise our own methodologies for analyzing myths and culture.

—PETER A. CAMPBELL
Ramapo College of New Jersey

Theatre & Mind. By Bruce McConachie. Basingstoke and New York: Palgrave Macmillan, 2013. vii + 82 pp. £5.99/$10.00 paper.

Bruce McConachie's *Theatre & Mind* is a new addition to the Palgrave Macmillan Theatre & series edited by Jen Harvie and Dan Rebellato. Each petite volume is intended to provide a general readership with a straightforward introduction to theatre's intersections with other fields of study. While envisioned for an undergraduate readership, *Theatre & Mind* serves as more than an overview of the field of cognitive studies in theatre; rather, it is a proposal to a new generation of practitioners and scholars to consider investigating the cognitive foundations of theatre. McConachie presents a compelling argument for cognitive studies in theatre, connecting the biological cognitive processes of human play and neocortical brain development to the processes intrinsic to acting and spectating.

McConachie begins with a discussion of the title word "mind," demonstrating not only its insufficiencies to describe the intended topic, but also our problematic cultural conceptions of it.

He notes that the word "mind" is problematic on two counts: (1) it is not indicative of the active process of cognition and consequently strips the mind of its interactive properties; and (2) it suggests a Cartesian separation between the body and the mind, between feeling and thinking, a notion that is antithetical to both cognitive studies and theatre. The principle that frames this book and the larger body of cognitive scholarship is that the mind, like theatre, is both embodied and interactive, which seems to make both fields natural corollaries to each other. McConachie advocates that theatre scholarship and practice must move beyond poststructuralist paradigms and behaviorist perspectives in order to join the current cognitive conversation, and more importantly to move our understanding of theatre and its processes forward.

The book draws from McConachie's larger body of work and that of other leading scholars in cognitive studies. His essay is organized around three main areas: playing, acting, and spectating, which guide the reader from the fundamental cognitive functions in human evolution into in-depth examinations of the same cognitive processes in actors and spectators of theatre. Through analyzing theatrical processes, McConachie demonstrates how cognitive operations inform theatre participation and practice. While just breaking the surface of cognitive studies, he maintains the integrity of its complex ideas and makes their concepts comprehensible to a general reader. McConachie also provides a list of publications that informed his essay, including works by both prominent cognitive studies scholars and performance theorists.

McConachie introduces readers to the fundamental cognitive functions in a concise tutorial on human evolution, focusing on the key cognitive theories involving the processes of empathy, emotions, conceptual blending, and role-playing, each of which is a critical survival skill that evolved out of hominid and human play. Starting with the impact of play on the human brain, he leads the reader through 50,000 years of cognitive development and demonstrates that our ability to pretend has allowed us to move beyond developmental play and into theatrical performance.

Furthering his argument on the role of cognitive processes in theatre, McConachie then weaves cognitive operations into acting processes. He challenges the commonly held binary assumption that actor training is either mental or physical and argues instead that it is an embodied practice. He advocates that the methods of Jacques LeCoq and Michael Chekhov are favorable approaches as they link intentional physical practice with embodied emotional expression. He reminds the reader that the concepts explained earlier in terms of human evolution are central to the processes of acting. Improvisation and rehearsal require the additional cognitive process of decision control, another skill necessary for human survival as well as creating the embodied art of theatre.

The final section of this concentrated volume focuses on the spectator's processes of selective conceptual blending between actor and character, emotional engagement with narratives, and navigating individual and cultural memory. Entwined throughout his examination of the spectator is a thorough analysis of Tony Kushner's *Angels in America,* which helps to illustrate the multiple and complex processes at work in the spectator during a single performance of a play. McConachie situates the spectator within a larger performance network. While this network is grounded in evolutionary development from the foundational individual neural networks to broader social networks, the concept bears some similarities to the social constructions of poststructuralist thought. McConachie's closing remarks return to his original proposal to the reader to consider the adoption of cognitive science as a mode of inquiry into the processes of theatre.

Theatre & Mind is an excellent primer on the cognitive foundations of theatre. Practically speaking, it could easily be used as a companion text in broad-based theatre surveys, introductory performance studies courses, or literature seminars. The book's connections between cognition, evolution, and theatrical processes are bold, plausible, and intriguing. McConachie strikes a good balance in content. While providing adequate depth into the study and application of cognition in theatre, he scratches just enough of the surface to spark the reader's curiosity for further exploration into the field.

—SHAWNA MEFFERD CARROLL
State University of New York at Plattsburgh

Audrey Wood and the Playwrights. By Milly S. Barranger. Palgrave Studies in Theatre and Performance History. New York: Palgrave Macmillan, 2013. xiv + 220 pp. $85.00 cloth.

In *Audrey Wood and the Playwrights*, Milly S. Barranger documents the life's work of a play agent who shaped American theatre over the course of forty years, until she slipped into a coma in 1981 at the age of seventy-six. Rather than follow a strict chronology, Barranger structures Wood's biography playwright-by-playwright in order to focus on Wood's developmental influence on the writers she represented. As the daughter of a successful theatre manager, Wood grew up immersed in the theatrical world and developed the ability to sense intuitively whether or not a play held commercial value. Barranger begins with Wood's early professional experience, from initiating contact with George Pierce Baker seeking names of up-and-coming playwrights to her business and marital partnership with casting agent William Liebling. As the most famous literary agent to represent American playwrights, her life deserves documentation; writers such as Tennessee Williams and Maurice Valency dedicated their published works to her in gratitude, she received the Richard L. Coe Award in 1981 for her contribution to the theatre, and a stage at the Jack Lawrence Theatre in New York City bears her name.

Material about topics such as intimate relationships or personal weaknesses found in typical biographies is missing here; instead, we discover the writers Wood advised, the plays she brought to production, and the criticism she offered. Barranger acknowledges the difficulties of writing about a person on whom so little documentation survives and focuses instead on Wood's instrumentality in linking playwrights to producers and directors, noting how "the agent is the unheralded handmaiden who facilitates the writer's career and sees to the affairs of business with a mixture of compassion, wisdom, and efficiency" (171). Barranger concedes that an authors' agent is largely "invisible" to the actors, the critics, and the audience; at times, it seems that Wood is absent from her own book. In one chapter, for example, detailing how three of her clients—Bertolt Brecht, Yip Harburg, and Jay Gorney—testified before the House Committee on Un-American Activities, no mention is made of Wood's perspective on the proceedings. Much of the book's excitement comes from anecdotal stories of working with her husband, a casting agent, to find the right director and actors for specific plays, such as when they convinced Elia Kazan to direct Tennessee Williams's *A Streetcar Named Desire* and recommended Marlon Brando for the leading role.

Since the agent resides primarily on the sidelines of her writers' accomplishments, Wood's professional success can only be appreciated by witnessing all the behind-the-scenes coaching she did, and Barranger's book provides a long-overdue summation. She explores how Wood approached each writer as a potential client and traces their ensuing relationship over the years. Wood had an innate ability to determine a successful play by "a green light flashing in her head" (25), and she would write playwrights succinct feedback indicating her belief in their talent. Nonthreatening to insecure playwrights, she possessed a soft but brisk demeanor, and she negotiated tirelessly with directors, producers, and the burgeoning Hollywood film industry to ensure her clients got the best deal for production rights and royalties. Her propriety appeared in the way she dressed and conducted herself, including once reproving Charles Laughton for receiving her one day lying on his bed with rumpled trousers, unbuttoned shirt, and bowl of fruit balanced on his chest. She maintained rules about reading manuscripts herself rather than having the playwright read them aloud to her (as they frequently offered to do) and insisted that no actor receive billing above a play's title.

Investing in an artist's creative output is a precarious business, and several times Wood experienced authors turning against her and blaming her for their soured careers, most notably Tennessee Williams and William Inge. She showered attention on Williams. In addition to arranging his domestic and international rights and royalties, she paid his monthly rent in New York and his taxes, made charitable contributions on his behalf, and monitored his sister's personal bank account. Thus it was particularly hurtful when he accused her of neglecting his career and ended their relationship. She nurtured Inge's career, too, and assisted his entry into rehabilitation for alcoholism, but he later blamed her for the poor reviews *A Loss of Roses* received. We get little insight into her hurt feelings, though, beyond a key line: "In the theater, what seems a rational solution often does not apply to the emotional problems of creative people" (94), illustrating the agent's difficult position drawing negotiations between industry and imaginative activity. Although Barranger quotes Wood sparingly, colleagues and friends of Wood noted her indomitable spirit, perspicacious wit, and blunt speaking style. An example of her fortitude and financial savvy occurs when her husband's illness necessitated that he relocate; she took the lead in searching for a university appointment in a warm environment conducive to his health and quietly initiated the sale of the "Tennessee Williams–Audrey Wood" correspondence to the University of Texas. In a later chapter, Barranger suggests Wood's businesslike demeanor belied her deep affinity for her clients when she draws a connection between Brian Friel's play *Faith Healer* and Wood's own understanding of artists' periodic loss of confidence.

During her forty-year career, Audrey Wood represented over a hundred writers, many of them noteworthy for challenging theatrical norms. Her role as an author's agent shaped midcentury theatrical experimentation, for without her support certain important plays might not have been staged. Robert Anderson's *Tea and Sympathy*, with its adulterous relationship and implied homosexuality, had a successful run after Wood found the right producing body (Playwrights' Producing Company) and director (Elia Kazan). She recognized

Audrey Hepburn as the ideal fit for the mermaid in Maurice Valency's translation of *Ondine*, and she convinced Shirley Booth to perform in Inge's *Come Back, Little Sheba* (Booth would eventually win an Oscar for the film adaptation). She determined needed changes in the original production of Arthur Kopit's *Wings*, and she gathered a production team responsive to the monologic format of Friel's *Faith Healer*. Because of her astute efforts, plays unusual in their structure or content received sensitive productions and found receptive audiences. Ultimately, Barranger effectively proves that Wood should be credited for her part in shaping the contemporary American stage.

—MIRIAM M. CHIRICO
Eastern Connecticut State University

Acts of Manhood: The Performance of Masculinity on the American Stage, 1828–1865. By Karl M. Kippola. New York: Palgrave Macmillan, 2012. 272 pp. + 19 illustrations. $98.00 cloth, $85.95 paper.

In *Acts of Manhood: The Performance of Masculinity on the American Stage, 1828–1865*, Karl M. Kippola examines thoroughly how and why nineteenth-century theatre audiences and artists, in particular Edwin Forrest (1806–1872) and Edwin Booth (1833–1893), replicated and manipulated idealized manly models. Along with his exploration of antebellum America through analyses of "dramatic, literary, and instructional" texts that produced and reproduced the American man in this period, Kippola also considers in his book "archival materials, political cartoons, popular novels, portraiture, conduct manuals, melodramas, and burlesques to trace the shifting meanings and signifiers of manhood" (7). To redress a dearth of book-length work on the dynamics of white masculinities on the antebellum American stage, Kippola thoroughly reconstructs Forrest's and Booth's lives and works, situating them within their historical, political, and social contexts, and linking their masculinities and identities to issues of nationality, race, culture, class, gender, and education.

In the introduction, "A New Race of Men," Kippola provides a brief examination of pre-1828 dramatic and performance practices, surveying the influences of John Philip Kemble's (1757–1823) and Edmund Kean's (1789–1833) acting styles as well as the dominance of British actors on the American stage, such as Thomas Abthorpe Cooper (1776–1849), George Frederick Cooke (1756–1812), William Charles Macready (1793–1873), and Edwin Booth's father, Junius

Brutus Booth (1796–1852). As context for the rest of the study, and drawing from Judith Butler's and Michael Kimmel's theoretical debates on the "multiplicities of masculinities" (2), Kippola also establishes in the introduction that "far from being stable and fixed, masculinities are man-made, fluid constructs, which are continually adjusting to evolving expectations and demands" (2), and that his book focuses primarily on two conflicting constructions and representations of masculinity: "*intellectual self-control* and *passionate action*" (3). Throughout the book, Kippola argues convincingly that Forrest's "rugged individualism" and Booth's "effete intellectualism" (5) represent these two opposed strains of manhood.

The book is organized into five chapters designed to map these different representations of white manhood. In the book's first chapter, "Act Like a Man: Images and Rhetoric of Reconstructed Manhood," Kippola examines how public figures adapted their performance of gender to meet the changing needs of the country. Addressing a wide range of contributing factors—from rhetorical style to political cartoons and portraiture—for understanding the antebellum masculine performance, Kippola looks into the performance of masculinity of the "most visible and influential figures of the period" (22) from John Quincy Adams (1767–1848) to Andrew Jackson (1767–1845). The book's first chapter establishes a context for examining the relation between the performance of manhood in the public sphere and that represented on the American stage.

In the following three chapters, "'A Glorious Image of Unperverted Manhood': Edwin Forrest as Masculine Ideal," "A Masculine Identity Worth Dying For: The Astor Place Riot," and "Decorum and Delicacy: The Feminized Manliness of Edwin Booth," Kippola investigates Forrest's and Booth's opposing strains of masculinity on and off the stage. Kippola introduces Forrest as America's most popular American-born actor from 1828 to the late 1850s, resulting from his appeal to working-class audiences and the staging of works that promoted nationalism and represented distinctively American masculine characters. To support his analysis, Kippola examines Robert T. Conrad's *Jack Cade* (1835), staged by Forrest in 1841, and focuses on how Forrest's manly model inspired emulation by his audience. Kippola also investigates Forrest's personal life, including the tensions between Forrest and William Charles Macready that led to the Astor Place Riot, "both a political and theatrical spectacle…of nineteenth century masculinity" (92). Contrastingly, Kippola studies Booth "both as a 'feminine' and a 'masculine' figure" (117), who, in the late 1850s, eventually supplanted Forrest's popularity as the country's most renowned actor. Kippola analyzes Booth's masculinity as a reflection of a changing vision of idealized American manhood, increasingly "built on refinement, repression, and sentiment" (117) and the accompanying transformation of the theatre experience from riotous to thoughtful.

In the book's final chapter, "Impossible Genial: The Masculine Transformations of John McCullough," Kippola examines the career of McCullough (1832–1885); despite being Forrest's protégé, McCullough's manly model differed considerably from his mentor's. In spite of emulating Forrest's external performance, McCullough's manly model incorporated instead "simplicity, nobility and moderation" (147) to meet the gradual changes of his middle-class audience and its desire to adjust behavior to achieve social acceptance. Kippola examines McCullough as a transitional figure "between the unrefined muscularity of Forrest and the intellectual gentility of Booth" (170).

Kippola's book ends with an examination of masculine performance beyond the Civil War, in particular of the processes of exclusion of Native American, African American, nonwhite immigrant, and lower-class models of masculinity as necessary to the construction of a privileged white manhood.

On balance, in *Acts of Manhood*, the first book-length exploration of masculinity on the antebellum American stage, Karl M. Kippola demonstrates the importance of Edwin Forrest and Edwin Booth in making visible the struggle to define and establish models of masculinity. Critically engaging, theoretically stimulating, and comprehensive in scope, Kippola's examination of how these particular theatre artists generated and manipulated models of the ideal man on the Antebellum American stage makes a valuable contribution to theatre and men's studies.

—FRANCISCO COSTA
University of East Anglia

Theatre Noise: The Sound of Performance. Edited by Lynne Kendrick and David Roesner. Newcastle upon Tyne: Cambridge Scholars Publishing, 2011. x + 227 pp. $59.99 cloth.

This book begins by acknowledging the simple binary of hearing and seeing implicit in the history and practice of theater, a binary that also motivated some of the founding texts in the field of sound studies, such as R. Murray Schafer's *The Soundscape*, first published in 1977. *Theatre Noise: The Sound of Performance* seeks to move beyond this binary by questioning the concept and phenomenon of "noise" and its ramifications in live theatrical performance. Editors Lynne Kendrick and David Roesner note that noise is often defined "*ex negativo*," as that which it is not: not sound, not music, neither signal, nor *logos* (xv). Drawing from musicology, film theory, the philosophy and sociology of sound and voice, and phenomenologies of listening, their interdisciplinary project seeks to locate within the sonic encounter of the theater event an investigation of the possible meanings and performative implications of "certain aspects of theatre noise, including those that might be excessive, unwanted or unintended, not meant or not meaningful" (xvi). French philosopher Michel Serres's words resound (he is quoted and referenced several times) throughout this anthology: "There is noise in the subject, there is noise in the object. There is noise in the observed, there is noise in the observer. In the transmitter and in the receiver, in the entire space of the channel... It is in being and in knowing. It is in the real, and in the sign, already" (*Genesis* 61, qtd. 12). As a basis from which to question what sound design, production, and reception do and have done in theater, this statement's resonance is put to provocative use in this book.

In their introduction, Kendrick and Roesner make the case for theater as "a unique habitat for noise" (xv), a location that highlights the "friction between signal and receiver, between sound and meaning, between eye and ear, between silence and utterance, between hearing and listening" (xv). Theater noise emphasizes the *process* of experiencing a performance, the chiasmic relationship between what is listened to and how it is heard. Noise is not unique to theater, but Kendrick and Roesner argue that theater provides an especially potent place to question what noise—in its actual acoustic sense and as metaphor—is and does.

The book contains eighteen chapters written mostly by European and French Canadian theatre designers, directors, performers, musicians, and researchers from a variety of academic disciplines, arranged not by theme or topic but rather like an "audio patch bay where a diverse range of inputs and outputs are interconnected in multiple ways with coloured cable" (xvii) or like using the "shuffle" function on one's playlist. While perhaps conceptually clever, this method of arrangement may not immediately engage the reader interested only in a specific subtopic, such as voice or silence. However, in the book's introduction Kendrick and Roesner offer something like a roadmap to the many connections possible in the book. They make a conscious effort to frame the project as a provocation to further thought, research, and experimentation, doing so through contradictions, overlaps, loops, and polyrhythms. When ideas presented in one essay return in a different context, becoming the background noise from which a new chapter's signal may emerge, the book's method and topic come together. Themes addressed in the book include silence; the materiality, embodiment, and vocality of theater noise; semiotic aspects of theater noise; relations between theater noise and both sight and site; and audiences and the act of listening in the theater. The chapters give penetrating treatments to material ranging from issues of technology in the history of theatrical sound (Larrue, Collins, Vautrin, Roesner, and Bovet) to differing conceptions of voice and its possibilities in the theater (Lagaay, Myers, Verstraete, Dunbar, and Kendrick).

For the reader for whom the topic might be a new area of scholarship, the first chapter, written by Ross Brown, offers a brief but excellent overview of the challenges and opportunities offered by theater sound. The first crucial issue is aurality. As Brown explains, "Any meaning made and exchanged through sounding and hearing is contingent, always, on an aural presence at the eventual end of the signal chain" (4). The implication of sound's necessary interpretation is that what is understood is always dependent on a cultural framework. One is only capable of hearing what one's cultural background has prepared one to hear, creating the "potential to mishear" (4). In addition, hearing runs continuously while one listens. Any signal that is actively attended to emerges from a background of noise (or silence) that is passively heard. Accordingly, "Sound must therefore be understood as ontologically distracting, and theatre must be understood, not as an uninterrupted programme of reception, but as a continual oscillation between engagement and distraction" (6). However, Brown's broad conception of theatre noise, which "valorises the background...the noise that is an inevitability of sentience" (11), is called into question in George Home-Cook's detailed phenomenology of listening, where "background noise is not the 'world' but the *ground of perception*" (98), and in Kendrick's own chapter, focusing on what she calls "applied aurality" in theatre by deaf artists. Using Jean-Luc Nancy's *Listening*, Kendrick writes: "This theory of subjectivity through resounding, not necessarily hearing, reveals how deaf actors might perform their own subjective 'non-hearing' identity" (186).

Theatre sound as an area of critical scholarly focus has only just begun. *Theatre Noise: The Sound of Performance* attends to and theorizes recent and past works in the theatre that have and are self-consciously bringing attention to sound that is excessive or unexplainable and to the multiplicity of ways to hear and listen and, in so doing, is helping to establish the field's foundation. Noise in the theatre is not that which gets in the way of understanding the event and its cultural repercussions, but instead may be attended to as culturally, philosophically, and politically significant. Let us hope that this excellent volume is a catalyst for further work in this burgeoning area of theatre and performance studies.

—DANIEL C. DENNIS
Ohio University

BOOK REVIEWS

The Cambridge Introduction to Christopher Marlowe. By Tom Rutter. New York: Cambridge University Press, 2012. xiv + 149 pp. $75.00 cloth, $19.95 paper.

In *The Cambridge Introduction to Christopher Marlowe*, Tom Rutter neatly guides the reader to a solid understanding of the life and works of this seminal Elizabethan playwright. With his deep passion for and knowledge of Marlowe, Rutter crafts a series of fascinating chapters using an expressive writing style.

Rather than gravitating primarily to Marlowe's death and *Doctor Faustus*, Rutter engages with the playwright's full body of work and the shaping events of his life. Instead of a chronological approach, he arranges the chapters to best illustrate the historical contexts of each subject. Rutter gives *Tamburlaine*, *Doctor Faustus*, and *Edward II* their own chapters, as they require the most contextualization. *The Jew of Malta* and *The Massacre at Paris* are linked in a single chapter via their subject matter, and *Dido, Queen of Carthage* gets grouped with his poetry because together they represent frequently sidelined aspects of Marlowe's work. The most discussed play in the book is not *Faustus* but *Tamburlaine*; Rutter argues its major significance to the Elizabethan theatre as well as its importance as a platform for Marlowe's dramatic voice; he wants contemporary readers to understand it as a better representation of Marlowe's critical place in the Elizabethan theatrical world than *Faustus*. These chapters are bookended by an opening chapter on Marlowe's life and his historical environment and a concluding chapter exploring the approaches taken to his work by selected critics and theatre professionals following his death.

One of the major draws of the book is Rutter's ability to provide the introductory reader with a historical lens through which to conceptualize the religious and political atmosphere in which the playwright lived. In two pages (9–10), he develops a succinct view of the Protestant Reformation that colors the cultural climate in which Marlowe's works were witnessed. Rutter devotes much analysis to the political implications of representing national leaders on stage in the sixteenth century. His thorough exploration of the stakes involved in representing religious viewpoints outside of the Church of England—whether Catholic, Muslim, Jewish, or atheist—as well as English nationalist sentiments following the defeat of the Spanish armada in 1588 convinces the reader of the visionary, poignant, and sometimes tolerant ideas Marlowe conceived in an era marred by religious turmoil and political uncertainty.

Perhaps Rutter's most exciting revelation is how much we actually know about Christopher Marlowe. Due to his financial and legal troubles (perhaps troublemaking is more accurate), a treasure trove of legal documents exposes a great number of certainties that help us understand the innovative playwright. Rutter points out Marlowe's brushes with the law as evidence for his argument that Marlowe's writings deliberately oppose the value systems inherent in the Elizabethan era. The introduction includes a four-page section of key dates spanning seventy-five years, most taken from legal documents. This is incredibly helpful since the book, for the most part, is organized to focus on one or more works of Marlowe rather than a given time period; the chronology allows the reader to accurately place Marlowe's work in a proper historical context.

Rutter carefully navigates the waters of comparison encircling Marlowe and Shakespeare. Instead of crafting a "Marlowe is better" head-on collision, Rutter often acknowledges his own admiration for Shakespeare while simultaneously examining how Marlowe's writings and, perhaps just as importantly, the Elizabethan public's reactions to Marlowe's writings, influenced the Bard. Shakespeare receives only cursory mentions, used in *The Cambridge Introduction* to better help the reader relate to Marlowe, due in large part to the reader's presumably more familiar relationship with Shakespeare's plays and poetry. Shakespeare's indebtedness to Marlowe is made clear; Marlowe did not need Shakespeare as much as Shakespeare needed him, regardless of how today's readers and theatregoers may conceive of these Elizabethan writers.

My only real criticism stems from the absence of synopses of Marlowe's plays. As this text is titled an introduction, the inclusion of synopses could serve to orient Marlowe novices and perhaps even those revisiting his work. It is possible that this was an editorial decision, but it is strange considering Rutter himself notes: "The teaching of Marlowe tends to focus on the plays, in particular *Tamburlaine*, *Doctor Faustus*, *The Jew of Malta* and *Edward II*, with the result that his other works can get sidelined" (99). At least the sidelined works should have received such synopses (by the author's estimation, *Dido, Queen of Carthage* and *The Massacre at Paris* fit this bill, not to mention his poetry).

This introductory text could fit into any graduate or upper-level undergraduate course on Elizabethan literature, Elizabethan history, theatre history, or even creative writing, as Rutter often explores how Marlowe expertly crafted blank verse. It compliments any library seeking a comprehensive look at the major playwrights of the Elizabethan era. It also functions as an object lesson to individuals focused on the classic Renaissance mode of learning. Marlowe did not limit himself to one literary area or even one profession. The fact that *The Cambridge Introduction to Christopher Marlowe* transcends disciplines (creative writing, history, literature, theatre) provides readers with a sense of the standards of education in the sixteenth century and how they shaped the art, literature, and the overall cultural fabric of the Elizabethan era, specifically through the period's most notorious author.

—RODNEY DONAHUE
Texas Tech University

Stage Designers in Early Twentieth-Century America: Artists, Activists, Cultural Critics. By Christin Essin. New York: Palgrave Macmillan, 2012. xiii + 200 pp. $85.00 hardcover.

Relatively little has been written on American stage design, and even less on the theoretical, social, cultural, and political underpinnings of designers' practices. Published studies are generally limited to coffee-table books of renderings and photographs of the work of seminal designers (i.e., Boris Aronson, Jo Mielziner, and Orville K. Larson's multidesigner study); a few autobiographies (e.g., Lee Simonson); mentions of designers in texts on production companies or on producers/directors; and practical "how to" design and technology texts. Drawing inspiration from Arnold Aronson, Marvin Carlson, Una Chaudhuri, and others, and focusing not on rudimentary aspects of stage design like drafting and rendering but on the designer's interaction with economic, social, and political movements, Christin Essin's *Stage Designers in Early Twentieth-Century America* begins to fill this void. She successfully sustains her strategy of examining the design artist as activist, author, cultural critic, entrepreneur—even cartographer (literally, metaphorically, and semioticly)—as she moves from chapter to chapter, situating designers within the intellectual and cultural contexts of their time.

Essin argues convincingly for her choice of case studies: (1) to recuperate lesser known designers (e.g., Aline Bernstein, Joseph Urban), (2) to contextualize from a historiographical perspective the extratheatrical work of design icons (e.g., Robert Edmond Jones's Paterson Strike Pageant poster and Norman Bel Geddes's pre-Disney *Futurama*, World War II models, and innovations in department store window dressing), and (3) to offer alternative analyses of canonical pieces (i.e., Mielziner's designs for *Death of a Salesman*). A short introduction, "Design as Cultural History," precedes a body organized into five chapters: "The Designer as Author," "The Designer as Cultural Critic," "The Designer as Activist," "The Designer as Entrepreneur," and "The Designer as Cultural Cartographer."

Chapter 1 emphasizes how designers' works reached audiences not only in attendance at productions but through the written word, as practicing American stage designers began to articulate their theories in publications like *Theatre Arts Monthly*. Although she did not publish design criticism or theory, Aline Bernstein is included in this chapter because of the ways in which she claimed authorship through autobiography and fiction—including a children's book—reaching a different and arguably large readership outside the theatre profession.

In chapter 2, Essin deftly explicates nuances of the New Stagecraft—more abstract or nonrealistic styles of production, initiated on the Continent and first popularized in the U.S. by Robert Edmund Jones, "father" of American stage design. She masterfully negotiates a style conundrum as she explicates how Belasco-type realism could thrive in the face of modernism. Essin implies that designers in the 1910s and 1920s, when the field was new in the U.S., were selective in their choices of scenic elements, foreshadowing what later would be termed "selective realism," exemplified by Jo Mielziner's work. She gently massages longstanding principles of the production process such as serving the playwright's intentions and supporting directorial concepts, stating that "designs convey meaning guided by *but* beyond them… By bringing their own impressions of a landscape to a production, designers imbue dramatic texts with meanings not necessarily present before being translated to the stage" (55). These ideas resurface later in the book, in chapter 5, when Essin examines *South Pacific* in light of not only how Mielziner's initial watercolor influenced Hammerstein's lyrics, but how the designer's romanticized interpretation of the Pacific perpetuated exoticism of the geographic region.

Chapter 3 examines the work of designer-activists: Jones's Paterson Strike Pageant designs, including his World War I poster, and Bernstein's community outreach work at the Neighborhood Playhouse, emphasizing the notion of designer-as-worker with Howard Bay at the Federal Theater Project. Here, and throughout the book, thick and evocative descriptions of production designs, exhibits, and projects guide the reader through Essin's readings of stage designs, not merely as blueprints for production or as works of art, but as projections of cultural and social ideals. I might quibble with the paucity of illustrations were I not well aware of the cost involved in incorporating renderings and production photographs in a scholarly manuscript.

In chapter 4, Essin addresses substantive ways in which designers affect a broader consumer audience. In defining *scenographic entrepreneurship* as "a process of dramaturgical interpretation, visual representation, and material practices" (133), Essin alludes to the similarities between design for the stage and design for the marketplace. Her examples include the influence of Urban's

Follies designs on bedroom décor in terms of both line and color ("Urban blue") and Bel Geddes's product design exemplified by his invention of the white stove, ubiquitous in post–World War II kitchens across the U.S.

Including analyses of *South Pacific* and *Fiddler on the Roof*, Essin's chapter on the designer-cartographer intertwines semiotics, geography, intercultural communication, gender theory, and diaspora studies. Her phrase "scenographic cartography" evokes "the stage as a canvas for orienting and territorializing" (171), both figuratively and literally, through the designer's representation of place.

Stage Designers in Early Twentieth-Century America exhibits extensive and outstanding archival research, critical insight, unique perspectives on the material covered, and clear, fluid prose. Essin offers a model for future scholars to apply in design history research. From a cultural studies standpoint, she draws attention to the designer as participant in and reflection of the sociopolitical landscape in which they reside.

Essin's study reaches beyond a niche readership of those who study, practice, and/or teach stage design. As she emphasizes, design history, with its attendant artifacts—production renderings, models, photographs, programs, and so on—has been overlooked, even though it is a "gold mine" for theatre historians, practitioners, and theoreticians alike. Essin's work is also valuable to cultural historians and to American history scholars who may bypass the traces of theatrical production as viable evidence in examining the past. Essin's employment of vocabulary from union activism, marketing, and geography illustrate her cross-disciplinary approach to theatre studies.

Essin's book is a call to action for recognition of the vitality of stage designers—past, present, and future—yes, as artists and craftspeople, but more importantly as citizen-artists who offer lenses through which to view a multiplicity of critical and cultural intersections and encounters.

—ANNE FLETCHER
Southern Illinois University

British Avant-Garde Theatre. By Claire Warden. New York: Palgrave Macmillan, 2012. 232 pp. $85 hardcover.

Claire Warden's most welcome addition to the history of British alternative theatre closes with a discussion of modern documentary theatre and the expressionist aspects of writings by Sarah Kane and Howard Barker that show the lingering influence of a "distinctly British, distinctly theatrical" strand of avant-gardism from the early twentieth century (4). In particular, the expressionist aesthetic vocabulary and social commentary noted by Michael Billington in Simon McBurney's 2010 production of *A Dog's Heart* (a Russian opera based on the novel by Mikhail Bulgakov) allows Warden to return to *The Dog Beneath the Skin*, a 1936 collaboration between Christopher Isherwood and W. H. Auden performed by London's Group Theatre, which receives close analysis at the start of her study and becomes a touchstone in subsequent chapters. Both plays concern a human being who comes to see the world through a dog's perspective and therefore must consider radical social change. These shows represent a theatrical modality that for Warden distills the central avant-garde quest to promote both political and aesthetic change.

Joint Stock Theatre Company performed Howard Barker's fragmented tragedy *The Power of the Dog: Moments in History and Anti-History*, which is set in Stalinist Russia and whose title also invites a comparison with Bulgakov's anti-Stalinist satire, in 1984. Warden's frame for her study resolutely sidesteps looking at aesthetically and politically pointed work in this range of the century's chronology—the period she covers runs from 1914 to 1956—but the heart of her discussion runs from T. S. Eliot's *Sweeny Agonistes* (1934) and Auden's *The Dance of Death* (1935) to Ewan MacColl's *Uranium 235* (1946). Her concern with the status of the category of historical avant-garde work today motivates her final thoughts, but her real goal lies in analyzing a specific body of work from the Group, the Worker's Theatre Movement, the Theatre Union, and Theatre Workshop in order to narrate a trajectory made invisible by a lack of models about a British avant-garde sensibility in theatre to parallel the work done along those lines in regard to poetry, the visual arts, and music (6).

Overall, her tight focus serves her as she navigates distinctions between literary modernism and a theatrical avant-garde and faces down the awful and ill-informed commonplace (see, for example, Christopher Innes's *Modern British Drama: The Twentieth Century*) that the British theatre saw no avant-garde movement. The depth of Warden's documentation about specific shows and the relationship of her case studies to her theoretical framework about performance-based histories bear fruit, especially in her demonstration of dialogues between local theatre scenes and innovations overseas. This is an excellent piece of scholarship—confident, detailed, and bold. The only losses attributable to this model concern two issues: the porousness between events of the 1920s and the 1930s and Warden's vocabulary for analyzing the avant-garde sensibilities, acknowledged or unacknowledged, of work across the 1970s and

1980s, as with Joint Stock mentioned previously. Warden's attentiveness to the impossibility of hard boundaries around ongoing aesthetic dialogues is strong, but in her second chapter, her focus consigns events and artists of the teens and 1920s, like Edward Gordon Craig or Adolph Appia, to the status of antecedents in a way that feels disjunctive from their ongoing influence.

In tune with contemporary historiographical models that are as concerned with rupture as they are with continuity, Warden favors the idea of rhizomatic relationships of events in which links and fractured genealogies emerge and diverge. Her chapters run not by chronologies or themes but by categories of performance elements. In exploring the characteristics of British avant-garde theatre, she first considers approaches to dramatic structure. Here, she pulls apart the issues of plot and naturalism that usually drive dramatic categories and focuses on techniques of fragmentation. She connects ideas about naturalism to Brechtian, episodic structures and draws attention to a British trajectory of epic or nonlinear naturalism, noting how naturalism grounds progressive political critique and how nonlinearity matters to the avant-garde project of transforming audience perception (50–54).

Chapter 2 focuses on staging conventions and reading space as political. Warden tracks the use of platforms and constructivist structures, the use of projection and lighting innovations, and the prevalence of cages and prisons in avant-garde scenography. In this section, she is particularly good at detailing how groups "were solving theatrical (and, in some ways, ethical) problems in comparable ways" despite diverse points of departure (20). Warden's third chapter turns to language use and follows up on her early problematizing of the idea that there are distinct "poetic" and "political" traditions in British writing. Working through issues of canonicity and adaptation and tactics of declamation, dialect, and verse, Warden smartly distinguishes how often experiments with language undertaken in a working-class register are deemed political while those done in an upper-class mode are considered poetic. Warden also provides an excellent analysis of the use of taps, knocks, and drums in experimental dramaturgy to complement a general understanding of schrei performance in expressionism and unpacks the dynamics of word and image in regard to avant-garde texts. Warden closes her study by looking at the categories of character and genre, and her work here on cross-generational influences, intertextuality, and performance genealogies vindicates her decision to focus on a versatile and multifaceted performative history, in the sense Erika Fischer-Lichte uses it—that is, a history that is "dependent on reciprocal, shifting relationships between audience and actor, and the various elements of the *mise-en-scène*" (20).

This study accomplishes several feats in addition to establishing the presence of British avant-garde theatre: it provides exemplary readings of how the work of Brecht, Meyerhold, and Piscator circulated in international influence; it frames Rupert Doone as a figure in need of further study; and it establishes Ewan MacColl as a figure to stand alongside the strong body of Joan Littlewood scholarship published in the last decade by Nadine Holdworth. Warden acknowledges the troublesome nature of her subject matter: some early-century avant-garde work can seem dated and juvenile; it can be hard to provide a total vision about a sector held together by nothing more than the sense of being "united in being against" (94), yet she has succeeded in writing a sophisticated, integrated treatment that conveys the urgency, heterogeneity, and necessity of such theatre history.

—SARA FREEMAN
University of Puget Sound

Readings in Performance and Ecology. Edited by Wendy Arons and Theresa J. May. New York: Palgrave Macmillan, 2012. 243 pp. $95.00 hardcover.

Throughout history, nature has certainly created a lot of drama, but is nature drama? As part of a larger conversation on nature and culture, the editors of this volume readily admit that the arts, especially theatre, "have traditionally been conceived as the activity that most divides humans from 'nature'"(1). As such, the essays in this book focus on rethinking the relationships that exist or are possible between theatre and nature. They term this approach an "ecological perspective," hoping to inspire both artists and scholars to pursue related work. The essays in the book employ a primarily materialist framework in order to address ways in which theatre has used "nature" as part of its content (part of an approach in literary studies coined "ecocriticism"), together with exploring considerations of the nonhuman in performance and what theatre means and does to the environment. The book is divided into thematic sections with essays that "speak to, and sometimes challenge, one another," hoping to engage the reader in an "open-ended and lively debate" (7).

The five individual sections of the book suggest how an ecocentric lens might be applied to many different fields within theatre. The first parts, "Ecocriticism and Dramatic Literature" and "Animals and/in Performance," focus on examining how nature, as an elemental force and then as a living nonhuman character, appears in and affects drama. The first two essays in Part I concentrate on how the environment was dramatized in American and Canadian theatre during the first half of the twentieth century. Barry Witham writes about environmental disasters in the 1930s through a thoughtful analysis of three lesser-known American plays from the period that "serve as cautionary tales for the twenty-first century" (21). In contrast, the plays discussed by Nelson Gray explore how settlers and First Nations peoples were intrinsically connected to their environment in such a way that it might bring humanity together via a shared sense of place. The third chapter, by Robert Baker-White, foreshadows the exploration of animal characters in the next section because it focuses on the human/animal dyads in Tennessee Williams's *Glass Menagerie* and Maria Irene Fornes's *Fefu and Her Friends*. Baker-White argues that reading each play through the lens of "the animal" provides "a means of reimagining possibilities for human interaction" (33).

In Part II, each author argues for the interdependent relationships between humans and animals. Una Chaudhuri begins with the dubious yet iconic image of a pair of polar bears "stranded" on Artic ice that have become central characters in the social and political drama surrounding global climate change. In her compelling essay, Chaudhuri weaves together theory, artistry, and science in order to show how drama reveals the similar threats that face polar bears and human children as to "give voice to the shared animality on whose recognition the future of so many species depends" (57). In the next essay Baz Kershaw describes a site-specific, three-day performance at the Bristol Zoological Gardens in England, where performers alternated among portraying visitors, zookeepers, primatologists, and feral humans. The performance explored how humans, as yet another primate species performing together with monkeys, chimpanzees, and others, form a "global 'performance commons'"(60) that ties together aesthetic and scientific communities. In contrast to the previous two essays, which focus on contemporary performance and art, Derek Lee Barton writes about how a giraffe that was imported from the Nubian Desert to Vienna in 1828 inspired many displays and images. The "giraffe demonstrates how the otherness of animal bodies has, from time to time, served to consolidate social and political boundaries" (77).

Part III, "Theorizing Ecoperformance," provides a general introduction to the larger discourses of ecology and theatre as they relate to aesthetics, politics, and social theory. On one hand, locating this chapter in the middle of the book situates it in a position resembling its rhetorical function—providing an overview of the central theoretical language necessary to the essays surrounding it. On the other hand, it might have been better placed at the beginning, giving the reader a foundation in the stakes raised by the others. In the first essay of this part, Bruce McConachie draws from the theories of John Dewey to describe the uncomfortable relationship between ethics and evolution as expressed in performance in order to "suggest that all artistic practice that successfully foregrounds body-environment interactions is always ecological" (93). Next, Kathleen M. Gough articulates the interdependence of culture and environment through a little-known musical that offered dark foreshadowing of the volcanic eruption and cultural fallout on the Caribbean island of Montserrat in 1997. Finally, Arden Thomas writes about dancing with nature through examining the work of Anna Halprin and Eeo Stubblefield. Each of the three chapters in this part provides rich analysis and descriptions of performance while engaging with a rich variety of critical and cultural theories.

The final two parts of the book are rooted in activism and practical approaches to creating ecologically informed theatre. In Part IV, "Ecoactivism and Performance," the authors apply ecology as a historiographical tool for framing histories of theatre. Sara Freeman uses three anti-nuclear plays from the early eighties to "(re)tell" a history of British alternative theatre where the plays look forward as "nascent ecodramas, rather than last-gasp remnants of old-style agitprop" (127), and Meg O'Shea focuses on embodied performance as intervention by writing about a Canadian group that tours a play about sustainability on bicycle. In contrast, Sarah Ann Standing foreshadows the next part by examining the aesthetics of ecoactivism in order to inspire theatre artists to imagine new ways of creating theatre.

Part V, "Case Studies in Green Theatre," presents practical guidance about how artists might create environmentally responsible productions. Downing Cless writes about directing, Anne Justine D'Zmura examines the devising process, Cornelia Hoogland explores sound design, Justin A. Miller looks at recycling and theatrical production, and finally Ian Garrett proposes how theatre can reduce its carbon footprint. Each essay provides a careful examination of a case, or cases, in which the artists engaged in theatre that was responsive to and responsible for the environment. The epilogue by Wallace Heim attempts to "think ahead" in response to all the essays in the volume, finally concluding that criticism can and should move between disciplines, as well as scholarship and theatrical practice.

I do wish that each part had an introduction to better situate the larger field that the essays address and to provide greater synthesis than the introduction and epilogue are able to do on their own. Unlike many edited collections, however, the level of scholarship and writing is consistently high and gives voice to both senior and junior scholars together with graduate students. Overall, this book provides an excellent introduction to the arguments and scope of a growing and exciting field of theatre studies.

—JENNIFER GOODLANDER
Indiana University

Walking on Fire: The Shaping Force of Emotion in Writing Drama. By Jim Linnell. Carbondale: Southern Illinois University Press, 2011. 144 pp. $29.95 paper.

Playwright and professor Jim Linnell's book on the relationship of emotion to dramatic structure is a playwriting guide as well as a contribution to theories of dramaturgy and affect. Linnell's play analyses and writing exercises are a heady alternative to "how-to" playwriting texts. The author's premise is that playwrights need to stop worrying about how to write and start focusing on why they write. The book's key concept, "emotional form," refers to plot as the "internal emotional structure…the writer gives to a narrative" (28). Such emotion-driven plots are built from characters whose unresolved fears and desires result in onstage actions. Playwrights who craft characters with this interplay of fear and desire at the forefront will write plays in which character drives the action.

Linnell historicizes contemporary dramaturgies by elucidating their connection to Freudian psychoanalysis. Chapter 1, "The Seeds of Emotional Form," lays out the argument that fuels the method. Inspired by personal experiences, playwrights use and create emotional form through confronting their own and their characters' moments of crisis, loss, and resulting self-knowledge. Linnell explains: "What we call our character is a skin laced tight to contain the desires and feelings that press against the comfort of our status quo. The writer, understanding emotional form, uses events like a scissors to snip away the laces binding the truth until it cannot be contained" (33). Chapter 2, "The Fire Hose and the Nozzle," elucidates the relationship between character, conflict, and action, offering a different metaphor to explain the way characters are undone by events that threaten loss; like a fire hose, character contains and expels action through the nozzle of conflict.

Chapter 3, "The End Is Where You Started," offers useful advice for playwrights struggling with plot, especially in choosing (or, as Linnell would put it, discovering) an ending. This is the author at his clearest, offering practical ways to make decisions about plotting. Although his approach is theoretical, even philosophical, Linnell offers exercises to put his theory of emotional form into action. These exercises are designed to unearth the writer's (and thus a character's) life "below the neck": "The Writer's Inventory" is a template for accessing dreams and memories; "Finding Trouble" is an inside-out automatic writing practice designed to let writers discover rather than manufacture dialogue. Other exercises offer methods for making choices about plot: "Ask the Character" and "Atom Smashing" are two ways to generate possibilities for action—by asking characters questions and listening to the answers and by letting the mind wander through an open-ended set of answers to "what-if" questions, respectively.

Chapter 4, "Collaborating with Calamity," identifies the audience's role in the creation of emotional form, that is, an approach to the construction of narrative that is driven by characters' emotions. To alienate or exclude audiences from the process of playwriting is to ignore a key collaborator. The author reminds us of Aristotle's articulation of what constitutes tragedy, focusing on the audience's experience of pity and fear, catharsis. Just as Aristotle counts catharsis as a desired result of tragedy, so the audience is an essential component of the creation of emotional action by the playwright. Linnell ties this observation to the Greeks' vital connection to playwrights and plays of their own time period, in contrast to what he identifies as our own disconnection from living writers and their works. He argues that this is especially true in university theatre programs, spaces that can potentially serve as laboratories for testing new works but that tend instead to choose plays based primarily on their historical significance. This critique of university department season selection processes is not contextualized fully enough to be altogether convincing. Nonetheless, Linnell's feelings on the subject come from an evident passion for new plays and playwrights. Chapter 5, "The Practice of Fire Walking," is an afterword that reinforces the book's major components, using Tony Kushner's *Angels in America* as an exemplar.

Particularly effective are Linnell's extended analyses of how emotional action works in specific plays, such as Athol Fugard's *Master Harold...and the Boys* and Harold Pinter's *The Birthday Party*. A strength of Linnell's theory is that it applies to many dramaturgical models, especially those commonly thought to diverge from traditional Aristotelian plot structure. Rather than making exceptions for such writers as Samuel Beckett or Harold Pinter, Linnell maintains that playwrights who diverge from what some would call linear structure are especially driven by emotional form. Indeed, the emotional conflicts these writers' characters experience can be particularly threatening, given that they inhabit worlds where notions of time and space are foreign or dreamlike, or where the reasons behind their actions remain hidden and mysterious to the audience.

Although Linnell's play analyses are a strong point of this study, aside from one concise, insightful analysis of Sarah Kane's *Blasted*, Linnell all but excludes plays written by women from his set of case studies, a fact made more conspicuous by his reliance on noncontemporary theorists such as Aristotle and Freud whose dramaturgies are not expressly feminist. Nonetheless, as a method of dramatic analysis, Linnell's Freudian model is apt as well as sound; Freud, after all, charts his own theories of subject formation in stages analogous to dramatic conflict. In the final analysis, the absence of female writers and theorists is a productive absence for the resistant reader, causing us to wonder whether a feminist dramaturgy would trouble Linnell's argument. Nevertheless, Linnell shows that the history of dramatic forms is a history of the emotions that shape our lives and societies, and this makes his study a vital contribution to the field of theatre studies, especially to models of dramaturgy that question the separation of form from emotion.

—JEANMARIE HIGGINS
University of North Carolina at Charlotte

The African American Theatrical Body: Reception, Performance, and the Stage. By Soyica Diggs Colbert. Cambridge: Cambridge University Press, 2011. xi + 329 pp. $99.00 cloth.

Soyica Diggs Colbert's *The African American Theatrical Body: Reception, Performance, and the Stage* examines the topic of the black body by analyzing multiple types of performance narratives. Utilizing African American theatrical and literary traditions as prophetic sites of engagement, Colbert refutes historically accepted assumptions about black bodies in performance. She scrutinizes works by dramatists including Suzan-Lori Parks and Lorraine Hansberry as well as works by literary figures such as W. E. B. Du Bois and Zora Neale Hurston. According to Colbert, these writers have engaged in the construction of dramatic narratives as "rites of repair." While recent scholarship seeks to elaborate the African American experience through the exploration of social rather than performance models, Colbert's central method of analysis recuperates theatrical texts. She demonstrates that such narratives provide an understanding not only of African American literary traditions but also of lived experience.

While psychoanalytical theory and critical race theory guide this work, at its core Colbert's study thrives through the suggestion of repetition and reproduction as the "DNA of black expressive culture" (20). Colbert's discussion is reminiscent of the work of sociologists Ron Eyerman and Cathy Caruth, who have written on the tensions present in the aftermath of cultural trauma and how those tensions in turn resonate through collective responses to such trauma. Caruth's account of a psychoanalytical theory of trauma suggests that not the experience of trauma but rather its remembrance produces traumatic effect, and both Caruth and Eyerman believe that trauma is mediated through various forms of representation. These concepts resonate with Colbert's work on repetition, and it is the specificity of Colbert's chapter-by-chapter discussion of the collective traumatic experience of multiple African American bodies resonating through fully rendered theatrical representations that solidifies much of her book.

The African American Theatrical Body is constructed of seven chapters, each vital in the author's journey toward a reconstruction of how the African American body is read within both dramatic and literary narratives. The first three chapters address the presence of specific acts of reproduction, recuperation, and reenactment to reclaim African American identity and build black resistance structures on narrative terms. Colbert explores Hansberry's *A Raisin in the Sun* as a site whereon both audiences and readers learn to deploy strategies of "perpetual deferment," investigates Du Bois's *The Star of Ethiopia* for a better understanding of gender specificity as recuperative, and demonstrates that Hurston's *Color Struck* and its vernacular forms are a method of critique in bourgeois versus folk narratives. In subsequent chapters, Colbert further highlights the ability of various performances and actions to reorder identities by illuminating Hughes's *God's Trombones* as a sermon, Baldwin's *Blues for Mr. Charlie* as a collective mining of "ghostly pasts" (192), and the plays of Amiri Baraka and August Wilson, through similarly prophetic hauntings, as pathways to the rituals of repair. In each instance, cohesively constructed dramatic narratives render forth countless pathways toward engagement.

Discussions of either the African American or black body and its ability to perform as both part of and apart from narrative attempts to elaborate, conceal, and at times negate its affect have long remained a subject of performance scholarship. Whether through the use of memory, text, or embodied practice, the black body resonates as a subject of interest and a tool for continued engagement. Performances by African American bodies have long attempted to avoid or engage the restrictions of spectators and audiences seeking to limit the movement of those same bodies. In Colbert's exploration of Parks's *The America Play*, Colbert identifies instances of "symbolic reordering" (5) functioning solely through narration as moments of engagement which "renders the black theatrical body flexible" and, further, engages how performance moves through bodies as equally viable motivating narratives. Through her study of that flexibility, Colbert draws attention to what Parks identifies as a specific artifice referencing what Parks views as the show of U.S. citizenship. Colbert maintains that it is through such action that an existing black theatricality reveals the ability of performance to highlight "mechanics of spectacle" (1) present in multiple instances of black stage performance. Again referencing Parks's *The America Play*, Colbert reveals the presence of a resonating "mimetic blackness" (1), one that disrupts the passing down of black theatricality across multiple generations. In this way, Colbert argues, each of the plays discussed "troubles genealogy" (1).

In the end, Colbert focuses on the question of what is accomplished by the living black body during acts of performance and how such performances can assist in clarifications of a distinctly African American literary space.

—KEITH BYRON KIRK
University of Houston

Queen of Vaudeville: The Story of Eva Tanguay. By Andrew L. Erdman. Ithaca, NY: Cornell University Press, 2012. x + 310 pp. $29.95 cloth.

Andrew L. Erdman's *Queen of Vaudeville* stands as an extension of his previous book, *Blue Vaudeville*. In his earlier text, Erdman examined the disjunction between the refined image of vaudeville put forth by vaudeville magnates and the risqué material often presented on their circuits, with headliner Eva Tanguay as one of several performers challenging vaudeville's family-friendly label. *Queen of Vaudeville* is a biography of Tanguay, tracing her life from her Quebecois roots to her death in 1947 and illuminating the characteristics that made her popular with audiences and unpopular with managers, stage hands, and other performers. Above all, Erdman emphasizes Tanguay's individuality as "a rousing model of human visibility" (14), a powerful charisma that compensated for any deficiency of talent.

The text is divided into twelve chronological chapters, in addition to an introduction and an epilogue. The first chapter covers Tanguay's birth in 1878 in Quebec and her childhood in Holyoke, Massachusetts, as well as her first public performance. Here, Erdman lays out many of the threads he will follow throughout his book, including her father's death, her experiences as a Canadian expatriate in New England, and her illegitimate daughter. Chapter 2 focuses on her first major successes on Broadway, *My Lady* (1901) and *The Chaperons*

(1902). Here, the author explores the development of Tanguay's ability to sell her persona to an audience while also marking the first appearances of her professional jealousy and wild romances, both of which would continue throughout her career.

Chapter 3 marks Tanguay's transition to vaudeville, where she would make her greatest impact, particularly with her trademark song "I Don't Care." Introduced in *The Sambo Girl* (1905), Tanguay would include this song in her vaudeville act, although after many years it became clear that the song "was also a burden" (72), as audiences demanded it at every performance. Her move to vaudeville marked the beginning of a journey that would elevate Tanguay to "the most famous headliner on the North American vaudeville circuits" (75). In chapter 4, Erdman shows how Tanguay learned to harness her image and market it to maximum effect. With her publicist and lover, C. F. Zittel, she created an air of mystery and transgression, drawing audiences to her with astonishing power, most clearly through her staged betrothal to Julian Eltinge, America's premier female impersonator, which did much to enhance both of their careers.

Chapters 5 through 7 deal primarily with Tanguay onstage. Chapter 5 describes her participation in the Salome craze during the first decade of the twentieth century. Her performance was quite popular, and her efforts to claim sole ownership of the Salome dance only heightened her public persona. Chapter 6 focuses on the rise of Tanguay imitators, most notably Gertrude Hoffman, a competing Salome dancer and very popular comedian in her own right. Tanguay used these imitators to increase her own profile, attacking them and asserting her uniqueness in newspapers. Chapter 7 covers her time in the *Ziegfeld Follies* of 1909, in which she replaced Nora Bayes and used her influence to have a young Sophie Tucker fired. In each of these chapters, Erdman notes numerous affairs—perhaps none more scandalous than an alleged dalliance with black performer George Walker—and run-ins with the police and with other performers. These incidences, Erdman suggests, were a part of Tanguay's irrepressible individuality, but also alienated her from her colleagues.

Chapters 8 and 9 deal with two of Tanguay's most disastrous relationships. In chapter 8, Tanguay is wooed by a mysterious man known as "Prince Charming" who turns out to be a conman, taking a great deal of money from Tanguay and leaving her heartbroken. Chapter 9 follows a similarly ill-fated relationship, this one with a dancer named John Ford (no relation to the film director), an alcoholic who took her money and ran off. Along with these tales of romantic woes, Erdman also addresses Tanguay's influence on a young Mae West, who saw Tanguay as a model of transgressive femininity, as well as Tanguay's growing devotion to Christian Science.

Chapter 10 marks vaudeville's decline and film's rising popularity. As Erdman writes, "Eva was still the top star of vaudeville. But it was unclear how long vaudeville itself could withstand the competition" (194). Tanguay made one feature movie, *The Wild Girl* (1917), only a moderate success. She had little choice but to return to vaudeville where she continued to earn money but had to work harder to earn the same amount. Chapter 11 follows Tanguay's decline, which included another failed relationship, plastic surgery, declining health, and a sham marriage to her twenty-five-year-old accompanist which ended after less than four months. Chapter 12 brings Tanguay's story to a close with an account of her final decline and death, which came on January 11, 1947.

Erdman's study provides a very thorough investigation of Tanguay's life, conducted through a wide range of evidence. This is particularly difficult, as many vaudeville performers did not leave much in terms of personal papers, meaning researchers like Erdman must reconstruct past events through newspapers, interviews, second-hand accounts, correspondence with living relatives, and other evidence. Moreover, the prose is quite readable and does not require an extensive knowledge of popular entertainment.

However, this general accessibility suggests that this text may be better suited to a popular rather than scholarly audience. The author includes several sections covering performance forms or significant figures that, while helpful, tend to cloud the focus on Tanguay. For novice readers this information is helpful, but for those with previous knowledge of vaudeville and musical comedy, these sections run a bit long. There is also some difficulty with sourcing, as attribution can be rather vague due to the author's effort to reduce the number of footnotes. The most significant issue, however, is the author's occasional tendency to slip from conjecture to assertion. The most glaring example is Erdman's speculation that Tanguay's father was an alcoholic. Unlike Ford's alcoholism, which is more readily supported with specific evidence, the author clearly states that the "evidence is circumstantial" when dealing with Tanguay's father's alcoholism (35). Yet throughout the text, his alcoholism is treated as an accepted fact, which does not sit entirely comfortably. More careful wording would likely have avoided this problem.

This text is a valuable biography of an important female vaudevillian, an area of scholarship that has seen increasing interest from researchers but still requires much more attention. That said, this book should reach a wider audience and bring more attention to an important figure in the history of American popular culture.

—FRANKLIN J. LASIK
University of Missouri

BOOK REVIEWS

Molière on Stage: What's So Funny? By Robert W. Goldsby. New York: Anthem Press, 2012. xx + 202 pp. $39.95 paper.

Among Theatre Communications Group's annual listings of the ten most-produced plays on the professional American stage since 1994–1995, a play by Molière makes the list only once: *Tartuffe* in 2006–2007. Robert W. Goldsby's book just might be the impetus to give us more Molière. Goldsby's long experience as an actor and director of the Molière canon undergirds his passion for the plays and his generous-hearted understanding of the personal motives and relationships behind them. In seventeen chapters grouped into four "acts" that loosely correspond to phases in Molière's life and career, the book intertwines biography with textual and production analysis of the plays as vehicles for the stage.

Goldsby's warm association with Molière goes back to the Comédie-Française's 1947 revival of *Le Misanthrope* in which wartime Resistance hero Aimé Clariond reprised his role as Alceste. As a student on the G.I. Bill in the 1940s, Goldsby had the good fortune to attend the play's first postwar performance. The communal intensity of "joy and grief" (4) generated that evening led to a theatre career that included chairing the Department of Theatre, Dance, and Performance Studies at the University of California, Berkeley, and directing professionally. Eleven plays by Molière in fifteen different productions (including some in his own translation) figure among the 153 productions Goldsby has directed. He writes about Molière from intimate acquaintance.

The first brief chapter summarizes Molière's life up to 1658 when he won the favor of Louis XIV along with the means to settle his troupe in Paris. The lively writing throughout the book yields abundant nuggets like this: "[Molière] learned that though he loves tragedy and tragediennes his true talent is making people laugh, even, unfortunately, in the tragedies" (10). Subsequent chapters each analyze dramaturgically one or two plays in chronological order even as they continue tracing Molière's biography in relation to his work. The method involves frequent use of the phrase "we can imagine" as Goldsby deftly ties dramaturgical tidbits to what was apparently going on in Molière's personal life. Yes, Molière loved women, and Goldsby shows how the playwright's passions led to the great roles he created for actresses. Through Tartuffe's attempted seduction of Elmire, Arnolph's doting on young Agnès, and Alceste's helpless fixation on Célimène, "Molière confronted on stage his own passion for Armande" and turned his "deepest feelings" into a "subject for laughter" (62), even—as in the case of Agnès—when Armande Béjart did not play the role she inspired.

Beyond the biographical material and the analysis of Molière's plays for the stage, the book functions as a kind of theatregoing memoir or vicarious experiencing of important productions and directors (and even a range of translators) of the plays from the original creations to our own time. For example, chapter 14 on *Les Fourberies de Scapin* (1671) celebrates Jacques Copeau's 1920 production with Louis Jouvet playing Géronte, Jouvet's 1951 production with Jean-Louis Barrault as Scapin, and Goldsby's own 1958 Berkeley production for which he used the translation by Lady Gregory. The dramaturgical analysis constitutes a directorial case study in putting farce on the stage. Goldsby's analysis of the act 2 scene in which Scapin dupes Géronte incorporates snippets from Lady Gregory's dialogue as well as examples of farcical devices like the "bright idea," the "turn and go" exit, the "magic prop"; and then Goldsby moves on to the famous "sack scene" and breaks it down into ten playable beats with fine fodder for any director.

Chapter 7, which covers *Tartuffe*, includes case studies of "brilliant entrances" (53). Chapter 8 on *Dom Juan; ou, le Festin de Pierre* shows how directors like Stephen Wadsworth and Jacques La Salle milk the comic and dramatic potential in an exit from the stage. Chapter 10 on *Le Misanthrope* offers serious subtextual insights. After the final exchange between Alceste and Célimène, for example, the famously defiant exit by Mademoiselle Mars in the nineteenth century is offered as one among several possible ways for Célimène to play the moment.

The seventeen chapters are complemented by ample notes, a bibliography, an index, a chronology of the plays discussed, and forty-six illustrations. The illustrations are small, often three or four on a page, and information is scanty in their captions, but they convey a sense of production approaches through the ages. On the whole, this is a book for theatre practitioners and for anyone looking to understand why Molière is one of the top classic playwrights—one who deserves the kinds of staging that Goldsby shows us. Part of the pleasure of *Molière on Stage: What's So Funny?* is the sense it conveys of how much fun it must have been for Robert Goldsby to write.

—**FELICIA HARDISON LONDRÉ**
University of Missouri—Kansas City

BOOK REVIEWS

Direction. By Simon Shepherd. Basingstoke, Hampshire, U.K.: Palgrave Macmillan. 2012. ix + 238 pp. $85 hardcover, $32 paper.

Direction by Simon Shepherd is one of a series of books entitled "Readings in Theatre Practice" that aim "to gather together both key historical texts and contemporary ways of thinking about the material crafts and practices of theatre" (viii). Each of the books in the series is devoted to one of the crafts of the theatre, including sound, clowning, puppetry, light, direction, voice, costume, and construction. Shepherd is the author of the book about directing as well as the editor of the series. As such, he emphasizes in the preface to the series that it is not another "how-to" of theatrical crafts, but rather an investigation into concepts and tools "not just for the doing but for thinking about theatre practice" (viii), with the goal of recognizing the multiple and conflicting viewpoints therein.

Shepherd's investigation into directing, as it has emerged in European and American theatre, is both thorough and lucid, teasing out the complexities of its historical development as well as the multiple ways in which it has been practiced and perceived. This is no small feat, given the elusive nature of an activity that seems to defy definition, description, or even name. But Simon revels in such complexities, making them the subject of his book. When, for example, he recognizes the dominant view that the director emerged as a separate and distinct role with the rise of Modernism in the late nineteenth century, he makes it his purpose to introduce counter narratives, including how many of the responsibilities associated with the role have been undertaken by others going by different names at different times and in different cultures.

Shepherd organizes his investigation of complex narratives and counter narratives about directing into five parts. The first part is a brief introduction to some of the historical antecedents for "the process of organizing a performance: both getting it on the stage and shaping its contents" (9). The discussion ranges from the *metteur en jeu*, who "sets up the play, creates the game, leads the entertainment" (10) in sixteenth-century Passion plays to what Gordon Craig, in 1905, called a stage manager, by which he meant someone who could bring together all the elements of the theatre in harmony. By the end of this introductory section of the book, Shepherd makes clear that what interests him most, and what he will return to over the course of the rest of the book, is the notion that "organization may be the critical and defining activity in directing" (16).

The second part of the book shifts to a discussion of conflicting assumptions in our own time about what directors do, how they do it, and how they come to occupy the role. Again, lack of agreement is the focus of this discussion, as Shepherd presents just how far apart opinions range with regard to these topics, provoking questions: Is directing primarily creative or interpretive? Is it about inspiring with vision or managing time, space, people, and money? Can or should directing be taught, or is it something one comes to through acting, stage managing, or other backgrounds? What assumptions lie behind the multiple ways directing happens, from forming and leading a company to researching a script, and more?

The third part of the book turns back to historical accounts of directing, this time with the intention of showing that there are divergent narratives about its emergence. For example, balanced against the Modernist notion that someone was needed to organize a visual whole at a time of cultural alienation during the Industrial Revolution is the idea that directors, as we tend to think of them today, are not relevant, given that the theatre has prospered for centuries without them. Or, another example, colliding with the Marxist critique that directors can be seen as part of the rise of the "Professional-Managerial Class," whose main function was the "reproduction of capitalistic culture" (88), is the notion of an "aura" of directing that sees directors as the guardians of the "spirit" of a play (91).

The fourth part of the book is a fascinating exploration of the multifaceted ways in which directors author text, when, that is, we understand "text" to mean more than the actual script. Directors thus "author" productions in as much as they integrate all the theatrical elements and produce something beyond the script. For example, Belasco and others edited scripts to suit their own theatrical sensibilities, and some directors, including Harley Granville Barker, published notes about their work for public consumption. Also, some directors author movement and space based on their own aesthetic response to the script, while others author themselves, in a sense, putting forward their philosophies, methodologies, politics, or personalities through their work and behavior, especially in rehearsal.

The fifth and final part of the book brings home the argument that, for all the shifting definitions and perceptions of directing, there is, nevertheless, one defining feature, which is that directing creates the relationship between the thing produced and the means by which it is produced, that is to say, between art and organization. Shepherd's argument is convincing. By organizing the show, he says, the director structures and manages the relationships among those who create it. Of course, organizing a production can happen in different ways, and Shepherd is vigorous in his approach to detailing them: by following organizational principles, as Reinhardt did in structuring his theatre according to the repertory system; by training actors, as Stanislavsky did; by following ideologies, as Théâtre du Soleil has done; and by adopting certain attitudes toward actors in the rehearsal space. Shepherd sees in these and other examples that what is staged is an accumulation of the ideology, structure, and relationships—that is, the organization as created by the director.

—LEWIS MAGRUDER
Miami University

Dramaturgy of the Real on the World Stage. Edited by Carol Martin. New York: Palgrave Macmillan, 2012. vii + 309 pp. $95.00 hardcover, $29.00 paper.

This anthology of essays and performance texts forms part of the Studies in International Performance series edited by Janelle Reinelt and Brian Singleton. The series focuses on how performance crosses borders and interacts between varying nations and cultures. *Dramaturgy of the Real on the World Stage* continues in this vein by exploring the performance of theatre of the real, sometimes known as documentary theatre, in multiple locations across the globe. This anthology offers a look into how these performances of real events are created and portrayed on international stages. Martin structures the anthology into two sections: the first includes essays that focus on theatre of the real performances, and the second features actual texts of performances in either their entirety or partial construction. Through both the essays and recorded texts of the performances, readers can gain insight into other cultures' performances of reality.

Carol Martin, in her introduction as well as her essay "Bodies of Evidence" that follows, defines theatre of the real, discussing its multiple titles from docudrama to verbatim theatre and theatre of fact, and how the slightest variation in nomenclature alters exactly what can be expected of the performance. She emphasizes that theatre of the real for an American audience is derived from actual texts and testimony. Witness accounts, court documents, and other factual evidence are used as a starting point, and the expectation of such a performance is that it offers a near reenactment of actual events. In the beginning essays, Martin notes that what is true about American theatre of the real may not be so internationally. Other cultures may view documentary theatre as witnesses telling their actual stories, as visual performance art, as commentary on the actual cultural event(s), or as imagined reenactments. She also notes how today's theatre of the real intersects both the global and the local in its creation.

The first section includes essays discussing theatre of the real performances across the globe. "Toward a Poetics of Theatre and Public Events: In the Case of Stephen Lawrence" by Janelle Reinelt examines a theatre of the real performance in the United Kingdom. *The Colour of Justice* centers on the brutal stabbing death of a black youth, Stephen Lawrence, by five white youths, and follows his parents' journey to gain some form of justice. Reinelt's essay thoroughly dictates the events of the actual hate crime and its aftermath and then describes the documentary theatre performance. The following essay moves the reader geographically from the United Kingdom to the Middle East. Wendy S. Hesford's "Staging Terror" delves into two separate performances: *Inconvenient Evidence* and *Guantánamo*. *Inconvenient Evidence* premiered in Tehran, Iran, in the form of multiple roadside murals depicting the abuses of Iraqi detainees by American soldiers in Abu Ghraib as shown in released photographs. It later traveled to New York in the form of photographs of the murals displayed at the International Center for Photography. *Guantánamo* premiered in London as a documentary play based on the letters of Guantanamo detainees who were found innocent. Both of the pieces Hesford discusses display the brutal events occurring behind the "victories" of America's War on Terror.

The next essay in this section is Yvette Hutchison's "Post-1990s Verbatim Theatre in South Africa: Exploring an African Concept of 'Truth.'" Hutchison primarily reviews the work of the Truth and Reconciliation Commission (TRC) that worked to address the actions and wrongs of apartheid. From the TRC, actual interviews from both victims and oppressors are used to create multiple verbatim theatre pieces, such as *REwind: A Cantata for Voice, Tape and Testimony* found in the text section. "Reality from the Bottom Up: Documentary Theatre in Poland" by Agnieszka Sowińska (translated by Benjamin Paloff) explores Polish theatre of the real that uses factual and historical sources as inspiration for the creation of a text. The essay explores this style through different examples, such as High-Speed Urban Theatre and Paweł Demirski's work. The final essay, "The Scripted Realities in Rimini Protokoll" by Florian Malzachar, focuses on the German performance group Rimini Protokoll and their use of actual people telling their own stories via a mix of scripted and improvisational storytelling.

The second section of the anthology contains actual theatre of the real texts, each preceded by an introduction. The texts included in this section are: *REwind: A Cantata for Voice, Tape and Testimony* by Philip Miller from South Africa's TRC; *Is.Man* by Adelheid Roosen, a piece centered around honor killings in Holland's Turkish communities; *Three Posters* by Elias Khoury and Rabih Mroué, which takes a look into the filming of a suicide bomber's final message; *The Files* by Teatr Ósmego Dnia, satire of reports by the Secret Security Service about their theatre; *Don't Be Surprised When They Come to Burn Your House Down* by Paweł Demirski, a piece focusing on communist remnants in Poland; "Excerpts from the Plays of Vivi Tellas"; and *Art, Life & Show-Biz* by Ain Gordon, an exploration of show business and art in America.

Dramaturgy of the Real on the World Stage is an excellent book for any scholar interested in theatre of the real or in global performance. This book is written for scholars with a previous knowledge of either field, and the essays' vocabulary and subject presentation require a developed understanding of theatre of the real. The anthology would benefit from a stronger connection between essays and texts. Martin discusses a connection among them in her introduction through their global connections, but within the rest of the anthology these connections are not emphasized. Ultimately, however, this anthology is an important addition to theatre and performance scholarship as it strengthens knowledge of theatre of the real and adds to an understanding contemporary and global works.

—**WILLIAM PALMER**
University of Missouri-Columbia

Doomed by Hope: Essays on Arab Theatre. Edited by Eyad Houssami. New York: Pluto, 2012. xvi + 189 pp. $29.00 paperback.

To say that Arabic drama has been understudied and insufficiently taught in the Western academy is at best an understatement. For years, stereotypes about where performance occurs and the relationship between Islam and live theatre, as well as a lack of basic language skills and cultural knowledge, have worked to leave a blank space in scholarly endeavors, with northern Africa left out of studies of African drama and southwest Asia ignored in many books about Asian performance. *Doomed by Hope: Essays on Arab Theatre* comes as a welcome work addressing this critical area at a time when the Arab world, in general, and Syria, in particular, are receiving increased global attention.

The collection is not alone in its attempt to bring more scholarly attention to Arab drama, but what separates Eyad Houssami's edited work from recent studies by his peers is the effort to bring scholarly and artistic voices together to reconstruct an archive of Arab performance from Cairo to Damascus to Kuwait. Additionally, as the title of the book indicates, the collection also represents a desire to bring greater attention to the late Syrian dramatist Saadallah Wannous, who stated of theatre and politics: "We are doomed by hope, and come what may, today cannot be the end of history" (4).

The focus on Wannous is the more straightforward part of the project, with Edward Ziter and Asaad al-Saleh writing about *Soirée for the 5th of June*, Rania Jawad writing about *The Elephant, the King of All Time*, Rabih Mroué discussing *The Rape*, and Sulayman al Bassam previewing his impending French production of *Ritual for a Metamorphosis*. Notable in all of these discussions is the consistency with which artists and scholars continue to turn to Wannous for his theatrical innovations and challenges to the Syrian state, both before and after Hafez al-Assad came to power in the early 1970s. Toward this end, Ziter notes that *Soirée*, a play about Syria's crushing defeat in the 1967 Six Day War, "is remarkable for its insistence that the event be taken as an opportunity to define a Syrian identity in defiance of a state that had rendered its population deaf and dumb" (11). Similarly, Mroué, when discussing a conversation between Syrian and Israeli characters in *The Rape*—a conversation that could land one in jail outside of the theatre—argues: "I posit that the theatre is a space of probability, a space in which one can play with the law, a space to break taboos and destabilize rigid beliefs in order to hold accountable ourselves and others" (115).

Of course, such idealistic proclamations are not new in critical writing about theatre. However, one of the strengths of *Doomed by Hope* is the breadth of performance activities that are used to support such claims. These include Dalia Basiouny discussing her documentary performance *Tahrir Stories*, Katherine Hennessey overviewing emerging artists in Yemen, Meisoun Ali looking at new theatre in Syria, Zein Daccache describing her experience with prison drama in Lebanon, and Joseph Shahadi and Margaret Litvin expanding the frame of Arab drama by looking at performances in the Palestinian diaspora and Arab and Muslim arts festivals in the United States, respectively.

These chapters represent a broad range of materials and styles and at times create a desire for more careful citations, contextualizing, and theorizing by the authors. For those who are not specialists in the Middle East, it may be frustrating to find claims about literacy rates in Egypt or historical events in Syria sometimes referenced without a source that can be consulted, either for fact-checking or increased understanding of the varied local contexts. Additionally, many of the contributors exhibit a comfort with the phrase "Arab Spring" that Syria's multiyear civil war would seem to undermine.

Despite this, what the diversity of perspectives does allow for is a sense of the breadth and depth of contemporary Arabic drama that challenges many stereotypes about predominantly Arab nations and the theatre found within them and their diasporic communities. Many of the authors also argue for, and at times provide examples of, the possibility of a dialectical relationship with the audience through unconventional performances. Basiouny, for one, makes clear that the real-life and immediate nature of her work became a starting point for conversation: "Audiences wanted to share their own stories and testimonies of the revolution, blurring the line between audience and performer, as both have become enlivened in a society awakening to a new wave of activism" (52).

In the face of these hopeful moments, the authors also create a catalogue of the challenges to contemporary performance in many of the countries under discussion. These include censorship, inexperienced playwrights, lack of appropriate performance spaces, cost of attending performances, inflexible bureaucratic structures, and the pressure to conform to nationalist ideologies. In explaining her turn to prison drama, Daccache states clearly: "I was bored of theatre in Beirut" (103). But what al Bassam says of the previous generation of theatre artists perhaps also holds true now: "Bad times for living: rich pickings for theatre" (125).

In his foreword, acclaimed Lebanese novelist Elias Khoury notes: "It is in Syria that the Arabs have taken themselves most by surprise… Their creativity has transcended the conventional boundaries of protest…and Syrians have transformed their demonstrations into weddings of freedom, with popular music, song, chanting, and dance. Cell phone cameras have transformed into tools of documentary" (xiv). Khoury's assessment points to the challenge for theatre artists engaging with the Arab uprisings: how to make work that matches the power, creativity, and confrontations to conventional thought occurring in the streets outside the theatres. What Houssami's collection reminds us is that this is not a new question, that what we see unfolding in the contemporary moment has a historical context, and that Arab theatre has always been a space for engaging these questions.

—**GEORGE POTTER**
Council for International Educational Exchange Study Center, Amman, Jordan

BOOK REVIEWS

Shakespeare and His Contemporaries. By Jonathan Hart. New York: Palgrave Macmillan, 2011. xiii + 254 pp. $85.00 cloth.

It is easy to embrace Jonathan Hart's *Shakespeare and His Contemporaries* as a valuable resource in the realm of Shakespeare scholarship. The breadth of Hart's background as a Shakespeare scholar is evident in the thoughtful and detail-driven evidence he examines. He breathes new life into the viewpoint that history and drama are never static and await reinterpretation.

This book definitively promotes Hart's premise of "decentering" (1) Shakespeare in his own time. He uses historical narrative as context for appreciating the complex role that Shakespeare played in the theatrical landscape of Elizabethan England. Hart thoroughly establishes the importance of Shakespeare's literary contemporaries Christopher Marlowe and Robert Greene, who likely influenced Shakespeare's writing before and during the time he began to earn public accolades. To quote Hart, "The power of Marlowe's dramatic language is another way of remembering that Shakespeare lived among great contemporaries and that the drama of Renaissance England and English Literature would be remarkable without Shakespeare" (6). Hart celebrates the central position Shakespeare's writing has attained in both historical and dramatic written history through effective analysis of Shakespeare's body of work.

In chapter 1, a thorough review of history during and after Shakespeare's lifetime is informative regarding both the struggles and eventual expansion of England's influence. Hart discusses not only those countries gaining global power in the late sixteenth century but also the tenuous position of Elizabethan England. Shakespeare's England had not yet attained its status as a world power, and the English language was not central to international trading communities. Hart succinctly explains how Spain was the dominant player in Europe's expansion until the defeat of the Spanish Armada in 1588 and connects the growth of the slave trade to Spain's gradual decline. He clearly communicates how European countries used skewed facts regarding Spain's participation in the slave trade when translating documents about expansion and colonization into English, French, and other languages.

In chapters 2 and 3, Hart underlines and contextualizes the significance of Shakespeare's contemporaries, particularly Marlowe and Greene. In comparing these two men's bodies of work with Shakespeare's, Hart reminds us that Marlowe was murdered at the age of twenty-nine, and Greene died at thirty-five. Shakespeare's longevity gave him twenty-plus years to generate additional works. Even so, Marlowe has been credited by Algernon Swinburne as being "the father of English tragedy and the creator of English blank verse" (187). Hart concurs that without a Marlowe there might not have been a Shakespeare.

When Shakespeare's First Folio was divided into the headings of tragedies, comedies, and histories, a number of Shakespeare's plays now considered romances were categorized as comedies. Hart constructs a strong case for the category of romances as a valuable critical tool. He not only examines how Shakespeare's *The Winter's Tale* (ca. 1610) must be viewed as a romance but connects this argument to Greene's *Pandosto, The Triumph of Time* (1588), which served as a direct source for *The Winter's Tale*. Hart scrutinizes *Pandosto* in its own right as a romance. He states that "Greene wrote romance in a well-established critical and poetic context that justified the ways of romance to those who admired Aristotle and the ancient views of literature" (64).

In chapter 4, Hart goes further in his discussion of comedy and romance by succinctly defining two aspects of Renaissance comedy as "romantic pastoral" and "satirical comedy." He deeply analyzes Guarini's *Il Pastor Fido* (1590), Shakespeare's *As You Like It* (1599) and *Twelfth Night* (1600–1601), and especially Calderón's *No hay burlas con el amor* as his examples of romantic pastoral comedy. Ben Jonson's *Volpone* (1607) and Molière's *Tartuffe* (1664) are dissected as the prime examples of satirical comedy. When comparing these two aspects of comedy, Hart analyzes what uniquely defines these plays as comedic while also examining their historicity.

In chapter 5's discussion of narrative, theory, and drama, Hart surmises that "playwrights have always valued and used narrative with dramatic results" (107). He reflects on Ross Chambers's book *Story and Situation: Narrative Seduction and the Power of Fiction* and the idea that to separate stories from their actual telling or, in the case of drama, the performance, does a disservice to the apprehension and appreciation of narrative. Hart focuses on four primary functions of narrative: exposition, suggestion, compression, and address. When examining these four functions, he discusses insightful examples not only from Shakespeare but also from Rabelais, Swift, Montaigne, Dostoevsky, and Thomas Mann, to name a few.

As Hart continues his detailed discussion of narrative in chapter 6, he links it to the irony and historical references found in Shakespeare's tragedies. Cervantes and Rabelais are cited as Shakespearian contemporaries who display playful attitudes toward plot. Hart discusses the formalist notion of how plot differs from story and the ways in which dramatic plotting can rearrange historical events. He also explores how Shakespeare's First Tetralogy informed his

Second Tetralogy and how both were informed by the writings of his Elizabethan contemporaries.

In chapter 7, Hart's passion for and knowledge of the history that is intricately woven into Shakespeare's history plays becomes evident. He effectively reviews Renaissance plays from the perspective of Shakespeare and his many contemporaries as well as from a contemporary knowledge base. This passion and drive fuels his discussion of Shakespeare's romances in chapter 8. When discussing *The Winter's Tale* and *Cymbeline* (ca. 1609), he draws meaningful references to his earlier discussion of Greene's *Pandosto*.

Overall, Hart's prose is both poetic and compact, and he guides his readers through the text with concise and informative introductions to each section. The book is an enjoyable read and is also organized to serve as a functional source of reference. Lovers of history and drama alike will enjoy Hart's extensive collection of textual and historical analyses that reconsider Shakespeare's influence in relation to his professional counterparts while honoring his influence as an individual.

—JANE PURSE-WIEDENHOEFT
University of Wisconsin-Oshkosh

Words, Space, and the Audience: The Theatrical Tension between Empiricism and Rationalism. By Michael Y. Bennett. New York: Palgrave Macmillan, 2012. 190 pp. $85.00 hardcover.

Michael Y. Bennett's *Words, Space, and the Audience* begins as an investigation of the title's three theatrical elements and the ways they make meaning in the theatre. Citing the ideas of Gay McAuley, Bert O. States, and Richard Bauman, Bennett examines the "ever-present *tension* between empirical and rational ways of understanding a play" (8). Bennett uses these explorations and examinations to determine how much of an audience's understanding emanates from "new, *a posteriori*, sensory experiences," and how much arises from "reason and *a priori* knowledge" (11). Bennett structures his book around four canonical plays and offers historical and philosophical context for each, paying close attention to the ways contemporary intellectual energies infiltrated them. The results are mixed, as he occasionally strays from his thesis and often relies very heavily upon literary close readings of the plays' texts. Still, Bennett's work proves to be a valuable contribution for charting the overlap between philosophy and theatre, an overlap that could prove elucidating to scholars of dramatic literature and reception theorists alike.

Bennett takes considerable care in chapter 1 to model the substructure he will employ in subsequent chapters, mapping the philosophical and historical terrain Oscar Wilde traversed and surveyed in writing *The Importance of Being Earnest* and *Salome*. Bennett most successfully achieves what his thesis promises in this first chapter, as he blends discussions of British Idealism, Sartre's notion of "bad faith" (plucked from his *Being and Nothingness*), Bauman's "consciousness of doubleness" in performance, and the spectator's gaze to "examine the performance of *being* or *not being*" (17, 42). Bennett capably analyzes the shifting ontology of the plays' primary protagonists through close readings of the playtexts, augmented by brief discussions of a pair of relatively recent productions. If Bennett's book has one overarching weakness, it is the paucity of such performance analyses. This is not an insignificant deficiency, considering that "space" and "audience"—as two of the primary makers of meaning in performance and production—are suggested mainly through philosophical invocation, rather than descriptions and evocations of embodied practice. Bennett does not engage consistently enough with the work of States and McAuley, which would have proven indispensible in connecting Bennett's philosophical project with theatre practice, both past and present.

When Bennett does offer production/performance examples, however, they are provocative and most closely approach his stated purpose in the introduction. One example is his discussion of three different productions of *Waiting for Godot* in chapter 3. Bennett triangulates the three productions to underscore the theatrical tension between *being* and *doing*, figuring these two poles as separate methods for the construction of competing ontologies, which he associates with rationalism and empiricism, respectively (91–92). Additionally, in chapter 4, Bennett briefly discusses two productions of Albee's *Who's Afraid of Virginia Woolf?* Unlike his discussion of *Waiting for Godot*, however, Bennett's choice of citations in this chapter mainly highlights thematic differences in the productions rather than focusing the reader's attention on the production's use of *space* and *gesture* as he did in chapter 3. As such, his analysis in chapter 4 remains relatively unmoored from theatrical practice. This is not to say his insights are without merit, rather they simply rely too heavily upon what the text may *suggest* about embodied performance practice and thus often slip into speculation.

Much of what occupies Bennett throughout are his efforts to translate the philosophical environments of each time period—late Victorian England, post–World War I Italy, post–World War II France, and the United States during the Cold War—into the two philosophical camps to which the title and introduction refer. Much of the book, in fact, is occupied with this recurrent theoretical gesture as philosophers and philosophies such as Hume, Hegel, Sartre, Camus, Austin, neo-Hegelians, positivism, Wittgenstein, and pragmatism are ushered into these two opposing camps. The terms "empiricism" and "rationalism" are, as a result, stretched very thin and come to embrace a variety of divergent philosophies. In placing these philosophies under general philosophical headings, some of their nuance is lost as Bennett occasionally deemphasizes the historical exigencies that necessitated or contributed to their development. Some of this might be explained by Bennett's contention that "each of these plays first appeared in a place and time that represented a crossroads in history and philosophy" (25). At times, Bennett overemphasizes the recurring historical pattern—empiricism and rationalism contending—rather than fulfilling his promise to "show how words and space in front of an audience 'create' meaning" (12).

Though Bennett struggles to connect McAuley's work—which relies heavily upon embodied practice, theatre spaces, and audience-performer-spatial dynamics—with his close readings, his insights into the philosophical currents that run through playtexts is intriguing. Considerations of the rehearsals and performances of these written texts might have served to illuminate these currents more fully while simultaneously strengthening the book's cross-disciplinary appeal. As Bennett suggests in his conclusion, which includes an interview with Coco Fusco, "the subject of performance studies with regard to this book is an afterthought" (125). Nowhere else in the book does Bennett so closely approach his stated purpose of engaging with the primary theatrical elements—space, word, and audience—to calibrate how meaning is made in the theatre than in this conclusion. Though he begins promisingly enough by invoking the work of anthropologist/performance theorist Richard Bauman, he soon relegates performance studies to an afterthought. If Bennett had begun his book with the questions and considerations that Fusco's interview raises, hewn more closely to his avowed purpose, and engaged more extensively with McAuley and other performance theorists, he may well have succeed—as he wished to—in bridging the disciplinary bounds between the "disparate fields of drama/theatre, history, and philosophy" (24). As it is, however, *Words, Space, and the Audience* functions less as a substantial study of theatrical practice than as an extended close reading of competing literary and philosophical texts.

—ADAM SHEAFFER
University of Maryland–College Park

BOOK REVIEWS

Acts of Gaiety: LGBT Performance and the Politics of Pleasure. By Sara Warner. Ann Arbor: University of Michigan Press, 2012. 296 pp. $55 cloth, $29.95 paper.

In *Acts of Gaiety*, Sara Warner offers a crucial reevaluation of politically resistant feminist and lesbian/gay performances from the 1960s to the present; in so doing, she traces a performance lineage that complicates the rise of queer theory in academia on the one hand and the concomitant turn of LGBT movements to conservative social agendas on the other. Warner opens with two central theses. First, she argues that queer theory, with its focus on the disruption of sexual categories, tends to read earlier contestations of gender and sexuality as essentialist, thereby obfuscating the disruptive effects of these earlier interventions in their historical moments. Second, she argues that this historical forgetting looms large in the current alignment of LGBT activism with neoliberal political goals that contrast sharply with the agendas of earlier feminist and lesbian/gay activists.

In response to these academic and political developments, Warner recalls specific "acts of gaiety," performances profoundly disruptive in their moment but largely ignored in historical narratives at present. Such scandalous acts challenged norms of sex and gender while likewise critiquing poverty, racism, and international imperialism. Given her focus on the obvious exuberance generated by these past acts of gaiety, Warner at times overlooks the joy to be found in present-day performances—including those that uphold some aspects of the status quo while contesting others. Consider the lesbian couple who fully acknowledge the social and economic privileges that accrue to legal marriage, yet still beam for the camera after obtaining their marriage license. Still, Warner rightly recuperates the earlier "acts of gaiety" she details in her text, as they offer a crucial opportunity to rethink the scholarship and politics of the present.

Warner offers careful case studies of acts of gaiety, beginning with the early theatrical exploits of radical feminist and lesbian Valerie Solanas. These days Solanas is best known for trying to assassinate Andy Warhol, but she also wrote plays, confronting prejudice against women and lesbians in her efforts to enter the Off-Off-Broadway scene of the 1960s. Warner offers a valuable reading of the early Solanas play *Up Your Ass*, long thought lost but found by Warner through painstaking archival efforts. The play follows butch lesbian Bongi Perez as she flirts with women, hobnobs with drag queens, turns a male trick in the bushes, and cavorts with a homicidal housewife. As Warner observes, the trashy sexual satire of *Up Your Ass* holds its own with the plays that won Jack Smith and Charles

Ludlam fame on the 1960s Off-Off-Broadway circuit; the fact that Solanas was blocked from producing her play testifies to the obstacles faced by women and lesbians even in the ostensibly freewheeling Off-Off-Broadway scene.

Next, Warner confronts battles over same-sex marriage by contrasting the current drive to legalize such marriages with the disavowals of marriage by feminist and lesbian/gay activists in the late 1960s and early 1970s. Warner wins kudos for tackling this contentious issue, but the immensity of the topic calls for a book of its own; here Warner risks flattening history in her shorter chapter-length study. Consider how Warner contrasts two "zaps"—quick, guerilla-style disruptions of institutional places and practices—during the early years of gay and lesbian activism. The first was a 1969 zap by politicized lesbians called The Feminists, who occupied the NYC Marriage License Bureau to decry marriage as a mode of female subjugation. The second was a 1971 zap by men from the Gay Activists Alliance, who stormed the same Bureau to agitate for same-sex marriage rights. Warner deftly analyzes the actions of these two groups. Yet to conclude that the two zaps "reflect a fundamental difference between lesbian feminists and gay men over the issue of marriage at a key moment in LGBT history" (90) elides the fact that other gay men were busily critiquing marriage at this time. Indeed, Warner effects such an elision when she approvingly quotes a critique of marriage from the famous "Gay Manifesto" of 1969, without noting in the body of the chapter that it was written by Carl Wittman, a prominent male homosexual activist of the era.

Warner follows with a study of Jill Johnston, an influential dance critic of the later twentieth century and an "enfant terrible" of the feminist and lesbian movements of the 1970s. Today, Johnston is best remembered for her 1973 book *Lesbian Nation*; Warner reminds us, however, that she was also famous for her provocative public performances, in which she affirmed her link to feminist and lesbian activism while challenging the strictures she found to inhere in the activist movements themselves. Warner documents, for instance, an occasion in 1970 when Johnston took a topless swim at a poolside fundraiser for NOW—during a speech by NOW cofounder Betty Friedan. For Warner, such acts by Johnston are formative of a "Lesbian Nation" not beholden to the ideologies of nation-states, but forged instead through alliances of affect and activism. In a crucial counterpoint to her chapter on marriage, Warner ends her study of Johnston with an account of the unconventional civil union Johnston held with her partner Ingrid Nyeboe in Denmark in 1993, a ceremony that invites us to outfit such rituals for new purposes.

The next chapter takes for its starting point the cartoon 'zine *Hothead Paisan*, produced by Diane DiMassa from 1991 to 1996. The series followed the adventures of a "homicidal lesbian terrorist" who wreaks havoc on the heterosexist establishment. Warner praises the series for offering readers an opportunity to imagine themselves in the shoes of Paisan herself, then follows her account of the 1990s 'zine with an astute analysis of a musical theatre version of the series at the 2004 Michigan Womyn's Music Festival. Warner discusses her own reservations about the production in light of the War on Terror that had ensued from the September 11 attacks; specifically, she notes that the 2004 performance occurred mere weeks after the release of photos from the Abu Ghraib prisoner abuse scandal—photos that, to the shock of many, prominently featured women among the abusers. Warner argues that tropes of terrorist violence within the 'zine demand rethinking after Abu Ghraib. Crucially, Warner does not disavow the impetus of the performance; rather, she calls for renewed analysis of performative fantasy in the lesbian imaginary, the need to revisit such fantasies in response to our historical moment.

The final chapter details the return of the Five Lesbian Brothers to professional theatre with their 2005 production of *Oedipus at Palm Springs*. This adaptation of Sophocles features lesbian couples who meet for a weekend at the resort town; catastrophe ensues when a younger woman is revealed to be the daughter of her older girlfriend. Warner notes that this *Oedipus*, viewed as conventional tragedy, received mixed reviews. Yet Warner calls the play a dark comedy; she argues that it acts as an extended "cynical tendentious joke," a term Freud used for a joke that channels unconscious self-hostility into self-deprecating humor. For Warner, *Oedipus* plays a wicked joke upon lesbians who mimic heteronormative family dynamics: "By adopting these same rituals, protocols, and sacraments of straight society, these characters are bound to the structures and strictures that govern them, including the incest taboo" (178). Warner offers a compelling analysis of the play and its reception. Yet she looks to Freud for a theory of jokes and their unconscious underpinnings, while also calling into question the incest taboo that, for Freud, undergirds all unconscious operations. This use of Freud embeds a tension in the chapter that I would like Warner to unpack in future work.

In her conclusion, Warner urges recuperation of acts of gaiety like those she has examined, the better to confront the present political moment. These recuperated acts can counter the forgetting of history endemic to queer theory, while contesting the neoliberal bent of current LGBT activism. True, there are a few occasions where Warner, in advancing her argument, overlooks the messy complexities that inevitably arise from radical political performance. But readers should take these occasions as spurs to their own inquiry into the text, rather than flaws within the text itself. Warner demonstrates that acts of gaiety inspired substantive political change in decades past. Today, in a vastly changed political landscape, could the revival of such acts inspire radical political action once again? As a queer leftist myself, I bear an abiding interest in this question; Warner gaily invites us to seek answers in our teaching, our performance, and our activism.

—ALAN SIKES
Louisiana State University

BOOKS RECEIVED

Angelaki, Vicky, ed. *Contemporary British Theatre: Breaking New Ground*. New York: Palgrave Macmillan, 2013.

Bailey, Marlon M. *Butch Queens Up in Pumps: Gender, Performance, and Ballroom Culture in Detroit*. Ann Arbor: University of Michigan Press, 2013.

Bak, John S. *Tennessee Williams: A Literary Life*. New York: Palgrave Macmillan, 2013.

Bartels, Emily C., and Emma Smith, eds. *Christopher Marlowe in Context*. Cambridge: Cambridge University Press, 2013.

Becker, Florian N., Paola S. Hernandez, and Brenda Werth. *Imagining Human Rights in Twenty-First-Century Theatre*. New York: Palgrave Macmillan, 2013.

Bennett, Susan. *Theatre & Museums*. New York: Palgrave Macmillan, 2013.

Billingham, Peter. *Edward Bond: A Critical Study*. New York: Palgrave Macmillan, 2013.

Bowles, Norma, and Daniel-Raymond Nadon, eds. *Staging Social Justice: Collaborating to Create Activist Theatre*. Carbondale and Edwardsville: Southern Illinois University Press, 2013.

Buccola, Regina, and Peter Kanelos, eds. *Chicago Shakespeare Theatre: Suiting the Action to the Word*. DeKalb, IL: Northern Illinois University Press, 2013.

Chambers, Claire Maria, Simon W. du Toit, and Joshua Edelman, eds. *Performing Religion in Public*. New York: Palgrave Macmillan, 2013.

Chinoy, Helen Krich. *The Group Theatre: Passion, Politics, and Performance in the Depression Era*. New York: Palgrave Macmillan, 2013.

Crémieux, Anne, Xavier Lemoine, and Jean-Paul Rocchi, eds. *Understanding Blackness through Performance: Contemporary Arts and the Representation of Identity*. New York: Palgrave Macmillan, 2013.

BOOKS RECEIVED

Crespy, David A. *Richard Barr: The Playwrights' Producer.* Carbondale and Edwardsville: Southern Illinois University Press, 2013.

Cummings, Scott T. and Erica Stevens Abbitt, eds. *The Theatre of Naomi Wallace: Embodied Dialogues.* New York: Palgrave Macmillan, 2013.

Demastes, William W. *The Cambridge Introduction to Tom Stoppard.* New York: Cambridge University Press, 2013.

Dolan, Jill. *The Feminist Spectator in Action: Feminist Criticism for the Stage and Screen.* New York: Palgrave Macmillan, 2013.

Dudeck, Theresa Robbins. *Keith Johnstone: A Critical Biography.* London: Bloomsbury Methuen Drama, 2013.

Durham, Leslie Atkins. *Women's Voices on American Stages in the Early Twenty-First Century.* New York: Palgrave Macmillan, 2013.

Farfan, Penny, and Lesley Ferris, eds. *Contemporary Women Playwrights: Into the Twenty-First Century.* New York: Palgrave Macmillan, 2013.

Faroqhi, Suraiya, and Arzu Öztürkmen, eds. *Celebration, Entertainment and Theatre in the Ottoman World.* New York: Seagull Books, 2014.

Feldstein, Ruth. *How It Feels to Be Free: Black Women Entertainers and the Civil Rights Movement.* New York: Oxford University Press, 2013.

Fletcher, John. *Preaching to Convert: Evangelical Outreach and Performance Activism in a Secular Age.* Ann Arbor: University of Michigan Press, 2013.

Fliotsos, Anne and Wendy Vierow, eds. *International Women Stage Directors.* Urbana: University of Illinois Press, 2013.

Gil, Daniel Juan. *Shakespeare's Anti-Politics: Sovereign Power and the Life of the Flesh.* New York: Palgrave Macmillan, 2013.

Gluhovic, Milija. *Performing European Memories: Trauma, Ethics, Politics.* New York: Palgrave Macmillan, 2013.

Grantley, Darryll. *Historical Dictionary of British Theatre, Early Period.* Lanham, MD: Scarecrow Press, 2013.

Hagher, Iyorwuese. *The Kwagh-hir Theater: A Weapon for Social Action.* Lanham, MD: University Press of America, 2014.

Hopkins, D. J. and Kim Solga, eds. *Performance and the Global City.* New York: Palgrave Macmillan, 2013.

Hutchison, Yvette. *South African Performance and Archive of Memory.* New York: Palgrave Macmillan, 2013.

Jones, Chris. *Bigger, Brighter, Louder: 150 Years of Chicago Theatre as Seen by Chicago Tribune Critics.* Chicago: University of Chicago Press, 2013.

Kear, Adrian. *Theatre and Event: Staging the European Century.* New York: Palgrave Macmillan, 2013.

BOOKS RECEIVED

Lim, Eng-Beng. *Brown Boys and Rice Queens: Spellbinding Performance in the Asias*. New York: New York University Press, 2014.

Lindfors, Bernth. *Ira Aldridge: Performing Shakespeare in Europe, 1852–1855*. Rochester, NY: University of Rochester Press, 2013.

Liu, Siyuan. *Performing Hybridity in Colonial-Modern China*. New York: Palgrave Macmillan, 2013.

Machon, Josephine. *Immersive Theatres: Intimacy and Immediacy in Contemporary Performance*. New York: Palgrave Macmillan, 2013.

Magelssen, Scott. *Simming: Participatory Performance and the Making of Meaning*. Ann Arbor: University of Michigan Press, 2014.

Magnat, Virginie. *Grotowski, Women, and Contemporary Performance: Meetings with Remarkable Women*. London: Routledge, 2013.

Mahala, Macelle. *Penumbra: The Premier Stage for African American Drama*. Minneapolis: University of Minnesota Press, 2013.

Malia, Scott. *Giorgio Strehler Directs Carlo Goldini*. Lanham, MD: Lexington Books, 2014.

McCleave, Sarah. *Dance in Handel's London Operas*. Rochester, NY: University of Rochester Press, 2013.

McCutcheon, Jade Rosina, and Barbara Sellers-Young, eds. *Embodied Consciousness: Performance Technologies*. New York: Palgrave Macmillan, 2013.

McDaniel, L. Bailey. *(Re)constructing Maternal Performance in Twentieth-Century American Drama*. New York: Palgrave Macmillan, 2013.

McInnis, David. *Mind-Travelling and Voyage Drama in Early Modern England*. New York: Palgrave Macmillan, 2013.

Menon, Jisha. *The Performance of Nationalism: India, Pakistan, and the Memory of Partition*. Cambridge, U.K.: Cambridge University Press, 2013.

Mulready, Cyrus. *Romance on the Early Modern Stage: English Expansion Before and After Shakespeare*. New York: Palgrave Macmillan, 2013.

Nevitt, Lucy. *Theatre & Violence*. New York: Palgrave Macmillan, 2013.

O'Connor, Jacqueline. *Documentary Trial Plays in Contemporary American Theater*. Carbondale and Edwardsville: Southern Illinois University Press, 2013.

Peschel, Lisa, ed. *Performing Captivity, Performing Escape: Cabarets and Plays from the Terezin/Theresienstadt Ghetto*. London: Seagull Books, 2014.

Picart, Caroline Joan S. *Critical Race Theory and Copyright in American Dance: Whiteness as Status Property*. New York: Palgrave Macmillan, 2013.

Pickering, Kenneth, and Jayne Thompson. *Naturalism in Theatre: Its Development and Legacy*. New York: Palgrave Macmillan, 2013.

Prentiss, Craig R. *Staging Faith: Religion and African American Theatre from the*

Harlem Renaissance to World War II. New York: New York University Press, 2014.

Prizant, Yael. *Cuba Inside Out: Revolutionary and Contemporary Theatre.* Carbondale: Southern Illinois University Press, 2014.

Salata, Kris. *The Unwritten Grotowski: Theory and Practice of the Encounter.* London: Routledge, 2013.

Solga, Kim. *Violence against Women in Early Modern Performance: Invisible Acts.* New York: Palgrave Macmillan, 2013.

Solomon, Alisa. *Wonder of Wonders: A Cultural History of "Fiddler on the Roof."* New York: Metropolitan Books, 2013.

Stevenson, Jill. *Sensational Devotion: Evangelical Performance in Twenty-First-Century America.* Ann Arbor: University of Michigan Press, 2013.

Stubbs, Naomi J. *Cultivating National Identity through Performance: American Pleasure Gardens and Entertainment.* New York: Palgrave Macmillan, 2013.

Syssoyeva, Kathryn Mederos, and Scott Proudfit, eds. *Collective Creation in Contemporary Performance.* New York: Palgrave Macmillan, 2013.

Syssoyeva, Kathryn Mederos, and Scott Proudfit, eds. *A History of Collective Creation.* New York: Palgrave Macmillan, 2013.

Thornbury, Barbara E. *America's Japan and Japan's Performing Arts: Cultural Mobility and Exchange in New York, 1952–2011.* Ann Arbor: University of Michigan Press, 2013.

Varney, Denise, Peter Eckersall, Chris Hudson, and Barbara Hatley, eds. *Theatre and Performance in the Asia-Pacific: Regional Modernities in the Global Era.* New York: Palgrave Macmillan, 2013.

Waldron, Jennifer. *Reformations of the Body: Idolatry, Sacrifice, and the Early Modern Theatre.* New York: Palgrave Macmillan, 2013.

Wiles, David, and Christine Dymkowski, eds. *The Cambridge Companion to Theatre History.* New York: Cambridge University Press, 2013.

Wills, Garry. *Making Make-Believe Real: Politics as Theatre in Shakespeare's Time.* New Haven: Yale University Press, 2014.

Witham, Barry B. *A Sustainable Theatre: Jasper Deeter at Hedgerow.* New York: Palgrave Macmillan, 2013.

Young, Harvey. *Theatre & Race.* New York: Palgrave Macmillan, 2013.

CONTRIBUTORS

DEANNA TOTEN BEARD is the associate chair of the Department of Theatre Arts at Baylor University, where she also serves as the graduate program director. Dr. Toten Beard holds an M.F.A. in dramaturgy from Stony Brook University and a Ph.D. in theatre history from Indiana University. She is the author of *Sheldon Cheney's Theatre Arts Magazine: Promoting a Modern American Theatre, 1916–1921*. Dr. Toten Beard is also the editor of the *Texas Theatre Journal*.

CHRYSTYNA DAIL is an assistant professor of theatre history in the Department of Theatre Arts at Ithaca College. Her research interests include U.S. social activist theatre and performance, the intersections of race and politics in performance during the Cold War, labor theatre, twentieth-century Ukrainian theatre, and witchcraft on the American stage. She has presented her research at the meetings of the Association for Theatre in Higher Education, the American Society for Theatre Research, the Society for Terrorism Research, the International Federation for Theatre Research, the Mid American Theatre Conference, and the American Literature Association, and has published in the *Journal of American Drama and Theatre* as well as *Performing Arts Resources*. She is completing work on a book about Stage For Action.

TANYA DEAN is a D.F.A. candidate in dramaturgy and dramatic criticism at the Yale School of Drama, where she also received her M.F.A. Her current research focuses on fairy tales and folklore in European theater. Her recent publications include contributions to edited collections such as *The Routledge Companion to Dramaturgy*, *Radical Contemporary Theatre Practices by Women in Ireland*, *That Was Us: Contemporary Irish Theatre and Performance*,

CONTRIBUTORS

and *Interactions: Dublin Theatre Festival 1957–2007*; and to journals such as *Irish Theatre International*, *Theater*, and *Journal of the Fantastic in the Arts*. Her production work as dramaturg includes *The Yellow Wallpaper* by Charlotte Perkins Gilman (Then This Theatre Company, Dublin) and *The Glass Menagerie* by Tennessee Williams (Long Wharf Theatre, Connecticut), and she served as artistic director for the 2012 Yale Summer Cabaret.

KRISTI GOOD is an adjunct professor of dramaturgy and script analysis at Carnegie Mellon University's School of Drama. Her research interests include the work of Irish playwright Sebastian Barry, cognitive science and performance, and global theatre of trauma and human rights. She is an active member of the Association of Theatre in Higher Education, the Mid-America Theatre Conference's Playwrighting Symposium, and the American Conference for Irish Studies.

ANSELM HEINRICH is a lecturer and the head of Theatre Studies at the University of Glasgow. He is the author of *Entertainment, Education, Propaganda: Regional Theatre in Germany and Britain between 1918 and 1945*, and *Theater in der Region: Westfalen und Yorkshire 1918 bis 1945*, and he has coedited a collection of essays titled *Ruskin, the Theatre, and Victorian Visual Culture* with Kate Newey and Jeffrey Richards. His next project is a book-length study on theatre in Europe under Nazi occupation during World War II. Other research interests include contemporary German theatre and performance, dramaturgy, and cultural policy.

BETHANY D. HOLMSTROM is an assistant professor of English at LaGuardia Community College, City University of New York. She received her Ph.D. in theatre from CUNY Graduate Center. Her dissertation, "Producing Memories: Staging the Civil War in US Culture, 1867–1908," examines the competing narratives of Civil War memories on stage, considering how race, ethnicity, gender, and history were performed. She has begun research for a second project on contemporary war reenactments, exploring the intersections of commercialism, tourism, and education in these performances. Her work has been published in *Youth Theatre Journal*, *Journal of American Drama and Theatre*, and *Theatre Journal*.

LISA JACKSON-SCHEBETTA is an assistant professor in the Theatre Arts Department at the University of Pittsburgh, where she both teaches in and directs the Ph.D., M.A., and B.A. programs. Her research focuses on theatre and performance in the Americas and Spain, formations of ethical and global citizenship, and community-academic partnerships. She earned her M.F.A. from Virginia Commonwealth University in 2006 and her Ph.D. from the University of Washington in 2010. She has previously published in *Theatre History Studies*, *New England Theatre Journal*, *Modern Drama*, and *Revista Iberoamericana*, among others.

DAVID JORTNER teaches theatre theory, dramatic literature, and directing at Baylor University. He received his Ph.D. in theatre and performance studies from the University of Pittsburgh in 2003, with specializations in Japanese theatre, American theatre, and theatre theory. Dr. Jortner is the coeditor of *Modern Japanese Theatre and Performance* and has published essays in the *Asian Theatre Journal* and *Tirai Pangung*. In addition, his essays have appeared in several edited volumes, including *Rising from the Flames: The Rebirth of Theatre in Occupied Japan* and *Revenge Drama in European Renaissance and Japanese Theatre*.

HADDY KREIE is currently pursuing her Ph.D. in the Department of Theatre and Dance at the University of California, Santa Barbara. She received her M.A. in theatre studies at Florida State University. She studies performances of memory in Francophone Africa.

GENE A. PLUNKA is Dunavant Professor of English at the University of Memphis, where he teaches courses on modern and contemporary drama. He has published sixty essays and book reviews on the modern theater. His books include *Peter Shaffer: Roles, Rites, and Rituals in the Theater*, *The Rites of Passage of Jean Genet: The Art and Aesthetics of Risk Taking*, *Jean-Claude van Itallie and the Off-Broadway Theater*, *The Black Comedy of John Guare*, *The Plays of Beth Henley: A Critical Study*, and *Holocaust Drama: The Theater of Atrocity*.

LI-WEN (JOY) WANG received her Ph.D. in drama and theatre from UC Irvine/UC San Diego in 2013. She earned her M.A. in drama from National Taiwan University, where she also served as an adjunct professor of theatre and drama in 2014. Her intellectual interests include theatre and war as well as political theatre.

ARIEL WATSON is an assistant professor of modern and contemporary drama at Saint Mary's University in Halifax, Nova Scotia. Her work focuses on the anxieties of metatheatre and reflexivity, as well as on theatrical representations of mental illness and the psychotherapeutic exchange. Portions of these projects dealing with Sarah Kane, Joe Penhall, Conor McPherson, Tennessee Williams, and Harold Pinter have appeared in *Modern Drama* and *Text and Presentation*.